# A FRONTIER LANDSCAPE

# A Frontier Landscape

## The North West in the Middle Ages

*N. J. Higham*

WIND*gather*

PRESS

*A Frontier Landscape: The North West in the Middle Ages*

© N. J. Higham, 2004

*Published by*: Windgather Press Ltd, 29 Bishop Road, Bollington,
Macclesfield, Cheshire SK10 5NX, UK

*Distributed by*: Central Books Ltd, 99 Wallis Road, London E9 5LN

*British Library Cataloguing-in-Publication Data*
A catalogue record for this book is available from the British Library

ISBN 0-9545575-6-5

Designed, typeset and originated by Carnegie Publishing Ltd,
Chatsworth Road, Lancaster
Printed and bound by Alden Press

# Contents

*For my family*

# Acknowledgements

This volume has grown out of a fascination for landscape history which originated in my school days. At university, my interest in the medieval economy was encouraged by Dr (since Professor Sir) Ian Kershaw, and this became allied to archaeological research interests in the North West of England under the influence of the late Professor Barri Jones, who exuded an unfailing enthusiasm for landscape archaeology of all periods. I have researched various different parts of the region, from northern Cumbria to southern Cheshire, over a thirty year period, and this project was first conceived a decade and a half ago, in collaboration with Professor Jones and Dr Denise Kenyon. However, for a variety of reasons, it has taken a very long time to bring this volume even to the preliminary and conditional conclusion which is presented here.

My understanding of the regional landscape has been encouraged both by the many individuals who contributed so richly to the research programmes which I directed and co-directed in Cumbria (1973–78) and then at and around Tatton Park (Cheshire, between 1978 and 1987), and also by numerous members of the Medieval Settlement Research Group, among whom I would particularly wish to acknowledge the stimulus and advice provided by Professor Chris Dyer, John Hurst, Dr Brian Roberts, Chris Taylor and Dr Tom Williamson. I have benefited from the discussion of particular local issues with Penny Anderson, the late Professor Owen Ashmore, Christine Barratt, Dr Paul Booth, Dr Chris Crowe, Sarah Davnall, Professor Jeffrey Denton, the late Professor John Dodgson, Dr Patrick Greene, Dr Mary Higham, Dr Denise Kenyon, Dr Chris Lewis, Mike Morris, Dr John Smith, W. John Smith, Dr Alan Thacker, Rick Turner, Simon Ward, Richard Watson, Rhys Williams and Dr David Wilson, over a period stretching back to the late 1970s and 1980s. Wide-ranging discussions with Jill Collens, Mark Leah and Adrian Tindall (Cheshire County Council), Dr Mike Nevell (University of Manchester Archaeological Unit) and Peter Ilet (Lancashire County Council) have been fundamental to the process of writing up during 2001–03. Dr Denise Kenyon kindly provided unpublished plans of ridge and furrow in western Cheshire and Dr Colin Phillips made available material from the *New Historical Atlas of Cheshire* prior to publication. I am extremely grateful to both of them. The photographs in the book are by and large my own. Additional aerial photographs were very kindly provided by Adrian Olivier and Peter Ilet, both of whom spent considerable time and energy providing me with the benefit of their enormous expertise at various times. Photographs of Norton Priory were provided by Dr Patrick Greene and Norton Priory Museum. Stephanie Jackson retyped drafts written in the 1980s. Dr Paul Holder assisted my use of the John Ryland's University Library and Richard Purslow, as publisher, has been forever helpful and supportive throughout the later stages of the project. My colleague, Dr Steve Rigby, very kindly read an early draft of the volume and suggested many improvements which I have incorporated, but some too which I have not. To all these and many more, I am exceedingly grateful.

Over several years, it is my family who have had to bear the brunt of the writing up process, who have accepted with patience the need to visit remote corners of the region and to take photographs of what they often felt were unprepossessing landscapes. It is to them that I dedicate the finished product.

Notwithstanding these very considerable debts, all opinions and views expressed herein are my own, and so too are any errors.

# Illustrations and Tables

........................................................................................................................

**Colour plates** (*between pages 148 and 149*)

**Figures**

*A Frontier Landscape: The North West in the Middle Ages*

## Tables

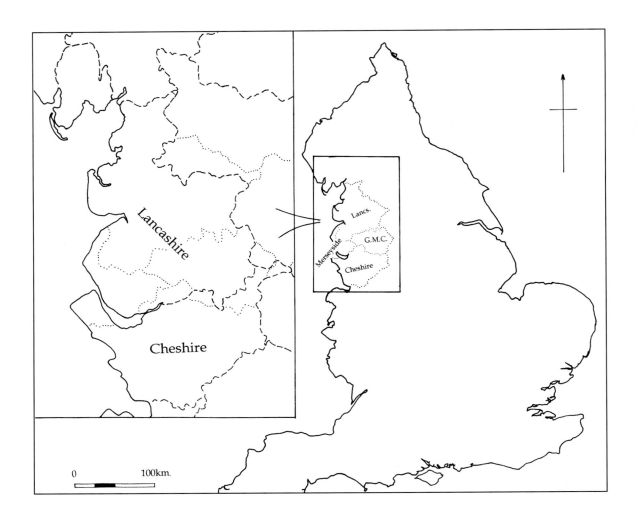

0   100km.

Lancashire

Cheshire

Lancs.

G.M.C.

Merseyside

Cheshire

# The North West and Landscape History

This volume offers a brief introduction to the medieval landscape of one region of England, the North West. For these purposes, the term 'medieval' will be taken to cover the period stretching from the late eleventh to the early to mid-sixteenth century. Regional boundaries are difficult to adhere to with any precision, but for present purposes the North West is defined primarily by reference to the post-1974 counties of Lancashire, Cheshire, Merseyside and Greater Manchester (Figure 1). There are a series of minor differences between this configuration of the region and medieval Lancashire and Cheshire, and one major one: notwithstanding occasional mentions, this volume does not pretend to cover Lancashire North of the Sands (Figure 1, inset). Where historical data is being mapped or tabulated, with this exception, the pre-1974 shires are utilised, but care is taken to differentiate between references to the medieval shires (including Lancashire only from the late twelfth century), and the post-1974 re-organisation.

## The physical setting

The North West region comprises the lands south of Cumbria between the Central Pennines and the Peak District, to the east, and the Irish Sea, to the west, with the valley of the river Dee providing an approximate western boundary further south, where Cheshire borders Staffordshire and Shropshire. This region is approximately 140 km (86 miles) north–south, and at most around 80 km (50 miles) west–east, forming an irregular oval or egg-shape. Alternatively it can be defined as the catchments of a series of river systems, from north to south, the lower Lune (the upper reaches lie in Cumbria), the Wyre, the Ribble and Douglas, the Mersey and the Dee (Figure 2). The coast-line is heavily indented, with a series of wide estuaries flanked by mudflats, alluvial marshes and/or mossland, by which these rivers enter the sea. Much of the coastline slope has broad mudflats and tidal sands, the most extensive being those in Morecambe Bay. In very general terms, the land slopes naturally from east to west, but locally the topography is far more erratic than this would suggest, with outliers of the uplands reaching well into central and southern Lancashire. The plain is far broader, and extends far further to the east, in Cheshire and in the Manchester embayment than further north.

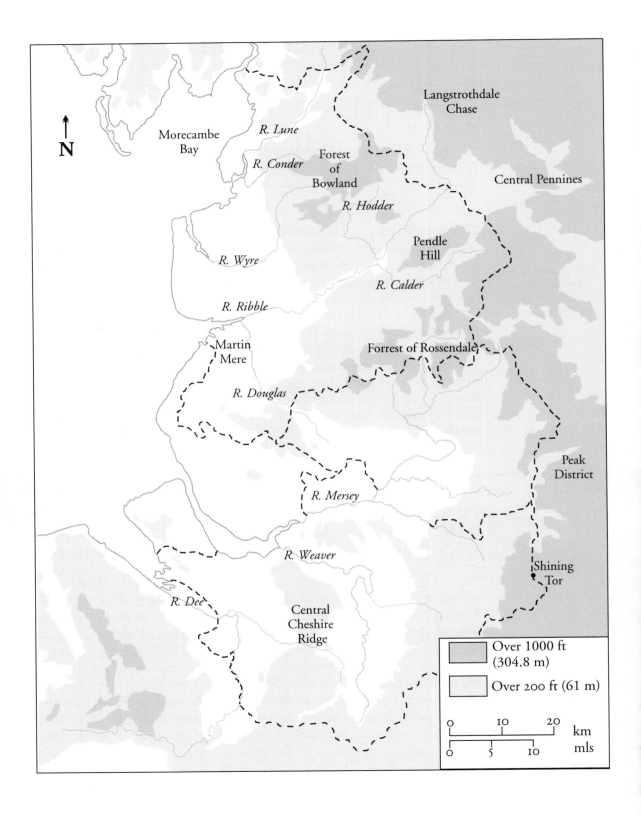

Morecambe Bay

R. Lune

R. Conder

Forest of Bowland

R. Hodder

R. Wyre

Pendle Hill

R. Calder

R. Ribble

Martin Mere

Forrest of Rossendale

R. Douglas

R. Mersey

R. Weaver

R. Dee

Central Cheshire Ridge

Langstrothdale Chase

Central Pennines

Peak District

Shining Tor

Over 1000 ft (304.8 m)

Over 200 ft (61 m)

N

0    10    20    km

0    5    10    mls

FIGURE 2 (*opposite*).
The topography of the
North West: rivers,
valleys and uplands.

FIGURE 3.
Chat Moss: a detail
from the air showing
old peat diggings.

Most of Cheshire forms the most northerly part of the great plain, which extends across the counties of the north-west midlands. This plain consists primarily of impermeable or only slowly permeable glacial till (largely clay), with occasional pockets of sand and alluvium, but with sands and gravels along the river valleys. Some areas of sand are very free draining, resulting in heaths in the later Middle Ages and early modern period, although much of this has since been quarried. The plain is broken by a few outbreaks of sandstone, most particularly the Central Cheshire Ridge. More localised and less dramatic outcrops underlie Chester, for example, Halton, and Dunham-on-the-Hill. Mossland is present but comparatively localised, although Danes Moss (Macclesfield) and Congleton Moss were very extensive in the Middle Ages.

Further north, however, the low-lying and poorly drained Mersey Basin was heavily affected from later prehistory onwards by the development of extensive mosslands (Figures 3 and 4). Indeed, it was arguably the impediment to travellers offered by the mosslands, as much as by the river itself, which made this such a prominent barrier in the Middle Ages. The mosslands have resulted

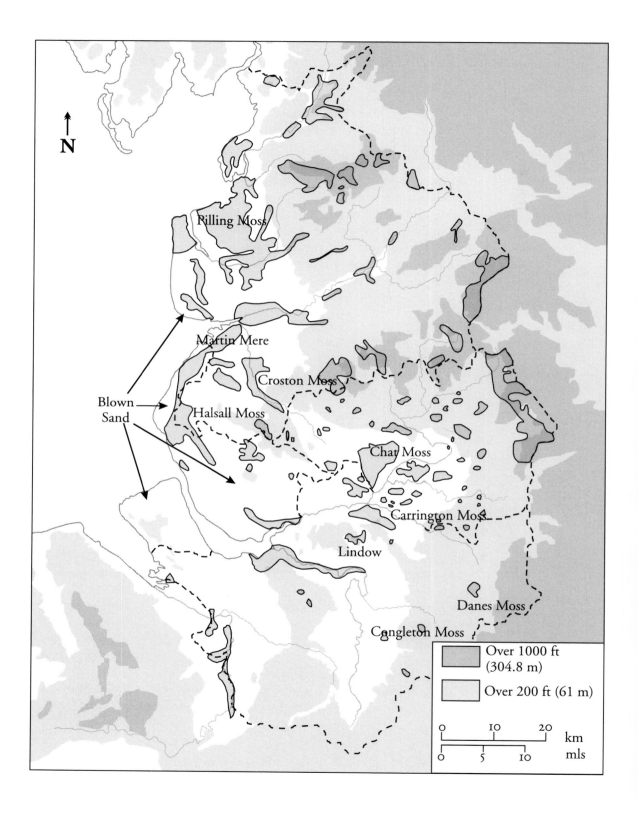

N

Pilling Moss

Martin Mere

Croston Moss

Blown
Sand

Halsall Moss

Chat Moss

Carrington Moss

Lindow

Danes Moss

Congleton Moss

| | Over 1000 ft (304.8 m) |
| | Over 200 ft (61 m) |

0        10        20
                      km
0    5    10
                      mls

from several environmental factors. Precipitation is comparatively high by national standards, with most of the lowlands experiencing around 1016 mm (40 ins). Levels increase both hill-wards and northwards, with Upper Wyresdale having the heaviest rainfall in the region with 1524–1778 mm (60–70 ins). Heavy cloud cover tends to reduce evaporation, leaving water on the surface, particularly in the much wetter period between July and January (Crowe 1962). Along the major rivers and on the coastal plain of central Lancashire, in particular, there are extensive areas of very low-lying, poorly drained terrain, often over clay-based podsols. The clay deposited by ice sheets over 10,000 years ago has resulted in a distinct shortage of well-drained tills, combined with comparatively flat lowland topography and very little calcareous soil. Only parts of Merseyside, a narrow belt of central Lancashire and parts of Lonsdale offered comparatively extensive land which was well-suited to arable in the Middle Ages, where Shirdley Hill sands, *et al.* provide free-draining soils. During later prehistory, increasing rainfall encouraged water-logging to occur where drainage was poor and the characteristic birch scrub and woodland which was widespread on these lowlands gave way to the growth of sphagnum moss and peat. This occurred first within particular drainage hollows such as kettle holes but spread outwards to cover extensive areas. The result is a patchwork of marshlands, developing on alluvium, and deep peat deposits, known as mosses, many between three and six metres thick, which can cover hundreds or even thousands of hectares, some of which have been developing for 8,000 years.

During the Middle Ages, many mosses were exploited as turbary, so as a source of fuel, and the moss skirtlands – where peat was comparatively shallow – for pasture. Peripheral enclosure pressed intermittently into the peatlands, incorporating small and shallow deposits into farmland, particularly when population levels were comparatively high. The deeper peat bogs were resistant to such processes, however, and posed considerable hazards still in the sixteenth century (Leland 1535–43):

> Chateley Moss [Chat Moss] a vi. Miles yn length sum [way] brast up within a mile of Morley Haul, and [de]stroied much grounde with moss therabout, and destroid much fresch water fische therabowt, first corrupting with stinking water Glasebrook, and so Glasebrook carr[ied] stinking water and mosse into Mersey Water, and Marsey corruptid caried the roulling mosse part to the shores of Wales, part to the Isle of Man, and sum into Ireland.

Such major expanses of lowland deep moss were not to fall to agriculture until the second half of the nineteenth century. Some were enclosed and improved for the purposes of profiting from rising food prices. Others in the Victorian era were utilised as a depository for night soil from the burgeoning urban centres and agricultural use only followed as a by-product. That process accounts for the presence at Chat Moss (Figure 3), and at Carrington Moss to the south, of exceptionally large quantities of late nineteenth-century pottery,

FIGURE 4.
The distribution of
peat mosslands and
marshland in the North
West.

5

glass, slate and other artefacts, on what are now among the most fertile agricultural parts of the region.

The drainage problems which led to the development of these extensive mosses are so widespread as to have impacted on the general character of the north-western lowlands. Chat Moss is merely one of the largest of these peat deposits, which stretched intermittently up the Mersey right into Manchester (hence Moss Side). Further widespread mossland occurred in Merseyside and western Lancashire. John Speed's map of 1610 contains few details of topography, but even he felt it necessary to include the vast mosses of Pilling and Marton in Amounderness, extensive coastal marshes occupying the whole of what is now Southport, and the great inland seasonal wetland of Martin Mere. When Celia Fiennes visited the area in 1698, she did not dare approach this Mere without a guide as night drew close, 'it being very hazardous for Strangers to pass by it' (Morris, ed 1947, p. 224) and it seems unlikely to have been less dangerous at an earlier date. Surviving place-names referring to moss and marsh both surround the extant mosses and marshes and mark the earlier presence of other smaller examples which have since been entirely lost to land improvement. Other areas had the characteristic black soils of the mosses, but deep peat had not developed. Such were, and are, often termed moors, and were a commonplace part of the landscape, being present in many townships and affecting numerous field names (with terms such as 'Black', 'Mossy', 'Moor') and both major and minor settlement names. Although tracts of rather better drained land do occur, much of this consists of blown sand, particularly along the coast of Merseyside and south-west Lancashire, and this terrain was also problematic during the Middle Ages. Overall, though, it is difficult to over-estimate the importance of mosses as a factor in the archaeology and landscape history of the region, particularly from the Mersey Basin northwards. A vision of this landscape in the Middle Ages must include the impression of a lowland zone across which perhaps 20 per cent of the total land surface consisted of peat deposits, moorland or marshland (Figure 4).

While other parts of England are also characterised by lowland peat – as are the Fen country and parts of the Humber basin – none experiences such high levels of rainfall and none has proved quite so much a challenge to archaeologists, in particular. In contrast, the Fens of East Anglia and Lincolnshire have seen dramatic discoveries in terms of settlement and land-use history over the last fifty years, which have impacted massively on our understanding of the landscape from late prehistory onwards. Such has not generally been the case in the North West.

The uplands provide a dramatic contrast. Comprised of faulted sand- or gritstones, the generally rounded fell country of the east of the region is rarely out of sight from the coastal lowlands. Great fingers of broken upland push out from the Pennines to form Rossendale, now on the borders between Greater Manchester and Lancashire, and the Forest of Bowland, between the Ribble and the Lune. The hills of the Forest of Bowland are by far the more extensive and the higher of these fell countries, rising close to 610 m (2,000 ft).

These upland areas are heavily eroded, however, with a series of deep and often dramatic valley systems. Further south, the Pennines provide a clearer boundary to the region, rising up above Macclesfield at Shining Tor to 559 m (1834 ft), with few breaks to allow traffic through, and few outlying satellite ridges, more like a wall demarcating the shire. The uplands, where rainfall was even higher, experienced similar problems of drainage to the lowlands with the same result, and peat deposits up to five metres or so thick have since developed on comparatively flat upland terrains along the Central Pennines. While the bulk of these deposits lie outside our region to the east, they form part of the boundary zone of the North West and must have been difficult to cross and quite treacherous to the unwary traveller in the Middle Ages (Figure 4). In this respect too, therefore, peat deposits help to define the region and its landscapes.

## Landscape history

Interest in and love for the English landscape has deep roots, but its systematic study came comparatively late – as an academic subject in the mainstream, landscape history has been largely developed over the last half century or so, by a mix of professional and amateur academics. An oft-quoted starting point was the publication by W. G. Hoskins in 1955 of *The Making of the English Landscape*, but this may be to confuse the attempt to construct a national history of landscape with the genesis of the subject as a particular type of scholarly exercise. That genesis lies in deeply researched local or regional studies, even before Hoskins's seminal work, which brought together a variety of historical and archaeological approaches to construct an integrated picture of the past within a particular space. Such studies were already being published by O. G. S. Crawford for parts of the south coast, and Arthur Raistrick, on the Yorkshire Dales, to offer two widely divergent examples, as early as the 1920s and 1930s. However, these in their turn should be viewed as a development of topographical and antiquarian studies published in the nineteenth century and before, with their roots in the works of antiquarians such as Leland and Camden in the sixteenth century, and William Stukeley in the 1720s. Landscape history is, therefore, a comparatively recent academic subject, but its origins go back over several centuries.

The study of the historic landscape draws too on the long tradition of more widely owned interests in the English countryside, its aesthetics, heritage and its preservation, which led, *inter alia*, to the establishment of the National Trust in 1895. The message here is very clear: landscape is to be used and studied, but it is also to be enjoyed, and the processes of our understanding its evolution and the ways in which hundreds of generations have left their mark upon it can only add quality to that enjoyment. As Bill Bryson recently remarked (2000): 'the English countryside is an exceptional creation – a corner of the world which is immensely old, full of surprises, lovingly and sometimes miraculously well maintained, and nearly always pleasing to look at.'

One of England's many surprises is the extraordinary diversity of landscape types in a relatively small area, but that diversity has not always been given the recognition in academic literature that it has warranted. Seventy years ago, scholars were only just beginning to recognise very broad divisions in the landscape. So Sir Cyril Fox (1932) distinguished 'Upland' from 'Lowland' England in his discussion of the interaction of environment, migration and cultural change in an archaeological context. The concept of an 'Upland' zone was not limited just to high ground but also included large areas of adjacent lowlands, including those of the North West. This was, therefore, a theoretical and symbolic division, rather than a mechanistically topographical one.

Over the same period, scholars researching early agricultural landscapes were seeking to plot the distribution of medieval and early modern open field by identifying diagnostic features in local records (as Gray 1915; Orwin and Orwin 1938). The result was a map of open fields with few examples in the North West (particularly Lancashire and Cumbria) and the South East (Kent to East Anglia). Concentrations of open field by this analysis coincided with regions that were recognised as 'champion' or 'planned' by the eighteenth century (at latest), in contrast with areas termed 'woodland' or 'ancient' (Rackham 1986, Figure 1.3). This terminology became central to the evolution of landscape history on a national level during the second half of the twentieth century.

From the 1950s onwards, efforts to analyse and interpret medieval rural settlement focused on precisely those nucleated settlements which were common in 'champion' regions, where most deserted medieval villages (DMVs) were being identified (Beresford and Hurst 1971). Attention centred, therefore, on a great belt of land characterised by nucleated medieval villages and extensive and highly organised common fields, stretching from Dorset continuously northwards to eastern Yorkshire and Northumberland. This central province (Figure 5) was much affected by large-scale enclosure, largely by Parliamentary private acts in the eighteenth century, resulting in modern day 'planned' landscapes.

During the 1960s and 1970s, this impetus placed considerable pressure on those seeking to examine landscapes outside this area, including those in the North West, to interpret what they found very much in terms of the established norm – of nucleated settlements and regular field systems. When these proved difficult to identify, the region fell into comparative neglect, with little research undertaken, particularly from an archaeological perspective. When efforts began to be made to review the peripheral landscapes on either side of the 'champion' countryside, they often tended to be lumped together, as if the fact of dissimilarity from the central, 'champion' country was their critical characteristic (Figure 5). This, in turn, encouraged the assumption that Cheshire and Lancashire necessarily had a settlement and landscape history which paralleled that of Kent or East Anglia, as if only two types of landscape were admissable.

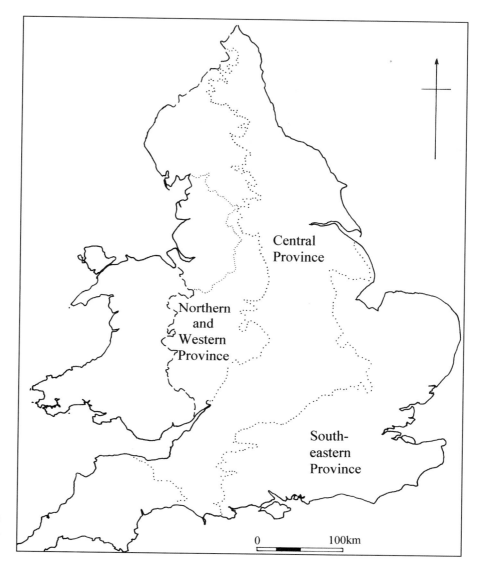

Central
Province

Northern
and
Western
Province

South-
eastern
Province

0          100km

FIGURE 5.
Landscape divisions
(after Roberts and
Wrathmell 2000), with
the North West region
marked in.

However, claims for the internal homogeneity of just two broad types of
landscape have never been particularly convincing. As Roberts and Wrathmell
(2000) have recently pointed out, the northern and western and south-eastern
provinces do have much in common – such as a high incidence of historic
woodland, of wetlands and a lack of parliamentary enclosure, but they also
have many differences. The north and west does not, for example, share the
large number of Roman villa sites and/or Anglo-Saxon pagan cemeteries that
occur in the South East, and it does have a noticeably higher incidence of pre-
English place-name survival. In many respects, therefore, it is helpful to
disentangle these two regions of England and allow them each their own landscape history, independent of one another.

The trend is now towards a greater consciousness of regional variety, with attempts to distinguish and discuss particular landscapes, so as to break down the vision of a single landscape history for all England. So, the national picture is increasingly being viewed as the sum of its parts (as Thirsk ed. 2000). There is no obvious limit to this drive to define ever smaller units of landscape as meaningful in their own right in historical terms, which finally emerged in the late twentieth century. So, for example, a new categorisation of countryside character by the Countryside Agency proposes a total of 159 areas across England (Figure 6), but still acknowledges the breadth of the characteristics used, and so the degree of local diversity which is still to be found within each area. The need to define landscape in greater detail in an archaeological perspective is driving the current English Heritage Landscape Characterisation Programme, which involves computerised mapping of fields of various types (e.g. Fairclough ed. 1999). The aim is to develop a quick and high level over-sight of 'the time depth and historic character of the present day landscape' (Fairclough 2002, 6).

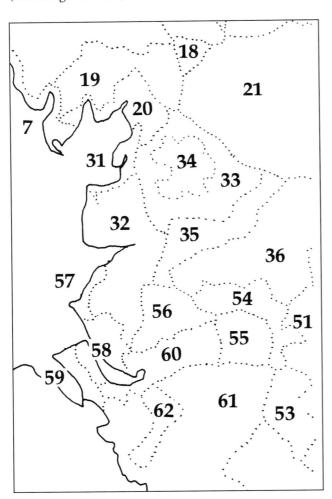

FIGURE 6.
The Countryside Character areas in the North West region as designated by the Countryside Agency:

*Key:*
7 West Cumbrian Coastal Plain
19 South Cumbria Low Fells
20 Morecambe Bay Limestones
21 Yorkshire Dales
31 Morecambe Coast and Lune Estuary
32 Lancashire and Amounderness Plain
33 Bowland Fringe and Pendle Hill
34 Bowland Fells
35 Lancashire Valleys
36 Southern Pennines
51 Dark Peak
53 South West Peak
54 Manchester Pennine Fringe
55 Manchester Conurbation
56 Lancashire Coal Fields
57 Sefton Coast
58 Merseyside Conurbation
59 Wirral
60 Mersey Valley
61 Shropshire, Cheshire and Staffordshire Plain
62 Cheshire Sandstone Ridge

Obviously, there is a tension herein, which has not yet been resolved, between landscape variability and the oversight of a large enough area to be capable of meaningful discussion in an historical or archaeological context. At the one extreme, it is valid to argue that only a very small land unit, such as a parish or manor, is a suitable vehicle for the discipline (see, for a particularly successful example, Dyer 1991; for the North West see Emery *et al.* 1996; Higham and Cane 1999). At the mid-way point are regional surveys, such as this one, and at the other extreme are national ones. Clearly, all these approaches have an important role in shaping the way the debate moves forward, all interact and all are necessary for the health of the overall research effort. The place of the regional study is particularly significant as the intermediate level in this hierarchy, since it is arguably at this level that the particular characteristics of any one part of the country, and variations within it, can best be explored. Additionally, regional studies share much of the geographical perspective of the Middle Ages, when local communities were generally highly conscious of their own manor, their own hundred and their own shire, and the agronomy and territorial organisation internal to them, but were comparatively disinterested in more distant parts of the kingdom. For social, economic and legal purposes, local communities interacted in various ways on a regular basis over short distances, and these interactions have some significance for landscape studies. So, for example, the exploitation and colonisation of the north-western uplands in the Middle Ages, as in the case of the Forest of Macclesfield (Plate 1), was closely linked with the role of the town and with systems of land-use and land management in the adjacent lowlands. Such patterns can be identified over the whole landscape, particularly where, as in the North West, there was widespread intercommoning on extensive wastes and wood pastures. A regional approach, therefore, has a particular value as an intermediate level of exposition between the purely local and the more broadly national. A regional perspective also provides an opportunity to gather together different types of evidence, drawn variously from history, historical geography, archaeology and historical ecology, to construct a picture of landscape development which is capable of contrast and comparison with other, and often very different, parts of the country, to the benefit of our understanding of both the whole and its many parts.

## The North West

Some English regional and sub-regional landscape histories have received considerable attention; others have not. In general, the south has fared far better than the north of England in this respect, and the North East far better than the North West. Indeed, landscape history had its genesis in the deep south, and was then taken up and developed as a discipline by those interested primarily in debates concerning open field and medieval villages, in the East Midlands (particularly Nottinghamshire and Leicestershire) and in Yorkshire. The north-western counties lay at a distance from this focus and long seemed to have little to offer its leading exponents. The scale of both industrialisation and urbanisation in and around both Merseyside and Greater Manchester, in particular, has had a considerable impact on the landscape, both directly and indirectly, and the area is far better known for its industrial archaeology than its medieval heritage (e.g. Ashmore 1982). So, for example, the researches of the 'Deserted Medieval Village Research Group', which was spawned by the project led by Maurice Beresford and John Hurst from the 1950s onwards at Wharram Percy (near Malton, Yorkshire), identified very few lost medieval settlements in the historic counties of Lancashire and Cheshire. Still fewer were either named or used as examples in the books written to share these new insights with a wider audience (Beresford and Hurst 1971; see also Rowley 1978). Indeed, the multi-authored volume which particularly celebrates the leadership which John Hurst and Maurice Beresford gave to medieval settlement studies (Aston *et al.* eds 1989) makes no mention at all of the lands between the Mersey Basin and the Lake District. One outcome, therefore, is virtual oblivion, as if the region was in some sense not part of medieval England, or at least not worthy of comment and of incorporation into wider discussions. Another common practice is to interpret local medieval settlement and building types by reference to excavated examples at a considerable distance from the region (see, for example, Astill and Grant eds 1988, Figure 3.1). One can appreciate the frustration of scholars faced by a poverty of the necessary data, but there are considerable dangers of misrepresentation in the extrapolation of information from one locale to a very different and much wider area.

The study of field systems has obviously thrown up similar problems. Since medieval and early modern field systems in the North West had little of the symmetry and scale to be found in, for example, much of Nottinghamshire, there has been some doubt as to how to approach the subject and how to interpret the remains. While substantial efforts have been made (as Davies 1960), the results have proved problematic to those seeking to establish a national picture, since they are complex in structure and difficult to integrate into a set of simple models. As a result, very few national surveys have found space for the inclusion of material from an area which differs so markedly from the 'champion' region (honourable exceptions are Baker and Butlin eds 1973; Hooke ed. 1985).

These are not the only difficulties of researching the medieval landscape of the North West. Other problems include the scarcity of parliamentary enclosure awards dealing with lowland common fields, which means that it is extremely difficult to establish the chronology of enclosure in the absence of the end point that such documents provide elsewhere. Nor are there many major manorial archives, such as have opened windows on the medieval estates of southern landlords, including numerous religious houses, the bishopric of Winchester and the archbishopric of Canterbury. Absent too is a substantial and easily identifiable material culture from the Iron Age, the Roman countryside or the early and central Middle Ages. The presence of archaeologically identifiable artefacts from those periods has enabled substantial results to be derived from field-walking in, for example, East Anglia or Northamptonshire (as R.C.H.M. 1975–82). Outside of late Anglo-Saxon Chester, pottery is not far short of non-existent until *c.* 1200, when several local wares begin to appear, and even now medieval pottery made in central and northern Lancashire is ill-understood. The archaeology of the region was long neglected, outside of its Roman forts and towns, largely due to the difficulties of locating and dating sites (as Iles and Newman 1996).

Against such a backdrop, it is hardly surprising that the medieval settlement and landscape history of the North West has been neglected, and has barely featured in national surveys or attempts to develop research strategies. That said, successive shifts in the research culture over the last quarter century have made the exploration of north-western landscape history an ever more feasible and exciting prospect. Within the region, the sense of frustration felt by archaeologists, in particular, began to dissipate with the adoption of aerial photography as a research tool during the 1970s. Seminal campaigns by the author and the late Professor Barri Jones (Higham and Jones 1975; Higham, N. J. 1979a), Adrian Olivier and Rhys Williams (1979), at the northern and southern extremities of the region, respectively, provided the beginnings of a new data base for an archaeological investigation of rural settlement. At the same time, extrapolation from existing vertical photographic cover began the process of mapping ploughing in the Middle Ages and the early modern period (Kenyon 1974, 1979). Thereafter, the inception of several new archaeological posts and ultimately archaeological units led in turn to new investments in field archaeology, which eventually enabled developer-funded archaeology to become well-established during the 1990s. The enthusiasm of those involved, allied to the resources which they have been able to attract, reflect a new and unprecedented level of commitment to the wider task of interpreting and understanding the historic landscapes of the region. Such have already begun to bear fruit via a number of projects (among many, see, for example, Greene 1989; Carrington ed. 1994; Emery *et al.* 1996; Nevell ed. 1999; Higham and Cane 1999; Higham 2000; Cowell and Philpott 2000).

## The lowland wetlands

While the archaeology and history of the north-western countryside has developed only rather slowly, vegetational history has been one of the great success stories of the region for much longer (as Birks 1965a, b; Hibbert *et al.* 1971; Tallis and McGuire 1972). Recognition of the special opportunities offered by the lowland mosses of the North West (as in Shimwell 1985) stimulated the inception of the government-financed 'North West Wetlands Survey', initially as a pilot study in 1987, which has attempted an integrated archaeological and palaeoecological survey of a wider region than is covered here, stretching from Shropshire to the Solway Firth. The bulk of this is now complete, and the resulting publications provide both a substantial data set and a series of land-use histories of considerable value. That said, the break-through which was anticipated, in terms of recognition of large numbers of new occupation sites, has not occurred. In practice, extensive field walking in and around the region's mosses proved far less rewarding than the corresponding expenditure of effort in similar locations in eastern England. The reasons are probably several: there is a marked scarcity of ploughed land and consequently the terrain is generally archaeologically opaque; the weakness of the artefactual record remains a major issue, and it may well be that population levels were generally lower in this region than in the Fen country throughout prehistory, as they were in the Roman and medieval periods.

The North West Wetland Survey has also, very understandably, failed to achieve something which would have been of inestimable value to the landscape historian, which is to provide a picture of the actual extent of the mosses at particular moments in time in the past. The process of land reclamation has been so lengthy and so extensive that mapping of historic mosses becomes ever less reliable as we move back before the series of comparatively accurate maps made in the decades around 1800. While the general picture is clear, the precise boundaries rarely are. Yates's Map of Lancashire (1786), gives an impression of the larger expanses of mossland then surviving, for example between Ormskirk and Eccleston (Figure 7), with a scatter of unnamed minor

FIGURE 7. Detail from Yates' *Map of The County Palatine of Lancaster*, made in 1786, showing the extensive mosses then still existing between Ormskirk and Eccleston.

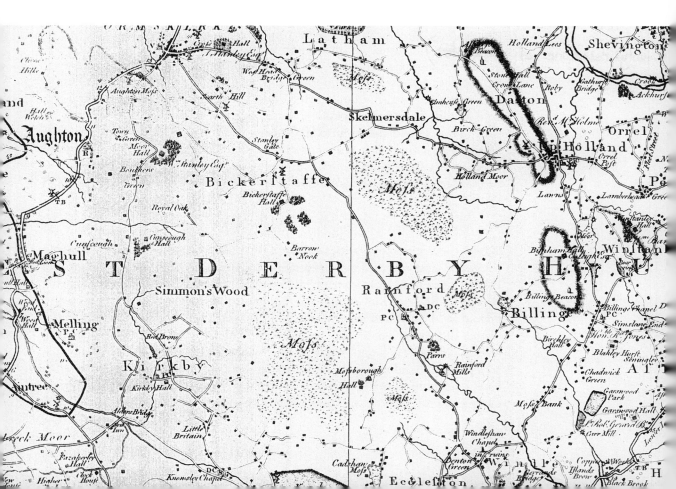

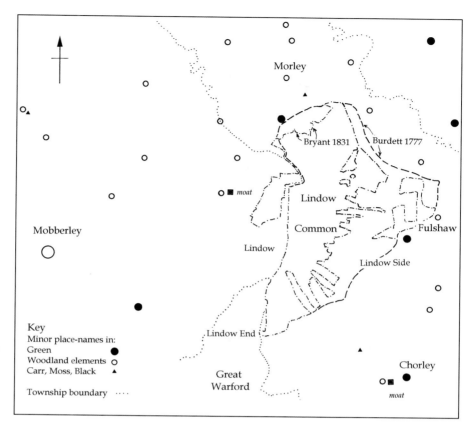

**Morley**

Bryant 1831     Burdett 1777

*moat*     **Lindow**

**Lindow Common**     **Fulshaw**

**Lindow**     **Lindow Side**

**Mobberley**     **Lindow End**

**Key**
Minor place-names in:
Green
Woodland elements ○
Carr, Moss, Black ▲

Township boundary ····

**Great Warford**

**Chorley**

*moat*

FIGURE 8.
Lindow Common as delineated by Burdett in 1777 and Bryant in 1831, in the context of an assarting landscape characterised by 'Green' and woodland-type place-names, dispersed settlement and moated sites.

settlements around them indicative of late settlement and enclosure. This imprecision regarding the extent of early mosslands is one which can be replicated right across the Mersey-Lune lowlands, as the following example will show. Lindow Moss (Plate 2) in northern Cheshire has become well-known nationally as the site at which 'Lindow Man', now conserved and displayed in the British Museum, was discovered during commercial peat extraction in 1984. It first appears on a map of Cheshire drawn by Burdett in 1777, named as Lindow Common. Burdett's mapping was not particularly accurate – he omits, for example, all of Lindow Common then in Mobberley parish – but what can be reconstructed on the eastern side runs significantly outside that enshrined in the next map available, Bryant's Map of Cheshire, produced in 1831. This suggests that the periphery of the Common was subject to considerable alteration from both land improvement and local communities exercising rights of turbary over just a fifty year period (Figure 8).

The inference would seem to be that Lindow, and by extension other mosses, were even more extensive in the Middle Ages than they were in Burdett's time, with marginal areas having been improved and enclosed both then and during the sixteenth and seventeenth centuries. We can make intelligent guesses at parts of this process at Lindow. The place-name Morley

('Woodland glade near/at a moor') is recorded around 1200 and may well have then been a comparatively new settlement, established on the slightly raised skirtland on the north side of the moss. It was one of numerous woodland and/or wetland place-names around the Moss. Growth of this settlement arguably pushed back the moss edge, and Morley Green was eventually (at an unknown but presumably later date) established between Morley itself and Lindow, on the very edge of the slightly raised topography on which the parent hamlet had developed. Again, there are several moated sites and numerous greens in the vicinity, both of which imply an assarting landscape in the later Middle Ages and\or early post-medieval period.

This picture of gradual and incremental but ill-defined improvement and enclosure on the edges of this medieval moss is probably typical of the process across the region. Small pockets of peat were largely dug out and exhausted during the Middle Ages, but the more extensive areas were far more problematic, and the efforts of medieval and early-modern communities affected only the periphery. The problem of definition of these lowland mosslands is, however, one which will continue to dog us throughout much of this volume.

## Current research and the North West

Towards the end of the twentieth century, changes occurred in the pattern and direction of research into landscape and settlement history at a national level, which had significant implications for the North West. In particular, the 1990s witnessed a switch away from open field villages as the principal focus of scholarship, in favour of more diverse patterns of dispersed settlement and ancient enclosure patterns. Beside these developments, attention has also centred on continuity in the landscape and the prevalence of long-term processes of rural management and exploitation. This shift was marked by the publication of a seminal work by Christopher Taylor (1983), which encapsulated the challenges then being formulated to established ideas about medieval settlements and their origins. Its arrival was also signalled by the formation of a new research vehicle, the 'Medieval Settlement Research Group', created by an amalgamation of the pre-existing 'Deserted Medieval Village Research Group' and the 'Moated Sites Research Group'. A particular focus of this group has been on patterns of settlement characterised by dispersal, leading to a study in some depth of parts of the south-east Midlands (Lewis *et al.* 1997, 2001).

Within this changing intellectual environment, the north-western landscape has the potential to make a distinct contribution to national debates. The presence in the region of pockets of landscape typified by villages and common fields (as in the valleys of the Dee and Lune and in parts of Amounderness) amid a wider pattern of dispersed settlements, hamlets, crofts, woods and open grazing (for the context, see Roberts and Wrathmell 2000), provides an opportunity to explore several significant issues. Why were open field villages established in the Middle Ages in some parts of the region, while elsewhere pre-existing habits of settlement continued to evolve without major re-organisation? Alongside this important debate and linked closely with it, the environmental marginality of this environment (from an agrarian perspective), with its high rainfall and extensive alluvial, blown sand and peat deposits, offers a chance to review the relationship between communities, variations in population during the Middle Ages, colonisation and the ways that resources were developed. The inception of a Malthusian crisis in late thirteenth-century England has long been a matter of debate (since Postan 1951, repr. 1973). The notion that population had grown to such a point that agriculture had been extended onto terrain which was insufficiently fertile to sustain long-term exploitation is of particular relevance to areas of late colonisation of often poor quality land, such as is widespread in this region. This study, therefore, asks why the expansion of settlement, which seems to have occurred quite dramatically here in the twelfth and thirteenth centuries, did not sow the seeds of its own demise, as it were. To pre-empt that discussion, it concludes that medieval agrarian practices in the region were sufficiently flexible to manage the environment available successfully, without any significant loss of productivity. Rather, the reverse seems to have been the case, with land improvement and economic specialisation occurring across the period, aided by the spread of markets, leaving an agrarian economy in 1500 capable of supporting a far larger population than that which was present in the eleventh century, despite significantly less favourable climatic conditions.

## A frontier landscape

The interaction between rural society and politics is a significant variable over the Middle Ages and never more so than in frontier regions. The North West was characterised as much as anything by its frontier status, containing as it did the early medieval frontier on the Mersey between the mid- to late Anglo-Saxon kingdoms of Mercia and Northumbria (Mersey means 'frontier river') as well as abutting the highly mutable political and cultural frontier with North Wales. A long coastline marked the edge of England towards the west, and both Chester, and then Liverpool, developed as ports to serve destinations in Ireland, Wales and the Irish Sea basin more generally. On occasion, the political and/or military power of Scottish kings also intruded into the region, as for example during the reign of Stephen (1135–54), and again in the early fourteenth century. The environmental marginality of much of the local landscape was compounded, therefore, by political and military pressures, which encouraged the development of a very particular type of regional community, and one which was unusually well-organised for war, often within patronage systems which were largely funded from outside.

**Conclusion**

This book is, therefore, offered as a contribution to the landscape history of medieval England, in the hope that it will help to highlight the opportunities for research in a hitherto largely neglected region of the country. It can only be an interim statement, of course, since so much work remains to be done. However, the initiative by the several county archaeologists to construct a new research framework for regional archaeology, which was launched in August 2001, should in the medium term provide the necessary intellectual cohesion to channel the research agenda over the next decade. In the meantime, it is appropriate that the particular landscape history of the North West be considered alongside that of other regions of England, if a more inclusive set of national debates is to emerge.

This study is also offered as a stimulus to those wishing to explore the particular nature of regional landscapes. Few currently study the pre-industrial landscape of the North West, in comparison that is with the Yorkshire Dales and Derbyshire Peak District, to the east, or the Midlands to the south. Yet the region contains perhaps a greater variety of landscape types (16 as defined by the Countryside Agency) than any other part of England of comparable size (Figure 6) and the scattered small towns and rural settlements of the lowlands and river valleys offer as interesting a landscape as any. If local variation has value, this is one of the richest landscapes in England. It is also, almost by definition, one which has developed over thousands of years. There are many, many, histories here, and much work still to be done, as we seek to break through the modern landscape in search of its origins over many centuries.

CHAPTER 2

# Settlement, Landscape and Community to 1070

The North West landscape only becomes entirely visible to the historian in the early modern period, when it can be divided into three sub-sets: the better-drained lowlands (largely between *c.* 9 m and 60 m); lowland mosslands and marshes; and the uplands, with their fells and steep valleys, which are largely on the east of the region. All were, of course, interwoven in the ways that they were utilized and had developed, and all had been influenced heavily by prevailing environmental and topographical conditions, and the constraints these imposed on settlement and land-use strategies. Unlike the Early Middle Ages, this was a commercialised landscape, with a considerable scatter of markets which enabled a degree of local specialisation to be sustained.

The first of these sub-types was characterised by a patchwork of fields and closes bounded by hedge and ditch, with small woods and copses scattered among the fields as well as long, narrow ribbons of ancient woodland along many water courses. Interspersed was a network of villages and market towns, some built around ancient churches, although hamlets and scattered farms were far more numerous, whilst some churches were comparatively isolated, away from other buildings. Roads and trackways snaked their way between, in places within hedges but elsewhere unenclosed, offering routeways to the traveller which were often heavily impeded by mud, with standing water trapped in deep ruts.

Extensive lowland mosslands remained until well into the industrial age, although most will have exhibited traces of heavy use by this period, as grazing and as turbaries, where peat or 'turf' was dug for fuel. Many small mosses had already been improved and had become agricultural land and even the greater ones had diminished in size as successive generations had undertaken drainage schemes and nibbled away around the edges, converting the skirtlands around old mossland or marshland to enclosed farm land.

Most of the uplands were at this point virtually unenclosed, with settlements huddled together within the valleys or on the lower slopes, each already forming a nucleus of irregular fields. These were beginning to exhibit the characteristic stone walling which was to spread out and take in a high pro-portion of the hill landscape, particularly during the later eighteenth and nine-teenth centuries, when Parliamentary enclosure would create new upland landscapes characterised by regular fields, new farmsteads, roadways and the quarries from which the necessary stone was extracted.

Areas of extensive woodland were few. John Speed's map of Lancashire, produced in 1610, marked numerous parks, the largest of which was Knowsley, but only one area, Simonwood Forest, a medieval forest between Knowsley and Ormskirk, was denoted as woodland. There were, however, numerous small stands of timber, heaths and thickets, and many streams and rivers were still fringed with ancient woodland, which also covered many steep slopes in the upper valleys of the western Pennines.

## Origins of the North West landscape

How ancient was this landscape? Answers to similar questions asked of other regions over the last two decades have emphasised the extent to which comparable early modern landscapes were rooted in a more distant past. Across England, much of the general pattern of settlement, clearance and land-use was already established in prehistory, with, in some instances, clear lines of development traceable back to the Late Stone Age (e.g. Taylor 1983; Jones 1986; Bettey 2000; Fowler 2002). Settlements have been occasionally peripatetic, of course, moving from one site to another under a variety of stimuli, and the numbers of inhabitants, and of settlements, have varied considerably over a long timescale. However, it is certainly no longer admissible to view the rural past as if conditioned just by a long succession of invasions and new settlements of entire peoples, as was generally believed half a century ago (as Hawkes and Hawkes 1947). Put simply, waves of incomers were not responsible for successive landscape revolutions, each wiping clean and reforming the landscape left by previous incumbents, whom they had exterminated or driven out, re-ordering it quite differently according to the agrarian practices they had brought with them.

Even where villages and open fields dominated the medieval landscape, no scholar would now argue that they originated with Anglo-Saxon immigrants in the fifth or sixth centuries, as was assumed before the Second World War. Rather, it is broadly accepted that the period during which they were developing lies between *c.* AD 900 and 1200. Where such developments were only partial and affected a small proportion of the landscape, as in the North West, the case for a general continuity of land-use and settlement patterns, beginning in prehistory and running into the Middle Ages, is obviously that much easier to make.

That said, there are considerable problems in establishing even the bare outlines of early settlement and land-use in the North West. Half a century ago, virtually nothing was known about the north-western landscape before the Middle Ages, and it was generally assumed to have been densely wooded. Beyond a scatter of enclosed sites, some of which have been termed hill-forts, there is still relatively little archaeological evidence of settlement prior to the Late Pre-Roman Iron Age and very little confirmed evidence for prehistoric or

Romano-British field systems (but now see Middleton *et al.* 1995; Collens 1999). Only in central Lonsdale, on the borders of Cumbria, does a 'dales' type of landscape offer the surface evidence of extensive remains from the Bronze Age onwards, which is best known at Eller Beck (Lowndes 1963, 1964; Higham, N. J. 1979a). In southern England, extensive field complexes defined by linear trackways (called 'co-axial fields') have been identified from the Bronze Age onwards, some of which have continued in use since the Iron Age to the present day (e.g. Williamson 1987). However, despite some speculation to the contrary, such complexes have not been identified with any degree of certainty west of the Pennines further north than Lichfield (Bassett 1992), and there can be no real confidence that the region was extensively enclosed even in the Roman period.

Yet, despite this lack of evidence for field systems, the last two decades have seen major advances, with several Mesolithic, Neolithic and Bronze Age sites being explored, and something like 60 late prehistoric and Roman period rural settlements now identified (see the several papers in Nevell ed. 1999). Characteristic of such discoveries is the double-ditched promontory enclosure at Great Woolden Hall (Irlam), identified from the air by the author in 1986 (Figure 9) and since excavated by the (then) Greater Manchester Archaeological Unit (Nevell 1999). This site, inhabited from the first century BC through the first half of the Roman period, occupied one of several small

FIGURE 9.
Late Prehistoric and Romano-British settlement at Great Woolden Hall, appearing as a double-ditched enclosure.

islands of relatively well-drained soil beside the Glaze Brook, but was almost surrounded by Chat Moss, Glazebrook Moss and Holcroft Moss. Prehistoric flints imply earlier activity and the post-medieval hall clearly demonstrates re-use of the same niche environment, although it is by no means clear whether or not there were significant breaks between these several occupations. Recent but still not fully published excavations on the site of Manchester Airport's second runway similarly revealed occupation of a raised, valley-edge site beside the River Bollin, in this instance primarily in the Bronze Age (Thompson 1999).

The pollen record indicates that widespread clearances for pasture were already occurring episodically in the lowlands early in the first millennium BC, some of which also exhibited traces of cereal pollen. A second cluster of such episodes late in the first millennium seems to have been associated with rather higher incidences of cultivation. At the same time, upland woodlands in Rossendale, around Featherbed Moss (Derbyshire) and Rishworth Moor (West Yorkshire) were all being cleared to provide grazing, perhaps on a seasonal basis, by the end of the millennium. This pressure on ancient wood-land seems to have been sustained throughout the Roman period and perhaps even beyond, with evidence of cereal production reaching on occasion into the high uplands. Farming was going on, therefore, and was arguably extensive, if not particularly intensive, with a widespread network of farms, some of which may well have had some enclosed fields. There is also a concentration of evidence of ritual killings and deposition in the late Pre-Roman Iron Age, Roman period or early Dark Age. The best known example is the Roman/sub-Roman period bog body (commonly known as Lindow Man) recovered from Lindow Moss in 1983 (Stead *et al.* 1986, Turner and Scaife 1995), but this is only one of three finds from this site, and others have come from Pilling Moss and Red Moss, Bolton. Further examples should, perhaps, be anticipated (Haselgrove 1996).

The Roman period witnessed the establishment of key nodal settlements in the region, with the foundation of forts and dependent civil settlements, such as Chester, Lancaster, Northwich and Manchester, and towns such as Middlewich. It is particularly important to stress the emergence of the Cheshire salt *wiches* in this context, although salt was already being exploited in the late pre-Roman Iron Age. Both Middlewich and Nantwich have provided considerable evidence of Roman-period extraction over recent years, and the latter is now beginning to offer the first slight traces of pre-Roman activity (Mike Nevell, pers. comm.). All these were to re-emerge as major centres around the end of the first millennium AD, albeit there is very little evidence of occupation during much of the Early Middle Ages. In addition, major roads were constructed between these Roman centres, many of which appear to have remained in use thereafter, and this would seem to be evidence for continuing traffic across parts of the region. Trackways had arguably long been a part of the prehistoric landscape, enabling both short and long distance trade to occur, for example in polished stone axes, metals, manufactured goods and salt. Occasional references occur to wooden trackways in the lowland peat bogs, as at Lindow, and Kate's Pad, near Pilling, which has been carbon dated to early in the first millennium BC, which imply that some constructed route-ways had even earlier origins than the Roman period.

The archaeology of this landscape is at its most problematic for the period separating the decline of Roman interest in the region, from *c.* AD 300, and the eleventh century, when Domesday Book provides a picture of sorts. This so-called 'Dark Age' period is particularly obscure in the North West. Outside Chester, where re-occupation is evident certainly from the tenth century onwards (Mason 1985; Ward 1994, 2001), only Heysham, Manchester, Tatton Park and as yet unpublished excavations at Irby and Moreton (Merseyside) have provided evidence of structures of the period with post-Roman iron work-ing additionally from Tarporley (Fairburn 2002). At Heysham, the parish church of St Peter's and the nearby ruins of St Patrick's Chapel, with its rock-cut cemetery, have both been dated to the eighth century (Plate 3), and the case made for a major monastic site (Potter and Andrews 1994; see also Taylor and Taylor 1965). This community, on the headland, might even have been com-parable to such focal church communities as Holy Island, Whitby or St Abb's Head in the North East. The presence of a hogback tombstone suggests that the site was still attracting patronage in the Viking Age. The Roman fort at Castlefield, Manchester, revealed traces of pits outside the gateway, which were initially assumed to be fifth century (Walker *et al.* 1986), but have recently been re-interpreted as possible evidence for the early tenth-century *burh* (Griffiths 2001). A scatter of coin finds plus the so-called 'Angel Stone' from the Cathedral imply some activity in the late Anglo-Saxon period. At Tatton, a large timber structure or hall has been excavated (Figure 10), which arguably belonged to the early sub-Roman period (Higham and Cane 1999), and the beginnings of a later, medieval settlement are thought to belong to a late pre-Conquest reoccupation (Higham, N. J. 2000). It should be noted, however, that the Manchester evidence was derived from the exploration of a Roman site, while work at Tatton was focused on the later medieval settlement: in both instances early medieval finds were essentially accidental. This underlines a central problem of researching the landscape history of this region. The absence of pottery between the Roman occupation and the High Middle Ages renders site identification extremely difficult. Although the culmination of this aceramic period was heralded by the tentative beginnings of Chester Ware early in the tenth century, it was only the much wider use of pottery by rural communities from around 1200 that certainly brought it to a close.

There has been some suggestion that the shape of cemetery or church enclosures may have some bearing on the date of their foundation, and in particular that curvilinear boundaries imply pre-Anglo-Saxon sites. Examples of churches set in circular or D-shaped enclosures are comparatively common in the region, occurring for example at Eccleston, Farndon, Christleton and Bowdon, Flixton and perhaps Manchester Cathedral. That said, the chrono-logical and cultural significance of this shape may not be particularly great,

FIGURE 10.
Tatton Dark Age
settlement: a massive
timber hall, dated to
the late-Roman and
early post-Roman
periods by carbon-14
dating, which lay with
other structures within
a fenced enclosure.

since examples can be found in most if not all parts of England, so arguments for pre-Anglo-Saxon church or cemetery sites cannot be pushed very far on this basis alone.

Another suggestion is that many of the minster churches of the region with names incorporating the element *burh* could, on the analogy of Bede's *Bancornaburg* (Bangor-is-y-coed), have been British churches, which were eventually re-named as part of the English takeover of the region (Higham, N. J. 2001a, b; for a wider context, see Brook 1992). Such names do not, however, occur among ancient parochial centres north of the Mersey, so if they do have any significance it is only within historic Cheshire.

The palaeobotanical record has provided another major resource, and is particularly important in the north-western region. This type of data provides some evidence of continuing settlement and land-use. While the pollen from woodland and scrub tended to increase as a proportion of the whole in carbon-dated diagrams from the region during the early Middle Ages, cereal cultivation is evidenced at Fenton Cottage on the Fylde (Middleton *et al.* 1995; Wells *et al.* 1997), and hemp or hops from two sites in the Mersey Basin. Demands made upon the local economy by the Roman military and others before about AD 300 seem to have dissipated thereafter, leading to a decline in levels of clearance and land-use and some regeneration of woodland.

The picture that emerges overall is of a very varied landscape already in the second half of the first millennium AD, with major centres already established, or being re-established, on the sites of earlier Roman occupation, and the main lines of communication already laid down. The old Roman roads ran across a comparatively well-wooded countryside. However, like many other areas characterised by woodland, there was a complex pattern of local clearances and settlements, plus extensive pasturage in use both in the woodland itself (as wood pasture), and seasonal grazing on and around some of the lowland mosses and parts at least of the uplands.

The region seems to have been barely affected by Anglo-Saxon culture prior to the conversion to Christianity, and has virtually no fifth- to seventh-century pagan cemeteries. The principal potential evidence for Anglo-Saxon paganism comes from the 'Harrow' (*hearg*) type place-names identified in south-west Lancashire (*Harhum*: Higham, M. 2003), and at Heswall on the Wirral peninsula in association with burial mounds which are probably prehistoric (Gelling 1992–3; Vibond 1992–3). These are curious outliers from the main distribution of this name type (Wilson 1985), and their close proximity to Scandinavian place-names may imply late formation in connection with Viking cult sites.

There are hints in the survival of pre-English place-names that this was a region where the Romano-British and sub-Roman inhabitants suffered little disruption from the upheavals of the early Middle Ages, staying in possession but becoming English by a process of acculturation (as argued by Gelling 1992, 53; Higham, N. 1993). However, there is a marked contrast between the rate of survival of British place-names south and north of the Mersey, with far more to the north in what became south-western Northumbria, then Lancashire. Taking wholly Brittonic names, 27 in Lancashire south of the Sands contrasts with just 10 in Cheshire (Coates and Breeze 2000), although, in Cheshire, some pre-English place-names retained significant status as the names of small parishes or townships (as Landican, Ince, Crew). There are virtually no pre-English names attached to streams, as opposed to rivers, as one might perhaps have expected from a region so close to Wales. All in all, the evidence suggests that anglicisation was comparatively successful. In Lancashire, by contrast, pre-English names or name elements are more numerous, and partly Brittonic names, in particular, include major parish names and topographical features (e.g. Manchester and Pendle both contain British elements). In some areas, as Warrington and Newton Hundreds (Figure 11), place-names which have a British element or refer to Britons are quite common. The latter can also be of high status, as, for example, the English-named Walton-on-the-Hill (which could refer to Britons, see below), which is an extensive parish in West Derby Hundred, but most here lie in rather wet and low-lying areas or on slight elevations within the mosses (Russell 1992). The incidence of minor names containing Celtic elements in Maghull, Ince Blundell and Burscough suggests a very conservative community in cultural terms. The unusual density of names derived from *eglës* (the Old Welsh derivative from Latin *ecclesia*) may imply that a British system of

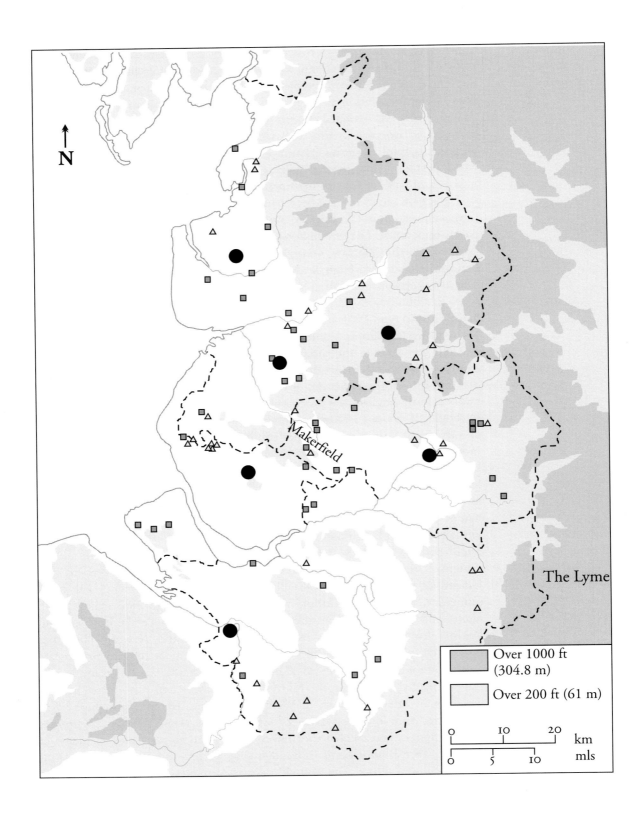

N

Makerfield

The Lyme

| | Over 1000 ft (304.8 m) |
| | Over 200 ft (61 m) |

km

mls

regional churches survived the takeover by Anglo-Saxon kingdoms in the seventh and eighth centuries comparatively intact. Between the Mersey and the Ribble, these 'eccles' place-names coincide with the Domesday hundreds in a way which suggests that those may represent comparatively ancient, 'British' units of territorial management (Barrow 1969). Only one such name occurs south of the Mersey (as Eccleston) and the only extensive Christian cemetery identified so far lies at Winwick near Warrington (Freke and Thacker 1987).

While the generality of Anglo-Saxon place-naming implies that the north-western communities conformed to English cultural norms and adopted the English language, there are hints that this process was uneven and in some parts comparatively slow. So, for example, late sound-changes in British are evidenced in the long vowel sounds found in Preese (Fylde), which may imply that British was still spoken in the eighth century. Place-names using the English term *walh* (meaning 'foreigner', 'slave') often occur on the periphery of large territorial units and may have arisen by reference to recognisably British communities (as Walton, Walton-le-Dale) although the term also occurs in Old English personal names. In West Derby Hundred, Walton-on-the-Hill is the focus of a very large parish, perhaps implying a wider 'British' landscape. The Scandinavian *bretar* ('Briton') is also found as an element in Merseyside (as Brettargh in Woolton and Bretland in Thornton (Russell 1992, 39)), implying the presence of recognisably 'British' communities as late as the tenth century (Ekwall 1918; Kenyon 1991). The large numbers of place-names in Cheshire linking *-ton* with either a directional term (as in Aston, Norton, Weston, Sutton) or a personal name (as in Tatton) may imply that a phase of re-naming coincided with an influx of Mercian administrators and estate-holders, at earliest in the later seventh century (cf. Gelling 1990; Owen 1997). The gradual process of cultural change in the region perhaps reflects its political marginality, lying as it did in the frontier regions of two great 'overkingships', Mercia and Northumbria, where these reached the Irish Sea. The presence of carved stones of characteristically Anglo-Saxon type does imply that these provinces were incorporated into the wider territorial organisation of the new kingships (as most spectacularly to be seen at Sandbach (Hawkes 2003; Figure 12), but see also examples at Lancaster, Heysham and Halton (Plate 4). However, there is barely any literary record of religious houses established here in the pre-Viking period (Chester is a possible exception: Thacker 1985), nor of any great concentration of early royal estates (although the place-name element *King* occurs at Kingsley in Cheshire).

The pattern of settlement and landscape is currently only understood at the most basic of levels, very largely via the interpretation of find-spots and place-names (see Kenyon 1991; Higham, N.J. 1993; Philpott 1999). The agricultural heartlands seem to have been characterised by settlement names (generally ending in *–ton*, *-ham* or *–bury*) and contained the majority of ancient church sites and high status settlements, but these were interspersed with more wooded terrain (commonly place-names ending in *-ley*), mossland, moorland

FIGURE 11.
Pre-English place-names, based on Coates and Breeze 2000, 369, 383, but including both possible and confident identifications, and with additions from Russell (1992). The large circles are 'Eccles' place-names; squares are wholly Brittonic or Welsh; triangles are partly Brittonic or Welsh.

FIGURE 12.
One of two stone cross shafts dating to around AD 800 in the Market Square, Sandbach, which arguably reflect the presence of an important church, perhaps a monastery, in the pre-Viking Period.

or hill country. Clusters of settlement-type place-names seem often to have been grouped in discrete territories, with woodland, mossland or upland-type names forming the periphery. The hundreds and wapentakes of Domesday Lancashire provide one model (Thorn 1991b), since they may well represent earlier, Northumbrian 'shires'. Similar units may be represented by some at least of the large parishes or estates which seem to have been paired to make up the hundreds of late Anglo-Saxon Cheshire.

There is some evidence for economic specialisation within large territories which are now discernable only by reference to the great medieval parishes of

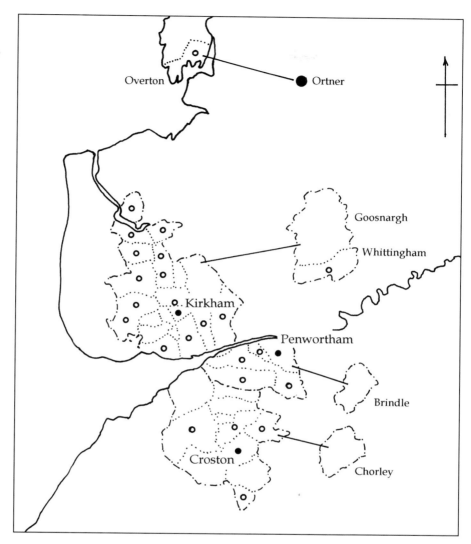

FIGURE 13.
Possible evidence for
early transhumance in
Central Lancashire,
based on lowland
parishes with detached
portions in the
woodland region.
Circles indicate a
settlement-type place-
name.

the region. The case has been made for agrarian specialisation in different townships in several of the Domesday hundreds in Cheshire (Higham, N. J. 1993), with some predominantly open landscapes and others woodland pasture. Further north, long distance transhumance may have influenced the shape of early parishes in parts of Lancashire, where, for example, Croston and Penwortham both included detached upland-edge townships (Chorley and Brindle respectively), which probably represent summer grazing. The place-name Ortner (Wyersdale) derives from 'Overton-*erg*', suggesting that it originated as summer pasturage attached to the lowland settlement of Overton on the west bank of the Lune estuary (Atkin 1985; Winchester 1993). Kirkham parish was similarly in two parts, with a western, lowland core characterised by settlement and wetland place-names, and a detached eastern portion centred on Goosnargh (another *erg* place-name) and dominated by woodland names (White Lea, Ashley, etc; Figure 13). These detached parcels seem in each case to reflect the needs of lowland communities where much of their immediately adjacent pasture was very low-lying and so periodically subject to flooding, thus necessitating the retention of grazing rights further inland, and generally in a woodland environment. South of the Mersey, place-names such as Knutsford Booths, Norbury Booths and Somerford Booths (from Old Danish *bōtih*, Middle English *bothe*) suggest the seasonal use of pasture but not necessarily at any great distance from the winter settlement. Across most of Cheshire, the variability of landscape was generally less, giving little encouragement to long-distance transhumance and a greater reliance on woodland pastures contiguous with more open and settled land. Similar patterns arguably occurred further north as well, in Salfordshire and Blackburnshire, for example, where local communities had access to nearby uplands, wetland grazing and/or wood pasture. In Salfordshire, there is a high density of settlement-type place-names (largely with the suffix *-ton*), which were presumably coined with reference to settlements within a lowland and locally cleared environment, but within a landscape which offered access to both mosses and dryer pastures on and towards the uplands. Further west, lowland woodlands seem to have been a more prominent feature. For example, the parish of Leigh (itself a woodland-type name) consisted of a core of topographical and settlement township names (Bedford, Pennington, Atherton), with woodland names on the edge which clearly reflect place-naming from the centre, as Westleigh (to the west) and Astley ('East-woodland clearing'), Tyldesley and Shakerley to the east.

Many boundaries which can be identified in the Middle Ages could easily have been in use for hundreds of years before the Conquest, but the difficulty lies in each instance in making the case. Clearly the coast and major rivers like the Mersey and Ribble were important territorial markers at all times, but the issue is problematic elsewhere. Place-names provide one important source of evidence. So, for example, the township name Macefen (Welsh 'boundary field') occurs on the edge of the core of settlement-type names in the parish of Malpas (*Depenbach* in 1086, arguably named after its boundary.). Beyond, a belt of woodland type township names occurs around the hundredal and shire boundaries to the south and east, which may imply that extensive wood pastures existed. Among these woodland names is the Celtic Iscoed. These two Welsh place-names suggest, but do not prove, that the general pattern of this landscape, and the territorial units which eventually emerged as the parishes of Bunbury and Malpas, were already present when Welsh was still the spoken language, so before *c* 800 (Higham, N.J. 1993, but see Dodgson 1967 for an alternative interpretation). Similarly, the modern place-name Tarvin means 'at the boundary river' (British Latin *terminum*, Welsh *tervin*: Dodgson 1966–67, III, 281), and occurs where the Roman road crosses the river. In the eleventh century the river (later known as the Gowy) divided two hundreds and it has been suggested that it had been a significant boundary in the Roman period

(Mason 1988). There are hints, therefore, that the boundaries of some major land units in medieval Cheshire were already old by the eleventh century, having been in existence even before the process of anglicisation took place.

To offer a second example, on the north-eastern edge of medieval Lancashire, Mary Higham (1999) has argued that the medieval bounds of the hunting preserve known as Burton Chase derive from an early pre-Conquest land unit. This was perhaps first documented as *in regione Dunutinga* ('[lands] in the region of the Dent-descendants/people'), granted to Bishop Wilfrid in the late seventh century. Again, British names feature around the boundary, including the Cant Beck and Pen-y-Ghent, both of which contain an element meaning 'boundary' in Old Welsh. The *Dunutinga[s]* should be interpreted as 'the people of the Hill', a terminology which in this locality should perhaps be identified with Ingleborough, on the top of which is a major late prehistoric hillfort (Plate 5). While the use of this nomenclature does not require that this territorial unit necessarily predated the Roman conquest, it certainly opens up the possibility. More particularly, it does suggest a pre-Viking region which should perhaps be compared with the *Wrocensætan*, the 'people of the Wrekin' (named from The Wrekin and/or Roman Wroxeter), in the north-west Midlands. The boundary of Burton Chase, therefore, may already have been in existence in something not far removed from its known, thirteenth-century form already for more than half a millennium, and quite possibly twice as long.

Other land units also look ancient. King Æthelstan's grant of Amounderness to the archbishop of York demonstrates that this was already an identifiable land-unit in the 930s. The Ribble estuary, like those of the Mersey and the Dee, is so difficult to cross that it was likely to have acted as a major boundary at an early date, separating Amounderness from the lands to the south. This would seem to tie in with the fact that the lands between the Ribble and the Mersey featured quite independently in the will of Wulfric, founder of Burton Abbey, around 1000, when they were apparently a single area of lordship, much as they were to be in 1066. Elsewhere, as in the hill country of eastern Cheshire, crosses may have served as pre-Conquest boundary markers (Sidebottom 2000).

## Scandinavians and the landscape of the North West

While national histories have rarely displayed much interest in the North West in the pre-Viking period, a large scale immigration of Vikings into the region in the tenth century has become an established 'fact' over the last century, one to which Anglo-Saxon historians have conceded considerable attention (e.g. Stenton 1943; Blair 1977; Loyn 1991). This view is based in part on the distribution of Viking Age sculpture, in part on hoards of precious metal (including the uniquely large example discovered at Cuerdale) but most of all on our understanding of place-names. Certainly, the central Middle Ages did experience a strong process of name formation in Old Norse, as witness the characteristic name elements such as the suffix *-by* (settlement), various personal names, *-kirk* (church), *-scough* (from *skógr* Old Norse 'wood') and *-argh* or similar (from *erg* Old Norse 'shieling', see above). This does suggest that Old Norse was a widely spoken language in parts of the region between around 1000 and 1200.

The case for large-scale Norse settlement was made most confidently, and argued most effectively, by Frederick Wainwright, whose interest in the region of his birth, education and subsequent employment (in southern Lancashire) never wavered (1945–6, 71):

> During the early years of the tenth century hordes of Scandinavians settled in north-western England ... They arrived in small separate companies seeking lands to cultivate rather than monasteries to plunder; it is highly unlikely that they were a 'great army' organized for and intent upon military conquest. It is generally believed that they came as peaceful farmers not as hostile warriors, although it would be easy to overemphasize this aspect of the settlement, for Norsemen in this age would be prepared at least to meet violence with violence.

Yet some doubt must be cast on Wainwright's assumption of large-scale immigration into the regional landscape, for several reasons. Firstly, there has been much disagreement as to the real extent of this process, with some scholars imagining that much of Cheshire, as well as all Lancashire, was affected. Neither of these generalisations can be justified on place-name evidence (Gelling 1995 for Cheshire; for Lancashire, see Tait 1908; Ekwall 1918; Wainwright 1975; Fellows-Jensen 1985; Kenyon 1991; Higham, M. 1995; Higham, N. J. 2004, Griffiths 2004). A minimalist interpretation should probably be preferred, which focuses exclusively on those areas where Scandinavian place-naming was concentrated. In Cheshire, this was almost entirely limited to the tip of the Wirral peninsula. Further north, Norse place-names are concentrated in an arc of land no more than about 20 km from the coast (Figure 14), with only a thin scatter further inland in the Lune valley, and up the Ribble valley, which was a major line of communication with York. Even where the heaviest concentrations occur, earlier place-names survive on the better terrain, as at Hambleton and Pilling, for example, and around the extensive mosslands of Over Wyre. Of the large, multi-township parish names, only Ravensmeols, Garstang and Ormskirk are constructed in Old Norse, and even the latter may denote the presence of an earlier church, implying that this was a renaming rather than a new foundation. Some minor parishes, with just one or a very few townships, have Old Norse names (e.g. Myerscough) or are Grimston hybrids (e.g. Flixton), but these are the exception and some may be comparatively late formations. Overall, the survival of Old English nomenclature at the parish level is indicative of at least a degree of continuity of settlement and organisation of the landscape.

FIGURE 14. Scandinavian place-names: the main distribution of major place-names is coastal, from the Dee northwards, with scattered outliers inland.

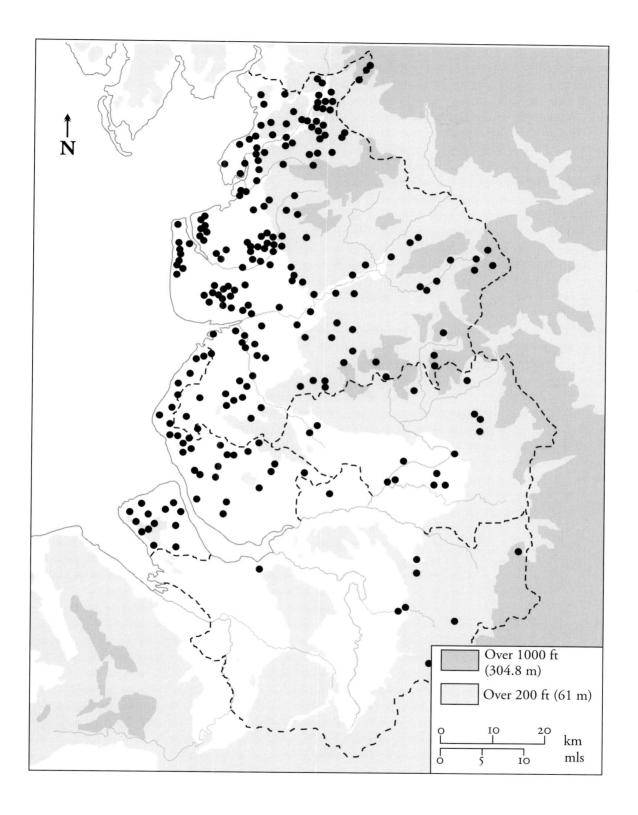

Secondly, the place-naming is not entirely consistent with incomers coming primarily from Ireland, as Wainwright supposed. Rather, there is far more evidence for Anglo-Danish influence in this process than had been thought thirty years ago, suggesting that some at least of the place-naming relates to the development of the Danish kingdom of York in the late ninth and tenth centuries, which encompassed Lancashire (Fellows-Jensen 1985). Names such as (West) Derby, Roby, Raby, Helsby, Kirkby and Crosby have few parallels in Ireland but fit easily into a pattern of place-naming emanating from the Danelaw. That said, there are sufficient Goidelic names (as Tarbock, Liscard, Noctorum and Arrowe, all in Merseyside) to substantiate the view that some incomers did come from either Ireland or the Isle of Man.

Thirdly, the assumption that language change *necessarily* implies large scale immigration is not entirely secure: it has recently been recognised that language, alongside other hallmarks of ethnicity or group identity, was to an extent negotiable during the Early and Central Middle Ages. Names which include both Old English and Old Norse elements are common (e.g. Kirkham, Sefton), which imply alteration of existing names. It cannot be ruled out, therefore, that a significant part of the place-naming process was generated by speakers of Old Scandinavian or a dialect of Old English much affected by Scandinavian, who were themselves, in part at least, descended from pre-Viking communities, but had, for a variety of reasons, adopted Old Norse as a *lingua franca* within the region. Some of the Viking name elements were still in use throughout the Middle Ages and entered Middle English, resulting in such odd-seeming place-names as Johnby, in Cumbria (the personal name 'John' only reaching the region after the Conquest, but then being combined with Old Norse –*by* meaning 'settlement').

The final reason for caution lies in the pollen evidence, which provides little scope for a large-scale increase in the total population occurring in the region in the tenth and eleventh centuries. Rather, the current state of knowledge would suggest that the landscape changed comparatively little during this period, generally continuing the patterns already established soon after the Roman era. So, for example, the well-dated diagram from Over Wyre indicates that the process of woodland regeneration which followed the Roman period peaked at some point between AD 670–990 and 1047–1280 (Wells *et al.* 1997). A comparable advance in arboreal pollen has been noted in several studies from right across the region (Oldfield 1963; Oldfield and Statham 1965; Birks 1965; Leah *et al.* 1997). This long-running reduction in farming pressure must place in jeopardy the assumption of a major Scandinavian colonisation, since such might be expected to have reversed this trend significantly earlier. What caused this apparent slump in land use remains a matter of debate. Some have looked to such military factors as William's Harrying of the North as a possible explanation (as Oldfield 1969), but the inception seems too early for this. Climate change remains a possible impetus, given the severe climatic deterioration which is generally dated to the middle of the first millennium. Disease may also be relevant (as suggested by

Hodgkinson *et al.* 2000), such as is likely to have been associated with a climatic downturn, and the series of plagues in the seventh century which were documented by Bede may have been a factor. Alternatively, lengthy political instability brought about initially by the collapse of Roman defenses in the fifth century and then by the destruction of the Anglo-Saxon kingdom of Northumbria in the ninth may have been the cause (Higham, N. J. 1986). The effect of the latter may have been to encourage regional communities to re-position themselves in terms of other societies spread around the Irish Sea, where a Norse culture predominated from the ninth century through to the end of the eleventh, at least.

Whatever the cause, the palaeobotanical evidence would seem to suggest that human pressures upon the landscape were comparatively light until about the twelfth century, and may have even decreased once the Viking Age had begun. Any influx of settlers during the tenth and eleventh centuries seems to have been at least balanced by an outflow from the region. Hints of the latter are preserved in the records of the St Cuthbert's community, which had eventually established itself at Durham. The abbot of Heversham and other members of the north-western elite sought a refuge there early in the tenth century from the attacks of 'pirates'. Such men may represent just the apex of a much larger exodus of western Northumbrians, and perhaps also north-western Mercians, from the region. This was not, however, ever likely to have involved the majority of the rural community, who, in Lancashire at least, were probably absorbed into the increasingly Scandinavianised society which now characterised the region.

Despite considerable work on place-names (Ekwall 1918, 1922; Wainwright 1945–6; Fellows-Jensen 1983, 1985, 1992; Kenyon 1991, *inter alia*), hoards (Graham-Campbell 1992, 2001) and metalwork (Edwards 1998), our under-standing of settlement and landscape in the region during the Viking Age remains extremely poor. One result has been that the North West has once again been neglected within the wider national debate in recent years. The region failed to command attention in the most recent collection of essays on Anglo-Scandinavian interactions (Hadley and Richards 2000), even though the front cover of the volume is illustrated by a photograph of one of the Viking Age crosses at Whalley on the upper Ribble. Excavated examples of Viking Age settlements have been identified both in southern Lakeland (Dickinson 1985) and adjacent parts of Yorkshire at Ribblehead (King 1978) but only Tatton has produced probable evidence of rural settlement of this period in the region (Higham N. J. 1998–9 and see below, page 135). Elsewhere in the North, there are signs of settlement nucleation and new settlement formation beginning within the Viking Age (see for example, Richards 2000; Hall 2001), on sites that would then be integral to the emer-gence of the medieval settlement pattern. The evidence from Tatton fits neatly with such hypotheses, but on present knowledge the wider case for the region remains to be established.

## Regional communities in the eleventh century

However complex the problems of interpretation (see, most recently, Roffe 2000), the Domesday Survey of the English shires undertaken in 1086 provides the earliest, chronologically precise source for the history of the North West. The administrative organisation that was enshrined in that work emphasises the existence of deep divisions within a regional community which was polarised between two parallel, and in some respects competitive, political hierarchies. The north-western Midlands was, in the mid-eleventh century, focused on the earldom of Mercia. By contrast, the heartland of the old kingdom and later earldom of Northumbria lay in an extended Yorkshire. Indeed, Lancashire had no independent existence at this date, the different parts of it having various connections with both Yorkshire and Cheshire (the term will be used here solely as a geographical indicator). Sustaining both earldoms lay deep-seated, regional loyalties founded in a long history of local and regional development that had, in the past, found expression under the aegis of earls whose interests did not necessarily coincide with those of the kings of England to whom they were responsible.

The most important of these divisions was that which separated the West Riding of Yorkshire (within Northumbria), from the shire of Chester, with those neighbouring areas of South Lancashire and North Wales that were appended to it (Figure 15). The boundary lay on the Ribble, with Preston and the large hundred of Amounderness forming the southern extremity of western Northumbria. Lancashire between the Ribble and the Mersey (*Ripam et Mersham*) was focused on six royal estates in 1066. In a region in which royal land was otherwise conspicuously absent, the king's tenure probably resulted from the conflict of interests between King Æthelræd and the leaders of the 'Five Boroughs', from whom southern Lancashire was probably retrieved for the crown in 1006 when Ealdorman Ælfhelm was murdered (Sawyer 1979). Southern Lancashire should probably be interpreted as appended to the Mercian earldom in 1066, but its precise organisation is unclear. Although there has been some suggestion that earlier Mercian influences were involved, it is probably pertinent that the local government and tenurial geography of the region seems to have been substantially redrawn in the early tenth century by Edward the Elder (Higham, N. J. 1989).

South of the Mersey, Cheshire was the most northerly of those Midland shires that were assessed for taxation purposes in hides, although a handful of entries for the county refer to carucates (a unit associated with Viking England) and there is a single instance of unhidated land (Tait 1916). South Lancashire, by contrast, was assessed in carucates but a note at the end of the first entry — the description of West Derby hundred — equates a hide with six carucates, presumably reflecting the imposition of a southern administrative gloss upon a community previously organised and assessed within Northumbria (Demarest 1923). Beyond the Ribble, assessment in carucates was standard. Land tenure in Lancashire, including the south, was dominated by thegnage or

FIGURE 15.
The North West in 1086: between the Ribble and Mersey, hundreds were focused on six great estates (solid circles); beyond the Ribble, the area was organised in similar multi-settlement estates (open circles) without hundreds. The early Norman castle and borough at Penwortham was probably the focus of administration for southern Lancashire. In Cheshire and parts of Lancashire, twelfth-century re-organisation of hundreds substantially altered their geography. The subsequent hundreds are in large print.

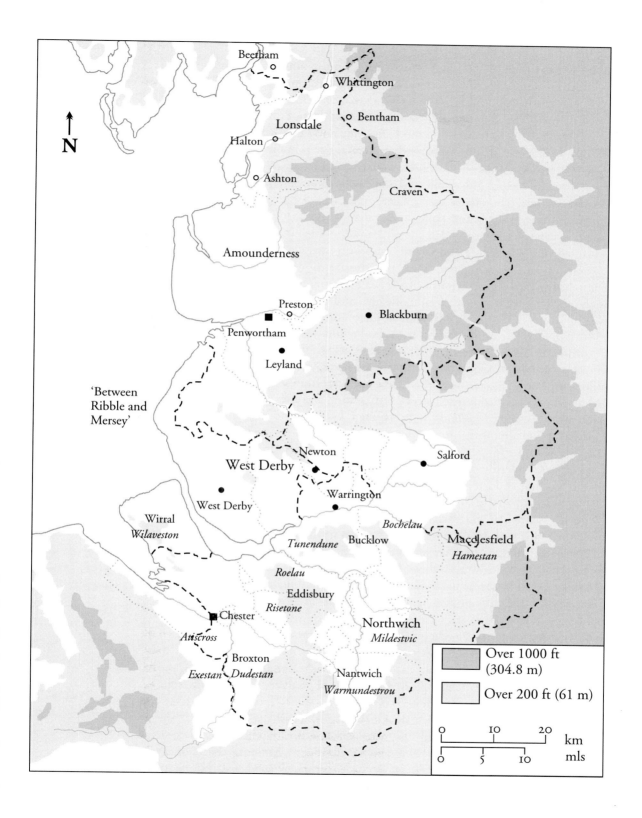

drengage, the basis of which was a payment of geld per carucate, a variety of boon works (in particular work on structures on the king's core estate and his hunting grounds), and subjection to the royal courts (for wider discussion, see Jolliffe 1926; Lewis, C. P. 1991b; Lewis, J. 2000). This differed considerably from forms of landholding which the commissioners came across in North West Mercia, where tenure of a vill seems not normally to have involved the obligation to perform such apparently menial tasks as boon works.

The frontier status of the north-western counties was no accident. The great, middle-Saxon kingdoms had developed out of core territories with substantial agrarian advantages, where relatively large populations could support strong military and political hierarchies. These hierarchies tested each other in whatever areas divided them, many of which by definition were disadvantageous. Lancashire and Cheshire were an obvious and perhaps the most obvious case in point, where the rival authority of Welsh kings traditionally competed with the pretensions of Irish Sea raiders and settlers and the increasingly anglicised communities of Yorkshire and central England. The region was the focus of a number of major military conflicts during the Viking Age, most famously including the probable site of the battle of *Brunanburh* (937) at Bromborough (Dodgson 1957; Higham, N. J. 1997). A Norse raid on Cheshire in 980 was one of a series which heralded the start of the Second Viking Age and Chester was presumably the port from which an English fleet led by King Æthelræd himself struck at Cumbria and the Isle of Man in 1000. The north-western Midlands were ravaged by Edmund Ironside and Earl Uhtred of Northumbria in 1016 and were adversely affected by a series of conflicts with the Welsh in the mid-eleventh century. In 1055 a Norse fleet was paid off at Chester by the earl for its part in a campaign which had culminated in the burning of Hereford.

Nor were all the military incursions temporary. Rather, the frontier with Wales in particular fluctuated erratically. The rewards obtained by King Griffith for his successful military intervention in English politics included the borderlands between the Dee and the Clwyd, parts of which (the area around Eyton) had previously been held by the Bishop of Lichfield and his men (Morgan 1978). It seems likely that the bulk of the remainder had previously been held by the earls of Mercia and represented in 1055, therefore, the price paid by Earl Leofric of Mercia for Welsh assistance against Harold Godwineson. In 1062–3, however, Harold and his brother Tostig launched an invasion of North Wales which destroyed King Griffith. According to Domesday Book, areas of north-eastern Wales such as Englefield were waste in 1066, and this presumably reflected the series of conflicts which affected the region over the previous decade.

Further north, the old British kingdom of Strathclyde included the historic county of Cumberland but, after the last British king died in 1018, it was absorbed into the new kingdom of the Scots, bringing the Scottish frontier with Northumbria far south of the later medieval boundary around Carlisle. Warfare between the Scots and the Northumbrians during the middle years of the eleventh century involved invasions from both sides, including one famous occasion on which Macbeth lost his throne. Northern Lancashire seems to have been severely affected by this process, although it is so badly recorded that it is rarely possible to be sure precisely what happened and when.

The North West was, therefore, a very volatile region, control of parts of which passed erratically between Anglo-Saxon, Welsh, Scottish and Norse elites during the later Anglo-Saxon period. Such a dangerous environment is unlikely to have encouraged much investment in the countryside or the expansion of peasant farms, and it is not surprising to find that much of later medieval Flintshire, for example, was heavily wooded at this date. A traveller to the region in the 1060s would have had to be careful to avoid active hostilities and will have seen extensive areas along the Welsh march where some at least of the farms had been burnt out, fields were un-ploughed and livestock few and far between. Further north, a similar picture of ruin and depopulation would probably have greeted a visitor to central or northern Lancashire, where Scottish armies seem to have undertaken a devastating raid around 1061 (Kapelle 1979, 93).

The great battles of 1066 did not immediately affect the North West, although many local men probably died at the defeat of Earls Edwin and Morcar at Gate Fulford, outside York, on September 20th. However, the accord reached between the Conqueror and these, the two most senior survivors of the late Saxon secular aristocracy, seems to have been unsatisfactory to both parties. Local unrest brought Norman forces into the north in 1068, and resulted in a war in north Mercia and beyond the Humber in 1069, which was concluded by King William's devastation of Yorkshire. The Northumbrian aristocracy may have been aided, as they had been in 1065 and 1066, by the followers of Earl Edwin in the north-west. Domesday entries suggest that much of Cheshire, Shropshire and northern Staffordshire was 'waste' when new Norman landholders took them over (Terrett 1962; Matthews 2003).

The east of Cheshire appears to have been particularly hard-hit, with numerous modest estates affected by the crisis. The manors of Longdendale were all, as late as 1086, still described as waste although they were valued at 40 shillings, only a quarter their value in 1066 (Morgan 1978; V.C.H. 1987). All still remained untenanted in 1086, a block of underdeveloped lands in the gift of Earl Hugh. In these circumstances, it seems possible that a Norman army entered Cheshire via Longdendale. The distribution of 'wasted' estates (i.e. estates producing no income) has led to attempts to establish a four-pronged progress across the county, broadly from east to west (e.g. Husain 1973). However, the contemporary road system, which was still on the Roman roads, provided the only feasible routes for what was probably a heavily encumbered body of armed men operating in unknown territory. Concentrations of 'wasted' estates around the Roman roads in the vicinities of Northwich and Middlewich and along Watling Street in Bucklow Hundred, for example, provide some support for such a model but fall short of proving it.

The opportunity to examine the 'wasting' of Cheshire in some detail derives from the provision of an additional valuation not available in some of the 'wasted' counties (including Derbyshire) pertaining to the estate at the date when the 1086 tenant obtained it. In Cheshire, it can reasonably be assumed that the enfeoffment of Earl Hugh with the county in 1071 was the effective starting point, although his disposal of 'waste' manors was still underway in 1086.

Within the later medieval county, there was little record of 'waste' in 1066. A handful of manors east of the Central Cheshire Ridge were stated to have then been 'waste' but these need have been no more than the victims of local catastrophe of a kind common where small populations subsisted uncomfortably close to the edge of genetic failure. In the west, a scatter of 'waste' or partially 'waste' manors were recorded in the Dee valley where they may represent indirect evidence of the dislocation that accompanied the Welsh campaigns of Earls Harold and Tostig in 1062 (Terrett 1962). As such, this incidence was only the outer fringe of a widespread devastation recorded at 1066 in the manors of north-eastern Wales, and in north-western Shropshire (Saunders 1954). Although this interpretation is to an extent contested, it seems probable that the rising incidence of 'waste' manors between 1066 and 1071 derived in part from the collapse of estate management caused by losses at Gate Fulford, but in part also by the actions of Norman soldiery. The outcome was a degree of dislocation in the agrarian economy that was only exceeded by contemporary Yorkshire (Hey 1986). Such was indeed described in graphic terms by Orderic Vitalis, who was born just six years later (Chibnall 1969), and who seems to have been well-informed.

In Cheshire, particularly in the less well-populated areas, substantial omissions concerning both 1066 and 1071 are characteristic of the Domesday Survey, perhaps implying that knowledge of landownership, land-use and values at those dates was only patchily available twenty years later. The valuation of numerous estates remained depressed below 1066 levels in 1086, although the total number of waste manors had then reverted to near the 1066 total. In the northern hundreds of Bucklow and *Tunendune*, for those manors for which figures are given, the gross loss of value between 1066 and 1086 was only 4s. 4d. However, manors where there was a recorded loss of value outnumber those with gains by 21 to eight, and the figures are distorted by the exceptional performance of Halton manor, at the centre of a major barony, where estimated value increased by the disproportionately high figure (by local standards) of 64s., to 104s. (Higham, N. J. 1982).

No estimate of value was recorded for lands subsequently in Lancashire at a stage intermediate between 1066 and 1086. As a result, the identification of Norman 'wasting' in South Lancashire is problematic. 'Waste' was recorded in 1086 at the capital manor of Salford and in Leyland Hundred (Morgan 1978), but not elsewhere in the area. Beyond the Ribble, Amounderness was described as very largely 'waste', with only 16 manors with any population at all in 1086. However, there is no clear evidence to suppose that this damage was inflicted by Norman armies and some commentators have preferred to blame the

*Table 1. Waste in Domesday Cheshire (based on Darby and Maxwell*
*1962, p.375; Hey 1986, table 1.2).*

| Date | Wholly waste | Partly waste | Total manors where waste was recorded |
|---|---|---|---|
| 1066 | 41 | 11 | 52 |
| Inception of current holder (?1071–86) | 135 | 27 | 162 |
| 1086 | 41 | 17 | 58 |

Scottish invasion of 1070, or another in 1061, or even poor management of estates far distant from their owners. A substantial group of manors in the Skipton area was also 'waste' in 1086 (Maxwell 1962) and it remains a possibility that this resulted from Norman soldiers passing from the Aire valley over the watershed into the Ribble basin. The 'waste' recorded in the hundreds of Leyland and Salford could document these Normans' march towards Cheshire and the Upper Mersey, but the case is far from compelling and other, more local causes should probably be preferred.

## Landholding, 1066–1086

In 1066, three of the most prominent and wealthy men in the land dominated landholding in north-western England. The King held Lancashire between the Mersey and the Ribble as six vast lordships, each coterminous with a hundred and each administered from a capital manor that seems to have been identical with the meeting-place of the hundred (Figure 15). Within each territory the local community was organised around a class of comparatively free, estate-holding thegns and 'drengs'. Their apparent lack of contact with their titular lord, the distant king of all England, can have encouraged little, if any, commitment to his political cause. It seems likely that social and political leadership of this community fell to such figures as the well-established Uhtred, occupying key estates in the comparatively affluent hundred of West Derby. Beyond the Ribble, earl Tostig held the most substantial and numerous of the vast, multi-settlement estates of North Lancashire alongside a handful of Yorkshire's senior aristocracy. These holdings were his, presumably by right of his tenure of the earldom of Northumbria, which lapsed in the autumn of 1065. Had more time elapsed between the Northumbrian rebellion that ousted him and the death of King Edward, we should expect that some at least of these estates would eventually have passed to his successor, earl Morcar, or his deputies. But for all practical purposes, this was a local society within which the regional land-owning elite provided the local administrators representing higher authority, with little contact from above.

Cheshire was a county of far more numerous, named tenurial units than Lancashire (277 places are named, many in relation to more than one tenurial unit), but amongst them, there stands out a minority of holdings by reason of their substantial size, carucage, tax assessment and value. Of the 15 estates assessed at five hides or more, Earl Edwin or his brother held eight, including four out of the highest-rated five. Fourteen manors were valued at £5 or more in 1066, of which six were valued at £10 or more. Of these 14, 12 were demesne manors of the earls, including all those valued at or above the higher sum. The central importance of the estates of Edwin and Morcar (who held the great manor of Acton and the 'waste' manor of Wheelock) is reinforced by the suspicion that in several cases both enjoyed beneficial hidation, meaning that their demesne lands were unusually lightly taxed. Neighbouring manors that appear to have been assessed for tax at a higher rate may, in some instances, have been bearing much of the tax burden of the earls' demesne (Higham, N. J. 1988a). This benefit can be detected also on the estates of the Abbey of St Werburgh in the Dee valley, of which the earls were the principal patrons. The value of the estates of the earls, as recorded by Domesday Book for the 'Time of King Edward', at £133, exceeded that of the next 25 wealthiest land-holders combined, and many of them, of course, like the bishop of Lichfield, were the earls' close associates. Edwin and his brother held many of the key estates around which society was organised, such as Macclesfield in the east, Acton in the south, Frodsham and Weaverham in the centre and Eastham in the Wirral.

Beneath these powerful families and institutions, a 'gentry-class' can be identified. Figures such as Gamel in Rochdale (who may be the same man as the individual of that name who held land in Poulton, Cheadle and Mottram), Edwin in the south-west of Cheshire and Alfward at Bowdon all held groups of manors and often controlled churches and such manorial perquisites as mills. Others seem to have been in the process of establishing themselves by service to the earls, as land agents, stewards, and so on, the same name occurring against numerous, but scattered and small estates (Higham N. J. 1995, 1997b). There was also a profusion of very small manors, either consisting of minor townships or fractions of a township. Such estates were often assessed at just one hide or less, with only one or a very few ploughlands, and many seem to have been little more than large farms held by freemen. Such include, for example, the manor of Norbury (now part of Stockport), held in 1066 by a 'free man', Brown, with four ploughlands but assessed at only one hide. The name Brown occurs with reference to four other manors in Cheshire, all of which are in the same area (Alderley, Bramhall, Chelford, Siddington), and all may refer to a single individual, but, even so, they totalled only five hides. At Norbury there was no demesne recorded: the manor was effectively a sub-tenanted estate held by an unnamed *radman* – a category of landholder specific to western England who owed riding services. He had three *cottarii* (cottagers who had no significant landholdings) as his workforce and a plough, an acre of meadow, extensive woodland and three enclosures. This was, there-fore, an example of a common type of small manor within the region, which consisted of one large farm with just a few cottages in addition, perhaps making up a small hamlet. Whether the *radman* should be viewed more as a tenant or as an estate manager is unclear but he probably acted in both capacities. The enclosures ('hays', so literally 'hedges', which were probably deer enclosures) imply that hunting was significant, which may be the reason Brown had put in what amounts to an estate manager. Brown also had substantial woodlands attached to other manors, and all his several holdings lay in the well-wooded landscape characteristic of eastern and southern Cheshire.

A rather different example of this type of small land unit further west is the manor of Thornton-le-Moors, on the Mersey lowlands near the Gowy estuary. This was assessed at two hides and had land for two ploughs, with half a ploughland in lordship. Two *villani* ('villeins', each normally holding a substantial peasant farm) and a *bordarius* (a near-landless tenant associated with woodland landscapes) shared 'half a plough' (probably a half team of oxen which would normally be combined with a demesne plough and half team). This was Stenketel's only manor in the shire in 1066, but there was a church and a priest by 1086, despite the tiny size of the potential congregation. The occupation of this and several other moss edge and very marginal sites on this estuarine skirtland suggests that some headway had already been made in terms of colonisation of the Mersey flood plain.

Throughout the North West, the church in its various guises was conspicuous by the poverty of its endowment. St Werburgh's was the only substantially endowed monastery. The bishops of Chester and Lichfield held five manors, in addition to which the minster church of St John's and the parish church of St Chad's at Chester held (or claimed) small, manorial interests. However, of these, only Tarvin (six hides and, with 22 ploughlands, valued at £8) was among the more substantial manors of the county. Elsewhere in Cheshire, church land was limited to small-scale endowments within manors held by the secular aristocracy. Most of the shire (excluding the northern Wirral) was divided into comparatively ancient parishes of considerable size, based on churches, often at places with *burh* (meaning 'stronghold', 'fortified site') as an element in the name (examples are Bromborough, Wybunbury, Prestbury, Astbury). These may reflect churches dependent on early estate organisation around fortified centres, particularly since *burh* was used locally for hillforts (as Eddisbury), but none has been identified. Alternatively, these names may denote church sites which predate the English takeover and refer instead to the enclosures surrounding Celtic churches, on the model of Bangor-is-y-Coed (Bangor-on-Dee), which was named by Bede in the *Ecclesiastical History* (II, 2) as *Bancornaburg* and which lies in Domesday Cheshire, in Maelor Saesneg (Higham, N. J. 2001a, b and see page 24 above). Other ancient parish names are topographical in formation (as Bowdon, Sandbach, *Depenbach* (Malpas)) or comparatively early settlement-type names (Frodsham, Weaverham), but a small minority are clearly later (Rostherne is a Viking Age name) and perhaps represent either the removal of a church to a new site or the re-naming of an existing settlement.

Between the Mersey and the Ribble, one, or at most two, churches held a carucate or two within the hundred. Elsewhere in England, church land often comprised something like a third of the total. In this respect, as in many others, the north-western counties were out of step with the main stream of developments across much of England, held back perhaps by the inadequacy of the local resource base and forming a frontier zone in the patronage of the secular political elite. The local community had little which they could afford to offer as an attraction to either religious communities or well-educated individual parish incumbents. The result was that vast, multi-settlement

FIGURE 16.
Whalley Churchyard: one of two standing crosses of the Viking Age still to be seen adjacent to the medieval church.

parishes were retained during a period when, elsewhere, they were rapidly fragmenting as landholders established local, manorial churches. Some early churches seem to have had connections with a British or Romano-British past. So, for example, the principal church of Domesday Salfordshire was at Manchester, while Walton-on-the Hill was probably already a major church in West Derby Hundred. Both place-names (as Preston, Kirk Lancaster, Ormskirk, Kirkham) and Viking Age carved stones (at Winwick, Manchester, Whalley) provide means of identifying which churches were in use, particularly in Lancashire where very few were named in Domesday Book (Figure 16), but the geography of religious sites cannot be safely established in full before the late thirteenth century (see below, page 200 ff.). It was an out-dated parochial organisation still based to a large extent on a few great parochial churches, which was carried onwards into the post-Conquest epoch, when the vested interests of the parochial clergy became progressively more stoutly defended.

## Conclusion

Domesday Book reveals a series of distinct but inter-connected late Anglo-Saxon communities in the region. Although no figures are available for 1066, these communities seem to have been comparatively sparsely settled on lands which were not particularly productive. Arable acreages were small, with much more land given over to pasture or barely used at all. Large parts of the region were upland fell country or lowland mossland or marshland, which were hardly settled. Woodland was still extensive, with settlements primarily small and scattered in a comparatively wooded environment, particularly along the Pennines. The area was vulnerable to the accidents of wars of conquest within England, as well as conflicts with the Welsh, the Irish Sea Norse and the Scots, and had been severely affected by warfare during the central eleventh century. Figures from the very apex of England's elite dominated land tenure, but few are likely to have been regularly present in the region in person and several, the king among them, are unlikely ever to have entered it.

However, Cheshire, north-eastern Wales and southern Lancashire, had a significance far beyond their wealth and populations at the core of the affinity of the house of Earl Leofric of Mercia, and as the hinterland of Chester, which was the major urban centre from which English kings sought to influence and even control communities around the Irish Sea. A high proportion of local adult males are likely to have engaged in the dramatic events of 1066–1070, and the consequent death-rate and dislocation of estates was probably similarly high. Afterwards, a process of rebuilding seems to have been required, which had some significance for the regional landscape and its history. However, the Conquest did nothing to alter the frontier status of the region, which remained for several centuries to come.

# CHAPTER 3

# Population, Environment and the Medieval Agrarian Landscape

The rural economy of late pre-Conquest Cheshire was the least developed of any of the then shires of England, although by comparison with that of the lands to the north of the Mersey contemporaries may have felt themselves to have been members of a relatively affluent society. By whatever criteria are adopted, tax assessment, ploughlands, ploughs or population, the north-western agronomy was unimpressive in its performance by comparison with most neighbouring shires (see Table 2).

*Table 2. The counties of Western Mercia at Domesday, plus Derbyshire: a summary of the assets of each shire listed in order of population size.*

|  | *DB Population* | *Hides and/or Carucates* | *Ploughlands* | *Ploughs* |
|---|---|---|---|---|
| Gloucestershire | 8,083 | 2,403 hides | – | 3,812 |
| Warwickshire | 6,656 | 1,480 hides | – | 2,238 |
| Shropshire | 4,907 | 1,255 hides | 3,078 | 1,809 |
| Herefordshire | 4,453 | 1,141 hides | – | 2,421 |
| Worcestershire | 4,341 | 1,302 hides | – | 1,986 |
| Staffordshire | 2,866 | 446 hides | 1,299 | 976 |
| Derbyshire | 2,746 | 681 carucates | 734 | 908 |
| Cheshire (excluding areas later in Wales) | 524 | 491 hides | 936 | 457 |
| Rank of Cheshire | 8/8 | 7/8 | 3/4 | 8/8 |

Based on Higham 1993, table 2, p. 204, Darby and Terrett 1954 and Darby and Maxwell 1962, with slight simplification.

Chester excepted, the region had failed to attract significant commercial activity and remained embedded within a cycle that was very largely dominated by local needs and parochial attitudes that saw no more than a small proportion of gross production escape from the estate on which it was created. Most of what did leave the local community arguably did so not by entry to a system of exchange but in kind, or as tax or as payment to a local and regional aristocracy whose use of that accumulated wealth did little to stimulate the economy. Stray finds of coins of the eleventh century are extremely rare in the region, suggesting that this was not an economy in which coinage played much part outside of the very few urban centres.

Investment strategies barely existed in the countryside. Where they can be identified, they took the form of monopolistic equipment or food-gathering enterprises associated with high status. The obvious examples of the former were the mills, of which 21 were recorded in Cheshire, including one that had, in 1086, been newly built, at Worthenbury. Investment in mills was only economic where the manorial lord could reasonably expect a flow of grain from either or both of demesne lands or tenants sufficient to justify the initial outlay and subsequent maintenance. Unless under-representation was commonplace, a reading of Domesday Book would suggest that these conditions were generally realised only on large estates, so that mills were, almost by definition, the property of lords with multi-settlement manors where numerous local farmers could be required to use and pay for the lord's mill. Earls Edwin and Morcar owned in 1066 a total of nine manors where mills were recorded in 1086, and all except the new mill at Worthenbury were probably already functioning before Edward the Confessor died. Others were dispersed in a fashion which implies that ownership of a mill should be acknowledged as an indicator of high status among estate holders in 1066. To give an example, the name Alfward occurs against several manors in 1066 around Dunham Massey and Bowdon, most of which had passed to Hamo, first Baron of Dunham, by 1086. The continuity of this local estate grouping would seem to indicate that all references to Alfward in this area are to a single individual, who effectively dominated the northern half of Bucklow hundred. This Alfward was the owner of a mill at Bowdon, which was presumably sited on the river Bollin, or one of its tributaries (Figure 17).

The only other evidence of mills at this date comes from place-names. Millington, also in Bucklow Hundred, occurs in Domesday Book, so the name 'mill-enclosure' or 'mill-farm' had clearly already become attached to the estate by this date. Millington Hall is perched on the edge of a narrow valley containing the physical remains of an old dam, which might indicate the site which gave the township its name. However, this was not a major estate in 1066, being just one ploughland taxed at half a hide and in any case 'waste' already in 1066, and no mill seems then to have been extant or at least worthy of mention. *Mill-* and *Milne-* occur in place-names in Lancashire, but none is recorded from such an early date as this.

Investment in food-gathering in 1066 consisted of fisheries, and enclosures in the woodlands for managing or trapping deer (see below, page 106). Fisheries were noted at 15 manors in Cheshire. The term appears to have carried with it an expectation of a particular scale of catch and therefore of value, but whether the yield of 1,000 salmon and the staff of six fishermen specified at the earl's manor of Eaton were typical is not clear. Again, the link with landowners of high status seems well established. Earl Edwin held five fisheries and a further four were attached to estates associated with the name

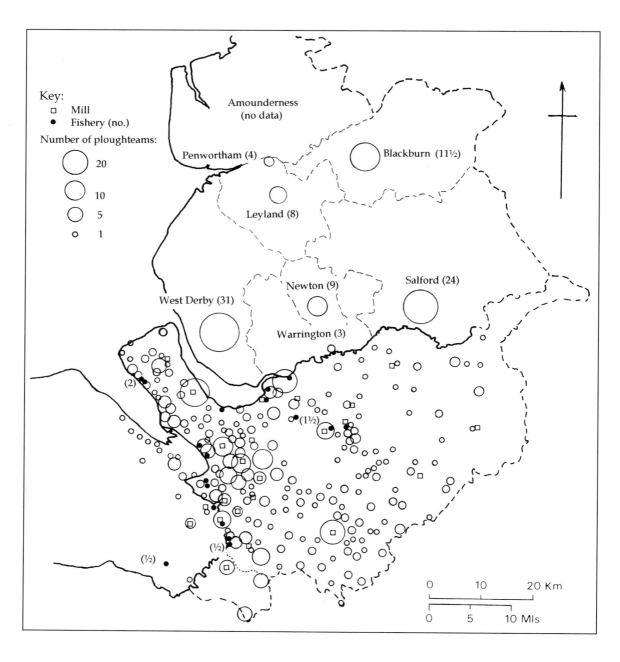

Key:
□ Mill
● Fishery (no.)

Number of ploughteams:
20
10
5
1

Amounderness (no data)

Penwortham (4)

Blackburn (11½)

Leyland (8)

Newton (9)

Salford (24)

West Derby (31)

Warrington (3)

(2)

(1½)

(½)

(½)

0      10      20 Km

0      5      10 Mls

Leofnoth – either a single individual or a very small number of figures holding important groups of estates on the Wirral and in Great Budworth parish. It seems clear that only fishing enterprises of considerable value were entered into Domesday Book, with the more normal run of minor rights and assets on local meres and rivers omitted. Major fisheries were highly valued and long protected by the earls, as their later charters make clear (e.g. Barraclough 1988, 159, no. 152).

Within the shire, a distinction as regards the presence of ploughs, plough-lands and manorial population should be drawn between the comparatively developed Dee valley and Wirral peninsula in the west, and the centre and east of the county, where Macclesfield (*Hamestan*) Hundred remained comparatively underdeveloped at the Conquest, with widespread woodland. For the former, the propinquity of the only significant urban community in the region, at Chester, and the most developed, most nucleated and most populated part of the hinterland was hardly coincidental. The factors which conditioned the foundation of Chester were primarily political but it seems likely that it was in part the commercial opportunities which were a by-product of that political initiative early in the tenth century which stimulated the local, agrarian economy in the west of the shire. At Domesday, Chester was one of the larger regional centres in England. If we assume a multiplier of around five to translate Domesday houses into total population, then *c.* 2,200–2,600 occupied the 487 houses which were counted in the city. Almost certainly, by the late eleventh century, the urban population, the port and the local hinterland had become inextricably linked in economic terms. There is, for example, no real likelihood that the local aristocracy and their households will have consumed the entirety of the local salmon catch. This was one local product that could have been traded by fishermen, reeves and estate managers into the urban markets and port facilities of Chester. The local salt industry provided the means by which the catch could have been preserved and traded further afield. Chester's mint was active throughout the tenth and eleventh centuries and was one of the more prominent in England in the mid- to late tenth century, suggesting a considerable flow of bullion through the port, presumably alongside a wide variety of goods (Dolley 1955; Hill 1981).

The population of the developing city was sufficient in size, therefore, to create in western Cheshire the first sizeable, extra-manorial demand for bulk foodstuffs since the Roman period. Taking a figure of *c.* 2,400 for the urban population and assuming around 3 acres per head would have been needed to feed them, it is clear that the town fields alone could not have fed the city (for the basis of this calculation, see Campbell 2000, 406–10). The product of around 7,200 acres would have been required. Grain production in the county arguably accommodated this demand. However, the scale of the harvest was still very low by the standards set by communities elsewhere in England and Chester may have been importing grain by sea even at this early date. Only three manors in Cheshire were credited with over 20 ploughlands. Of these, Tarvin was held by the Bishop, and Eastham and Acton by the earls. Including these, only 11 manors had over ten ploughlands and these were similarly concentrated in the hands of a minority of powerful men among the aristocracy and in areas where access to Chester was a feasible commercial strategy. Most lay in the Dee valley. Despite the difficulties posed to navigation on the upper reaches of the river once mills had been constructed at Chester (Hewitt 1929), a short boat trip might have carried any surplus to the urban market, or to the households of these landholders. Alternatively, carts or pack-horses

FIGURE 17.
Domesday ploughs,
mills and fisheries in
the North West. In
Cheshire (after Phillips
and Phillips 2002, 31),
the evidence is based
on estates.
In Lancashire it is
based predominantly
on hundreds, excepting
the castle and borough
of Penwortham, which
is recorded separately.

could have transported modest quantities along the old Roman road running in from the south from Whitchurch to the Dee bridge.

Prominent among these estates were those of Earl Edwin centred on Bettisfield, Iscoed and Worthenbury (later in Maelor Saesneg), and Christleton, Farndon, Malpas and Tilston further north within the Dee valley. Others lay on the Wirral, where the Earl's estates at Upton and Eastham were complimented by the Bishop's Burton estate, and significant ploughlands at Saughall, Caldy and Trafford. Whether they themselves consumed the surplus of their estates or sold it, the community of St Werburgh's was arguably obliged to bring the surplus of their demesnes at Huntington and Saighton into Chester.

More problematic is the commercial potential of the few estates accorded high numbers of ploughlands in the valleys of the Weaver and Mersey, or in the east of the county. The 30 ploughlands recorded at Acton (near Nantwich) and the 19 at Weaverham were both under the control of the earls and directly or indirectly associated with centres of hundredal government and the salt trade. The development of agriculture to levels which seem beyond the subsistence needs of the local community should perhaps be associated with the commercial opportunities offered by traffic in and out of these manors carrying salt. All three of the major *wiches* are likely to have stimulated an exchange economy, despite the absence in the Domesday Survey of any clear reference to local markets or fairs (Oxley 1982). Further north, the similarly multi-settlement estate of Halton was credited with 20 ploughlands. If any surplus was available, then road or river transport may have taken grain from this area to Chester. However, it remains possible that no such surplus was produced, given the large number of separate communities represented by this global figure and the needs of the elite household associated with Halton itself.

Opportunities for the lesser manorial aristocracy or their subordinates within the manor to avail themselves of market opportunities seem to have been very slight indeed, and progressively reduced with the distance from the few available markets. There is little evidence, beyond the name itself, that the several 'port' place-names in eastern Cheshire – the several Davenports and Stockport – were functioning as markets at this time, although the Davenport (arguably that in Middlewich Hundred, which is the sole 'port' name in Domesday Cheshire) sacked by the Irish Sea Vikings in the 920s had presumably been a place of some local significance.

## Domesday ploughs and ploughlands

The record of ploughlands in Domesday Book provides at best no more than a yardstick of agrarian potential in the opinion of local juries, and even this interpretation is controversial. The incidence of ploughs suggests that current use was significantly below potential, particularly in the eastern hundreds (Figure 17). In Cheshire, the impact of the dislocation and wasting of 1066–1070 had apparently led to the loss of substantial acreages, which were only just being brought back into cultivation in 1086. In only a small minority of cases did the number of plough teams in that year equal the stated number of ploughlands. These instances were concentrated in the west of the county, where the wasting may have been less severe, the local community more buoyant and the recovery therefore more swift. However, nationally, numerous manors were recorded in Domesday Book as having more ploughs than ploughlands and in Derbyshire, for example, the total number of ploughs recorded was greater than the total number of ploughlands. In all Cheshire, only the western manors of Farndon, Foulk Stapleford, Ness, Neston and Raby were overstocked with ploughs (Terrett 1962), although even here, in each case the excess was only a single plough. If there was any common cause linking them, it would seem to be the creation of sub-manors within the estate, rather than an expansion onto previously uncultivated land, suggesting that excess ploughs reflect inefficiencies in the use of capital rather than new investment in agrarian development.

Where vigorous reconstruction of the agrarian base is apparent, as for example on the 20 ploughland estate of Halton, this had not by 1086 yet reached, let alone breached, the assessment of arable potential accorded the manor. In some instances, there are signs that the process of reconstruction was in a very early stage when the Survey was made. This is at least a likely explanation for the curious pair of entries concerning Butley, held and being farmed by Wulfric. Here five ploughlands were recorded but the actual areas under cultivation was variously noted as a mere seven and/or 12 acres, illustrating the problems facing landholders attempting to bring back to cultivation lands lost since 1066, particularly in eastern Cheshire.

Taking the county as a whole, but excluding areas later in Wales (see Lewis 1991a, 3; Thorn 1991a), the assessment of ploughlands totals 936, but only 457 plough-teams were actively employed in 1086 (see Table 2). The apparent gap between potential and actual production was, therefore, a substantial one, even according to the perceptions of the late eleventh-century community, although it was less than in the North and East Ridings of contemporary Yorkshire. It may have been Earl Hugh's need to make proper provision for his supporters that led him to release to them a significant number of what had previously been comital estates. Whatever the reason, the transfer from an English to a Norman aristocracy weakened the near-monopoly previously exercised by the earls over the tenure of the large and strategically sited estates of the county, by establishing a number of local baronies focused on estates which had been held by Earl Edwin or his brother.

Agricultural activity is less easy to ascertain from the Domesday account of south Lancashire and impossible beyond the Ribble. No systematic estimate of ploughlands was recorded, if, indeed, it was ever attempted. 31 ploughs were said to be working on the lands of the hundred of West Derby but there were far more manorial units in the hundred (47 names occur, some more than once), so it seems unlikely that this fully reflects the actual level of agricultural production before the Conquest. Among the few specific estimates that were included was the identification of 15 ploughlands at, or dependent upon, the capital manor at West Derby and a further four at Huyton and Tarbock. In tandem, these were almost enough to accommodate the actual number of plough-teams said to be at work.

Elsewhere in South Lancashire, estimates of ploughs are even less reliable: in Newton Hundred only nine ploughs of the tenants were recorded, and in Warrington only the two ploughs on the demesne and the single plough of the manorial tenants at that site. The latter leaves the unlikely circumstance that the seven French tenants established there had not a single plough working their lands. Assessment of Blackburn, Leyland and Salford Hundreds appears more complete. However, the total of plough-teams recorded for Lancashire south of the Ribble was a mere 90½ active in 1086. While it seems unlikely that this is an inclusive figure, there is little reason to question the general picture of low agrarian output at Domesday (for a wider discussion, see Lewis 1991b).

The dislocation of the 1060s and 1070s may have been a serious economic set-back in the North West, but the impact was not uniform. In areas such as the hundreds of Macclesfield (*Hamestan*) and Bucklow (*Bochelau* and *Tunendune*) in the north and east of Cheshire, the consequences seem to have been both severe and long-lived. It has been suggested that it may have been this phenomenon which was responsible for the episodes of secondary forest rejuvenation identified but not securely dated in pollen cores extracted from Chat Moss, Holcroft Moss and Lindow Common on both sides of the Mersey (Birks 1963–4, 1965). However, this could be explained as easily by reference to disruption and economic recession throughout the Viking Age (as Hodgkinson *et al.* 2000 and see above, Chapter 2). Elsewhere in the region, devastation associated with the Conquest was of insufficient scale and duration to be recorded palynologically. However, this may be in part due to the concentration of pollen studies on the less-affected uplands of Rossendale and North-West Derbyshire (Tallis and McGuire 1972; Tallis and Switzur 1973; Bartley 1975), and the lowland wetlands, rather than an accurate comment on the state of the dryer lowlands.

## Domesday estates

The Domesday Survey has little information to offer concerning the organisation of agricultural activity, beyond its occurrence within estates which were in Cheshire termed 'manors'. These manors varied radically in composition. 'Classical' manors – as beloved by economic historians in the nineteenth and early twentieth century, with demesne, manorial tenants and free tenancies, did occur but can be identified in any number only in the west of Cheshire. Elsewhere land units were often no more than a handful of villein or bordar tenancies, or a single farm, either in demesne or sub-let to a comparatively free tenant. Only on a minority was there both demesne ploughing staffed by estate servants and plough-teams owned by the manorial tenants. On large manors, ploughs were often also owned by free sub-tenants and/or their subordinates, holding portions of the estate.

To give a specific example, Robert fitzHugh held the manor of Malpas in 1086 and had three ploughs on his demesne, and one bordar (*bordarius*: a peripheral tenant of low status) with no recorded equipment. He had sub-infeudated five men-at-arms, who had three ploughs on their own demesne lands and seven villeins with two and a half plough-teams as their tenants. A superficial reading of this account might invite the interpretation that there was a single community comprising 13 or 14 farming units of various sizes, and open the door to speculation that here were the conditions necessary for a nucleated village associated with open field agriculture. This must remain a possibility, but only a distant one. Malpas was one of the common examples of a Cheshire estate that encompassed what was eventually to emerge as a group of townships. Unlike Malpas itself (which is a rare French place-name – it was called *Depenbach* in 1086), most bore place-names that pre-date the Conquest and which probably existed as settlements at Domesday, if only as a single farm or tiny hamlet. The Domesday estate administered from Malpas probably included the townships of Macefen (a Welsh place-name), Bradley, Chidlow, Agden, Wigland, Wichalch and Stockton as well as the possibly (but not certainly) later names of Newton and Oldcastle. There is no evidence that the demesne ploughlands of Robert himself were situated at or close to his church and castle, but they may have been. So, too, may those of his unnamed men-at-arms, in addition to their holdings in Iscoyd, Worthenbury and Bettisfield, in what eventually became the southern portion of Flintshire. However, given the wider picture, we should not expect their tenants necessarily to hold lands physically situated in town fields clustered tightly around the modern Malpas. The description is ordered according to social ties rather than geography, and should be read in the context of Robert's other estates in the area, all of which were sub-infeudated (Table 3).

While the unnamed military tenants were probably normally to be found at or near Malpas, where their castleguard was owed, the other named French tenants seem to have had wider interests. Drogo was perhaps the same individual as held lands in Berkshire of Robert d'Oilly, who came originally from Les Andelys (Keats-Rohan 1999), while Humphrey is likely to have held lands at Halton, and a Roger held Poulton as a sub-tenant of Osbern fitz Tezzo. Edwin, in contrast, was a previous Anglo-Saxon landholder who had successfully transferred his allegiance from Earl Edwin to the incoming Norman lord. With around 70 households, so perhaps 350 individuals, spread across around 30 townships, this community was, in practice, widely dispersed in small hamlets and individual farms across the barony. Only at Malpas, Tilston and Cholmondeley were there groups of households which *could* have formed nucleated settlements (14 households, 13 and 11 respectively), but this supposition makes a series of assumptions that may be questioned. First of all, it assumes that the total number of households listed under Malpas were congregated there, which seems unlikely, and that each of the unnamed men at arms

*Table 3. Estates of Robert fitz Hugh in south west Cheshire
(Dudestan hundred)*

| Estate | Demesne Assets | Sub-infeudation and assets | Tax (hides) | Ploughlands |
|---|---|---|---|---|
| Malpas (*Depenbach*) | 3 ploughs; 1 *bordarius* | 5 men at arms with 3 ploughs 7 *villani* with 2½ ploughs | 8 | 14 |
| Tilston | 1 plough; 2 slaves; 4 *villani*, 4 radmen, 1 reeve, 1 smith, 1 miller, with 4 ploughs | | 4 | 8 |
| Overton | 1 plough | | 1½ | 2 |
| Cuddington | 2 *bordarii* & a plough with 2 oxen | | ½ | 1 |
| Edge | | Edwin: 1 demesne plough, 3 slaves | 2½ | 1 |
| Duckington | | Edwin: waste | 1 | 2 |
| Edge | | Edwin: waste | ½ | 1 |
| Cholmondeley | | Edwin & Drogo: 1 demesne plough, 5 slaves; 1 *villanus*, 3 *bordarii*, 1 reeve, 1 smith, with 1 plough | 2 | 4 |
| Hampton | | Edwin & Drogo: 3 *hospites* 'who have nothing' | 2(½) | 4 |
| Larkton | | Edwin & Drogo '1 man pays 12d, 1 *bordarius* pays 2s' | 1 | 3 |
| Shocklach | | Drogo: 2 ploughs, 2 ploughmen; 2 *villani* with 1 plough | 3 | 4 |
| Bickerton | | Drogo: 2 *villani* with a plough | 3 | 4 |
| Chowley | | Mundret: 1 plough 2 radmen | 1 | 1 |
| Broxton | | Roger & Picot: 1 demesne plough; 3 *villani* with 1 plough | 5 | 6 |
| Tushingham | | Humphrey: 1 demesne plough; 1 *bordarius* | 1 | 2 |
| Burwardsley | | Humphrey: 3 *bordarii* with a plough | 3 | 3 |
| Bickley | | Fulk: 1 demesne plough; 1 reeve, 2 *bordarii* with 1 plough | 1 | 3 |

were heads of households rather than members of the baron's household. In practice, the castle and church may have been comparatively isolated (Plate 6). Tilston was also a multi-township parish during the Middle Ages, and none of the other three townships then in the parish was named in Domesday, suggesting again that this is a well-disguised pattern of dispersed settlement. Cholmondeley may have been a second centre for the management of the extensive parish of Malpas, with the populations of several of its unnamed townships incorporated. At only Tilston and Cholmondeley is there any evidence of economic specialisation (a reeve, two smiths and a miller), but these could easily have been attached to a comparatively isolated estate centre. Dr Chris Lewis (1991a) made the same point regarding the manor of Christleton, which also lies in the agriculturally well-developed west of Cheshire. With very few exceptions, therefore, it seems safest to assume that the bulk of the population was living in isolated farms or small hamlets.

The organisation of Malpas and many other estates in Cheshire was, therefore, probably similar in some ways to contemporary estate structure in south Lancashire, consisting of a capital manor with only small amounts of demesne land surrounded by geographically distinct but tenurially dependent satellites. Since this pattern typifies large estates locally there is some reason to see in the North West during the Conquest period the type of estate structure that has elsewhere been termed the 'multiple estate' (Jones 1976).

To conclude, there is relatively little evidence in the Domesday Survey for the region which is consistent with the presence of large, nucleated villages with open fields, and some that directly conflicts with it. On those manors where the likely number of townships or other settlement units is close to the recorded population, there seems no place for assuming that extensive open fields can have existed in 1086, simply because the intermingling of strips would have been impossible. So, to use the same barony of Malpas as an example, just three large manors *could* have had both nucleated villages and large-scale open fields, although on balance none seems very likely, while the remaining 14 certainly *could not* merely by virtue of their tiny populations. Domesday therefore seems to provide oversight of a predominantly dispersed settlement pattern, with comparatively isolated farms and hamlets separated one from another by fields, pasture, woodland and considerable areas of inter-commoned 'waste' (Higham, N. J. 1988b). That is not to presume that strips were absent: contemporary plough technology and particularly the normal use of the eight ox plough team by the eleventh century – as the Domesday Survey clearly implies – meant that cultivation would already have tended to be organised in units which were comparatively long and narrow. Where hamlets existed, adjacent strips held by different individuals may have already formed the core of what would later develop as small open fields, but we cannot be clear that such were present, let alone common-place, on the basis of Domesday Book.

## Medieval ploughlands

There has been considerable difficulty in establishing an overview of agriculture in the North West in the Middle Ages. It has long been recognised that both Lancashire and Cheshire became counties characterised by enclosed fields held in severalty comparatively early, in comparison with the 'champion' country where open field was still extensive in the eighteenth century (Gray 1915). When Hewitt wrote his economic and social history of Cheshire, in 1929, it was without reference to open fields in the area. The recognition that such were, in fact, widespread in the county both in and before the Tudor period owes much to the work of a handful of researchers working shortly after the war (Chapman 1953; Sylvester 1956, 1958). Detailed research since then has elaborated many of the conclusions reached at that stage, in part via the use of new types of evidence, such as aerial photographs, which were then only just becoming accessible (Davies 1960; Youd 1961; Harris 1967; Elliott 1973; Kenyon 1974, 1979; Williams R. S. 1979, 1984; Thompson *et al.* 1982; White 1981, 1983, 1995). Modern research suggests that, by the thirteenth century, the largely pastoral rural economy of Cheshire described by William of Malmesbury, *c.* 1120 (Hamilton ed. 1870), had developed into a more mixed pattern of land-use with interspersed small open fields, closes, woods, pastures, mosses and meadows, albeit pastoralism remained an important element in the landscape.

Nevertheless, substantial problems of interpretation remain, most of which derive from the inadequacies of the surviving evidence, and difficulties of relating one type of evidence with others. Here we will survey the types of evidence available then try to draw some general conclusions.

Firstly, there is extensive physical evidence. Broad ridge and furrow, formed by ox-ploughing so likely to date before *c.* 1700, still covers significant areas of south-west and much of west Cheshire (Figure 18), and this was even more extensive prior to the rush to arable of the last two decades, which has led to wholesale destruction of the surface remains in some townships. There is much less evidence on the ground in central northern and eastern Cheshire. It is arguable that much more would have been visible had so much of this area not been either built over or ploughed during the modern period, a process which has effectively destroyed almost all surface evidence of medieval agriculture, for example, in the Mersey basin. In newly developed townships, such as Hurdsfield near Macclesfield, very small numbers of fields still retain broad ridge but are isolated by both later ploughing and the construction of an industrial estate.

North of the Mersey, ridges presumably once covered the dryer areas of south western and southern-central historic Lancashire and parts of the Ribble valley. Such can still be identified very occasionally even in pockets of rurality within the Merseyside conurbation, for example around Halewood, as soil marks, although it is impossible to demonstrate that the remains are medieval in date. Ridge and furrow seems to have spread wherever conditions were

FIGURE 18.
Broad ridge and furrow recorded from vertical aerial photographs along the eastern edge of the Dee Valley. Excluding only the marshy lands of the valley bottom, low agricultural ridges dominate the ground surface. These belong to a long chronological period but much has survived since the Late Middle Ages under permanent pasture. Blank areas include settlements, woodland, narrow ridge and modern cultivation, which is particularly widespread around Clutton (after plotting by Dr Denise Kenyon from vertical aerial photographs taken by Fairey Surveys Ltd).

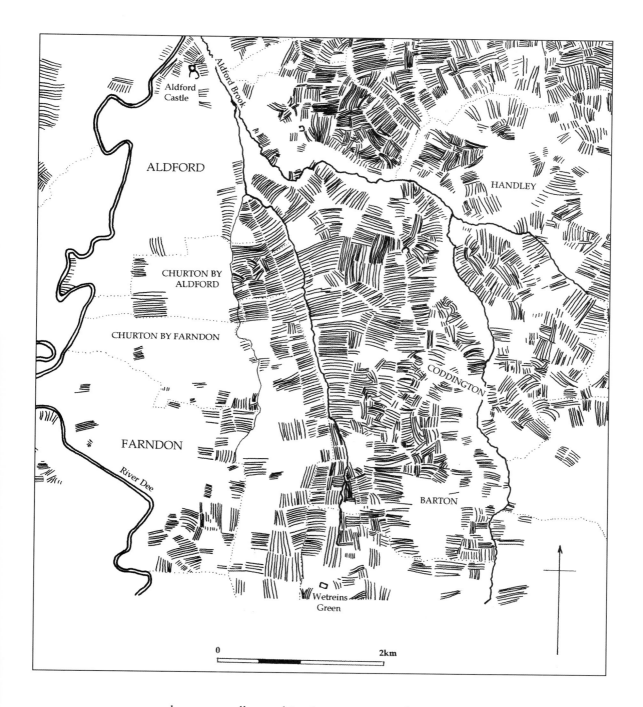

0                                 2km

adequate to allow cultivation to occur and it was arguably particularly valuable in this region for its drainage qualities, since cross-contour furrows helped
to channel excess surface water away into local streams. Ridges were developed
on many areas of marginal soils, specifically wet, lowland clays (e.g.
Wettenhall, Cheshire) and reclaimed marshland, where conditions were such

that the production of a crop was often a hazardous affair, and drainage a *sine qua non*. Some were probably also associated with meadowland used for the production of hay, as seems to have been the case on the banks of the Weaver at Acton. Even the Pennine edge reveals occasional evidence of broad ridge on very marginal soils indeed, as can be seen, for example, in isolated fields at Adlington and even on the edges of the Harrop valley.

Ridge and furrow is quite widely visible in the southern Lancashire uplands but most was formed in the late eighteenth and nineteenth centuries, when ploughing extended onto many areas which have since reverted to moorland (Figure 19). This tends to be comparatively short, straight and narrow, with a width of around five metres or less, rather than the eight to 12 metres which is common in medieval ridges. In Lonsdale there are several lynchet-systems (Figure 20), where ploughing in strips has formed terracing, and extensive areas of ridge and furrow are still visible, much of which is arguably medieval in origin (White 1983), such as those to be found around Sellet Hall, Whittington (Figure 21).

FIGURE 19 (*below*). Narrow ridge and furrow above Watergrove Reservoir, Wardle, Rochdale, which is associated with eighteenth- and nineteenth-century farms.

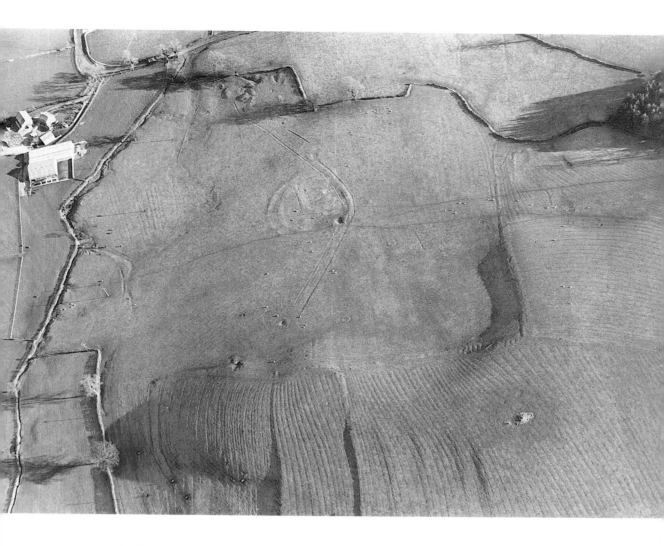

FIGURE 20 (*above*).
Several different periods
of ridge and furrow,
some overlying strip
lynchets but all
respecting a pre-
medieval settlement, at
Sellet, Whittington, in
Lonsdale.

PETER ILES, LANCASHIRE
COUNTY COUNCIL

In some areas, headlands can still be identified, where ploughs will have been turned to start back along the ridge. The ridges themselves are generally comparatively low, in comparison with some in the Midlands which can reach in excess of a metre from furrow bottom to ridge top. Many are quite long, however. Numerous examples are still discernable in excess of 200 m in west Cheshire, with some even approaching half a kilometre. At Eaton Park, on the banks of the Dee, an extensive pattern of long, curving ridges without any evidence of boundaries suggests that ploughing was present across a high proportion of the township prior to emparkment. Various sixteenth-century deeds suggest there was arable land at Eaton of, variously, 100 or 200 acres, associated with three or four messuages, which presumably refer to that part of this agrarian system that was then still under the plough.

Other types of physical remains include the fossilization of what would seem to have been open field strips in later enclosure systems. These are

FIGURE 21.
Lynchets at Over
Kellet, in Lonsdale.
Earthworks of this type
were formed by ox
ploughing at any date
from the Late Anglo-
Saxon period to around
1700, but many are
likely to be medieval.

PETER ILES, LANCASHIRE
COUNTY COUNCIL

apparent in several areas in both counties. Perhaps the most extensive and least problematic remains survive around the villages of Longton, Hutton, Little Hoole and Much Hoole, just south of the Ribble estuary, where predominantly north–south medieval strips are enshrined in the modern enclosure pattern, with enclosure apparently taking place, in part at least, during the seventeenth century (Winchester 1993). Later agricultural activity has removed virtually all traces of ridges, so it is only the shape of the modern fields which arguably reflects their origins. This group of villages has developed on a slight ridge of low-lying but comparatively well-drained land. Settlement is generally ranged down both sides of a single street, with Longton having a back lane parallel to the village street to the north. Open field once apparently stretched to the boundary of the township to the north, and to Meadow Head Lane to the south, where common meadowland was probably concentrated along the wetter land there. Angus Winchester (1993, 14–15) has explored the

documentary evidence for Longton in the thirteenth and fourteenth centuries
and located several field and/or furlong names by reference to nineteenth-
century cartography, leaving no doubt that intermingled strips were present
here. Marsh Lane provided access to the west to summer grazing on the
marshes of the Douglas estuary (Plate 8), and Moss Lane and others to the east
to the extensive mossland, which provided fuel, which separates this group of
settlements from Leyland (Figure 22). Outside the open fields themselves,
much of this landscape was probably intercommoned grazing in the earlier
Middle Ages, with the typically straight lines of the township boundaries being
imposed comparatively late, perhaps in combination with the planning of the
village itself and the laying out of its open fields.

Similar field systems indicative of past strip cultivation that have been
enclosed can be observed in the south west of the Fylde, at Freckleton,
Newton-with-Scales, Clifton and Elswick, in parts of Lonsdale and in the
upper Ribble valley at Pendleton. So, for example, an extensive area of long,
parallel, narrow fields characterises the junction of the rivers Wenning and
Hindburn at Wray, a nucleated fell-edge village near Hornby, which arguably
derives from medieval open field with strips up to 2,000 m long. In Cheshire,
evidence is widely scattered but generally less clear-cut, appearing at
Mobberley, for example, Leighton, Dunham-on-the-Hill and Alvanley. Such
'quilleted holdings' in the modern field system, resulting from piecemeal
enclosure of medieval strips, have been identified as widespread in west
Cheshire, where open fields have been suggested to have extended across more
than 75 per cent of many townships (Chapman 1953), but this may be over
optimistic. Even where substantial open fields can be detected, as at Aldford,
for example, it is common for neighbouring townships to exhibit none at all,

FIGURE 22.
Longton: an
interpretation of an
open field village in the
Middle Ages in Central
Lancashire, set within a
landscape in which
estuarine marshland
and inland mosses were
both extensive.

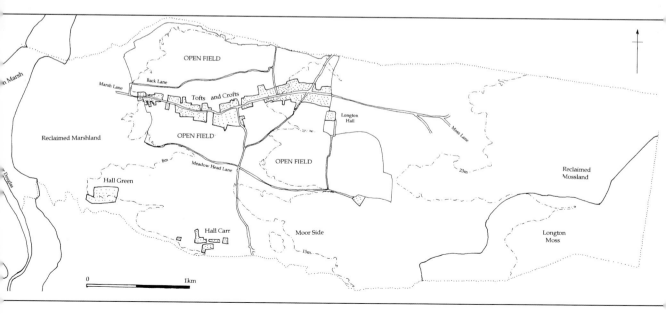

as Lea Newbold, in this instance (Figure 38, page 130). At best, open field was apparently present on only a proportion of manors, generally in connection with nucleated settlements.

Map evidence derived from the tithe apportionment of the mid-nineteenth century or eighteenth- and nineteenth-century estate maps provides a considerable scatter of evidence for remnants of strips, interspersed holdings and field names indicative of open field. The name 'Town Field' is particularly common and normally indicates a field held in several strips by various individuals. Other names use such elements as 'Butts', 'Flatts' and 'Loons', all of which refer to open field strips or ridges. A good example is Bunbury (Cheshire), where the tithe map of *c.* 1840 offers a group of field names clearly indicative of open field, one of which was then still in three strips (Thompson *et al.* 1982). Long selions cultivated with the eight-ox plough often formed a reverse 'S' shape in plan and this can be identified in field boundaries on later maps (e.g. John Hussey's map of Tatton, 1733: Higham, N.J. 2000; or the First Edition Ordance Survey map for Treales: Figure 38) or extant hedges (visible at Malpas and Raby).

Medieval documents make frequent reference to strips in lands or fields in a context which implies sub-division. So, for example, in the Swinehead Cartulary, numerous parcels of arable land are described as being within one or other of the furlongs or lands of Comberbach (near Northwich), and are defined by reference to neighbouring parcels owned by different individuals. 'Town field(s)', 'place-name-field' and/or 'field(s) of place-name' are widely documented from the fourteenth century onwards, in Cheshire, western Lancashire and the valleys of the Ribble and Lune (Elliott 1973).

It is not, however, an easy matter to make connections between these different categories of evidence and we should particularly resist the temptation to interpret the region by reference to stereotypes derived from elsewhere. The chronological disparity of these forms of evidence compounds the difficulties faced by the modern scholar seeking to understand them. Even for that inestimable part of the field remains which derives from medieval abandonment of arable, it is unlikely that more than a small proportion was last ploughed before the Black Death. Much of the surviving ridge is likely to derive from ploughing with oxen designed to improve pasture for dairying during the sixteenth and seventeenth centuries, rather than medieval arable, particularly where the ridges are very clearly bounded by existing hedge lines. Map evidence is today a copious and detailed source of evidence but this post-dates a long sequence of changes. Considerable caution should be exercised in attempting to relate evidence which comes predominantly from the eighteenth and nineteenth centuries to agrarian activity as it was before the Black Death (but for an excellent example of the use of maps in this context, see Thompson *et al.* 1982).

Despite these shortcomings, the evidence does suggest that, by about 1300, at latest, cultivation was widespread in much of the lowlands of the North West and pushing into both the uplands and the poorly drained moss or marsh skirtlands. In some instances, comparatively large-scale open field seems a reasonable interpretation of the available evidence. This would seem to be indicated at places like Longton, where the evidence suggests two large open fields. However, this is only one part of the picture and several other types of agrarian organisation occurred alongside. So, for example, the surviving field name evidence is linked only to relatively small pockets of open field (White 1995), with 'Town Field' type field names in the post-medieval period rarely extending beyond, at most, a score or two of acres. The extent to which communities cultivated their land in common, even in the arable areas of the region, remains far from clear. There is a strong connection between the degree of settlement nucleation which can be discerned and the survival of evidence for open field. It is noticeable that those townships where very little nucleation occurred (as Agden, Cheshire, or Culcheth, Lancashire, for example) seem to have had little or no open field at any date. Where there was settlement nucleation, as Clotton (Cheshire), for example, or Clifton (on the Fylde), open field could be extensive and evidence remain in the landscape to a late date. At the extreme, large and particularly urban communities could have large numbers of individuals owning strips, which could delay enclosure (White 1995): the open field at Frodsham was enclosed in 1784 and that of St Mary's on the Hill, Chester, was only finally enclosed by Act of Parliament, in 1805–7. Just as large complex systems survived late, so too are they likely to have developed early and in a more regular way than open fields associated with scattered rural communities.

The process of open field formation is wrapped in mystery, not just in this region but nationally. The rare instance of a documented planned settlement, such as Liverpool, provides the clearest evidence of a substantial re-organisation of land into extensive open field under the direction of a lord and his agents (Figure 23). Here, the medieval town fields survived comparatively intact until overtaken by urbanisation in the mid-eighteenth century, and the individual fields long remained visible even thereafter in the street pattern (Stewart-Brown 1916). Even here, though, there is evidence of later assarting, suggesting that the initial re-organisation of the first half of the thirteenth century did not satisfy the demand for arable over the next few generations. Otherwise, however, there is little direct evidence that the local appearance of small-scale open fields was something which was imposed on the community by manorial lords, as may have occurred in parts of north-east England, nor were they introduced by substantial cohorts of immigrants from regions where it was already practised. That said, there is some indication that lordship was involved. Nucleated settlements associated with Norman castles, such as Hornby, reveal evidence for apparently regular open field in early maps.

In very general terms, the field systems which were present in the North West are best interpreted as an agrarian system which developed over a long period under particular local conditions. Nationally, open field seems to have emerged as an integrated mixed-farming system in which arable and pastoral components could be managed in a complementary way, rather than competing for land (Fox 1981; Campbell 2000). What occurs locally is a

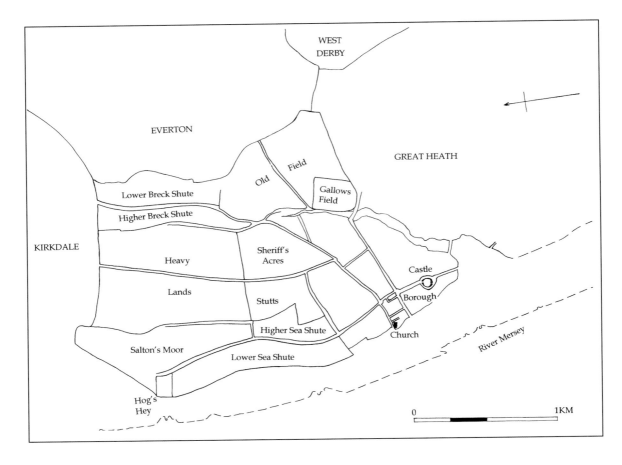

FIGURE 23.
Liverpool: a new
foundation of King
John in the early
thirteenth century,
combining a castle,
borough and port. Its
town fields are now
engulfed in the
nineteenth-century city
(after Stewart-Brown
(1916), with additions).

pattern of agricultural activity that embodied some of the classic characteristics of Midland open field but also displayed features more normally associated with very different patterns of land use. The widespread availability of extensive summer pasture reduced the pressure to systematise open fields to provide grazing on the fallow within a single ring-fence, which other communities without such resources experienced. Parts of the open field might be used as pasture at some times of the year but livestock were not necessarily free-ranging over the whole area, as often occurred elsewhere. Rather, fines recorded in the court rolls of Chatburn, Worston and Pendleton from 1377 onwards imply that animals were normally tethered or hobbled, and pigs ringed to stop them being destructive (Farrer 1897). Even manors such as Kirkham in Amounderness, sited among a lowland group of similarly settlement-named townships on relatively dry land, had open pasture of an acreage roughly equivalent to the ploughland (Shaw 1949). Grazing was not scarce until quite late in the period.

Secondly, land suited to agriculture was often not available in the large blocks necessary to develop extensive open fields, leading locally to comparatively small groups of strips interspersed with other types of land. The rotation of large blocks of the township's fields on a regular basis simply does not seem to have been a common practice. Thirdly, where large eleventh-century farms persisted as the dominant force in a township, there was little potential value in creating open fields with intermingled strips. Even where subsequent division of a small estate occurred, due to inheritance or sale, the result was more likely to be a cluster of smaller estates, each organised around a high status site or hall, than the creation of a village and open fields. The result was a fluidity of practices and local landscapes throughout the region, depending on specific, local environment conditions, tenurial factors at an early date and the numbers of individuals with access to land.

Much of the evidence is of ridges in small groups which are bounded by existing hedges, in contrast to the more extensive ridge and furrow of the core Midland counties, where enclosure hedges regularly cut across the physical remains of earlier ploughing. This is particularly common around the middle Dee valley, at places like Churton and Coddington. At nearby Grafton, banked trackways can still be identified as earthwork features weaving between closes containing broad ridges, and these should probably be interpreted as of medieval date. In those areas where this pattern developed most fully, agriculture was often extended to the manor boundary, so that the systems of adjacent manors physically abutted. Again, this occurred extensively in the area east and north of Farndon and south of Chester, as is obvious from the extant field remains (see Figure 18). It is also visible elsewhere on the better drained claylands and on small islands of sand and gravel supporting brown earths, where several manors shared access to limited expanses of agriculturally-attractive terrain.

However, it is difficult to distinguish between what should be interpreted in the medieval and early post-medieval periods as ridged closes and ridges within the open fields. Do the ridges visible today within modern fields reflect the cultivation of enclosed land, in crofts or closes, during the Middle Ages? Or did the piecemeal enclosure of open field occur in such a way that groups of adjacent strips, organised in furlongs, were eventually enclosed as single units? Much of the evidence is equally well-suited to either interpretation. What is clear is that there are comparatively few instances where later field boundaries clearly bisect ridges, which may suggest that current fields do often represent the boundaries of cultivation even in the Middle Ages. Many of these must then already have been closes, so not all ridges need equate with open field. So, for example, some town fields identified as late as the nineteenth century retain ridge and furrow, as at Aldersey (Cheshire), but this does not distinguish them from neighbouring closes, most of which are similarly ridged.

This observation introduces considerable difficulties into the process of interpretation. While in many parts of the Midlands, ridge and furrow generally equates with open field, this cannot be assumed in the North West, where much was arguably outside any communal regime. This observation may undermine some of the conclusions concerning the extent of open field in Cheshire which were made in the decades just after the Second World War.

Despite the widespread distribution of broad ridge and furrow, therefore, and the virulence with which it seems to have been created, there is comparatively little evidence of regular three or two field systems of the classic type found in the English Midlands (Gray 1915; Orwin and Orwin 1938). Where these did occur, they were characteristically either on terrain which was particularly well-suited to the practice (as at and around Longton) or on the estates of the church where long-lived and comparatively consistent estate management may have encouraged the standardisation of local practices. On the bishop of Coventry and Chester's manors of Tarvin and Wybunbury (Sylvester 1958), numerous quite disparate fields were organised into a three-course rotational system. However, this is far removed from the classic examples of such systems in the southern estates of the bishopric, where there would normally only be two, three or at most four open fields. Elsewhere, there may have been examples where the rotational system coincided with a reorganisation of land, both in west Cheshire (Sylvester 1956) and Samlesbury, for example, in the Ribble valley, which seems to have had a three field system in operation in 1336. At the baronial settlement of Halton on the Lune, the nucleus of the arable lands seems to have been four common fields totaling about 220 acres, and some of the outlying hamlets of the manor were also equipped with common arable. However, the arable at Halton lay in a single block, which is easily detectable on the First Edition Ordnance Survey Six–inch maps (Figure 38), lying to the north of the village. The same can be said of Newton, Clifton and Treales, on the north side of the lower Ribble (Figure 38), where each of the settlements were sited close to wetland and on the edge of arable. At Bare, on the coast, two common arable fields called the West Field and Bank Field totalled about 40 acres (Harris 1967), suggesting that only a small proportion of the total acreage of the vill was in open field.

Two- or three-field systems were, clearly, far from being the norm. In some of the less heavily populated and agriculturally less attractive areas, there are signs that a single field may have been in use, presumably perennially, on an in-field basis. Such seems to have been the case in many of the manors in which Furness Abbey received small grants of land in the twelfth century, predominantly in that part of Lancashire now in Cumbria, beyond the Sands. Elsewhere, where documentary evidence is copious, references occur to a bewildering number of fields. A rental of Vale Royal Abbey of *c.* 1334 mentions by name scores of fields in eight manors, some of which were jointly ploughed by cultivators from several communities (Brownbill 1914; Sylvester 1956). At Coddington, five fields have been identified and mapped (White 1981). At Speke, near Liverpool, a grant was made of half an acre in 'Le Schichefeld' defined by the highway and the lands of other cultivators, and similar grants refer to the 'Bonkefield', 'Adcockusfeld' and 'Okelotschech' in circumstances that require us to suppose that each was sub-divided (Lumby 1939). In 1086 the manor was assessed at only two carucates and valued at a mere 64*d.*, suggesting substantial economic development over the two centuries that followed. A series of documents in the Moore papers dating from

1293 to the 1350s refer to approximately a score of field names in and around Liverpool (Brownbill 1913). For example, a grant of 1316 conveyed two selions in the townfields of Liverpool, 'one in the Quithakris between the lands of Richard [the grantee] and of Alexander, son of Masse, the other in the Dalfield [Dalefield in other references] between the lands of the said Alexander and of Robert del Mosse'. This evidence does not fit the two- or three-field type of system and requires that we consider other patterns of arable management.

One possibility is that field names were undergoing replacement, resulting in a confusing profusion of names for what were perhaps only a small number of fields. We can set aside simple differences that derive from non-standardised spellings: for example, at Liverpool the 'Quithakris' (also the 'Quitacris') was probably the same as the 'Quitakirfield'. However, it is less clear to what extent 'Everstonedale', 'Coupedale' and 'Dalefield' were interchangeable. By the time the Liverpool townfields can be mapped (Stewart-Brown 1916) the fourteenth-century names had been replaced, although their layout may have changed little and the surviving names reflect an assarting landscape of improved moor and heathland. That contemporaries were aware that the open fields of the community had grown out of a recognisable nucleus finds support at Liverpool in the several references to the Old Field or its component parts – 'Little Holdefeld', 'Mukeleholdefeld' and 'Great Oldefield', but this may be due to the re-organisation associated with urban development. At Tarvin, four of the 14 identifiable arable units were called fields, similarly inviting the suggestion that these had at some stage formed a nucleus of customarily divided land, around which peasant assarting or lordly investment in land improvement slowly created new units (Sylvester 1958). In other locations, a similar profusion of field names is common, but does not seem to have been due to name changes. At Tatton (Cheshire), a tentative reconstruction of the open field suggested that the two manors of Tatton shared the well-drained, sand-based brown soils between them as open field, remnants of which can be identified on an estate map of 1733. These were divided into a number of separately named fields and furlongs, a minority of which were still locatable by name in the eighteenth century (Higham, N.J. 2000).

Name replacement does not, therefore, provide a sufficient explanation of the profusion of field names. An alternative solution may be that the terms 'field' and 'furlong' were used interchangeably throughout the region (as argued by Elliott 1973), with the meaning of 'a grouping of strips organized and managed in common'. The size was highly variable, from a handful to (rarely) a hundred or more acres, but several 'fields' or 'furlongs' could be immediately adjacent, or, alternatively, quite separate. The large number of 'field' names encountered should normally, therefore, be interpreted as referring to relatively small groups of intermingled strips managed within a collective regime. Many communities had just one, two or three such units, but others might have many more.

Holding strips was not confined here or elsewhere to parts of the open field or common meadows but occurred in addition within enclosures described as crofts. Croft names appear in this context in the Liverpool fields – 'the Morcroftes', for example – and it is likely that numerous units of sub-divided land originated as assarts, newly cleared from the 'waste' by individuals or small groups. Some north-western 'croft' field names may reflect the process of enclosure from existing open field. Others were incorporated in open field systems but retained the name (as at Liverpool). Others were never part of a communal regime but were held in severalty by individual farmers, and these were probably the commonest by far, particularly in areas where assarting was underway. Ridge and furrow is no proof of the presence of open field. In some areas, enclosed land held in severalty seems to have been a more extensive element of larger farms than strips in the open field, but the latter perhaps predominated on the holdings of the manorial peasantry (in Lancashire generally termed 'oxgangs'), where such existed, who had less opportunity to enclose significant parcels of land.

The organisation of whatever rotational system was in use seems, therefore, to have been based upon a unit of land of variable size, comparable to what might elsewhere have been described as a furlong within an open field. Local field systems accommodated the marginal nature of many areas. Some communities used the same specific parts of their land for crops each year, and grazed much of the remainder, often locating the settlement in between to help keep livestock away from the crops (as at Clifton or Newton). Elsewhere there could be a complex intermixture of arable with lands used for other purposes. In some areas, a long ley system of rotation was in use, in which agriculture was rotated with extended periods when the land was used as pasture. Although the terminology was not used very much within the region, this could operate as an infield/outfield system, with a small amount of land cultivated each year but different parcels of the outfield being ploughed for several years and then returned to pasture or meadow. For example, at Heaton Norris (on the southern borders of the Manchester barony) those responsible for the extent of 1322 were in some difficulty in establishing what was and what was not arable land: 'Certain acres of land and plats are of arable land, some of meadow land and some of pasture, and so meadow, arable and pasture cannot be separated because some are meadow and pasture and some arable land ...' (Farrer 1907). The total area under discussion was 225 acres attached to six messuages, suggesting that some at least of these were substantial farms. A not dissimilar description would have been apt when the tithe apportionment was undertaken in the middle of the nineteenth century.

A similar situation had arisen at Frodsham, one of the great, multi-settlement but single township estates of the earldom of Chester. There, the agricultural lands were divided before 1350, with the burgesses sharing town fields, alongside several bond settlements with their own field systems. Manorial demesne dominated the marshes, where drainage made advances in the early fourteenth century to allow numerous large but not regularly divided furlongs to be managed within a three-year rotation (Booth and Dodd 1979).

Scholars have long been encouraged to abandon attempts to impose a unitary model of open field origins on the stubbornly diverse regions of England (as Thirsk 1987). In the North West, there is scant evidence of the type of regularisation which was suggested by the Thirsk model of open field farming (Thirsk 1964, 1966; see also Titow 1965; Fox 1981; Williamson 2002). Instead, there emerges a tendency for field systems to remain polyglot, small-scale and unsystematised. This picture could additionally be complicated by sales of land units of all sizes from the half selion (or even the 'ferthyng') upwards, by the thirteenth century at latest, with land in each generation undergoing fundamental re-apportionment by inheritance, as well as expansion by assart (Miller 1975).

The result, by the late thirteenth and early fourteenth centuries, was a highly complex package of agrarian practices rooted in the economic and social customs of the specific community, both present and past, but with a powerful impulse towards expansion. Much ploughland was outside a regime even approximating to the Midland system, and more akin to the enclosed fields which we might recognise as typical of the regional landscape today. The croft or close, and rights to common pasture, not the open field strip, were in many parts of the region the more significant element in this agrarian economy. Control of enclosed land offered farmers the ability to make separate choices about land-use on an annual basis, which may have helped compensate them for the comparatively poor growing conditions, which were all that could be expected from the north-western environment.

Disputes over the right to plough up large areas of previously cultivated land (presumably ridged land) within the Cheshire forests in the fourteenth century remind us just how pervasive ridge and furrow must have been. Old ridges since lost to agriculture in the forests presumably derived from earlier assarts, which had since been abandoned, or even from cultivation prior to the afforestation of pre-existing settlements with arable in the eleventh and twelfth centuries. That some boonwork ploughing at least was undertaken by shared plough teams is illustrated by an entry in the court roll of Shotwick Manor for 1339, but the paucity of the evidence makes it impossible to assess whether this single reference represents normal practice in the region. Many farmers arguably had their own ploughs and teams of oxen, and the acreages to support them.

The comparative absence of regular two- or three-field systems thus seems to imply that the rise to prominence of agriculture was a comparatively late phenomenon. The scarcity of sub-divided fields in the late eleventh century is a matter of deduction (see above). The ubiquity of sub-divided but irregularly organised fields *c.* 1300 in the lowlands is broadly demonstrable from written evidence. It may be that the comparative irregularity that was a feature of the region was the product of swift but late agrarian development in an area which was not subject to heavy manorial obligations. Had demographic and economic changes not intervened, it is possible that increasing regularity would have been imposed on some local field systems from above. That at least was achieved on the eve of the Black Death on the Cheshire earldom's new manor of Drakelow, where a three-field regime was adopted, but even here the demesne appears not to have been intermingled with the lands of tenants of the manor (Booth 1981). Another factor, however, may have been the crops grown. All the evidence for both counties suggests that oats was by far the commonest grain crop, and would normally have been spring-sown. Spring cultivation allowed stock to graze the arable from harvest time for about half the year, reducing the need to set aside a significant proportion of the town lands as fallow for common grazing, particularly when combined with the widespread availability of pastureland outside the open fields in the summer months.

## Population and the expansion of agriculture

It seems likely that one factor behind a major agrarian expansion throughout the region during the period up to 1349 was a demographic rise of substantial proportions. Why this should have occurred is not precisely understood but this was a national phenomenon, with a population at Domesday of 1.1–3.0 million rising by 1300 to 3.4–7.0 million: a threefold increase (recent estimates are conveniently listed by Campbell 2000, table 8.06). Particular factors make it likely that the regional population rose even faster. Climatic conditions had improved significantly in the centuries immediately around the Conquest, and this had some potential to make farming more productive (Lamb 1972–7). In a region conditioned by high rainfall, low rates of evaporation and heavy soils, this arguably opened up considerable opportunities and served to raise thresholds of agricultural productivity to an extent sufficient to improve life expectancy within the community and offer to a larger proportion of families the opportunity to produce children at and above the rate necessary for replacement (for parallels see Razi 1980).

The local community had for long been faced by hostile political and environmental circumstances which arguably inhibited population growth and the Domesday population was arguably reduced by recent warfare. By 1086, it was also equipped with a heavy plough capable of creating ridges and so providing an element of surface drainage, although it is far from clear when this technology became available within the region (most recently, see the several theories grouped in Astill and Langdon 1997). When opportunities arose through greater political security and improving climate, the community was able to expand into the newly emerging niches of a changing habitat. By the second quarter of the twelfth century at latest, this community was arguably entering an expansive phase, which was quickened considerably by growing commercialisation, which occurred from the late twelfth century onwards, and which facilitated a degree of economic specialisation. This was to last until changing circumstances confronted a much-enlarged population in the second decade and, even more dramatically, in the second half of the fourteenth century.

The scale of demographic expansion that occurred was considerable but not precisely quantifiable. There is general agreement that, nationally, the rate of increase varied. It was lower in areas where the landscape was already extensively ploughed in 1086 than where relatively low populations were confronted by substantial untapped resources. So, for example, the expansion of settlement on the fen edges of Lincolnshire involved a population increase of five-fold or more (Hallam 1958, 1961). The North West was an area with an unusually low level of population in the late eleventh century where substantial expansion was feasible, and where virtually unlimited access to marsh, moss and upland could provide a living for families with little or no ploughland. It is likely, therefore, that population growth was on a scale similar to that occurring elsewhere in areas of low population per unit area, so well above the national average.

Reliable figures based on Domesday cannot be offered for the region, owing to the implicit under-representation of population in some Cheshire vills (Higham, N.J. 1982a) and the apparently large-scale under-recording of the Lancashire population. Commentators have suggested a total recorded population for Cheshire of 1951 (Brownbill 1901, followed by Hewitt 1929), or 1524 (Terrett 1962) – depending on the area excluded and the specific categories of population included. Hewitt computed a total population of 10,500–11,000. Russell (1948) argued for the much lower figure of 6,180 for Cheshire and South Lancashire, to which we might perhaps add 920 as an estimate for central Lancashire and Lonsdale to round it up to *c.* 7,000. Some later studies have queried the low rate of under-representation in Domesday population figures and the low multiplier adopted by Russell (e.g. Titow 1969). However, others have broadly confirmed his comparatively low estimate of national population at 1.10 m. The apparent omission of figures for many Cheshire manors, however, suggests that Russell's figures for the region may be too low. The estimated total of 7,000 should, therefore, be considered a minimum for the region. Using a multiplier of five, 1,524 households in what was later to be medieval Cheshire suggests a total population of around 7,620, to which we should perhaps add a further 20 per cent to compensate for under-representation, giving a total of *c.* 9,144, or perhaps 8,000–10,000, to provide a reasonable margin of error.

The number of households in Lancashire was probably higher than the totals which can be extracted from Domesday, but the scale of omission can be no more than inspired guesswork. There were approximately 250 'settlements' of variable status acknowledged by the Survey of which a proportion was supposedly unpopulated. West Derby was probably the most populous area, with around 61 thegns holding land in 1066 but only eight Frenchmen, 46 *villani*, one radman, 62 *bordarii*, two male and three female slaves were noted in 1086, suggesting a total of around 110 households at most. In Newton Hundred there were 22 households, in Warrington 15 and in Blackburn 'as many men as have 11½ ploughs', which is unquantifiable. 68 households, at most, can be counted in Salfordshire and 53 at Leyland, including the 21 at

Penwortham. Beyond the Ribble, no population figures are given. The total number in Domesday Book, even counting every French tenant, burgess (at Penwortham) and slave of either sex as a separate householder is therefore only around 280, to which some notional addition should be made for Amounderness, Blackburn and Lonsdale. Perhaps 400 households might be an appropriate base figure in 1086, suggesting a total population some five times bigger at around 2,000.

Faced with this intractable evidence, commentators have generally made higher estimates, apparently on the grounds that Lancashire's population just could not have been as low as this would suggest. Russell estimated a total population of 7,927, which assumes the unproven circumstance of an even spread of population across the north of England, so uses population density from east of the Pennines as a guide. A more recent estimate of 6,400–8,000 (Cowell and Philpott 2000) assumes a population marginally below 2.5 per square mile. However, while it seems reasonable to view the actual Domesday figures as representative only of a minimal estimate, the repeated assertions of the commissioners that parts of the region were exempt from dues, partly or wholly waste or largely depopulated, do imply that they are not so far off the mark as modern scholars have tended to assume. At Domesday, Lancashire's population probably, therefore, fell within the range 2,000–4,000. This would suggest a total population in 1086 for the whole region of only some 10,000–14,000, which, given the size of the region, is very low by comparison with southern or central England.

By 1300 this population had increased dramatically but it is very difficult to quantify this assertion. The earliest national figures available come from the poll tax figures of 1377, 1379 and 1381, but Cheshire was exempt and details only survive for a small proportion of Lancashire, and none from the fullest accounts of 1377 (Fenwick 1998, 436–78). Totals, however, do survive. In 1377, 23,880 were taxed. If 35 per cent of the population was then under 14, this computes to a total population for Lancashire of 32,238. If the young constituted 50 per cent, then the figure should be inflated to 35,820. Under-enumeration in 1377 has variously been computed at between 5 and 25 per cent but recent review of the process would suggest that the lower figure should be preferred (Fenwick 1998). This would suggest a figure for the shire of between 33,850 and 37,611, to which we might add a similar number for Cheshire, coming up with a total of *c.* 67,000–75,000, which is somewhat below that offered by Bennett (1983), at around 93,000. If the region suffered average losses in the Great European Famine of 1316–22 and the Black Death of 1348–51 (see below) then the regional population around 1300 should have been *at least* 1.7 to 1.9 times higher, that is in the region of 114,000–143,000. Acceptance of such figures would imply a population rise in the order of ten-fold between 1086 and 1300.

The basis for this calculation is peculiarly fragile, even by the normal standards of statistics for medieval England, particularly given the absence of poll tax figures for Cheshire. The results may be subjected to many levels of criticism, and caution alone would seem to suggest that such a rate of increase is unreasonably high. However, they do reflect the fact that there was an unusual opportunity for demographic growth in the region, which had as a starting point the lowest population densities in England below the Tees and culminated in population levels comparable to those found in Yorkshire, Shropshire and Staffordshire (Pelham 1969). The rate of growth must have been far greater than the cautious two-fold estimate offered by Hewitt (1929). Overall, it was surely far higher than the 36 per cent rise at Burton (in Wirral), in what was, in the eleventh century, the most developed part of the region (Booth and Jones 1979; Booth 1981). It should also be recognised that the total population of England *c.*1300 had probably reached something like five million (Campbell 2000) or even six million (Smith 2002). Against that backdrop, an estimate of 114,000–143,000 for these two shires in 1300 does not look outrageously high.

The Papal *Taxatio* of 1291 provides evidence for both Cheshire and Lancashire at the parish level for the distribution of the tax assessment. If we suppose that levels reflect, approximately at least, the relative prosperity of the local community, then mapping tax levied per acre of the parish offers the opportunity to identify the pattern of wealth distribution (Figure 24), and this probably reflects population levels per unit area quite effectively. As one might expect from the Domesday evidence, there was a distinct concentration of wealth at and around Chester, in the Dee valley, and another focused on Middlewich in the Weaver valley, where salt production supplemented agriculture. What is less predictable is the extent to which northern Lancashire had developed, with by far the largest concentration of wealth per acre in the parishes of Kirkham and Preston, with further foci at Warton, Claughton and Heysham. While particular circumstances arguably boosted the wealth of some communities – as fishing at Heysham, for example – these comparatively wealthy localities reflect the extent of agricultural development in those parts of the Fylde and Lonsdale which offered the best environmental conditions. Both areas have a comparatively high incidence of what seem to have been nucleated settlements with open field, and their distribution may imply that some lordships took an active interest in developing open field villages.

Whatever the precise rate of expansion, there is plentiful indirect evidence that a considerable increase did occur, enlarging old communities and peopling the landscape with a host of minor hamlets and farms, plus carving out space sufficient for new communities to emerge. New set-piece urban plantations on the Liverpool model (founded 1209) were not typical, but many small hamlets seem to have grown from nothing or from individual holdings to become villages. Additionally, large numbers of individual farms were built, often on land which had not previously been settled. While some of these eventually failed, many did not, and they account for the basic framework of the widespread scatter of rural settlements and minor sub-manors still visible in the landscape when the Ordnance Survey began detailed mapping.

The population of existing communities can on occasion be shown to have grown, in some cases exponentially. At Frodsham, for example, eight villeins and three bordars were recorded in 1086, suggesting a population of around 55. By 1349, the manorial community had grown to at least 32 households to which should be added a burgess community of about 43 households (Dodd 1982), implying a population now reaching *c.* 375. This approximately seven-fold increase may not have been unusual of old settlements and does provide an indication of the elasticity of the resource base available to the eleventh and twelfth century communities. The Vale Royal rental of 1334 suggests that

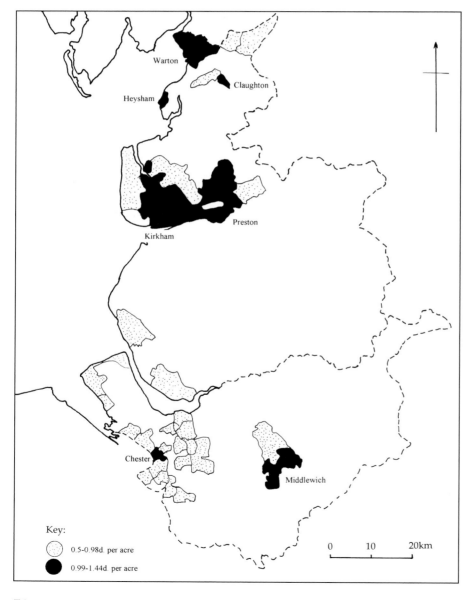

FIGURE 24.
The distribution of taxable wealth, by parish, from the Papal *Taxatio* of 1291. The comparative wealth of parts of central and northern Lancashire imply a particularly rapid development of the countryside in these areas since the late eleventh century (after Phillips and Phillips (2002), 39, with additional data for Lancashire provided by Professor Jeffrey Denton). The parishes are named in Table 6.

Key:

○ 0.5-0.98d. per acre

● 0.99-1.44d. per acre

0   10   20km

around 220 families then occupied holdings on five manors which had just eleven recorded tenants in 1086, again suggesting a very high rate of growth (a twenty-fold increase). Elsewhere, small-scale but successive expansion of agriculture at the expense of under-utilised land was widespread, effected by peasants as well as the comparatively affluent tenants and sub-manorial holders, who provided the nearest medieval equivalents to the yeomanry of Tudor England.

Examples of assarting are among the commonest types of indirect evidence for population growth, forming one of the most frequent subjects of disputes, court cases and accords. Many instances reached court because there was resistance from within the manorial community to enclosure of parts of what had been traditionally perceived as common pasture. Many court cases focused on the hedges, ditches and other boundaries with which cultivators defended their new assarts. For example, in the Lancashire assize Hugh le Sorreys claimed that the fence he had constructed at Wheatley (near Nelson, Lancashire) had been unjustly pulled down with the result that his crops had since been trodden down and destroyed. In defence of this action, John de Knol claimed that the fence came a long way into the pasture of the vill where it had never been before, so he had pulled it down. The verdict of the court was that three perches of the fence had been justly destroyed but that John should repair the remaining six perches. From the earliest records in 1196 onwards, final concords in the royal courts of Lancashire are studded with references to new assarts (Farrer 1899, 1901, 1903, 1907, 1915). There is no sense of any reduction in the rate of assarting even in the second quarter of the fourteenth century, following the mortality of the famine of 1316–22, when something like ten to fifteen per cent of the national population is estimated to have died. This would suggest that regional population was at very high levels indeed by 1300.

Numerous documents written on behalf of manorial lords stress their right to assart. For example, a survey written before 1292 on behalf of Robert Grelley, Baron of Manchester, defined the extent of the common pasture of the manor and his rights therein (Harland 1856–62):

> from the for[d] of Medelac [Medlock], by Saltergate, as far as to the hedge of Cleyton, which is situated upon the Saltergate, which descends from the house which was that of Alexander Franceis as far as into the Corn-broc and then descending as far as into the inclosure of Ardwick, and by the inclosure of Ardwick as far as into the bounds of Bexwic [Beswick], and by the bounds of Bexwic to the bounds of Bradeford, and by the bounds of Bradeford to the Saltergate. And Robert Grelle ... may enclose, till, build upon and ditch all the said land without impediment.

Elsewhere, numerous comparable documents established, defended, reiterated or divided the right to bring new lands into cultivation. The borough charter by which the burgesses of Altrincham were confirmed in their status demonstrates a greater interest in the lord's future plans for enclosure of hitherto common grazing than in any other specific issue (Ormerod 1882). By the late thirteenth century, most land that was easily accessible and physically well-suited to agriculture was already either in open fields or in closes held in severalty but under the plough at least in some years. However, the pressure to assart had by no means abated, and individuals and communities alike were turning to those areas where adverse environmental conditions or forest law had slowed the expansion of cultivation. The abbots of St Werburgh's were at the forefront of land clearance in the Forest of Wirral in the late thirteenth and early fourteenth centuries. Similarly, a rough draft drawn up about 1308 elaborated the boundaries of a plot of land in Little Budworth in the forest, that Warin de Grosvenor purposed to grant to his son Robert (Barker 1953). 'Ruding' field names and references to assarts, the ditches that formed their boundaries and the gruesomely named 'Dedecherlenche' make it clear that this particular landscape was one in which assarts both recent and old predominated. It is no accident that complaints to the king by the Abbot of Vale Royal included mention in 1299 of illegal assarts perpetrated by Richard son of Warin le Grosvenor in the vill of Over in the Forest of Mara in despite of a prohibition (Brownbill 1914). As population grew, assarting was an obvious strategy by which to feed, endow and profit from each new, larger generation. Once land had been enclosed from the waste it could be improved and used more intensively, so expanding the productive capacity of agriculture. Where pasture could be converted to arable, a five-fold increase in the calorific value of the food produced could be expected (Campbell 2000), translating into a substantial increase in the population capable of being fed from the land per unit area.

Where there was no forest land available to assart, better-off peasants, freemen and the local gentry were encroaching both legally and illegally on the wastes of many manors. The 1322 extent of the manor of Manchester claimed that Sir John Byron and Sir John de Longforde had taken advantage of the minority of Thomas Grelley to enclose illegally 100 acres of the 356 acres of common pasture at Brownedge, so as to convert it to arable. By 1300, the Cheshire sanctuaries at Rudheath and Overmarsh, which had earlier been open heaths where incomers to the shire had been able to camp in order to seek protection from the earls, were extensively enclosed and cultivated.

The defendant in an interesting court case concerning Over Kellet claimed that his 'approval of the waste' was sanctioned by the Statute of Merton. In response, the plaintiff pointed out that the approved waste lay not in the woods but among the plough lands of the vill 'where no waste is and the Statute of Merton should not extend to such places'. The defendant then claimed that custom allowed the joint owners of vills to break up and approve parts of the pasture adjacent to their arable land but the court eventually found for the plaintiff. In a similar case concerning land at Wiswell, Beatrix de Blakeburne was successful in her defence of two new, small enclosures taken from the open field on which she had constructed buildings for her cattle. Her appeal to local and customary practice was then enshrined in the court record: 'the custom of the county is that any villagers may approve their arable land near their messuages and the vills where they dwell for the purpose of building such cottages'. Such practices had important implications for the piecemeal enclosure of open field in the region.

Vast areas of lowland moor and mossland existed in the region in the eleventh and twelfth centuries. By the late thirteenth century, cumulative encroachments upon it, along with extensive digging of peat or turf as fuel, had brought many of the smaller deposits close to exhaustion. At Salford, the landholdings of many free tenants consisted very largely of parcels enclosed and improved from the local moorland, and the process was still underway in the second decade of the fourteenth century. The same applied in the case of small mosses like Sink Moss at the north-western extremity of High Legh (Cheshire), around the skirts of which inhabitants of the now shrunken hamlet of Sworton near Swineyard Hall were actively extending their crofts.

Along the estuaries and major river valleys, monastic communities and other landowners ventured to reclaim marshland, as on the west coast at Cockersand and along the Mersey at Norton, Ince and Frodsham. The process has parallels in other areas with extensive lowland wetlands, as the Somerset Levels, for example. In 1322, the peat moors of the manor of Manchester were considered to be close to exhaustion under the pressure of turf-cutting for fuel, combined with the appropriation, often without licence, of substantial parts of the remainder. However, other estates in the area appear to have become run-down in the 1320s, as was the case on Henry de Trafford's estate in Withington, where a low valuation of the farmland was justified on the grounds that 'the land and the meadow are of no value and lie in the waste among the gorse' (Farrer 1907), indicative, perhaps, of the agrarian crisis of the previous few years.

Substantial areas of woodland remained in the region *c.* 1100, including large but scattered tracts which lay outside the comital forests of Cheshire or the royal chases of Lancashire. Colonists entered into such areas as Fulwood, near Preston, and Burtonwood, near Warrington, in sufficient numbers to establish entirely new communities. A court agreement of 1332 concerning Burtonwood and two moieties of the manor of Warrington (Farrer 1903) referred to the inheritance of Henry de Boure in the wood, which included 45 tenements leased for terms of one, two or three lives. Where these leaseholders were identified by a place-name (19 instances) they all derived from the Mersey basin, the most distant coming from Rochdale. There is little evidence here, or elsewhere at this level within rural society, of colonists from distant communities outside the region, although there was certainly some re-location into Lancashire from Wales in the twelfth century, as the Norman conquests there evaporated (Davies 1987). Even so, the Cheshire barons were sufficiently interested in immigrants coming into Cheshire in the early thirteenth century to include access to them among the privileges sought and granted in the Cheshire *Magna Carta*. A substantial flow of incomers should probably be assumed, therefore, given that the area was the nearest thing to a 'Wild West' available to the medieval community within England. Such immigration from outside the region can be demonstrated at present in the nascent boroughs, the religious community and among holders of substantial free tenements, so it is perhaps the difficulties of the evidence which tends to conceal incomers among the regional peasantry.

## Lords and peasants

During the twelfth century, the owners of great estates across England generally leased out their demesne lands and took their share of profits from the countryside in the form of rents and the proceeds of justice. This generality does not, of course, cover all major landholders, since new monastic orders such as the Cistercians preferred direct exploitation to leasing. However, it holds in most cases and accounts to some extent for the scarcity of manorial accounts in the twelfth century. Conditions changed, however, in the thirteenth century, which witnessed a long-term shift in the balance between costs of production and prices to the advantage of the producer. By the end of the century, prices had risen to 100 per cent above, and wages 75 per cent below, their long-term averages (Campbell 2000), fuelled in part by a significant increase in the money supply but more particularly by a substantial rise in population (Britnell 1993). In response, most landowners took back control of their demesne lands in order to profit directly from market conditions. In the North West too, the great estates engaged actively in the market, promoting numerous new settlements based on a pastoral economy in previously under-utilised terrain, particularly in the uplands (see below, page 113–19), and engaging in demesne farming in several lowland areas. Demesne lands were taken in hand across much of lowland Lancashire, for example, and by the abbots of St Werburgh's around Chester.

However, this resumption of demesne farming may have been less enthusiastically undertaken here than elsewhere. Grain production will arguably have been less profitable for many landholders, owing to poor environmental conditions. High rainfall, low evaporation rates, poor drainage, a predominance of heavy clay soils and a shortage of light loams characterised the region. Additionally, there was a high incidence of oats, yields from which were always much lower than from wheat or barley (see below). The principal thrust of new, direct exploitation by the great lordships in the region lay, therefore, in the pastoral economy, not arable production, and in the exploitation of larger acreages rather than better management of existing lands.

So, for example, at the death of Henry de Lacy in 1311, 100 acres of demesne at Tottington and 183 acres and one rood at Haslington, were let for 4*d.* per acre (Farrer 1907). At Colne, 551 acres were let to diverse tenants and at Standen 80 acres of demesne and 36 acres of meadow. At Halton, 54½ acres of demesne were let in 1295–96, and this was the first year that the Earl's oxhouse had been leased, suggesting recent abandonment of direct farming. There were at that date still a few livestock on the demesne at Widnes, with some evidence of increasing numbers by 1304–5, but this was primarily a cattle farm, without significant arable. The direct management of just four acres of meadow and sale of 11*d.* worth of apples at Congleton in 1294–95 demonstrates just how minor a part of the whole enterprise demesne farming had become.

Many of the great estates had also been organised at a time when labour was so scarce that lands, and often entire manors, were leased out or sub-infeudated wholesale. The earldom of Chester is a case in point, having let go control of many of the great demesne manors which the Anglo-Saxon earls of Mercia had retained, apparently in order to provide adequate support for the network of baronies which was required for social and military purposes. The sequestration of the earldom by the crown in 1237 will not have encouraged demesne agriculture on what remained, since the royal lands were among the most likely to be sub-let. There was virtually no regular week-work owed to their landlords by manorial tenants in the North West. During the thirteenth century this will also have meant that demesne agriculture will have been very largely dependent on paid labour. However, the value of week-work has probably been exaggerated nationally (Britnell 1993; Rigby 1995), and there is some evidence to suggest that it was an exceptionally inefficient method of staffing the demesne (e.g. Stone 1997).

Elsewhere in England, a significant shift towards leasing is rarely observable before the second quarter of the fourteenth century (Campbell 2000), and demesne farming remained widespread up until 1376. In the North West, however, there seems to have been a reversion to leasing out demesne lands at a comparatively early date. At Frodsham, for example, several lengthy tenancies of the estate pre-date the Black Death (Booth and Dodd 1979). On most estates of absentee lords in Lancashire it had become customary to lease all or the bulk of the demesne to diverse tenants at will by the 1290s and this had become established practice hallowed by long tradition by 1348. The principle was stated in an extent of the glebelands of Bolton-le-Sands made in about 1320 (Farrer 1907):

> Be it remembered that it is more expedient to demise the demesne lands to farm than to hold them in the lord's hand; ... it is well to retain as much of the better land as will suffice for one plough and to demise the residue to farm.

That such sentiments were being voiced in the region by those on whom the great clerical and secular estate owners relied as managers, says little for the life-expectancy of demesne farming after the Great European Famine of 1316–22, particularly once Scottish raids had begun to add to the difficulties already caused by cattle murrain.

Relations between lords and even their manorial tenants were rather different from those which were normal in the champion country of the Midlands, where regular labour services were either levied or commuted for cash payments. The relationship is best exemplified by a consideration of efforts made in the second quarter of the fourteenth century by the abbot of Vale Royal to raise income from his tenants. His approach was not to impose week-work but to tighten oversight of inheritance, entry fines, heriots and mulcture (payments for use of the lord's mill), which was to exacerbate relations between tenants and lord in the best documented manorial conflict to occur in the region – on the manors of Darnhall and Over. These estates had been part of the demesne of the earls of Chester, falling to Henry III and thence to Prince Edward, after the death of the last earl in 1237. Subject to distant lords, the manorial tenants had enjoyed a long period during which supervision by the manorial court had been lax. In all practical respects the mid-thirteenth century occupiers had inherited what amounted to free tenements or holdings on Ancient Demesne.

That this was not, in fact, the case was brought home to them in 1266 when Prince Edward gave this small group of manors to his new monastic foundation at Darnhall, which was later translated to Vale Royal. The under-endowed monastery had little option but to exploit all available rights so as to maximise its revenue, and these included enforcing their version of local manorial custom on their tenants. In 1329, the manorial bondsmen of Darnhall were sufficiently antagonised by the claims of the abbot to take to arms. Even after most had surrendered, ten were sufficiently obdurate in their opposition that they were placed in shackles at Weaverham. The last to abandon the struggle, Hondekyn, son of Randolph de Holden, fled from the manor with his cattle and chattels, only to be taken and imprisoned by the abbot. During the following decade, the discomforted tenants laid their case before the Justiciar of Chester and, failing there, carried their petition via a series of misadventures to the king in parliament at Westminster and sought in addition the aid of the Queen. Failing to obtain relief, they ambushed the abbot and his party in distant County Rutland and several fell on both sides in the ensuing mêlée. Despite their consistent opposition, the tenants were eventually forced to submit to the abbot and admit themselves bondsmen and as such ineligible to take their grievance beyond the manorial court (Brownbill 1914).

The issues were substantive and the grievances of the tenants very real. Both sides spent considerable sums on the case and it seems clear that some at least of the tenants were men of substance, able to bear the costs of suing through the royal courts as well as travelling widely in their pursuit of justice. The conflict derived from the very different perspectives of a long-privileged, manorial tenantry and a new, local and impecunious manorial lord. Despite the blood shed in open conflict on the road, none of the tenants was subjected to capital punishment by the several courts and they obtained considerable sympathy for their cause from the Crown, but no redress.

The manorial customs which the abbot imposed focused particularly on the transition of property from one generation to another, and the various perquisites of lordship, as the following extracts from the custumal drawn up by the monks show (Brownbill 1914, 118):

Also, when any one of them dieth, the lord shall have all the pigs of the deceased, all his goats, all his mares at grass, and his horse also, if he had one for his personal use, all his bees, all his bacon-pigs, all his cloth of wool and flax, and whatsoever can be found of gold and silver. The lord shall have all his brass pots or pot, if he have one (but who of these bond-tenants will have a brass pot for cooking his food in?), because at his death the lord ought to have all things of metal. Abbot John granted to them in full court that these metal goods should be divided equally between the lord and the wife of the deceased on the death of every one of them, but on condition that they should buy themselves brass pots ... Also it is not lawful for the bond-tenant to make a will, or bequeath anything, without licence of the lord of the manor.

No other conflicts between lords and their tenants elsewhere in the region were so well-recorded. References to the manumission of villains are uncommon and bondsmen do not appear to have been particularly disadvantaged compared to free tenants. Once the villeins of the Cheshire barons were freed of military obligations by the Cheshire *Magna Carta* in the second decade of the thirteenth century, it may be that villein status offered certain advantages. Those at Darnhall were, however, expected to keep watch around the abbot's hall in the event of war.

## The rural community, crops and the standard of living

It is notoriously difficult to estimate the standard of living of those actively involved in the agricultural process. Nationally, it has been argued that population levels had reached a point in the late thirteenth century where there was significant under-employment and many had been forced by rising prices to trade down to poorer and cheaper foodstuffs (Dyer 1989). Any such conjecture in an area starved of long-running estate documentation is necessarily speculative and can be based on no more than anecdotal and indirect evidence. However, changing population levels certainly shifted the balance between land availability and mouths requiring food. In such circumstances, subsistence might eventually have been threatened and it might be imagined that Malthusian checks could have emerged as a mechanism for the control of population size (for recent data, see Smith 2002). However, it is also clear that the flexibility of local agrarian practices and management, allied to the increasing development in the region of market opportunities and the commercialisation of the economy (in general, see Britnell 1993), enabled the regional community to sustain much higher than average rates of population growth. For some, with access to capital, the period probably saw living standards rise rather than fall, as mechanisms for exchange and increasingly accessible urban markets encouraged economic specialisation to spread into the countryside and replace the largely subsistence agronomy of the eleventh century. Assarting, new enclosure and land improvement were arguably the keys to these processes, with widespread use of drainage to enable difficult terrain to be used more extensively. Marling was also in use by the thirteenth century, which was a practice that was certainly considered valuable at a later date for improving yields (Hewitt 1923).

There does seem to have been some expansion in the number of individuals with strips in the open fields, and a consequent decline in the size of their holdings. By the late thirteenth century, only a minority of the manorial community held full bovates. At Frodsham, it has been estimated that 6.3 per cent of the bond community held 30 per cent of the available acreage, leaving about 50 per cent of holdings with a half bovate, and 19 per cent with only a quarter bovate (Dodd 1982). Of course, many of the smallholders could presumably have sold their labour to their neighbours or within the adjacent borough, but the price of labour had fallen dramatically at this time, just as grain prices were rising. The economic position of such families was clearly worsening.

The bovate was a unit of land which had its origins not in land measurement but in an estimate of subsistence capacity. It was that unit of landed resource which an eleventh or twelfth century community deemed sufficient to support a bondsman and his household. It should be equated with the Lancashire oxgang – that unit of land which enabled a proprietor to contribute a beast or its equivalent to the plough-team. Given the highly variable quality of agricultural land in the region, it is hardly surprising that both should have been elastic measures. At Halton (Lancashire), an oxgang had 9 acres and two roods in the common fields but would generally contain, in addition, acres in closes derived from assarts not incorporated into the common fields (Harris 1967). At Overton, ten oxgangs each contained 12 acres, two contained eight acres, one contained 18 acres and one 22 acres (Farrer 1915). South of the Mersey, a bovate at Shotwick was only three acres (Sylvester 1956). In all these cases, the acre represented a customary measure. This was also highly variable within the region. The Cheshire acre probably derived from a unit of forest measurement based on a perch of the unusual length of 24 ft, as opposed to the more normal 16½ ft, giving a customary acre substantially more than the statute acre (Maitland 1907; Hewitt 1929). In South Lancashire, a similar measure was commonly used. North of the Ribble, the customary perch varied, but was probably more commonly 21 ft, similar to the customary measure found across the remainder of the northern counties of England, perhaps derived from a Northumbrian original (Smith 1958).

These large customary acres represented a general recognition of the poor quality of the land in this region and the consequently greater area necessary to support a peasant household. A 12-acre bovate in South Lancashire had a total land area of something approaching 30 statute acres, but contemporaries evaluated such a holding as equivalent to, at most, a 10 to 15 statute acre holding in southern England.

Low yields were consequent upon climatic conditions, which threatened the rural community with an incidence of harvest failure far higher than was the case in regions of better drainage, less rain and a lower incidence of cloud cover. The same conditions encouraged the community to sow the low yield crop, oats, because it was less sensitive to harvest disruption by rain. So at Accrington in 1295–96, the de Lacy estate spent just *6d.* on reaping corn (i.e. wheat), but *5s. 9d.* cutting oats (Lyons 1884). At Standen Grange in 1304–5, a harvest of eight quarters and five bushels of wheat, plus three quarters and three bushels of barley contrasts with 189 quarters and six bushels of oats. Sales of wheat from the same estate in 1295–96 were a mere *5s. 5d.,* compared with oats to the value of £10 17s. 7½d. The expected gross yield from oats per seed was regularly less than 2.5, in contrast with wheat, where a five-fold yield could normally be expected. However, yields recorded on the estates of Bolton Priory in nearby Craven (West Yorkshire) suggest that oats could be relied upon to give a return when all other crops failed (Kershaw 1973a). Net yields of over 20 bushels per acre could be achieved by using heavy seeding rates in Norfolk (Campbell 2000, 331) but it seems unlikely that such high outputs were often achieved in the North West. At Ightenhill Grange in 1304–5, 27 quarters of oats were harvested but 11 quarters had to be set aside for seed (Lyon 1884), implying a yield of only 1:2.45. At Standen Grange in 1294–95, 51 quarters from a gross yield of 121 quarters and 6½ bushels were held back for seed, again implying a yield of less than 1:2.5. The discovery at Audlem, in South Cheshire, of a grain-drying kiln full of oats underlines the significance of this comparatively low yield crop to the local economy.

On the better arable lands of the Cheshire lowlands and south-west Lancashire, oats were, however, used in rotation with wheat, barley, peas and other pulses. In central Cheshire, the Vale Royal manors were certainly capable of producing wheat. A corrody sold to one Richard, son of Ralph de Bradford, provided him with a loaf of white convent bread each day as well as a flagon of better ale (made from barley) and 'kybecht' or black bread, made from oats (Brownbill 1914). Oats, rye and barley were all grown at Macclesfield (Tonkinson 1999). When Edward I required supplies for the Scottish war, Cheshire was expected to provide considerable quantities of wheat and malt-barley. 'Wheat', 'barley' and 'bean' all appear in medieval field- and place-names in several localities within the region (e.g. Wheatley and Barton, Lancashire; Bancroft, *Benfurlong*, Cheshire).

In other parts of the region, wheat was, however, rarely sown. In Macclesfield Hundred little grain other than oats was grown, and oats was virtually the only grain sown in the uplands of eastern Lancashire. There can be little doubt that the normal bread grain of many of the north-western peasantry, in particular, was oats. When Edward I ordered a purveyance for the war in Scotland in 1306, Lancashire was one of only three counties from which no wheat was demanded (the others were Devon and Cornwall). 1,000 quarters of oats were to be provided, and 100 live oxen – the only such mentioned and in contrast to the carcasses to be brought from Devon and Cornwall. Wheat was imported to Chester with some frequency from Ireland, although much of this trade was probably linked to the provisioning of armies and garrisons, or may have been necessary to compensate for local, royal requisitioning during the conquest of Wales (Hewitt 1929). The remainder was probably consumed very largely within the city. In most years we should expect the rural community to have been self-sufficient in grain, if rarely capable of exporting much of a surplus.

In such circumstances, any fragmentation of the customary bovate might carry with it serious consequences for the sustenance of the manorial community (Titow 1969). The real extent of such fragmentation is difficult to assess despite the clear signs at Frodsham. The ten Overton 12-acre oxgangs were, in 1348, apparently rented by the inhabitants of 12 messuages, an 18-acre oxgang was held by three tenants and the 22-acre oxgang by two tenants. References to part oxgangs are rare in the few surviving Lancashire court rolls, despite the quarter oxgang that comprised a minor part of the inheritance of Ellen, relict of Thomas le Palmer at West Derby (Farrer 1901). At Great Marsden, for example, 12 customary tenants held 12½ oxgangs, at Little Marsden, four held 3½ oxgangs and at Padiham 25 held 24 oxgangs (Farrer 1907). A superficial reading of such figures suggests that in general the oxgang or bovate had not suffered significant sub-division over the preceding two and a half centuries. It could even be argued that the oxgang had been augmented by the addition of new assarts to the benefit of the manorial community. However, this may be to misuse the evidence. The Lancashire court rolls concentrate their attention on the interface between the lord and the manorial community. It is arguable that a village aristocracy of the type identified at Frodsham occupied this interface and was responsible for the rents of the oxgangs. Beneath this layer of society was a community of sub-tenants and cottagers. At Clitheroe, landholdings comprising a single messuage with or without a handful of acres were common. Although this was a small town, it seems unlikely that all such tenants made a living from trade or manufacture. At Overton, 7½d. was answered for by the reeve for the rents of tenants 'for diverse dwellings within the lordship, holding neither lands nor tenements, to wit for reaping corn ...' (Farrer 1915). In 1295–96, new rents at Halton included a plot of pasture in the Marsh let to bordars for the first year. At Singleton, in 1323, 24 bondmen had 28 oxgangs, paying 14s. 3½d. per oxgang, but a further 13 cottages brought in another 21s. 6d. At Rygeby, nine cottages were let for 9s. 8d. (Farrer 1907). By 1300 it is clear that there was a landless stratum present within the rural population. We cannot say how many people were in this position, but they were probably numerous and they may have been under-employed.

Among some communities evolving within newly assarted areas, cottagers or smallholders can be identified, although the special conditions here may have offered enhanced employment opportunities. At Brownedge in Manchester barony, in 1322, new cottages were being built on plots of pasture of between one and two acres. At Burtonwood, by Warrington, 45 tenancies included 21 containing no more land than one or more messuages (29 and a moiety in all) and a further nine with less than five acres attached (Farrer 1903). A minority held the bulk of the productive lands and parts of this were arguably sub-divided and sub-let, such as the six messuages, 40 acres of land, three acres of meadow and 20 acres of wood held for a term of three lives by

Gilbert de Haydock and his family. Below landholders of the ilk of Gilbert there presumably existed a substantial majority who were obliged to feed themselves by paid labour. Even so, the total of 51½ messuages implies a community of approximately this number of households and a population of 200 to 250 persons, supported by an arable extent of about 243½ acres (customary), nine acres of meadow and 114½ acres of wood. In years when economic opportunities allowed the whole community access to these resources, via paid labour for instance, there was probably enough to go round. When other factors affected the harvest, it is difficult to see how the less privileged members of such communities could hope to escape dearth.

While the economic fortunes of some rural households may have fallen to a precarious level by the late thirteenth century, this was a matter of declining access to land and work, not dropping yields. The village aristocracy was arguably able to exploit the rising market for grain. If wages locally followed the national trend, then they were depressed to low levels by the comparative availability of labourers in the early fourteenth century, and established farmers with sufficient capital could take up the substantial local demesne lands available at lease and work them with cheap labour. Rent for the oxgang varied, depending both on the size, and on the extent to which customary services were commuted within the rental, but an annual rent of 2–3s. was common in Lancashire, with or without a day's ploughing, a day's harrowing, a day's reaping and carriage of the lord's grain and millstones (as at Gorton: Farrer 1907). An in-coming tenant could be expected to pay an entry fine as high as 10s. for a messuage and oxgang at Ightenhill. However, that it was paid underlines the economic capacity of this minority of comparatively wealthy tenants, who should be seen as the Lancashire equivalent of the bondsmen of Vale Royal, or the bovate tenants of Frodsham.

A tier above these villagers on the social ladder was both widespread and populous in the region, holding enough land to be substantial farmers and significant rentiers. The origins of these men may lie in the radmen and other free but often un-named Domesday tenants, such as 'free men', thegns and drengs, who escaped demotion to the ranks of the manorial tenantry, augmented by the over-production of children by the local aristocracy and gentry who sought to provide land for their younger sons. Such was the origin of Swineyard Hall, for example, a moated hall occupying an environmental niche between the Shirdley Hill Sand of Sworton Heath and a small lowland moss, Sink Moss, neither of which were completely enclosed until an Act of Parliament tidied up the township in the early nineteenth century. Given the name, the site had once presumably been used as a pig-pasture until it was occupied by a cadet branch of one of the two Legh families of High Legh in the early fourteenth century (Figure 25).

The Swinehead Chartulary, made in 1619 but containing copies of numerous medieval charters, provides a vivid insight to this landscape just before and after the Black Death. The family had interests in pannage, house-bote and haybote in the woods of High Legh, and common of turbary and

FIGURE 25.
Swineyard Hall: a
moated capital
messuage of the Later
Middle Ages, at the
head of a new manor
consisting of assarted
land on and around
former woodland,
heath and moss at the
northern end of High
Legh, Cheshire.

pasture on the moss, but it was particularly involved in assarting and enclosing new lands from the waste on the moss skirtland. The following undated early fourteenth-century grant provides a flavour of the agrarian system which was developing:

> a certain assart called Le Part with the moor called le Pratmore within these demises ... from the assart of Henry de Houlgreve in breadth near the way coming from Leigh to the land of Hugh the son of Adam de Leigh, and in length from the aforesaid way as it appears nigh the land of the said Hugh to the furthest part of Holme meadow against hay hatch, and so from the longest part of Holmeade it doeth extend into a croft of Henry de Houlgreve which is called the Bincroft [Beancroft] and from the Bincroft it doeth extend unto the capital land ...

The Leghs of Swinehead were amassing a small estate in this northern quarter of High Legh township, with outliers elsewhere, which eventually amounted to 12 messuages, 300 acres of land, 30 acres of meadow, 100 acres of pasture, eight acres of wood and 40 acres of turbary. By 1319, the estate included a water mill, and in the following century the family began to claim manorial status. Given that the two manors of High Legh at Domesday combined had only three *servi*, one villein and two *cottarii*, with one plough, the area of Sworton and Swinehead at the northern end of the township is most unlikely to have been inhabited at all on a permanent basis in the eleventh century. Indeed, this and the nearby Northwood, on the opposite side of Sink Moss (which also developed as a sub-manor), were probably well-wooded in 1086, given that the estate was credited with woodland one league long and half a league wide, with an enclosure. What we see here, therefore, is a process of intensification of land-use, with woodland swine-pasture giving way to a permanent settlement practising mixed agriculture, surrounded by fields and equipped with a mill. The whole enterprise was being driven by the needs of an under-endowed minor gentry family to make marginal land pay.

The flexibility of this agrarian system, combined with the widespread availability of under-used land capable of improvement, encouraged the emergence of holdings of 100 acres and more, as the more successful within this community obtained control of increased areas of land by assarting, engrossment and enclosure. It is likely that it was the free and aspirant-gentry within the rural community who were responsible for much of the reclamation. They had the economic power to invest capital in land improvement and the connections and negotiating strength to obtain access. When the holdings or acquisitions of such individuals can be seen in the court rolls, they were generally characterised by a variety of different types of land, capable in combination of supporting mixed farming. For example, in June 1315, William, son of Richard de Urmston, came to an agreement concerning six messuages, a mill, 40 acres of arable, two acres of meadow, 40 acres of wood and 3*d.* in rent in West Legh (Farrer 1903). Similar agreements in 1323 and 1322 listed, respectively, two messuages, 40 acres of land, 200 acres of wood, 100 acres of pasture and 100 acres of moorland at Goosnargh, and 40 messuages, 440 acres of land, 20 acres of meadow, 300 acres of wood, 400 acres of turbary and two parts of a mill at Burtonwood. The sums that changed hands in some of these cases were in excess of £30, requiring us to believe both that these transactions represented land sales and that individuals at this level of society and above had access to cash or credit sufficient to pay such sums.

## Plague, population and the agrarian landscape, 1350–1540

Statistics are unavailable for the population of the North West in 1349 and the numbers lost in the Black Death. Indeed such statistics are nationally reliant on small samples, based either on specific communities or on sections within society which may have been less than characteristic of the whole (Smith 2002). The evidence for Cheshire was collected by Hewitt (1929) and has been augmented by more recent work on court rolls (Booth 1981; Tonkinson 1999). For Lancashire, the evidence was collected for the Victory County History (1908), and by France (1938). It is unfortunate that what might have been the most detailed surviving records – an ecclesiastical court case in North

Lancashire over mortuary payments – are seriously flawed by obvious approximations and poor arithmetic (France 1938 places rather too much reliance on these figures). Where figures are available for specific communities, as is the case for the tenants of Macclesfield, the population seems to have dropped dramatically, with numerous holdings vacant in 1349 and being grazed by the livestock of neighbours (Tonkinson 1999, 77). Although these instances are anecdotal and may, therefore, be unrepresentative, there is general support for a death rate nationally of between 40 per cent and 50 per cent of the population. There is every reason to think that the local community shared equally in the disaster.

Particularly where there were large parishes, the unprecedented death rate of successive plagues caused major problems in the disposal of the remains. Chapels such as that at Didsbury or St Nicholas at Liverpool (in 1361) were licensed for burial for the first time. Here and elsewhere the plague deaths hastened the acquisition by chapels of full parochial rights, if only immediately on a temporary basis. There is some evidence that the local community was subjected thereafter to the national pattern of cyclical plague (e.g. Razi 1980; see also France 1938). The population of Macclesfield was dropping once more in the late fourteenth century, after a rally in the 1360s and 1370s. There was official recognition of the virulence of an outbreak in the early 1420s, particularly at and around Lancaster. This may imply that the regional demographic trend after 1350 was at best characterised by short periods of slow growth – supposing that birth rates rose – followed by plague-induced decline. At worst, no such growth episodes occurred, birth rates failed to respond to plague deaths and the population stayed at or close to the levels of the 1350s for something approaching two centuries. If, as some evidence suggests, new outbreaks of the plague particularly affected the young, then a consequence may have been change to the age profile of the community in favour of non-child-bearing age groups, which may have long delayed a sustainable demographic revival.

Total population may have begun to recover slowly in the late fifteenth century, as the incidence and severity of recurrent plague subsided (Bean 1962–3), and certainly increased rapidly over the course of the sixteenth century (Wrigley and Schofield 1981). Even so, local outbreaks of plague could be severe. That which occurred at Liverpool in 1540 brought a reaction similar to that of the London authorities in the 1660s (France 1938). In 1506 a 'great deal of sweating sickness' was reported at Chester and an epidemic occurred in 1517 when 'grass growed in the streates of the same cittye' because of the flight of the population (Flenley 1911).

The sole, nationally relevant source for the size of the population in the generation after the Black Death is the returns of the Poll Taxes of the period 1377–81. However, Cheshire was not subjected to these taxes. Population figures have been computed from the Lancashire returns for 1377 and 1379, suggesting a population of *c.* 67,000–75,000 for the region (see above but note the discussion in Bennett 1983). This figure is based on data which is far from being representative and may err substantially. Thereafter population probably fluctuated around a mean, which altered little until, at earliest, the last quarter of the fifteenth century, when indirect evidence (of prices) implies the beginning of a demographic rise, which was eventually to become substantial. We should expect the estimate of population in 1379 to have risen by around one hundred per cent by the reign of Elizabeth I, going up particularly steeply in the decades around the mid-sixteenth century. In 1563, the population of the region was in the order of 143,000 (based on Phillips and Smith 1994). This figure comprises a Lancashire total of *c.* 82,000, significantly higher than Cheshire with *c.* 60,000.

These figures provide the first evidence that Lancashire's population had overtaken that of Cheshire, but this may have occurred as early as the four-teenth century. The rise of Lancashire reflects both its greater land surface and its consequent scope for improvement and assarting to accommodate new farming units, and the growing importance of textiles to the late medieval and sixteenth-century rural economy.

The immediate consequences of the Black Death included a sudden rush of tenancies onto the land market. Where court records survive, most holdings were rapidly re-let, suggesting that considerable reservoirs of potential tenants existed in the mid-fourteenth century, unable, before the plague deaths inter-vened, to obtain sufficient access to land. However some dislocation was unavoidable. At Macclesfield, 46 holdings failed to provide a rent in 1348–9 but only six holdings remained un-let by 1355. A surfeit of land over tenants had re-emerged by the 1360s, when the Black Prince's officials found it impossible to lease the iron works and coal mines of the manor 'for lack of farmers' or maintain the level of income from the manorial mills (Booth 1981, Tonkinson 1999). At Rudheath and Overmarsh the Prince's official had considerable difficulty in finding tenants for the holdings of deceased farmers and the matter was not aided by the release onto the market of the demesne of the manor of Drakelow in 1355. Neither area would have been considered good land and may have been unattractive to potential tenants who were enjoying an unprecedented opportunity to choose between alternative hold-ings. Elsewhere, it was necessary to group several holdings together and thereby let a similar amount of land to a smaller number of tenants. At Macclesfield, increasing numbers of farmers held sufficient land for subsist-ence, while some, like John Cresswall, held over 60 acres (Tonkinson 1999, 111). Other tenancies were re-let on easier terms, expressed in waived entry fines, less rigorous conditions of tenure or lower rents.

During the first few generations after the crisis, the distribution of the pop-ulation and of wealth appears to have varied little from the patterns established in earlier centuries. In Lancashire the general distribution of wealth as evi-denced by the returns for the lay subsidy of 1334 probably changed only slowly throughout the century. The basis of taxation rapidly became ossified, and therefore loses any value for comparative purposes (Glasscock 1975). Within this pattern, the agricultural south-west, particularly in the vicinity of Crosby and Widnes, was by far the most heavily taxed, followed by the remainder of

West Derby Hundred, Preston and southern Lonsdale. Almost certainly the large mosses and the uplands in the east remained comparatively sparsely populated well into the sixteenth century. However, some areas of the lowlands, which had been thinly settled in 1086 were obliged to pay considerable sums towards the Cheshire mize (Bennett 1983). The assessment on which that tax was based was made shortly after 1346, so reflects the distribution of wealth immediately prior to the Black Death. Not surprisingly, the overall level was comparatively modest and the higher rated areas were concentrated in the west of the shire plus the Weaver valley (Phillips and Phillips 2002, map on p. 33). However, for a vill such as Lymm to be assessed at 72s., and neighbouring High Legh at 66s., implies a comparative improvement in their relative demographic and economic performance when compared with Dee valley communities. These figures presumably reflect the fact that, already in 1086, these were both large, two-manor townships, and High Legh had expanded to include two new (sub-)manors by this date, with significant populations occupying land which had been waste at Domesday. Numerous vills remained comparatively impoverished and under-populated, particularly in the east of Cheshire and along the Central Ridge, where many communities were assessed at less than 20s.

## Labour, land and tenancy

The century after 1350 was the century of opportunity for those of the under-privileged who had the good fortune to survive the high mortality of the Black Death and the successive plagues thereafter. The ranks of the labouring poor were depleted by recruitment into the boroughs and into rural tenancies, as well as by death. The result was a significant shortfall in the numbers of labourers locally available for hire. To the extent that wage rises were consequent upon a labour shortage, this phenomenon can be identified. The Statue of Labourers was enforced within the region with some vigour, bringing in to the Crown and Duchy a valuable addition to flagging levels of income. In Cheshire, at least, most of those presented preferred to pay a fine, to avoid further legal process from the sheriff's court in each hundred to the court of the justiciar at Chester. Those indicted included craftsmen, such as smiths, cordwainers (shoe-makers) and a cartwright, as well as agricultural workers and a number of rural weavers or websters. It appears that numerous employers were prepared to pay both men and women wages higher than prescribed by law. The effect of the legislation is likely to have been no more than an inconvenience to the minority who were arraigned, for each of whom we must assume numbers who avoided accusation.

Several factors made the issue of wages a sensitive one within the region. Low levels of customary labour services meant that even before 1349 those running large farms were more dependent on paid labour than in other parts. In practice, few major fourteenth-century landlords were heavily committed to direct exploitation even before the Black Death. However, for the ranks of the local gentry and wealthier 'yeomanry' who made up the large, middle tier of landholders there was little option but to employ labourers if production was to be maintained. When grain prices fell in the late fourteenth century, many local proprietors abandoned agriculture and converted their lands to pasture. A more affluent community nationally probably meant that demand for the products of pastoralism was more buoyant than that for grain, which may have given some advantage to a region which had traditionally under-produced the latter but exported the former.

Local peasants were not generally motivated to rebel against the labour legislation. Most bondsmen were not required, even in the early fourteenth century, to engage in regular week-work as a condition of tenure. In practice, much boon work had already been commuted to a money payment and many manorial tenants already held additional tenancies in the old demesne lands (e.g. in the Lancashire estates of the Duchy). For such tenants, the issue of wages was not pressing. Indeed, the successful among them were more likely to be hiring labourers than to be offering themselves for hire. It may have been to encourage the supply of labour for their own use that a series of manorial tenants were building cottages on plots of land as small as one rood in Chatburn (Farrer 1897, 5–6).

The situation was more critical for those who customarily employed significant quantities of wage labour. Those responsible for the income of the great lords adopted new, more defensive, estate management policies after the mid-century. The few large estates with substantial demesne tended to reduce their exposure to the increased risk of direct exploitation of the land. The prime example is that of the earldom of Chester, where Booth (1981) has documented the rapid decline of demesne activity at Drakelow, Frodsham and Macclesfield. At Frodsham and Macclesfield there are signs of investment in demesne sheep and cattle in the decades after 1350, but in neither instance was this maintained, and by the late fourteenth century most of the assets of the earldom were leased. The flight from direct exploitation was also underway among the monastic estates of the region, with a growing reliance on income from rents of land and other assets by the late fourteenth century.

An exception to this pattern may have been the abbey of Chester. The abbot complained that his *nativi* had been in arms against him in 1381 (Bennett 1983). Cheshire was not subject to the poll taxes which provoked the so-called 'Peasants' Revolt' in the South East. However, the abbey was a major and long-established landowner with estates almost surrounding the principal market for local produce at Chester. There are some signs that it retained a significant degree of direct control over the produce of these estates rather longer than its neighbours. It may be that the conflict between the monks and their tenants was stimulated by the inability of the latter to exploit changing economic circumstances when all around them others appeared better able to do so. It has been noted that those men who were named as rebels were the holders of substantial rural tenancies in 1398, and the conflict may have been between two groups of potential employers as much as between lord and peasantry.

As a general statement, it is fair to say that villeinage withered away in the region relatively rapidly after the Black Death. Having never existed widely in the more extreme form which a Midlander would have recognised, bond tenure was replaced by a multiplicity of shades of tenancy 'at will', for lives or for a term of years. The precise conditions of such tenure varied from manor to manor and from tenancy to tenancy. Copyhold – tenure supported by a copy of the manorial entry – was being established in the region by the early sixteenth century. Some landlords, including the Stanleys, were converting customary tenure to leasehold during the 1530s, at considerable advantage to themselves, and the fear that this would spread may have helped fuel the Pilgrimage of Grace. The ancient, legal distinction between bond land and free tenements declined as types of tenure became increasingly flexible. By a new agreement dated 1351, the Duchy reduced the level of servile obligations for many of its Cheshire tenants around Halton (Bennett 1983) but the tenants of the manor of Ashton-under-Lyne were still required to perform boon service in 1422 (Bowman 1960).

The land which the aristocracy released onto the market was in large part taken out of cultivation: there is substantial direct and indirect evidence which implies that grain was to an extent replaced both by sheep and cattle, although sufficient presumably continued to be grown to provide for the local population. The result was an ossification of ridge and furrow, which survives particularly in southern and western Cheshire (see Figure 18). The area remained one of mixed farming (cf. Flintshire: Booth and Carr 1991, lxxvii), but the acreage given over to wheat, barley and more particularly oats shrank, while pasture was extended.

This process was associated with the shrinkage of rural settlements, many of which contracted to a handful of tenements or a single farm. For example, the excavated medieval tenements at Tatton were abandoned not during the creation of the deer park in the mid-eighteenth century but during the second half of the fourteenth century or, at latest, the early years of the fifteenth. The settlement pattern that replaced it in the early sixteenth century was centred on a new hall (Tatton Old Hall) constructed at some distance from the supposed site of the thirteenth-century manor house and presumably located by its builders with a significantly different set of objectives in mind. Elsewhere, many manors had shrunk to a single farm or manor house; in perhaps half the vills of the region there was no resident manorial lord (Bennett 1983). Several of these abandoned or shrunken sites have been identified from the air, such as Spurstow and Overton (near Malpas), or the shrunken site of Bruera (Williams R. S. 1984). Others can be deduced from later map evidence (Chapman 1953) or from lost place-names – see for example the loss of *Faudon* on the edge of Peover Heath. That said, the large numbers of abandoned villages which are such a common theme in central England simply do not occur in the North West, where most desertions seem to have been moated platforms, individual farms or very small groups thereof (Figure 26).

FIGURE 26.
Hough Hall moated platform at Hoo Green, Mere, Cheshire (after a contour survey by Tony Garbutt): the earthworks of a short-lived capital messuage of the Later Middle Ages. Excavations in 1988 revealed a well-preserved, late medieval oven and the clay floors of ancillary buildings. This may have been Strethyl ('Street-hill'), the residence of Richard de Venables and Isabel his wife in the reign of Richard II. It is a good example of a small moated platform, typical of many in the region.

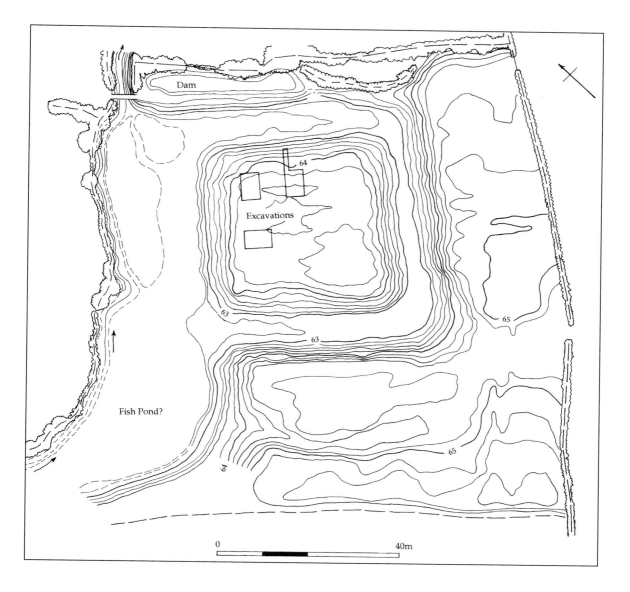

Dam

64

Excavations

63

63

65

65

Fish Pond?

64

0                                    40m

The farming practised by this reduced scatter of occupiers was still mixed agriculture with an emphasis on livestock. The simplicity of the inventory attached to the will of Matthew Legh of Swinehead in 1512 is such that a great deal of rounding up or down should be assumed. However, after setting aside a debt owing of £20, the assets were noted under eight headings. Cattle and horses made up half the headings and 56 per cent of the value against a mere 14 per cent of the value of corn and hay. Matthew seems to have been growing grain enough for his own needs but producing cattle for market and this was probably typical of many of his countrymen in the fifteenth century. His rather more successful contemporary, the courtier William Brereton, was engaged in animal husbandry (largely cattle) on his own account and sending both his stock and that of others to market in London and Coventry (Ives 1971). Even so, he had demesne grain lands at Holt and a lease of corn tithes, which brought him a substantial income.

Most holdings comprised land of several different types, without the concentration of strips which was commonplace in the Midlands. Enclosed land, often in small, piecemeal assarts or crofts and tofts, made up a significant proportion of the land of most communities, and most also had access to significant, albeit diminishing, un-enclosed commons. So, for example, when Nicholas Robynson died at Chatburn in or before 1496, his manorial tenancy comprised

> a messuage and garden, with one acre of waste[,] twenty acres of land and a half, and half a rood of rodeland [assarted land], four tofts, and fourteen acres of land and meadow, and half an acre of land of demesne land, with the appurtenances.

When Thomas, his son, died in 1508, the holding was larger and even more diverse:

> 1 messuage, 17 acres of oxgang land, one acre of land of rodeland, with the appurtenances, in the town of Chatburn ...; 1 messuage, 3 acres of land of rodeland, with the appurtenances, called Mandebell Croft, 3 acres of land of rodeland, with the appurtenances, called Heyles, and half an acre of land lying upon Hallflat, and half an acre of land lying in ffoxhoult Redez, and half a perch lying at Grayston, and two acres of land lying near to Green Lane ..., and one acre of land lying in Middilwode Hey, and 10 acres of land called Peche and Weteacre, with the appurtenances, within the township of Chatburn, and half an acre of meadow lying in Barkergaite, in the same town ... (Farrer 1897, 16, 29).

This mix of different types of land provided a comparatively flexible basis for agrarian change during the later Middle Ages and beyond. The withdrawal from demesne cultivation of the great estates removed one of the major forces for the maintenance of customary practices. Reduction in the numbers of cultivators within many open field systems and the abandonment of some arable in favour of pasture led necessarily to the decay of town fields. Changes in the demographic profile of the region also perhaps resulted in pressure for a rapid transformation of local field systems. Characteristics of an enclosed landscape had always been present but they now became increasingly dominant, as livestock farming took over arable. The diversity of open fields within the region much reduced the type of social opposition to change which was the experience of many other regional communities elsewhere in England.

The process of enclosure is, however, difficult to document. Within the old arable, there seems to have been an extremely low incidence of confrontation or dispute. Most open fields shrank or entirely disappeared leaving little trace over the next few centuries and almost all was gone before the era of Parliamentary Enclosure in the eighteenth and nineteenth centuries (Davies

1960; Youd 1961). Against the background of increasing public concern on a national level, a royal commission was appointed on 28 May 1517 to investigate what enclosure had taken place over the previous quarter century, what land had been converted from arable to pasture and what settlements had been depopulated. The results for Cheshire have survived (Leadam 1897) but are almost perfunctory, with hundredal juries reporting a very low level of enclosure. For example, the Bucklow Hundred jury reported that Sir Philip Legh had put a pale around a park of two acres which had been cultivated, and a handful of other cases were raised, but no vill, hamlet, farm, building or cottage had been thrown down or made ruinous.

While the field evidence points to wholesale but piecemeal enclosure of open field, therefore, this survey provides remarkably little evidence that this was in practice occurring. We must conclude either that enclosure had hardly begun in the region by 1492, or that it had already occurred and that the process was proceeding by this stage without significant conflict, with vested interests in what remained reasonably secure from threat. Of these two options, the second seems preferable.

Certainly, much open field did survive the reign of Henry VIII. The vills around Rochdale, for example, were still utilising town fields in the late sixteenth century (Wadsworth 1919–22) and much of the common field of Stockport was enclosed by amicable agreement in 1712 (Giles 1950–1). The last remnant of open field at Ashton-under-Lyne, Lees Field, was finally enclosed in 1841 (see the contemporary plan in Bowman 1960, 24), but had shrunk to a mere 13 Lancashire acres already by 1592. The open fields of Carnforth were still functioning in the eighteenth century, and many other instances can be detailed (Youd 1961). However, there are signs that much of what had existed in 1349 was already enclosed by 1540, or was shortly to be enclosed. The open field system has been described as being 'in decay' in the sixteenth century (Davies 1960), but that may be to over-emphasise its pre-plague cohesion and systematisation. The area subject to open field at Bare (Lancashire), for example, was a mere 40 acres in the mid-sixteenth century, in an area where numerous closes were shared by more than one proprietor or used simultaneously for more than one function (Chippindall 1939; Harris 1967). Such closes might either be stages in the removal of land from open field, or they may be a parallel development.

Despite the apparent equanimity of the Cheshire jurymen, much conversion of arable to pasture was underway, although not necessarily in the quarter century before 1517. Scattered documentary evidence illustrates the process of enclosure by exchange and agreement at Farndon Hay in 1491 and Carden in 1506 and 1619 (Chapman 1953). Parts at least of Liverpool town fields were enclosed in the mid-sixteenth century. An endorsement to a thirteenth-century deed in the Norris collection notes that Sir William Norris 'in his time brought the town field into close'. He died in January 1567 (Lumby 1939). By 1540, the process or conversion and enclosure was well-established in the region.

In many areas it is possible to trace open field or furlong names identified before the Black Death in estate documents of the seventeenth and eighteenth centuries, where they appear as names attached to enclosed fields or as the characteristic 'flat', 'loon', 'butt', 'dole' or 'acre'. It is common to find that broad ridge conforms to the modern field boundaries, as tends to be the case, for example, in the middle Dee valley. This need not imply that these ridges are post-medieval. Many probably reflect the retention of the same field units as pastures in the new era. The reason probably lies in the small size of open fields, many of which were no larger than was required of a pasture, and most of which were presumably already protected by ditch and hedge. As a result, many open fields arguably passed into the era of enclosure simply by the act of pasturing of livestock through what had previously been the growing period, and the failure to cultivate. The result would be a gated pasture, rights over which might then be exchanged or purchased to establish tenure in severalty. Elsewhere modern fields contain several groups of ridges, running in different directions (Figure 27), or post-medieval boundaries actually cut through ridge and furrow, although the last is unusually rare in the region compared with parts of the Midlands.

The medieval attack on marsh and moor relaxed but did not cease in the decades after the Black Death. Despite the presumed population drop, there remained sufficient demand for new assarting to occur on the Duchy of Lancaster's Salfordshire estates. Fines for the building of new houses on the lord's waste are a common feature of surviving rolls in the fifteenth and early sixteenth centuries and farms without open field lands existed, as in Richard Radcliffes's holding south of Catlow (Colne) in 1478, which contained exclusively rodeland and 'new improvement'. The rate of survival of vaccaries in the Trough of Bowland, Upper Bleasdale and Wyresdale, which had been first documented around 1300, is impressive evidence for continuing settlement and exploitation of these upland edge sites.

The late fifteenth and early sixteenth centuries witnessed renewed pressure on the wetlands of the region and a new beginning to the process by which the major mosses were systematically reduced in size and smaller ones entirely improved. Illicit turf digging and removal outside the manor (as sales, etc.) is a common complaint, and numerous cartloads were sometimes involved. New enclosures, new farms and/or new houses all encouraged improvements. Many field names are suggestive of newly improved wetland. In some instances, drainage activity caused disputes between rival, local proprietors. Such an incident broke out in the spring and summer of 1491 at Ince (Lancashire) where Sir Thomas Gerrard was attempting to drain and enclose Ince Moss with a ditch over 40 roods (around 200 m) in length (Fishwick 1896). The attempt stimulated a confrontation between Sir Thomas and another claimant of the freehold, who brought the matter to the court of the Duchy to complain about a series of increasingly violent incidents.

Throughout lowland Lancashire, mossland remained extensive, making up a large proportion of many holdings. An inquisition at Warrington in 1496, for example, found that Sir Christopher Standish died seized of a moiety of the manor of Harperhey, eight messuages, 200 acres of (arable) land, 100 acres of pasture, 20 acres of meadow, four acres of wood and 300 acres of moor and turbary (Fishwick 1896). Local place-names (such as Moston, Blackley and Boggart Hole Clough) still reflect the spread of peat soils on the east side of the river Irk in this manor. Such reserves of unenclosed terrain offered immediate benefits as a source of fuel and pasture and provided a reservoir of land, much of which could be drained, enclosed and leased, as demographic pressures and inflation made such developments increasingly attractive to landlords in the mid sixteenth century.

FIGURE 27.
Broad ridge and furrow around Higher Daleacre, on the borders of Bradwell and Moston, near Winsford. Ridges have clearly influenced the pattern of later enclosure but in several areas ploughing in different directions lies in the same fields.

## Conclusion

The North West witnessed both exceptional levels of population growth between 1086 and 1300 and a significant shift towards a market economy. In the late eleventh century, farming was very largely subsistence based and levels of labour input, capital investment and overall activity were all very low by comparison with other regions of England. Additionally, Cheshire at least was severely affected by the dislocation of estates as a consequence of the Conquest and earlier warfare had impacted to an unknown extent on other areas.

Before 1100, the rural population was very widely dispersed in very small settlements, with little in the way of open field agriculture being practised. The number of open fields increased dramatically over the next two centuries, with many vills having numerous examples. However, continuing access to widespread common grazing reduced the pressure that might otherwise have been experienced to systematise these ploughlands and the uneven nature of the terrain meant that few areas were well-suited to extensive arable fields. The result was a very varied landscape, in which small open fields were much more common than large ones, and were regularly interspersed with other types of land, including pockets of woodland, moss and marshland, pasture and meadow. This society was characterised by low levels of manorialisation and a tendency for great estates to obtain the bulk of their income from the profits of manorial courts, rectories, mulcture and rent, although direct management of farming did expand significantly during the thirteenth century, particularly in the uplands.

Population growth before the Black Death also fuelled the processes of assarting, land improvement and conversion from pasture to arable. This was a period which witnessed an unprecedented assault on what hitherto had been little used or waste areas, and the development of numerous new small estates and settlements. The marginality of this regional economy in the eleventh century perhaps offered considerable opportunities for expansion thereafter (but see Bailey 1989 for a critique of the concept of medieval marginality). This process was spearheaded in part by landlords keen to make profits from underused land, and wealthier peasants played a significant role. However, the local gentry and larger free tenants were arguably responsible for heading up this expansion of the rural economy into new lands, which they converted from marginal woodlands or waste lands to clusters of new and profitable farms. Much of the rural landscape of the North West today bears the marks of these changes.

# Woodland, Forest and Pasture

## Woodland

Throughout the Middle Ages, mixed deciduous woodland was the natural vegetation of the North West, if human interference be discounted. A cursory examination of the valleys of central Lancashire, the Cheshire Plain or the still extensive mosses at Lindow or Barton, for example, is enough to reveal even today the continuing and persistent capacity of oaks, ashes, birches and alders, in particular, to re-colonise under-utilised areas. The low levels of population in the region at Domesday were enough to guarantee that extensive woodland existed. It would be going too far to describe the whole of both counties as wooded with localised clearances but there can be little doubt that woodland was widespread and covered a significant proportion of the land surface.

In addition, some trees were clearly significant landscape features. Numerous examples were used in charter boundaries in the Middle Ages and earlier ones gave rise to such place-names as Ashton ('Ash tree settlement'), Agden ('Oak valley') and Acton ('Oak tree settlement'). The community of *Warmundestrou* (later Nantwich) Hundred, in one of the most densely wooded parts of eleventh-century Cheshire, met at 'Warmund's Tree'. That said, there are very few trees now living which can confidently be assumed to have been growing during the Middle Ages. The oldest specimen is arguably the ancient yew in Astbury churchyard, which is thought to have been there for over a millennium and may even pre-date the church. Another yew at Eastham was probably planted during the Viking Age. A very few deciduous trees may have begun their lives before the Tudor age, such as the Marton Oak (Figure 28), a pollarded specimen over 14 m in circumference, so perhaps 500–1,000 years old, but now entirely hollow and surviving in three separate fragments, or the several ancient, stag-headed trees to be seen around Coddington. However, even the Marton Oak was not primary as regards the settlement around it: Marton takes its name from the mere, now drained but remembered in a series of field-names, which used to lie immediately to the north of the medieval village. Most of the great oaks of the region, however, such as the magnificent oak at Arley Green, are likely to have been saplings no earlier than the sixteenth century. Although woodland management locally certainly did include coppicing in the later Middle Ages, coppiced stools, with a thicket of side-shoots growing from a single root complex, are far less visible today in

FIGURE 28.
The Marton Oak, an ancient pollard likely to have been growing within the village since the Middle Ages.

this region than in south east England, where they are often the oldest living things in any particular neighbourhood (an example in Epping Forest is illustrated in Muir 2000).

Woodland was an important resource throughout the Middle Ages, being cropped in a variety of ways and for numerous different purposes, among which was the provision of fuel for the salt industry at the *wiches* of central Cheshire. It has been estimated that the Droitwich salt-pans each consumed 23 wagon loads of wood per year. In 1086 it is unclear just how many salt-pans there were in Cheshire but it should probably be estimated in scores, suggesting that considerable acreages of woodland in the centre and south of the shire must have been managed to provide the 500–1,000 wagon loads of fuel that would have been needed annually. This yield will have increased substantially over the following two centuries and it seems likely that extensive

FIGURE 29.
Woodland as recorded in Domesday Book. The Cheshire evidence (after Phillips and Phillips 2002, 31) is recorded by estate, the Lancashire evidence by hundred, but Warrington Hundred had no record of woodland.

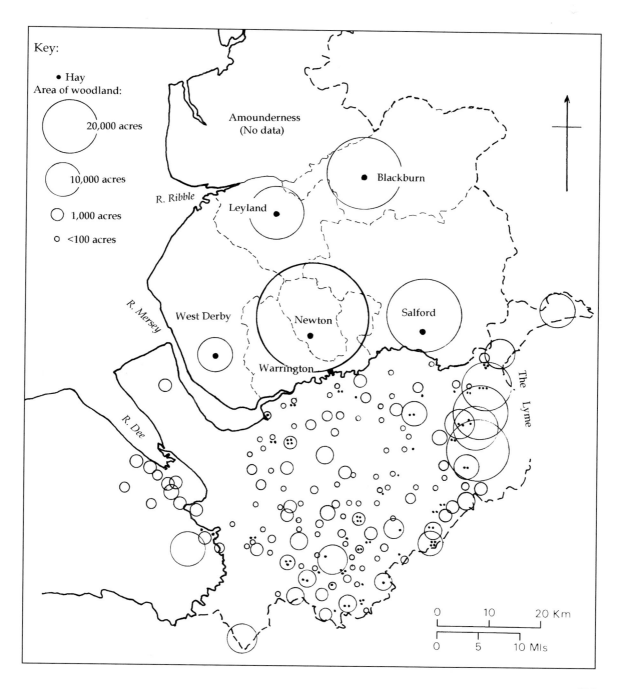

woodlands were managed and coppiced around the valley of the river Weaver. There was probably coppicing at Bollington, and pollarding on the woodland pastures of Coombs, both in Macclesfield Forest (Tonkinson 1999), as well as elsewhere, but documentary evidence is sparse. At the dissolution, Whalley Abbey was in possession of several substantial stands of timber, including one

Key:

● Hay
Area of woodland:

20,000 acres

10,000 acres

1,000 acres

○ <100 acres

Amounderness
(No data)

● Blackburn

R. Ribble

Leyland

R. Mersey

West Derby

Newton

Salford

Warrington

R. Dee

The Lyme

0    10    20 Km

0    5    10 Mls

of 16 acres within Whalley Park, and these were being coppiced on cycles of up to 20 years (Hulton 1847).

While the Domesday Survey cannot be relied upon as an accurate description of landscape, there is sufficient reference to woodland to provide general support for the conclusion that trees covered a significant part of the landscape south of the Mersey. Woodland was a major but under-reported component of numerous manors in eastern Cheshire, particularly in and around the Lyme, and also on the heavy clays of the southern plain along the county boundary with Staffordshire (Terrett 1948), where fuel for the Nantwich salt industry may have derived (Figure 29). In the far west, the comparatively well-developed economy of Wirral and *Dudestan* Hundreds had already, by the late eleventh century, resulted in widespread clearance of standing woodland as demand for timber, fuel and grazing competed for scarce resources. There is some evidence to suggest that in the Wirral peninsula many hitherto wooded areas were becoming heath-land under this pressure.

There is plentiful place-name evidence for woodland in the region, most commonly from township and minor names ending in '-ley' (from *leah*, Old English for a wood or a woodland clearing) or '-wood'. Such names often occur in significant groups, which may be interpreted as areas which were noticeably well-wooded at some stage in the mid- to late Anglo-Saxon period. These 'woodland' place-names are particularly common around major territorial boundaries. In Cheshire, these tend to occur in groups or belts of land around the perimeters of ancient land units such as the parishes of Malpas and Great Budworth, and *Warmundestrou* hundred (comprising the early parishes of Acton and Wybunbury: Higham, N. 1993; Figure 30). In Lancashire, a smaller proportion of township names contain woodland suffixes, although numerous minor place-names do. These tend to occur along the broken, intermediate lands between the lowlands and the hill country, in the hundred of Leyland and the western part of Blackburn, then around the boundary between the hundreds of Salford and West Derby (so Mawdesley, Chorley, Tunley, Knowlsey, etc.). Woodland-type township names are scarce both around the great mosses of the west of the medieval shire, where sixteenth century observers reported a marked lack of trees, and in areas such as Salford Hundred and Lonsdale, where settlement place-names dominate.

As early as the eleventh century, many of these woodland areas seem to have been occupied and clearance was probably active. In Lancashire, at least, parts of the landscape outside the arable lands of the numerous small estates held in thegnage or drengage formed common lands accessible, in return for a rent or render to the hundredal court, to any member of the shire or hundred (Jolliffe 1926). That said, there do seem to have been customary rights exercised by particular communities or landholders over individual grazing lands. The movement of stock into and out of areas of woodland pasture on the edges of the lowlands led to the development of meandering long-distance trackways, some of which are probably now enshrined in the minor roads of parts of central Lancashire. It has been suggested (Atkin 1985) that distinctive

FIGURE 30. Woodland township names: these are particularly common in Cheshire but in Lancashire settlement names tend to dominate at the level of township and parish, with woodland names more numerous as the names of hamlets or individual farms. Squares indicate names indicative of The Lyme.

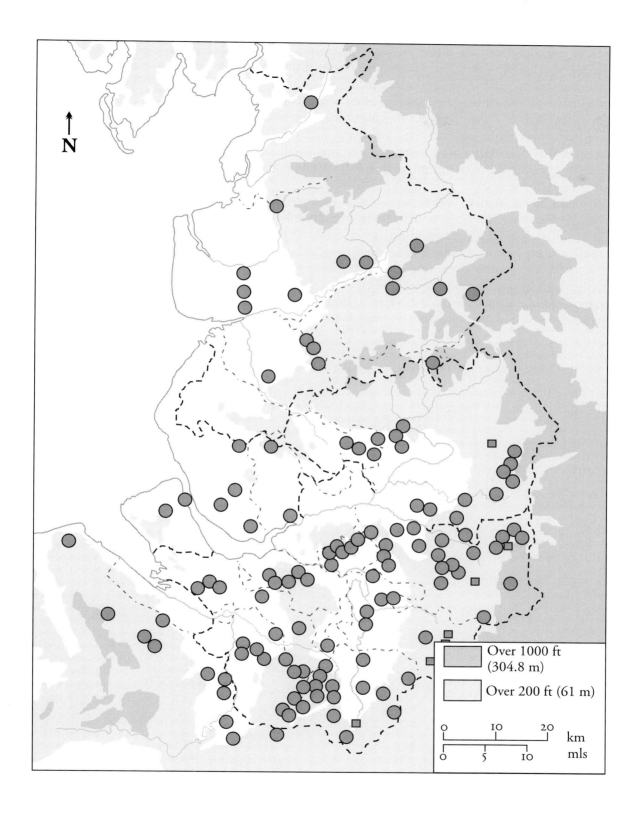

Over 1000 ft
(304.8 m)

Over 200 ft (61 m)

0        10        20    km
mls
0     5      10

double enclosures can be identified from nineteenth-century maps, which developed as an early element in the management of this landscape. Of each pair of enclosures, one was arable and divided between several small farms, the other pastoral and in single ownership, often of high status. Examples have been identified at Tunley in Wrightington and at Charnock Richard, where they may represent the core of livestock farms or vaccaries of a very early date. These primary enclosures are distinguished in part by the size of field banks and the apparent age of perimeter hedges, in part by the presence of funnels for the control of stock.

To take North Tunley, Wrightington, as an example (Figure 31), the mid-nineteenth-century landscape is characterised by meandering lanes, although these run predominantly north–south rather than east–west, crossing gently rolling country. By the standards of Leyland Hundred, this is an upland area. The settlement pattern is entirely dispersed. The place-name Tunley means 'settlement in a woodland enclosure', which seems entirely appropriate in this context. Minor names are indicative of a woodland landscape with small pockets of mossland, interspersed with small hills. A 'stock funnel' can be seen

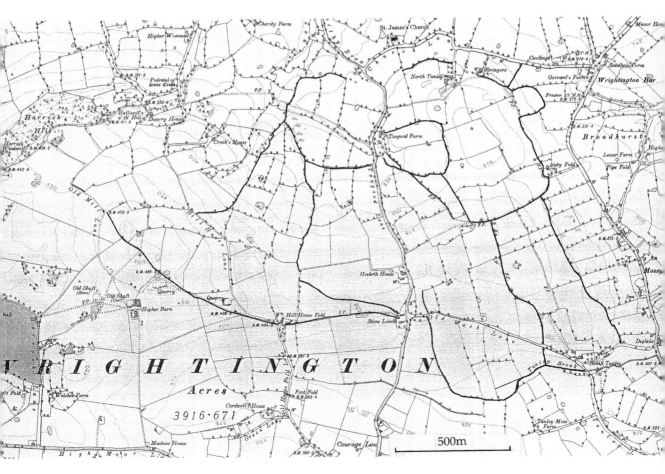

focused on Stone Leach, which could have been used to manage animals entering specific grazing lands, although other origins for these particular boundaries are equally possible. The fields are comparatively irregular, so typical of an area of woodland assarting, and seem to have developed over a very long period. Early enclosures appear to have existed, characterised by continuous boundaries and/or massive hedge banks, centred on Toogood Farm and North Tunley. These may represent hays or woodland enclosures for either livestock or deer (see below) in the Central Middle Ages, intended to delineate the higher, dryer ground and exclude the mosses to the south and east. Streams, too, played a primal role in the sub-division of this landscape. As enclosure took place thereafter, however, early enclosures and boundaries were engulfed in a much wider process of piecemeal enclosure from wood pasture, which remains the dominant characteristic of local field systems, and it is not at present possible to be entirely confident as to the early evolution of this landscape.

Although there are now few substantial tracts of deciduous woodland in the North West, numerous small pockets of trees sustain a rich ecosystem, which implies that many are fragments of ancient woodland. Characteristic plants of the ancient woodland floor include wild garlic, dog's mercury, wood anemones, native blue bells and celandines, which flower successively during the late spring and early summer. Ancient woodland is most common in long ribbons, occupying the slopes of river and stream valleys, in locations where the steep gradient or wet conditions have deterred clearance for agricultural land use. Examples can be found around Charnock Richard, along the various tributaries of the Mersey in the lower Pennines, such as the Tame, Goyt and Etherow, and along the Bollin and its various tributary streams, such as Burleyhurst Wood, just south of Manchester Airport. These densely wooded, often steep little valleys provide natural breaks to farming and regularly feature as boundaries of manors, townships, parishes and hundreds. Many woods have changed very little since first being mapped in the eighteenth or early nineteenth centuries. Poynton Coppice, a linear woodland nestling in the valley of a tributary stream of the Bollin, provided pit props to the local coal mining industry in the nineteenth century. It is rich in ground flora even though it contains no trees in excess of 200 years old, although traces of coppicing survive, and has long divided the manors and townships of Poynton and Adlington. On occasion, it seems that such streams have become boundary markers only by default: in the neighbourhood of Arley Hall, extensive medieval woodland, which is still reflected in local farm names, formed a belt of wood pasture on flat clayland between the pre-Conquest Cheshire hundreds of Tunendune and Bucklow, and may well have been inter-commoned as wood pasture. These woods were cleared as part of the thirteenth- and fourteenth-century expansion of settlement and agriculture associated with the establishment of the sub-manor of Northwood (see page 87) and a very minor water course, just a metre or two wide, was then used to mark the boundary between High Legh and Aston-by-Budworth.

FIGURE 31.
Tunley and Wrightington, in Leyland Hundred, based on the Ordnance Survey Six Inch Lancashire Sheet LXXXV NE 1894, copied under licence: the nineteenth-century field system derives from a long history of enclosure, the early elements within which can to an extent be identified, and are somewhat speculatively picked out by thicker lines. This is a typical woodland field system, characterised by meandering lanes, dispersed farms, moats, woodland-type names, small-scale moors and mosses, and irregular fields.

There was considerable interest among the Anglo-Saxon and early Norman landholders in woodland enclosures, in part at least for deer management. A total of 104 'hays' (from Old English *(ge)hæg*, Middle English *hay, hey*, 'fenced-in enclosure') were noted among the assets of 49 Cheshire manors, normally in association with woodland, and at Weaverham and Kingsley it was specifically stated that they were connected with roe-deer – a creature of dense woodland and glade pastures (discussed in Terrett 1962). Manors where more than one 'hay' was present were most commonly held before the Conquest by the earls or others of the elite, as Macclesfield, for example, but numerous examples occur elsewhere on the manors of the relatively well-wooded south and east of the county. Some of the many current place-names containing this element may indicate the site of the eleventh-century enclosures (as at Whalley Heys and Lower Heys in Macclesfield: Davies 1976; Park Wood and Wood Hay in Adlington: Liddiard 2003), but there is some confusion with the Old English *hege*, 'a hedge', which could divide any fields. Hawks' eyries were often associated with them and were clearly a significant asset among the late-Saxon and early Norman aristocracy. These were numerous in the North West, as compared with other parts of medieval England, and particularly prominent in the Cheshire Domesday (see Liddiard 2003 for a discussion). Some examples of these early enclosures may be traceable: Liddiard, for example, suggests that the field remains of a later deer park at Baddiley, which is followed by part of the township and parish boundary, may be the Domesday 'hay' (Figure 36A), but the remains of most such enclosures seem to have been swept away by successive re-organisations of the fieldscape during the Middle Ages and beyond.

Above the Mersey, the thegns of West Derby at Domesday held land by services which explicitly included building 'the King's halls, ... fisheries, *et in silva haias et stabilituras*' ('and in woodland the enclosures and deer traps'). In the other hundreds of South Lancashire, similar services applied, and the existence of further 'hays' is confirmed by the presence in Salford Hundred of 'many' in association with forest three leagues long and wide, and a hawk's eyrie, which may imply that some at least of the later baronial parks, such as Tottington or Blackley, already existed in some form. A 'hay' was to be 'made' (or perhaps 'maintained') each year by the men of Leyland in the extensive woodlands of the hundred. At ten leagues by six leagues and two furlongs, the woods of Newton, the smallest of these hundreds, were by far the largest, in theory at least far exceeding the size of the hundred. Eyries were mentioned but unnumbered, and hays not even noted, although such probably existed. We should be in little doubt that management of woodland for deer and hunting was already a significant feature of the regional economy in the late pre-Conquest period. Again, the coincidence of park and township boundaries might suggest that Barton Park (Amounderness) *could* have early origins (Figure 36B): the case for woodland enclosures in eleventh-century Lancashire must be acknowledged in principle, but is extraordinarily difficult to demonstrate in any instance. However, large woods remained a common component of particularly Lancashire court cases in the early fourteenth century, suggesting that they were both still present and also highly valued assets. So, for example, estovers (fallen timber) in 3,000 acres of woodland in Tatham, 'for burning and building, and making ploughs, ox yokes and wagons, in the manor of Ireby', were the subject of a final concord in 1317 (Farrer 1903), and a 200 acre wood at Goosnargh, very near Barton, was at issue in the same court rolls in 1323.

## Forests

While woodland is a term used specifically of tree-covered terrain, forest was a legal entity, not a term descriptive of the landscape but an area within which forest law was operative. In practical terms, the forest provided legal protection to beasts of the chase – red, fallow (once these arrived in the Norman period) and (initially) roe deer, and wild boar. Constraints upon human activity within the forest area and adjacent to it were designed to protect the beasts themselves, their habitat, sustenance and breeding cycle. Forest normally contained some woodland but all sorts of different land types and land-uses were present, including arable cultivation. The little evidence available implies that the forests of the North West in the hands of the earl in Cheshire and of several powerful lords in Lancashire were administered in most respects as if royal forests. That is at least the implication of the partial relaxation of elements of his forest code incorporated in the *Carta Communis Cestriensis* or *Magna Carta* of Earl Ranulph III in the second decade of the thirteenth century. Each unit of forest was 'policed' by a hierarchy of officials under a forester whose post was, in most cases, inherited and associated with specific families and manors. So, for example, the master forestership of Lancaster descended in the Gerner family based at Halton Castle, and the four foresterships of Delamere were held by the families of Kingsley, Grosvenor, Wever and Merton (Husain 1973).

There is every reason to believe that Earl Hugh shared the passion of his liege lord for the chase. Newly rich in land from his share of the spoils of conquest, the earl set aside substantial tracts for hunting. By so doing, he radically extended the forests of the late-Saxon earls with the consequence that his subordinates in some areas enjoyed a much-reduced access to hunting as an economic or leisure strategy. His successors defended this monopoly against the assaults of the local aristocracy, secular and clerical alike, as well as from the acquisitiveness of a land-hungry peasantry.

Earl Hugh took over a forest or chase at la Mara in the Delamere region from Earl Edwin, and this he extended at the expense of the manors of *Roelau* Hundred, five of which were noted in Domesday as containing forest or recently afforested land (Weaverham, Conersley, *Aldredelie*, Done and Kingsley to which should be added the waste manor of Eddisbury, which was central to the forest). Of these, all but Kingsley were comital demesne manors and described as waste when Hugh took control. That three of these manors should be place-names which cannot now be located is a tribute to the rigour of the policy pursued by the earl. The process of afforestation was not, therefore, inflicted upon a substantial local community but inserted into the process of economic reconstruction of a partially derelict landscape. It did, however, significantly reduce agricultural land in the area, representing a loss of 18 ploughlands in addition to the three hides at Weaverham placed within the forest.

A certain Dunning held Kingsley throughout the Norman transfer of estates and emerged in 1086 as a tenant of the earl. This may imply that he already fulfilled the role of comital forester of la Mara. A possible descendant, Ralph de Kingsley, was made master-forester in 1123. The name Dunning was recorded against five manors elsewhere in central and western Cheshire in 1066 and it is possible that all referred to a single individual. Gilbert the Hunter was a well-established tenant of the earl in Middlewich hundred in 1086 and may have been expected to assist the Earl in his pursuit of game in the southern parts of the forest (Mondrem). The twin forests could at a later stage be defined by the townships expressly within the forest, those with responsibility for the maintenance of the forest staff and those liable to customary taxes specific to access (Ormerod 1882; Husain 1973; V.C.H. 1987; Figures 32 and 33).

In the hundred of *Hamestan* the extensive areas of woodland attached to comital manors at Macclesfield, Adlington and Gawsworth imply the existence of hunting preserves in the late-Saxon period, which may have amounted in practice to a forest, and the afforested area was probably always very large in the Norman period, stretching along the Lyme from Romiley to Bosley, and Prestbury to the county boundary (Figure 33).

West of Chester, beyond the Dee, it was noted in the Domesday Survey that Earl Hugh had afforested all the woodland of the hundred of *Ati's Cross* (now incorporated in Deeside: Morgan 1978), making a discontinuous hunting preserve ten by three leagues in size. Despite the obvious convenience of this tract to a magnate spending time in the Dee valley and at Chester, it does not appear to have survived long, perhaps owing to the hostility of the important land-holders whose manors were seriously affected by the earl's action. Ralph the Hunter held the manors of Broughton and Soughton within this forest, and outside it the manor of Stapleford in *Dudestan* Hundred. It is possible that his presence implies the beginnings of a forest administration.

One further forest was created by the earls in Cheshire. Early in the twelfth century the hundred of Wirral was afforested, apparently as a punishment imposed by the third earl on a community that was notoriously unruly (Ormerod 1882). The disturbances peculiar to this community may have been a by-product of the complex manorial holdings typical of the area as well as a response to the exactions of the earls and St Werburgh's. The extent to which the afforestation involved depopulation of this, the most heavily peopled part of the county is unclear and we should beware too simplistic a view (Husain 1973). Exemptions existed from the beginning to protect the estates of religious

FIGURE 32. The Forests of Mara and Mondrem in central Cheshire (adapted from V.C.H. 1979, with additions). The forests of the Norman earls were developed from a hunting preserve of the pre-Conquest earls of Mercia.

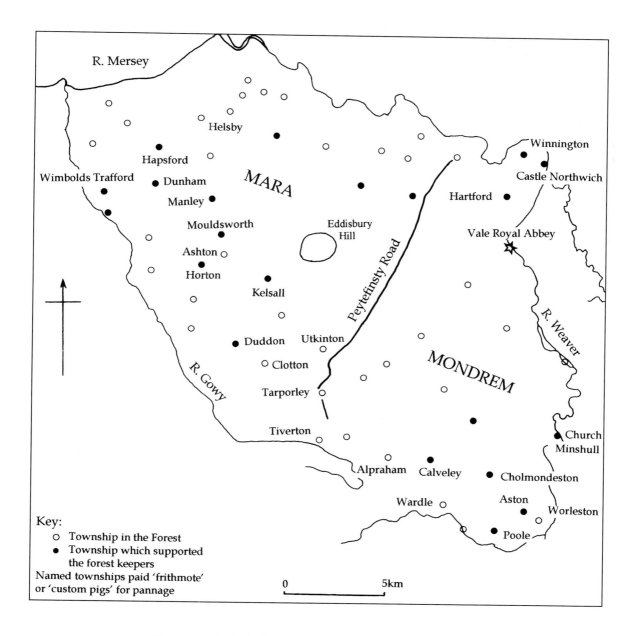

Key:
- ○ Township in the Forest
- ● Township which supported the forest keepers

Named townships paid 'frithmote' or 'custom pigs' for pannage

0 ———— 5km

houses and the bishop, all of which were substantially tenanted. The records of the proceedings of the forest court that are extant from the late thirteenth century imply a considerable population within the forest vills practising agriculture in a fashion not markedly constrained by forest law. However, if there was any serious intent to utilise this forest for the chase, real changes must have been necessary to allow some woodland to develop and to encourage game into the area. It is difficult to see how this could have occurred in an area so apparently devoid of woodland without serious dislocation of the local community.

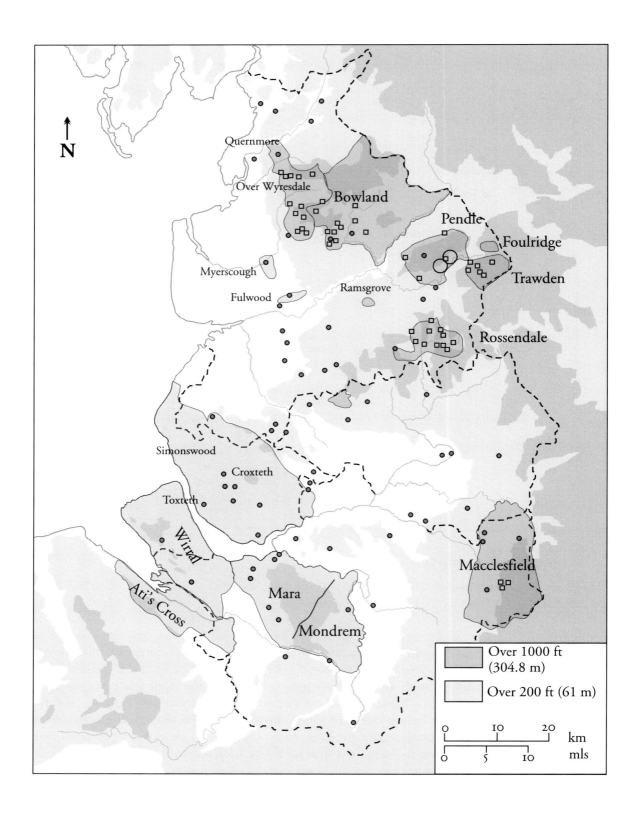

N

Quernmore

Over Wyresdale

Bowland

Pendle

Foulridge

Trawden

Myerscough

Ramsgrove

Fulwood

Rossendale

Simonswood

Croxteth

Toxteth

Wirral

Macclesfield

Ati's Cross

Mara

Mondrem

Over 1000 ft
(304.8 m)

Over 200 ft (61 m)

0          10          20
                                km
0        5        10
                          mls

North of the Mersey there is also evidence for the existence of forest at the Conquest. It may be that responsibility for those in southern Lancashire rested with King Edward – as dedicated a huntsman as his Norman successor was to be – although he is never know to have visited the area. It was forest (*foresta*), rather than just woodland (*silva*), that was described among the assets of the capital manors of West Derby and Salford. Despite the personal absence of the king, the nucleus of the forests of Lancashire probably owed something to the structure of his estates, and the landscape management of his principal tenants. The waste condition of so much of Lancashire beyond the Ribble provided circumstances in which the extension of forest into that region was a comparatively simple matter. Roger of Poitou took the opportunity during his two periods as tenant-in-chief of these lordships to extend his forest in the Toxteth area to all the demesne vills of his lordship as far as Makerfield. A grant to the de Lacy family of the honour of Clitheroe provided an opportunity in the twelfth century to create an extensive baronial chase in Blackburnshire and much of Bowland. Further north, Roger created a substantial forest based on his honour of Lancaster encompassing parts of western Bowland.

The estates of Roger of Poitou passed to the crown in 1102 and again by the elevation of Stephen of Blois to the throne in 1135. As part of the royal perquisites in the reigns of Henry II and his sons, the Lancashire forests were extensively increased in size at the expense of the interests of local families. For example, jurors in the reign of Henry III acknowledged that Croxteth, part of Hale, Simonswood, Kirkby, Altcar, Ince Blundell, Ravensmeols, Down Holland and Lydiate had been afforested in recent generations. Beyond the Ribble, forest law was extended to incorporate the entire hundred of Amounderness and most of Lonsdale (Shaw 1956; Grant 1991). In 1311 the forests of the Lancaster lordship were combined with those of the honour of Clitheroe to form a major element of the earldom and duchy of Lancaster.

The Norman forests acted as important reservoirs of game, timber and land, protected to an extent from other types of exploitation by their use by the land-owning elite for hunting. Their earliest role was therefore likely to have been as an amenity but it is clear that this process also allowed members of the social hierarchy to draw on forest resources, including timber and food. By the thirteenth century, however, the balance had shifted irrevocably away from private hunting, if that ever was its principal use, and the forests were used as a source of meat and pasture, and as a reservoir from which patronage could be dispensed. The enforcement of forest law was made to yield a substantial profit. Under increasing pressure from hunting and with a much-reduced habitat, boar were becoming rare, although 80 were taken from the Forest of Pendle in 1295 and dispatched to Pontefract. This sort of pressure proved unsustainable, however, and wild boar were probably only to be found within parks by the fourteenth century, and eventually died out even there. Royal control of Cheshire after 1237 encouraged the 'export' of deer from the forests; 40 were taken in La Mara and Macclesfield, salted and dispatched to the king at Westminster in 1239–40 (Stewart-Brown 1938). From the point of view of the crown, there was little difference between that process and the dispatch to the same destination of 91 cattle from the earldom in 1245. However, deer were also declining in numbers and, excluding roe deer, were eventually exterminated outside parks south of the Lake District, and even within parks many existing herds derive from imports from the continent (Aybes and Yalden 1995).

The decline in numbers of the beasts of the chase and the increasing intrusion of graziers and cultivators into areas of old woodland and the upland fell country created circumstances in which man and wolf came into open competition. The inevitable result was the extermination of the wolf population. King John rewarded the extermination of wolves in central Lancashire, and more were destroyed in Delamere. A wolf trap is recorded in Macclesfield Forest in the early fourteenth century, when there were probably still wolves in the Peak District (Tonkinson 1999), and other occurrences survive in such names as Woolfall. Place-names recalling the wolf are concentrated along the Pennine edge and in the Cumbrian and Lancashire uplands (as Wolf Fell, Wolfhole Crag, both in the Forest of Bowland), suggesting that these were among the last refuges of wolves during the later Middle Ages (the place-name evidence is explored fully in Aybes and Yalden 1995). Indeed, references to wolves in Lancashire in 1295–96 and 1304–5 provide the last reliable records of their presence (Yalden 1999), suggesting that Bowland and its environs may have been among the wolf's final strongholds in England.

Despite the primary purpose of the forests as a refuge for beasts of the chase, numerous communities lived within them. The constraints imposed by forest law stopped men from hunting, limited access for livestock to unenclosed grazing at those times when the deer were dropping their fawns and controlled the breaking of new ground to make assarts. In other respects, as applied to the agrarian economy, the forests were areas where local communities were expected at an early date to pay extraordinary fines such as 'frithmote' for access to pasture. Such payments were not unique to the forests – a triannual customary payment called 'beltoncow' was paid by the Overton and Skerton communities in 1348 for inter-commoning. However, within the forests they were combined with the exactions of forest courts administered by staff who often abused their positions of power and patronage for profit. Communities and individuals suffered considerable financial loss and inconvenience at the hands of courts and officials. For example, Nicholas de Wardle was arraigned for slaying a fat buck in Rochdale Forest and apprehended by the keepers by night, seized and dragged to Clitheroe Castle where a court fined him four marks. The Court of Wirral Forest in 1286 took action against entire communities in whose fields offences had been committed, often causing the oxen of the village to be driven off as a form of bail to ensure that plaintiffs attended the court.

Herds pastured within the forests of the North West were substantial. They comprised the livestock of forest communities, and of neighbours who paid for annual access to the forest and were fined for strays in the prohibited season. They included also livestock of the earls and lords of honours and the religious communities on whom they or their predecessors had conferred substantial privileges. The practice of using particular parts of the landscape as summer pasture seems already to have been widespread before the Conquest, giving rise in Lancashire and Wirral to place-names in *erg*, an element which is particularly associated with cattle pastures (as Kellamergh, Grimsargh, Anglezarke, Arrowe). The comparable element in the hill country was *saetr* (as Cadishead, Summerseat), with *thveit* ('-thwaite': as Rosthwaite) occurring north of the Ribble. Names in '-booth' occur across the whole region (as Goldshaw Booth, Dunnishbooth), deriving from very similar elements in Old and Middle English and Old Norse. Not all of these place-names need, however, derive from the pre-Conquest era, since Old Norse heavily influenced the Lancashire dialect, in particular, thereafter.

## Livestock and vaccaries

Little is known of peasant livestock in the region in the medieval period. Communities in and around Delamere and other forests made payments of pigs to the earl as the price of pannage (Figure 32) and in the thirteenth century these reached 139 and 400 in separate years (Stewart-Brown 1938), suggesting that very large numbers indeed were being pastured. Strays in Delamere in 1304–5 included 400 cattle, two oxen, 70 horses and 199 pigs. In September 1324, the hallmote of Colne imposed fines for the escape of 76 'beasts' (i.e. cattle), 17 horses and 20 pigs. The earl of Lincoln's steward at Halton let grazing for 155 cattle in Northwood in 1304–5. Pigs were by far the commonest of the escapes of the manor of Tottington in Salford Hundred in 1323 and at Ightenhill (Burnley) in the same year (Farrer 1901). At Macclesfield, by contrast, pigs only occur as strays in the forest in small numbers, in comparison with cattle and horses, although most peasants probably had one or two. In 1194, the sheriff of Lancaster had 120 breeding ewes on the demesne but, throughout the thirteenth and early fourteenth centuries, there seem to have been few really large flocks in eastern and upland Lancashire, in comparison with parts of Yorkshire and the Lakes. Where sheep can be identified in the uplands it is generally in very small numbers, such as the single beast of estray sold at Ightenhill in 1324. The scourge of wolves was arguably enough to deter graziers in areas where these were present from developing substantial flocks, at least until the late thirteenth and fourteenth centuries, when significant flocks begin to appear along the Cheshire Pennine edge. However, the incidence of fulling mills and of 'shepherd' as a by-name both imply that many small flocks of sheep existed in the region by 1300. A sheep walk occurs, for example, in Hackensall and Treesall, on the Lancashire coastal plain, in 1335 (Farrer 1903). The 65 named free tenants of Burtonwood and Warrington in 1332 included the occupational names of 'Webster', 'Herdman' and 'Shepherde' (Farrer 1903). Manorial ownership of fulling mills was the norm, and these were becoming widespread in the region already before the Black Death, as witness the several at Macclesfield by 1240 (Mills and Stewart-Brown 1938) and on the Irk at Manchester by 1282 (Harland 1861). Farmers were probably also interested in the manure that sheep could provide when folded on the arable: it was arguably in part the high incidence of pastoralism in the region that maintained the limited agricultural land in good shape throughout the period and enabled farmers to avoid dropping yields even while expanding their ploughlands.

Significant numbers of horses were detailed and occasional references occur to goats, a type of livestock of which some manorial lords were highly suspicious because of their omnivorous habits – they were prohibited, for example, at Ormskirk (France 1954), but were apparently common in the parish of Warton by the early sixteenth century, when they attracted Leland's attention. However, among the owners of great estates, at least, the principal livestock were cattle. A pastoral demesne enterprise was attached to the de Lacy's castle at Widnes, which was increasing in size in the late thirteenth century: in 1304–5 it had 50 cows, three bulls, seven steers, 13 heifers, 35 yearlings, seven oxen and 12 calves (Lyons 1884). However, the major development took place in the upland forest areas. Across the thirteenth century, if not before, the Crown, the de Lacy family, their successors and several of their neighbours took advantage of the buoyant demand for cattle and plough-beasts on their own estates and in the markets. Their stewards developed a network of cattle rearing stations, or vaccaries (vaccarii), in and around the valleys of the uplands particularly of eastern Lancashire. This process represents a substantial investment, and one which was consistent with the emergence of high farming visible more widely on English demesnes between c. 1170 and 1300. Estate managers developed novel economic activity in areas where environmental constraints and/or forest law had hitherto deterred the inflow of colonists dependent on subsistence agriculture and peasant initiative. However, although vaccaries were generally developed by the great estates, many were not being exploited directly even around 1250, with estate managers employing a mix of short leases and direct exploitation, perhaps as a hedge against poor returns from either sector.

The new vaccaries were generally sited close to the rivers in well-wooded valleys where small areas of arable, winter pasture and hay meadows could be developed and from which seasonal use of upland grassland was available. Their development represents a considerable effort to divide up the upland valleys into a maximal number of units and make them profitable. The total breeding stock of a vaccary was small, generally starting at a bull and 15 cows, although some had 40 or more, but these were only part of the stock at any one time. In those instances where an annual rate of increase can be calculated it was less than 20 per cent of the total stock and less than 40 per cent of the total of breeding cows (Tupling 1927). Gelded cattle were generally kept on the vaccary for four years to attain maturity before being exported to become plough-oxen. At any one time, a vaccary could therefore be expected to have a total herd of at least 75–80 beasts. In 1313–14 the Wyresdale vaccaries were stocked with seven bulls, 288 cows, 39 heifers, 38 'twinters', 115 stirkes and 119 calves. Although references to losses from wolf predation do occur, losses from murrain were, when calculable, nine times as high. The profit margin from these enterprises may not have been very great even at the height of demesne activity around 1250, although considerable gross revenues accrued to the great estates from their activities.

To provide an example, over a period of 18 months in 1246–48, eight and a half vaccaries in Upper Wyresdale were let to farm for £28 6s. 8d. Others were retained in demesne, from which 87 gelded cattle were sold as oxen for £34 16s., 27 poor cows fetched £6 1s., the sale of bulls grossed 30s. and other livestock brought in £4 4s. 6d. The hides of six cows, 11 bullocks, four heifers and 13 stallions earned 21s. 2½d. (Shaw 1956). The practice of leasing vaccaries seems to have increased steadily during the late-thirteenth century, until, by the mid-fourteenth century, at least half were regularly let; after 1350 the incidence of leasing was to increase even further to the point where the estate administration had effectively abandoned direct intervention in this area of production.

The vaccaries had considerable significance for the development of the structure of settlement in the upland margins of the North West. Their stock was generally leased to a keeper who took his profits from the butter, cheese and milk production, paid an annual rent and maintained the buildings under the supervision of an official of the lordship, termed in Lancashire a sub-instaurator. On the vaccary, the keeper had a staff of herdsmen, the *pastores* or boothmen, who lived in bothies near the central grange buildings or out on the pastures. From their activities derive many of the numerous livestock-related minor place-names of eastern Lancashire and, less commonly, of eastern Cheshire, such as Oxenhurst, Calf Clough Head, Ox Pasture End and Rams Clough, all in the Forest of Bowland. The herdsmen were paid in kind for their services with parcels of land, which they could cultivate and on which they could keep their own cattle, pigs and poultry and they were frequently among those who were fined for escapes into the forest. The stock keepers of Wyresdale were, for example, in 1258 fined £10 for 'manifold trespasses' (Shaw 1956).

Even though pastoralism only required perhaps a fifth of the workforce of arable land per unit of area, this entrepreneurial activity was directly responsible for the establishment of new communities in areas that had been slow to attract colonists and which might otherwise have remained virtually unoccupied. Development within an elaborate estate structure guaranteed these nascent communities markets for their surplus, protection from competitors and communication with the communities of the western plains. In such circumstances the difficulties of the terrain and the disincentives posed by forest administration were overcome. Areas which had barely been populated in 1086 emerged by c. 1300 with a network of pastoral-based communities, and vast acreages which had resisted economic exploitation were brought within the net of the medieval community. In 1297 in Wyresdale alone there were 20 vaccaries, of which half were retained in demesne and half let. Only one, Ortner, provides evidence of use as summer pasture by a lowland community before the Conquest (page 29), and some were certainly named in the post-Conquest era (as Abbeystead, Gilberton). The largest of those in demesne was stocked with 60 cattle. In the early thirteenth century, there were 21 listed (Farrer 1907), of which 15 names survive today as individual or groups of farms, and in upper Bleasdale a further four, all of which survive (Figure 34), and form the basic skeleton of the settlement pattern thereafter. Along the Tarnbrook Wyre, for example, a string of farms and/or hamlets bearing the

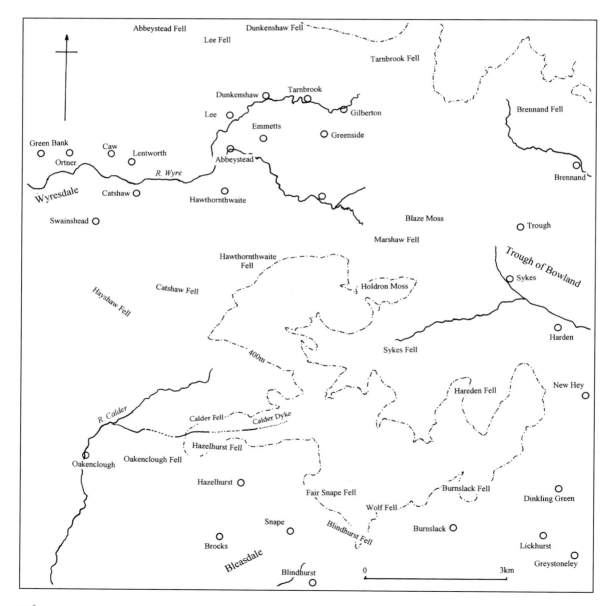

FIGURE 34 (*left*).
Vaccaries in Wyresdale,
Upper Bleasdale and
the western edge of the
Forest of Bowland.
Note the Calder Dyke
delineating the fells
accessible from
Bleasdale. The contour
is at 400 m.

FIGURE 35.
Higher Fair Snape,
looking towards
Hazelhurst, both
medieval vaccaries in
upper Bleasdale,
photographed from
Blindhurst Fell.

names of these vaccaries are strung out, all close to the stream, between half and one kilometre apart, suggesting a fairly heavy density of settlement foundation (Plate 7). The presence of the aptly named Wolf Fell looming above the vaccaries at Fair Snape and Blindhurst in Bleasdale puts into context the drive to eradicate wolves at this date (Figure 35). In the Clitheroe-centred forests of Blackburnshire, a yearly render of 100 marks (£66 13s. 8d.) came from 32 vaccaries in the chases of Trawden, Pendle, Rossendale and Accrington. The latter had a single, but exceptionally large breeding herd of 100 cows, but around half this number was more normal.

The vaccary system imported to the upland margins in the thirteenth century a pattern of settlement already dominant in much of the North West. This was a settlement system on the edge of long-established habitation, peripheral to the old nucleated settlements of the valley floors, such as Chipping. The communities comprised a scatter of farms and/or hamlets of different sizes, dependent on the scale of the work force, surrounded by a network of both perennially and seasonally used buildings, including summer lodges such as that built to accommodate those attending the cattle on summer upland pastures at Oakenwood. These sites eventually developed in various ways, some, such as Gilberton and Greenside, as single farms, but others as a group of neighbouring farms with related names (as Lower Emmetts, Higher Emmetts, Top of Emmetts), which emerged from the process of sub-letting and the sub-division of vaccaries, by or in the sixteenth century. Some eventually developed as hamlets (as Abbeystead, Tarnbrook), where a group of farms had cottages constructed around them to form a nucleated settlement. All today are dominated by stone buildings of the seventeenth, eighteenth and nineteenth centuries, but the general pattern has probably changed little since the late Middle Ages, although the enclosure of individual farms was largely a phenomenon of the early post-medieval period. Along with the assarting hamlets which were developing elsewhere in the northern uplands, these settlements were engaged in the intensification of pastoral land-use, via more intensive management, labour input and raised stocking levels, with only small amounts of new arable (cf. McDonnell 1986).

The valleys and valley sides into which this system intruded had, in the eleventh and twelfth centuries, been extensively wooded (Tallis and McGuire 1972). The progressive expansion of pastoralism led to a substantial decline in woodland cover (Mackay and Tallis 1994), under the pressure of grazing on young growth, the cutting of underbrush for winter-feed and of timber for the construction of new buildings or fuel. The comparatively treeless landscape typical of modern Rossendale or Trawden owes its inception to the vaccaries of the thirteenth century. Indeed, there is very little place-name evidence of woodland during the Middle Ages in Bowland, excepting the immediate environs of some upland streams and such minor names as Good Greave, a now virtually treeless hillside above the vaccary of Whitendale. Most, if not all, vaccaries included small enclosures used either for growing oats for consumption locally, or for keeping livestock away from hay crops. Several farm and field names (in 'hay', 'meadow' and 'holm' for example) reflect this practice. Such enclosures were already being assarted on the slopes of Longridge Fell, for example, by the early thirteenth century (Newman 1996), and gradually spread around the valley-bottom vaccaries throughout the hill country. Many vaccaries also gave their names to adjacent fells, and those of Upper Wyresdale, which are marked on the First Edition of the Ordnance Survey Six Inch maps, imply that each eventually acquired exclusive rights over considerable upland pastures as summer grazing. An earthwork known as the Calder Dyke can still be identified intermittently for some three kilometres separating the head-waters of the Calder from the Brock, running in part along the watershed between Hazelhurst Fell and Oakenclough Fell, to the south, and Calder Fell (Figure 34), and this seems already to have been present by the sixteenth century, when it was termed 'The Fence' (Shaw 1956, 375; Winchester 1993, 24). However, although some further undated cross-contour banks and ditches can be identified, above Tarnbrook for example, the uplands were probably largely unenclosed during the Middle Ages.

At its height, the organisation of demesne vaccaries was very complex. Accounts for the de Lacy vaccaries in 1304–5 were rendered to the steward and chief-instaurator at the manor of Ightenhill in the presence of the sub-instaurators, the keepers, Simon the geldherd, the keeper of the replacement stock, the keeper of the barren cattle of Accrington and the two keepers of the oxen. Male cattle were gelded at Accrington and Bakesden, in numbers of about 2,500 per year. Early in the fourteenth century, cattle pools existed, one at Reedley Hallows holding replacement stock en route to the vaccaries and another at Brericar holding cattle selected for replacement, en route to the butcher, the lord's kitchen or the market.

Cattle were not the only product of these forests. Horse studs were maintained in the Lancashire forests, at Quernmore and Ightenhill, and in Macclesfield Forest. In Lonsdale there may have been a long tradition of horse rearing, giving rise to the place-name Stodday near Lancaster. Elsewhere, the proprietors obtained revenue or other benefits from the export of venison, the felling of timber and the mining of iron. In 1315, for example, an iron mine in Calder Forest produced 780 'pieces' sold upon the account for 81s. 3d. (Farrer 1907). There were several iron forges in each of Midgley and Dane Wood, Macclesfield, in the second half of the fourteenth century (Tonkinson 1999). The smelting of ore could be carried out using local timber to make the necessary charcoal, and this added to other pressures on the upland wood-lands. However, these profits were irregular and there is little evidence of substantial mining activity within the region during this period.

## Parks and enclosed woodland

By the thirteenth century, the great aristocracy had focused their interest in beasts of the chase into parks within their forests, so freeing up the remainder for exploitation as demesne pasture. The lesser aristocracy had little access to the great chases and afforested lands of their superiors but they profited from stewardships and extensive areas within their own estates, both inside and outside the forests, were woodland or open waste and so available for economic development. Most such areas comprised in the eleventh and twelfth centuries the customary grazing lands of the manorial communities. As demographic pressures grew, so the regulatory role of the manorial aristocracy was converted to a proprietorial interest in such areas. This process was limited but not halted by the Statute of Merton of 1234. Economic conditions were such that sections within the community continued to compete for advantage as more and more land was enclosed for pasture or assart. The extent to which the local community was aware of the economic potential of unenclosed land is forcefully conveyed in an assignment of dower in Samlesbury and Mellor drawn up in 1336 (Farrer 1915). Wood-wards were expected to guard the common wood, and it was only under their oversight that housebold (building timbers), haybold (timber for fencing) and estovers (fallen branches for fuel) could be taken; improvements (i.e. assarts) were envisaged, turbaries (peat diggings) and an iron mine were in use, pigs could be pannaged and cattle grazed and there were wild birds to be caught; wild bees produced honey and wax, sparrow (and other) hawks might nest, and there was herbage to be cut. Iron and hives of bees were clearly goods which were traded regularly in the region's markets, appearing, for example, in the list of tolls charged at Manchester. Iron was mined in small quantities in several of the region's commons, as at Trawden in 1422–23, as well as *Sclatemynes* (Farrer 1897, 491), which were presumably exploited, in part at least by this date, for roofing materials.

In many areas, court cases resulted from the problems of defining property rights and the boundaries of manors. In some instances it seems likely that tenants of two or more vills had previously shared rights of common. This issue was particularly acute across the lowland wetlands, where numerous commons were mered and divided up during the later Middle Ages. Such was the basis of the dispute between Richard de Urmston and a group led by Jordan de Hilton in which the point at issue, a dyke, was declared to lie in Urmston rather than Flixton (as the defendants had claimed) and had, therefore, to be dismantled (Parker 1904).

Many local manorial lords set aside their own manorial woodland as chases and parks and then proceeded to develop hunting preserves and/or vaccaries, and take other profits within them. Parks were a common feature both within the forests and elsewhere. Musbury Park, for example, was an area of high moorland on Tor Hill (near Haslingdon), in Rossendale Forest, around which a four and a half mile (7.25 km) long paling was erected in 1304–5 (Tupling 1927). Such areas were enclosed to allow the proprietor exclusive control of the land. Subsequent use was generally as pasture but in some instances in the fourteenth century parks were rented out and cultivated. The primary function of most was as a controlled breeding and hunting ground for deer but many were exploited for herbage and other resources for a considerable profit.

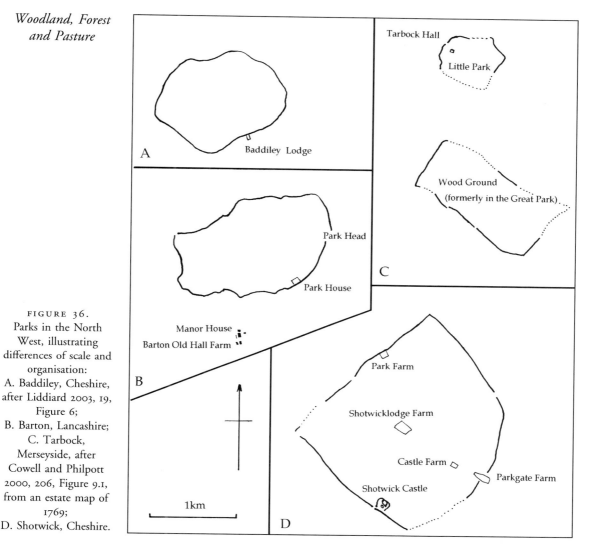

FIGURE 36.
Parks in the North West, illustrating differences of scale and organisation:
A. Baddiley, Cheshire, after Liddiard 2003, 19, Figure 6;
B. Barton, Lancashire;
C. Tarbock, Merseyside, after Cowell and Philpott 2000, 206, Figure 9.1, from an estate map of 1769;
D. Shotwick, Cheshire.

The tradition of constructing parks in the High Middle Ages in this region probably derived directly from the 'hays' of Domesday Book (see above), and like them they were particularly associated with wealth and social status. Ightenhill (Burnley) in 1311 was adorned with a park defended by a one and a half leagues long pale. At Widnes, the castle of the baronage was associated with a substantial park, around which a pale was maintained: 141½ roods of old paling were removed in 1295–96, and 13 roods of new paling and 27 roods of hedge set out. At Shotwick, the castle was adorned with a park in 1353, which dwarfed the remainder of the township and which required 13,500 palings from Ewloe Wood (Figure 36D). Recent trenching across the pale revealed a substantial bank still remaining. By the early fourteenth century, the barons of Manchester had developed similar facilities. Their park at Blackley had sufficient grazing for 200 cattle and a herd of 200 does 'for the lord's pastime with the deer-leap' (Farrer 1907), and Leland (1964 edition, V, 43) later noted that 'Wild bores, bulles, and falcons bredde in times paste at Blakele'. Elsewhere, the barons had also developed eight vaccaries in the woods and moors of Horwich. In 1282 these were already a valuable source of income (Farrer 1903):

> In the forest of Hopeworth there are 8 vaccaries and 1 plat which is not a full vaccary worth £19 per annum; pannage of the same forest with eyries of sparrow-hawks worth 40s. yearly; there are 3 foresters who keep the forest and shall have the escapes (of animals) giving 60s. per annum.

On other estates in the region, parks were frequently carved out of the peripheral 'waste' of manorial land, with or without royal licence. Ringway, which is now better known as Manchester Airport originated as a 'ring-heye' or 'ring-hedge', which probably encompassed the entirety of the small township which emerged in the post-medieval period. The Baron of Dunham Massey declared his intention to enclose a park in 1281 in the course of a dispute with his tenants of the manor of Hale, which began two decades before. In 1290, when he gave borough status to Altrincham, Hamo de Massey recorded his intention to enclose a deer park at Sunderland and this was done by 1353, although there is some dispute as to the location (Wilson 1987). Part of what had been the common woodland of the larger of the two manors of Tatton had been granted away to Mobberley Priory in the early thirteenth century. When the manorial lords recovered it, 70 years later, it was not returned to common but reserved as a park around which Richard de Massey successfully petitioned to divert the Knutsford road in 1288 (Higham N. J. 2000). In some landscapes, more than a single period of emparkment can be observed, with parks being enlarged, or a second park constructed. At Manchester, an 'old park' was directly associated with the castle site and later manor house, apparently before Blackley was developed as a park. Two parks existed at Tarbock in the thirteenth century, the pales of which can still, in parts, be identified (Cowell and Philpott 2000). The Little Park lay around the hall site, while Great Park was developed further south (Figure 36C). A 'new park' at Radcliffe was the subject of an indenture in 1338. During the late thirteenth and early fourteenth centuries, licences to empark were obtained from the crown for Anglezarke (1339), Ashton-under-Lyne (1337), Hoghton (1337), Leyland (1348), Over Kellett (1278), Roby (1339), Thurland (1302) and Thurnham (1315) in Lancashire alone, and the royal estate developed one in Bleasdale.

Parks were an important symbol of status, a valuable resource and an amenity, much valued by gentry families or those aspiring to that status. However, their distribution was uneven across the North West. In Lancashire, examples have been identified scattered widely across the central belt of reasonably well-drained terrain, where place-name evidence suggests that woodland persisted well into the Middle Ages. Others were established in the uplands and their vicinity, but few if any examples have been identified on or around the lowland mosslands of the west coast between examples at Toxteth and Roby, near Liverpool and Thurnham, near Lancaster. Here islands of dryer land tended to be dominated by nucleated settlements and open fields, so would have been costly to convert to parkland. Otherwise this relatively wet terrain was unsuitable for hunting, was virtually treeless and hardly had any hedges, even. In Cheshire an initial survey has identified fewer examples but there are numerous omissions and the distribution may owe more at this stage to the inadequacies of sources examined than any real dearth (see Cantor 1983), particularly given the number of 'hays' in Domesday Book.

The construction of parks and other enclosures often required substantial quantities of materials. While some were hedged, many were fenced with palings of split oak, set upon a substantial bank. Such banks can still be seen, for example at the south-western corner of Newton Park (near Wargrave), on the south-western edge of Lyme Park (Disley) and around Arley (Plate 9). Private woods were also, on occasion, defended by substantial earthworks, including both banks and ditches. A bank of around ten metres broad is still visible along the edge of old demesne woodland immediately north west of Adlington Hall (Cheshire), for example and a whole series of palisaded enclosures were erected in Macclesfield Forest during the fourteenth century. Their construction required large amounts of timber, much of which was necessarily obtained by harvesting the woods which were to be enclosed. Parks on the scale of Musbury made greater demands on local timber resources than the construction of a Roman fort would have done 1200 years before, in circumstances in which woodland rejuvenation was a great deal less likely. By 1346, enclosure around the Earl of Lancaster's park at Myerscough had reached the pale and responsibility for the upkeep of the perimeter and the wages of the parker were delegated to the occupiers of the adjoining plats of land (Farrer 1915).

## Waste

Far more extensive than parks were the areas hitherto considered 'waste' that were, in the period 1100–1349, enclosed from the common and brought into cultivation or an intensive pastoral regime, and from which the livestock of others were excluded. Between the Conquest and the Black Death, the shrinkage of common land and of under-utilised rural resources was one of the principal characteristics of the region. By that process, the population found room for expansion on an unprecedented scale. By controlling it, the aristocracy were able to make profitable some of the least rewarding estates in medieval England, and at the same time to endow religious houses and find support for their younger children. By the early fourteenth century, little that was cultivable or capable of supporting grazing remained unused. Common grazing lands were under considerable pressure and woodland was becoming in many areas a scarce resource to be husbanded and defended, already eroded by a lengthy and steady process of improvement (Miller 1964), and local communities were increasingly prepared to go to law to exclude livestock from outside. Even in the upland manors of eastern Lancashire, the manorial commons were gated by the late fourteenth century and tenants fined for excess animals found grazing there. Some tenants tried to compensate by grazing livestock in the lanes and verges, but found themselves fined for that as well, as John Pichaver found to his cost at Chatburn in 1425 (Farrer 1897, 13). In Macclesfield Forest the communities of the Forest had in theory equal rights to graze all areas which were open but in practice local groups strongly protested when neighbours put livestock onto pastures which they particularly felt to be their own.

Many old woodlands must have been in a position comparable to that of Fulwood, immediately north of Preston. An extent made in 1346 recognised existing improvements old and new which the burgesses had made in 324 acres beneath the King's 'hay of *Foghelwood*', their rights of pasture and haybold in the forest, and their right to reduce to tillage all the neighbouring moors up to within 40 perches of the coverts of the wood (Farrer 1915). Neither deer nor wood could long withstand pressure of that sort. The cutting and taking of greenwood (hawthorn or holly) and the felling of ash trees were both fined in the rural manors subject to the court at Clitheroe in the late fourteenth century (Farrer 1897, 2–3), and the crown was regularly using the woodland resources of Delamere to bestow patronage, by the gift of building timbers for example. By the standards of the time, the landscape was becoming full.

## Conclusion

In the last chapter we saw that a rapidly growing population, new and more intrusive management styles and an increasingly commercialised economy were expanding the agricultural lands of the North West between the Conquest and the Black Death. In this one, although there has necessarily been some overlap, we have explored the ways in which woodland was exploited, livestock grazed and wood pasture progressively enclosed or assarted. Forests spread locally to cover substantial parts of the region and were exploited by the elite in various different ways, many of which have left their mark on the landscape. Both within them and elsewhere, parks were also constructed, some of which can be still be identified on the ground. Perhaps the most important development was the spread of cattle rearing into the upland valleys, with the establishment of vaccaries in, for example, the fastnesses of Bowland, Wyresdale, Bleasdale and Rossendale. These established numerous small, permanent communities in old woodland areas where very few if any had existed for half a millennium or more, and began the process of constructing the modern landscape of the eastern edge of the North West.

Following the Black Death, the flight from direct exploitation by aristocratic or royal estates was most marked in the Lancashire forests. The vaccaries were never again to be directly exploited. Land in much of eastern Lancashire was leased off on attractive terms to whoever would take it (Tupling 1927). The officers of Clitheroe Castle were responsible for collecting rents for increasing numbers of holdings in the old vaccaries. For example, Overberdshaw vaccary in Trawden was mid way through a ten year lease to Edmund Parker and John Parker in 1422–23 (Farrer 1897, 491). The process of enclosure was accelerated by the wholesale policy of leasing adopted by the Duchy under Henry VII. Parks, vaccaries and moors were subdivided and leased and tenants increasingly came to hold by copyhold tenure (Hoyle 1987). In 1507 the 11 vaccaries and nine pastures attached to Clitheroe were let to 59 tenants and further new tenants were being admitted. In practice, the management policies pursued by the Duchy encouraged a substantial population rise within the old vaccaries by the early sixteenth century, as increasing numbers took advantage of the local availability of land, coupled with the growing market for wool and/or cloth. This demographic increase is reflected in the building of a new church in Rossendale in the reign of Edward VI, and the proliferation of farms and settlements throughout the uplands across the east of the North West. During the second half of the sixteenth century, much of Bowland was enclosed as farms and leased, as the Duchy took advantage of the demographic momentum and consequent rise in land values (Porter 1978). The park at Toxteth, which had for all intents and purposes been the property of the Stanley family since the 1440s, was disemparked and leased as numerous farms around 1590 (Booth 1993), and numerous other parks, such as Shotwick, followed suit, taking advantage of the opportunities now expanding for specialisation in the countryside. The open spaces which had been maintained or even created during the Middle Ages were losing ground still further, and what had been areas reserved for hunting, or at least for pastoral specialisation, were giving way to enclosed regular, planned fieldscapes, with only field and farm names hinting at the medieval landscape which was being replaced.

# CHAPTER 5

# Farm, House and Castle: Communities and their Buildings

## The structure of rural settlement

As has already been established, the small, eleventh-century population of North West England was scattered in communities that rarely comprised as many as a dozen families and were characteristically only a third that size, or as small as the single household. Similarities between this pattern, that of the Romano-British past and contemporary communities in Wales have led to suggestions that a causal link existed between the two or that the north-western communities operated within patterns derived from a 'Celtic' past (summary Higham, N.J. 1979). However, recent research into patterns of rural activity in other parts of England has tended to highlight similar, dispersed settlements throughout much of the Saxon period, and beyond. Villages as such developed comparatively late and in many areas not until the period c.900–1200, or not at all (c.f. Hoskins 1955; Beresford and Hurst 1971; recent work summarised in Taylor 1983; Lewis et al. 1997; Roberts and Wrathmell 2000).

Within this new research framework, it has become less necessary to seek for specific factors to explain divergence from village formation, and more necessary to identify factors leading towards nucleation, where such occurred. It does seem clear that the region was one in which environmental factors, accessible economic strategies and the lack of early demographic pressures combined to maintain a pattern of settlement that was characteristically dispersed, into the twelfth century and beyond (e.g. Lewis 1986; Higham, N.J. 1988b). Where a comparatively small proportion of the total land surface available to a community was organised as open field, the pressure to nucleate was naturally reduced. Particularly on the margins of settled areas, where population density was low and vills large, this pattern was accentuated, characterised by occupation of small niches of locally superior land within an environment which offered insufficient resources for large groups of medieval farmers to establish themselves at any one spot. Parallels with other, environmentally comparable areas of the North of England are both obvious and relevant for the late pre-Conquest period (e.g. Higham, N.J. 1986a; Winchester 1987).

Sustained demographic growth over a period of two centuries or more necessitated changes to the established patterns of settlement. Two strands of this development can usefully be highlighted. Firstly, the growth of individual settlements occurred, with the result that nucleated communities became more common in the area, particularly in areas like Wirral, the lower Dee valley and parts of the Lancashire lowlands where land quality was sufficient across considerable acreages for arable to become extensive and open field systems to be established. This process of nucleation may, in some instances, have been encouraged by estate managers. In parallel, dispersed settlement both intensified and expanded into new areas, such as the wide expanses of Rossendale or Wyresdale, as well as the periphery of many existing but under-populated estates (Figure 37).

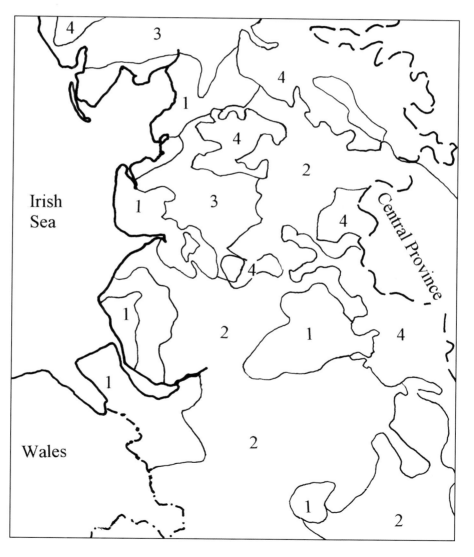

FIGURE 37.
The pattern of settlement types in the North West:
1) Mixed nucleated and dispersed settlements;
2) Occasional nucleated settlements, hamlets and farmsteads;
3) Very little nucleation, dispersed settlement;
4) Upland, medieval settlements only occur on the margins.
(Based on Roberts and Wrathmell, 2000.)

a) Aldford

b) 500m

c) Clifton

d) LEA NEWBOLD

e) BURTON / Burton

f) Halton

g) CHURTON / Churton

h) Treales

The first of these developments is partly evidenced in the emergence or foundation of substantial numbers of both royal and seigneurial boroughs during the period (see page 165 ff., Figure 84). However, nucleated villages also emerged on a minority of estates without the establishment of borough status. Such occurred particularly when rural communities were tightly controlled in their entirety by long-established landlords, such as St Werburgh's or the Bishops of Coventry and Chester – at Tarvin, Burton, or Wybunbury. Similarly, the lordship of Clitheroe included several strip field villages in the upper Ribble valley, such as Pendelton, and the groups of open field villages on both sides of the lower Ribble have already been highlighted (page 60–61). At Halton (Lancashire), a substantial village grew up on either side of the road running up the valley from the pre-Conquest church and Norman earthwork castle, and this nucleation, with its attendant open field, presumably reflects a seigneurial interest (Figure 38f). At Treales (Lancashire), a large nucleated settlement seems to have grown up on the local by-way, without any marked degree of regularity but strategically sited between mossland to the east and west, meadows to the south and arable to the north (Figure 38h).

In some instances, nucleated villages originated from failed boroughs. At Aldford, for example the Norman motte and church were complemented by a regular, planned borough, laid out on four roads on a near-square plan (Figure 38a). A very small but highly regular example of a planned village is Burton, also in the Dee valley, where fewer than 20 crofts are set out around a hall, with two roads forming a small square settlement, with the remains of open field still detectable to the south (Figure 38e). In Lancashire, the best examples are perhaps Newton (Figure 38b) and Clifton (Figure 38c). At Newton, two parallel roads imply a playing card shaped, planned village, which was sited strategically between open field to the north and the Ribble

FIGURE 38.
Examples of settlements in the region, after Ordnance Survey Six Inch maps, copied under licence:
  a) Aldford, Cheshire, a failed borough laid out south of the castle and church (Cheshire Sheet XLVI S.E., 1913).
  b) Newton, Amounderness, a two-road, four-row, nucleated settlement with open field to the north on the edge of the Ribble marshes (Lancashire First Edition, 1844, Sheet 60).
  c) Clifton, Amounderness, a highly regular, so probably planned, two-row village with open field to the north, again on the edge of the Ribble marshes (as above).
  d) Lea Newbold, Cheshire, a large moated site in a dispersed landscape (Cheshire Sheet XLVI S.E., 1913).
  e) Burton, Cheshire, a small, nucleated settlement exhibiting signs of planning, with traces of open field to the south (Cheshire Sheet XLVII N.E., 1912).
  f) Halton, on the Ribble, an apparently unplanned but large village stretching away from the pre-Conquest church and Norman castle up the road towards Hornby, with enclosed open field strips to the north (Lancashire Sheet XXX N.E., 1919).
  g) Churton, Cheshire, a village divided on Hob Lane between two townships exhibiting very different patterns of development in each (Cheshire Sheet LIII N.E., 1899, Second Edition). The northern township constituted a monastic grange, focused on what is now Grange Farm (off the map to the north), while the southern township developed as a regular, small village.
  h) Treales, Amounderness, a single street village without much evidence of planning, occupying scarce dry terrain, with open field to the north on the higher ground, meadow to the south, and mosses to west and east.

marshes to the south, on the very edge of dry land. Clifton was a larger, single street settlement, but in a very similar location and highly regular in plan. Both may well have been planted as part of a strategy of colonisation of the Ribble estuary lowlands. In these circumstances, manorial control over the organisation of the rural economy probably influenced the structure of the settlement that developed.

A particularly interesting example is the village of Churton (Cheshire), which was already in the eleventh century divided into two manors and was split between the parishes of Aldford and Farndon. The southern half of the village was laid out at some date as a single row of messuages with a back lane (Figure 38g), but the northern settlement was managed as a monastic grange from the short-lived Cistercian house at Poulton, based on Grange Farm, with settlement occurring on the village site only at a later date.

Such regular communities were limited to the better agrarian environments of the region and were arguably only representative of a minority of vills, surrounded by a network of smaller settlements consisting of manorial and sub-manorial hamlets and farms of all sizes. Some developed central place functions within this network, which led in some cases to the establishment of markets, as occurred at Burton on Wirral, but most were just substantial villages, with insufficient a market role to develop into towns.

Even on large and long maintained estates, a hamlet and farm-based pattern of settlement was common. This is characterised by the organisation in very small villages or hamlets of the bond tenants of comital manors such as Frodsham or baronial estates like that of Manchester, as well as in the many small manors or their satellites in the region. If we take a large parish, such as Great Budworth, the commonest pattern of settlement seems to have been townships with small hamlets and scattered farms, with only a few exhibiting nucleation (as Great Budworth, which is the principal example). Vills in which little agglomeration of settlement occurred were probably more common throughout the period than nucleated villages or rural market boroughs, as at Lea Newbold (Figure 38d), for example, Iddinshall or Huxley, in old woodland areas scattered among the nucleated townships of the Dee valley. Most small towns were surrounded by dispersed settlement, as for example, the twin boroughs of Knutsford. The study of settlement form in the area relies heavily on maps of the period 1700–1850, although, of course, the relationship between this type of evidence and medieval morphology is far from certain. Take, for example, the wonderfully detailed map made by John Earl in 1785 of the manor of Marthall cum Warford for William Egerton of Tatton Park (Cheshire Record Office. DET/1424/21). The largest concentration of settlement is just four farms (at Brook Farm). Elsewhere there are several pairs of farms and a single moated site (Moat Hall), and no hint that any medieval village had existed. That said, there are numerous straggling hamlets and very small villages visible on early maps, which seem to have derived, in part at least, from organic processes of growth, as opposed to formal planning. These are typical of assarting landscapes, particularly on the edges of old moss or

FIGURE 39. Alderley Edge (Cheshire): dispersed settlements in an assarting landscape between Lifeless Moss and the Edge, based on the survey made by James Heyes for John Trafford Esq., in 1771.

heathland. On the periphery of Lifeless Moss below Alderley Edge, a map of John Trafford's lands made in 1771 reveals a landscape of both recent and ancient enclosure stretching from Chorley Hall and Chorley Green via the nascent Alderley Edge village to Hough, a small agricultural agglomeration of holdings below the Edge (Figure 39). Three field names incorporating 'Ridding' adjacent to Alderley Edge imply medieval clearance of woodland. Alderley was first recorded as an estate in 1086. *Hough* is a topographical place-name, which refers to the slight elevation on which it stands. It was first recorded in the thirteenth century, but it is impossible to tell without detailed archaeological investigation to what extent this small and straggling settlement developed in the Middle Ages. Wilmslow is also depicted on this map, as a single street development, with no particular signs of planning, running south from the parish church. The name is clearly pre-Conquest (Wighelm's mound: Dodgson 1966–81, I, 220), initially denoting the church site alone but then extended to the village, which is only likely to have developed following the grant of what had previous been the core of the estate, at Foulshaw, to the Knights of St John early in the thirteenth century (Hodson 1974).

There is a noticeable lack in this area of the agricultural village-type frequently to be found in parts of the Midlands and the North East, consisting of farms in substantial numbers laid out in an organised fashion along one or more village streets. Many existing villages, like Rostherne (near Knutsford), derive not from nucleated medieval villages but from groups of tradesmen or artisans established during the demographic expansion of the period after 1500 and very largely after 1700, and others from industrial or proto-industrial development of the same period. Deserted or shrunken medieval settlements are often not of a size to be described as villages, rarely consisting of more than a single messuage or small cluster of such around a capital messuage (e.g. Williams R. S. 1984: examples in Cheshire are mapped in Phillips and Phillips 2002, 33; Figure 40). The more substantial groups of earthworks of this kind, such as those at Stock (near Barnoldswick), which are very largely post-medieval, are better explained as organically generated settlements rather than planned villages (Figure 41). Small villages such as Burton (in Wirral), Pendleton or the deserted site of Easington Lancashire), arranged around a green, remain the exception, and generally cluster together within particular groups of vills.

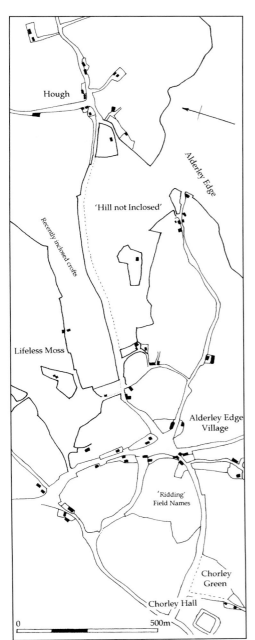

Hough

Alderley Edge

'Hill not Inclosed'

Recently inclosed crofts

Lifeless Moss

Alderley Edge Village

'Ridding' Field Names

Chorley Green

Chorley Hall

0      500m

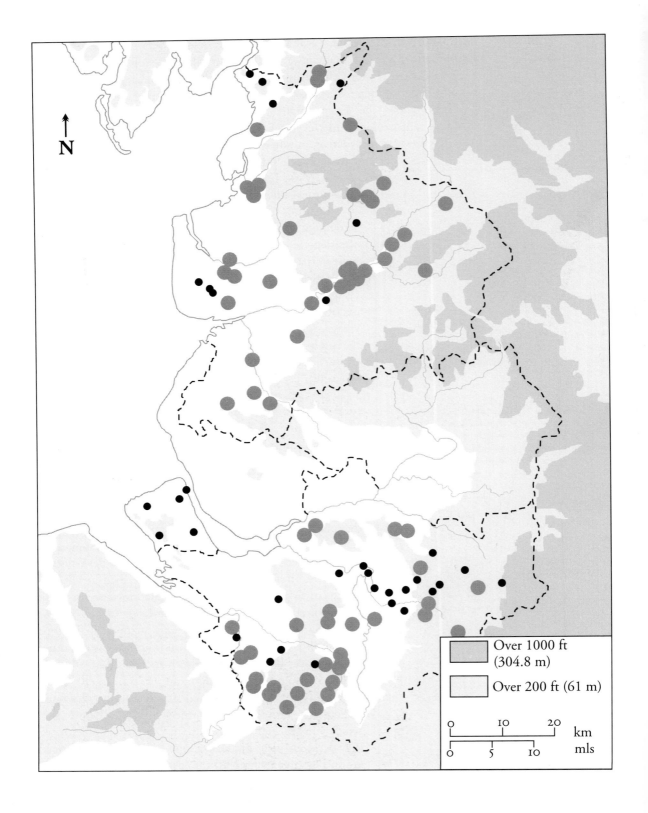

In old woodland areas, the expansion of population resulted in a pattern of settlement with marked similarities to the networks of farms found in other areas of late expansion, such as the Forest of Arden (Roberts 1968). Such networks were typical in the North West of lowland moor-side settlements, much of the Pennine edge landscapes of Blackburn, Macclesfield and Leyland hundreds and of the upland valleys where the mapping of medieval vills is particularly problematic (cf Winchester 1978).

## Buildings

Only Norton and Tatton 'village' sites have been excavated on a scale large enough to examine even as much as a single messuage of the period (Greene and Hough 1977; Greene 1988; Higham and Cane 1999; Higham, N.J. 2000). Of the two, Norton is the site with more evidence of planning. An estate map

FIGURE 40 (*left*).
Deserted and shrunken settlements in post-1974 Lancashire (after Newman 1996, 111) and Cheshire (after Phillips and Phillips 2002, 33). There are both deserted and shrunken settlements in Greater Manchester County and Merseyside, but the scale of industrial and urban development over the last two centuries makes mapping unrealistic.

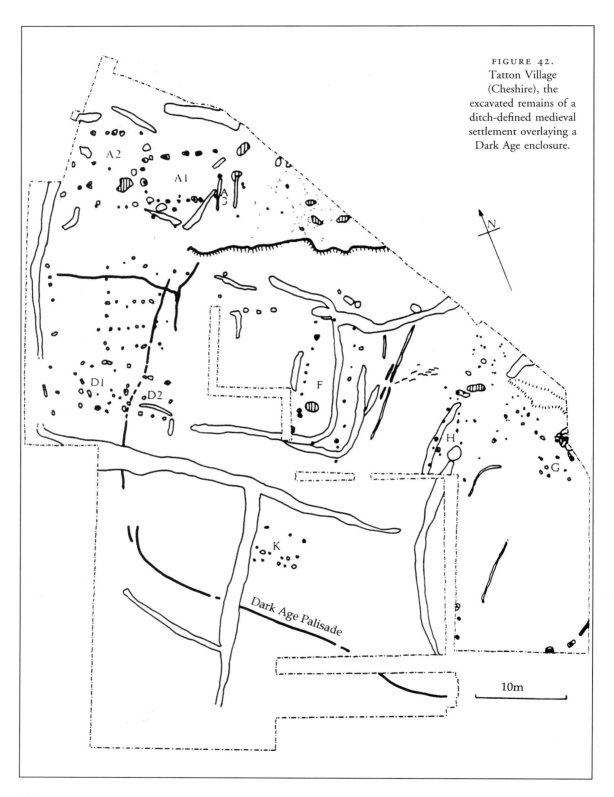

FIGURE 42.
Tatton Village (Cheshire), the excavated remains of a ditch-defined medieval settlement overlaying a Dark Age enclosure.

Dark Age Palisade

10m

of 1757 (Greene 1989, 27, Figure 14) shows a single street, dividing two rows of tenements of regular length and breadth, with transverse roads signalling the two ends of the village. This regularity may imply reorganisation by the priors. Tatton, in contrast, was in all probability a straggling settlement of the kind sometimes described as an 'interrupted row' (Dyer 1991) throughout its history, occupied by more or less farmers according to the pressures exerted by local demography and the elasticity of tenurial structures, with scattered halls and hamlets elsewhere in the township even in the Middle Ages. Excavation on both sites has been severely hampered by the near total absence of stratigraphy.

The site of 'Old Tatton' is one that was finally abandoned under the pressure of seigneurial emparkment in the mid-eighteenth century and the earthworks now visible are substantially those of a community active in the 100 years centred on 1700. Large-scale excavations between 1978 and 1987 concentrated on an area adjacent to the sunken road – the main relic of medieval occupation which is still visible – in an area which had been cultivated during the early eighteenth century. This revealed a group of small, medieval, timber-framed buildings constructed using earth-fast posts in individual post-holes (Figure 42). Most were constructed within and over the perimeter line of a pre-existing and already ancient, inhabited enclosure and large timber-framed hall (Figure 10), the presence of which underlines the continuing attractiveness of this site to rural settlers (see page 23–4).

The earliest, identified building of the medieval sequence was a slightly bow-sided structures 14.4 m by 4.6 m (maximum dimensions), probably based on ten paired posts set in holes dug rarely larger than 40 cm diameter or deep, with end posts supporting the gables (building F, Figure 42). The structure probably had an internal hearth, set off-centre in the southern half, and was aligned approximately north-east – south-west. No dating evidence was directly associated with it, a factor which pointed to an early date given the prevalence of thirteenth- and fourteenth-century material on the site. However, a sherd of 'Chester Ware' came from a re-deposited context nearby and a probably late-Saxon clay loom weight had found its way into adjacent cobbling. Both may have been associated with this structure. If so, the building may belong to the late pre-Conquest period.

The earliest attempts to differentiate areas of the site appear to have been by the construction of slight, stake-supported fences that were identified parallel to the building. In a later re-development, divisions were established on a more substantial scale. Ditches and drainage channels were dug, maintained and replaced in a relatively complex sequence from, at latest, the thirteenth century, into the middle of the fourteenth century. If, as seems likely, these represented both functional and tenurial divisions, then they were probably associated with parallel banks and hedges. In one area, shallow post-holes suggested that the perimeter boundary of a messuage, close to the entrance onto the road, had been strengthened by the addition of posts set in a bank, since ploughed away. The ditches were small, rarely in excess of two metres wide or half a metre deep, but there is some evidence that those digging them became increasingly concerned to drain water away from the site in the period around 1300, resulting in ditches of increasing depth. The 'Dark Age' saucer-shaped enclosure which medieval occupation superseded became a drainage problem at this stage.

Within the enclosures defined by the ditches and the sunken road, a series of buildings were constructed that were characterised chiefly by their small size and the simplicity of technique. The largest and most substantial was a rectangular building, A1, nine metres by five metres, built with posts set in individually dug post-holes arranged in six pairs but complimented by single posts at the gable ends to support the ridge. The lack of an internal hearth and the presence of shallow drains designed to remove liquids from the interior make interpretation as a cattle byre likely. Against the west gable-end was a far flimsier structure eight metres by 5.6 m (internally) with an internal hearth (A3). The two buildings shared a wall but not a roof – an arrangement found elsewhere on the site.

These buildings probably represent the house and byre of a member of the manorial community. The presence of cattle accommodation, and what has been interpreted as stalls for other livestock in the yard, suggests that it should be associated with some of the adjacent closes and, perhaps, selions in the open fields. This may be the messuage of a family with a holding equivalent to a virgate or a moiety of the same, and does not look like that of a landless or near landless cottager.

In this context, the artefactual evidence from the messuage is significant. No medieval coinage was discovered, metalwork was extremely sparse and consisted of no more than a handful of nails and small iron objects such as rings for harnessing, and pottery reached the site in only small quantities, limited forms and in the later period of the occupation. If a significant surplus existed, these families disposed of it by means which are so far archaeologically unidentifiable. Their buildings were certainly not allocated conspicuous resources. Most of the upright, oak timbers were squared but generally of small size, rarely exceeding c. 15–20 cm across. Almost no stone was used – the total absence of surface outcrops in the township meant that building stone had necessarily to be imported and this did not occur on the site until the late fifteenth century at earliest, and more likely the sixteenth century, when the Old Hall was constructed on padstones. There is no evidence of the material used to fill the panels between the timber frames, nor traces of an interrupted cill-beam. Surviving late-medieval, large houses in the region utilised clay-daubed wattles, the daub consisting of marl and/or clay mixed with water, chopped straw and dung and coated with lime-wash (Singleton 1955). Excepting the lime-wash, these materials would have been locally available to the Tatton community. However, if wattle and daub was used, it appears to have been without any means of securing the base. It is possible that some of these buildings may have relied to an extent on clay walls of the type that emerged in the vernacular traditions of South Lancashire (e.g. Singleton 1955;

Taylor 1884). There are references to 'turf cots' in the court rolls of Clitheroe, suggesting cottages built of peat blocks or turves in some of the rural manors in the parish of Whalley. Roofing was almost certainly with thatch of osiers or straw – the former would have been available from the adjacent stream-side and the latter was a ubiquitously available resource. That said, stone slates were being quarried from the upland commons by the fourteenth century, so some buildings were then being roofed with gritstone, albeit none was found here.

Small buildings built largely of earth, modest timbers and straw were presumably the habitation of the majority, who may often have shared their floors of beaten earth and clay with their fowls, pigs and livestock. A comparable tradition of buildings has been identified on the Solway Plain, which derived from the medieval period but lasted into the eighteenth century, perhaps owing to the insecurity created by cross-border conflict (Brunskill 1962). The vernacular tradition these buildings represent is characterised by a pragmatic commitment to local materials, all of which could probably be both obtained without money changing hands and erected without specialist assistance.

The less recognisable buildings excavated at Norton were in this and other respects directly comparable, with zones distinguished by drainage ditches and buildings largely defined by earth-fast posts, with a date range that extended from the thirteenth and fourteenth centuries to the seventeenth century (Greene and Hough 1977). Given the availability of local sandstone, it is not surprising that undressed stone was used rather more here than at Tatton, but it appears to have been adopted to do little more than provide some dwarf walls on which timber-framed structures were then erected, slightly removed from the damp earth.

Elsewhere, excavation along the corridor of the A5300 in Merseyside revealed the ground plan of a multi-unit but somewhat irregular, timber-framed building, some 15 m long, which seems to have provided accommodation for both humans and animals, at Brunt Boggart, Tarbock (Cowell and Philpott 2000, see plan on page 129). Again, this was associated with drainage ditches. The building was abandoned and sealed within the Middle Ages.

Documentary evidence implies that similar vernacular styles were in use across the region. A lease of a house at Garstang laid upon the lessee the obligation to uphold it with thatch and daub but any 'great' timber (i.e. frames) would be the responsibility of the lessor (Lumby 1939). The Duke of Lancaster gave the monks of Whalley in 1360 two thatched cottages built of oak ribs in *Ramsgreve* in the Chase of Blackburn, with land of various categories which was presumably farmed by the occupants. Construction in timber remained the norm at this level of society even on the Pennine edge into the post-medieval period and beyond and the cruck frame and similar structural techniques had a long history in the north-western counties at all levels among the rural community. A survey of Hornby Castle (*c.* 1579–85) makes it quite clear that the tenant farms were almost all still centred on houses constructed in the cruck tradition. Sizes varied from a modest four bays to upwards of a dozen. The exception was the 'fair tenement' of William Bennison 'newly built with stone having 10 bays …' (Chippindall 1939). With this house, the 'great rebuilding' was beginning to reach into the countryside of the region, but timber-framing remained the normal method of construction in and around the Mersey basin throughout the seventeenth century.

## Farm buildings

By the late medieval period, it is clear that roofed accommodation was regularly provided for the plough oxen, horses and some other livestock on holdings at all levels of society. This can be traced in the upland areas of Lancashire, among manorial tenants and on the great demesne vaccaries, as well as in the old agricultural lands of the plain. A new shed for cattle was constructed by the Duchy administration at Bacup on the grand scale, from timber and reed straw (Tupling 1927). The tenants of Burscough Priory at Coppull, in the mid-thirteenth century, agreed to build an aisle-less building, largely of oak, measuring 30 ft (9.1 m), as well as maintain an existing barn. The buildings constructed by Beatrix de Blackburn at Wiswell as easements for her cattle were probably on a scale closer to the Tatton byre and the function they were intended to serve was presumably similar. Buildings for a variety of other storage purposes were also largely of timber, perhaps on the same lines as Worden Old Hall – originally constructed as a barn with timber-framing and panels of wattle and daub (Glass 1982). The survey of the Hornby estate listed numerous 'outsetts' or farm buildings on the tenant farms.

Structures intended for special uses were also common in the region. The small number of mills noted in Domesday grew rapidly until examples were present on at least a very large minority of manors by 1300 (e.g. Bott 1984). The majority of these were water mills, taking advantage of the large number of streams and rivers in the area fed by substantial rainfall in the eastern uplands. These were constructed with, and possibly on, dams of timber and earth, which were frequently the subject of litigation because of the flooding caused up-stream. Most were built and owned by the manorial aristocracy who imposed the obligation of grinding their corn on tenants and used their monopoly control of such equipment to increase revenues from their estates, as well as provide flour for their own households. The near monopoly of the earls in Cheshire as evidenced in Domesday was rapidly eroded as many lords of small estates sought to raise income by this means. To date no example of a medieval mill has been excavated in the area, although work at Tatton in 1986 and 1987 examined a substantial cross-valley bank, which had been constructed on peat which provided a calibrated date of AD 970–1270. This was clearly medieval and, despite some doubts, was interpreted tentatively as a mill dam (Higham, N.J. 1998–9; Figure 43).

Evidence from other regions suggests that mills and associated earthworks could be sophisticated and substantially engineered, with the development of

a single site occurring over a long time scale. The documentary references to corn mills that occur throughout the region may imply that 'multiple mills' were in use, with two or more pairs of millstones running from a single dam. On some manors, the quantity of grain was sufficient for two grain mills to be operating in tandem, as was occurring at Halton on the Lune when the widow of William Dacre died in 1324. References also occur to both windmills and horse-mills. Richard Butler, for example, left an estate in 1323 which included a horse-mill in Warrington as well as a windmill on his demesne lands (Farrer 1907). The same combination of wind and horsepower had been harnessed at Broughton (Lancashire), but when Gilbert de Singleton died the horse-mill had fallen down and the windmill was broken (Farrer 1915). On balance, it seems likely that most corn, throughout the region, was, by the thirteenth century, ground by water power but windmills were common across the lowlying west of Lancashire, where the natural fall of local streams was insufficient to power water mills. Fulling mills were also spreading by the thirteenth century.

Other structures were erected and maintained by the rural community or individuals. Many local by-ways crossed small streams and rivulets by plank bridges, such as those that carried tracks or paths from Tatton to Mobberly and Knutsford. Elsewhere more substantial bridges had to be maintained. That which crossed the Dee at Chester was already the responsibility of the

FIGURE 44.
The medieval stone
bridge spanning the
Dee between Farndon
and Holt.

County in 1066, when it arguably formed part of the defences of the *burh*, and was to be the joint responsibility of the City and Shire thereafter. Medieval stonework survives to an exceptional degree in the bridge linking Farndon and Holt (Figure 44) and at Warrington and Stockport (from *c.* 1370) bridges carried traffic across the Mersey. Fish traps were constructed from stakes and wicker on all the major rivers of the region and small boats were used by fishermen and others on the numerous meres and rivers.

## Castles

There is no clear evidence that defensive sites of any kind were constructed between the tenth-century *burhs* of Cheshire and southern Lancashire (Higham, N.J. 1988c; Griffiths 2001) and the castles built from 1069–70 onwards. Notwithstanding, the status of a late-Saxon thegn was consistent with the ownership of a defended house with a gatehouse and some of the numerous, local place-names in *-bury* (e.g. Bury, Pendlebury) may reflect sites of this stature. The possibility remains that late-Saxon sites in this region may in the future be identified with the characteristics of 'proto-castles', at King Edward's Penwortham and West Derby, or Orm's Halton, for example.

The early Norman aristocracy were few in number, foisting themselves upon a hostile, if chastened, local community. Those who could concentrate sufficient resources built castles. In the North West, early examples were so-called 'primitive' castles (Cathcart King 1988), built entirely of timber, earth and turf, small versions of the kind excavated extensively at Hen Domen (near Montgomery, Barker and Higham 1982). Such castles could be erected rapidly, using only the materials immediately to hand. Most in this region, but by no means all, were constructed with two major components, a motte and a bailey. The motte was an earthen and turf mound, in some cases constructed around the upright timbers of a wooden tower, which was separated from the bailey by a ditch. Mottes were typically small in size compared to the bailey and probably used primarily as a watch tower or as the place of last resort in the event of an attack. The bailey was a defended courtyard, normally surrounded by a ditch and earth and timber bank, in which the normal business of the site was conducted in and around ranges of timber-framed buildings set within the defences. The occupation of such a site might be of long duration, with numerous phases of structural replacement or refurbishment, and only a minority of sites were later developed as masonry castles.

The initial phase of construction might encompass both motte and bailey, or only a single element. At the coastal site of Aldingham (Cumbria), excavation by Davison showed the initial, early twelfth-century defensive work to be a simple ring-work 40 m in diameter. This was later remodelled to form a motte to which was appended an outer enclosure or bailey (Wilson and Hurst 1968). It has been suggested that West Derby castle was similar in plan to the primary phase at Aldingham. In contrast, at Gisburn there is no trace of a bailey and it is possible that this site never constituted more than a defensive mound.

Our understanding of these substantial monuments remains only partial. Excavation of a half section through the presumed motte at Newton (Lancashire) failed to identify any structural evidence, the mound consisting of sand. The bailey had been destroyed in the process of constructing the nearby M6 motorway (Hollos 1987). More recent exploratory work by Chester Archaeology at the motte and bailey at Aldford (Cheshire) has found signs of cleaning out of the castle ditch well into the thirteenth century, but no clear evidence of the Norman period of occupation.

The earliest, documented example of a castle north of the Mersey is that at Penwortham, near Preston, which was already built by 1086 at the caput of the estate recently held by Roger of Poitou. The physical remains of the site consist of a small earth motte perched above the Ribble and earthworks, now under trees, adjacent to the church. Lancaster was, at Domesday, nothing grander than a subordinate part of the estate based on Halton, the site of the estate church, and the primary castle site. Penwortham, with twin castle and borough, was the most highly developed of the Lancashire estate centres among all Roger's erstwhile estates in Lancashire. The site replicates the site of Chester – defending and exploiting a navigable river, on comparatively well-drained, raised land but close to the best crossing point, sited at the interface with the as yet untamed communities north of the river (for a possible tenth-century *burh* site here, Higham, N. 1988c). The site was marginalised after Roger received Lancashire beyond the Ribble and it declined in status in the twelfth century, when it became the centre of the minor Bussel barony.

Chester Castle was initially constructed by King William, at the close of the campaign in which he took direct control of Cheshire (1069–70). It was this castle that was to form the focus of Earl Hugh's great honour, despite the absence of any reference to it in Domesday Book. The castle was constructed on an artificially raised spur on the edge of the Dee, close to the town bridge, immediately outside the perimeter of the city walls. Successive rebuilding has almost entirely remodelled this area since the eleventh century and only brief glimpses of much of the site have been possible (e.g. Strickland and Rutter 1980/1). The earliest surviving stone fabric belongs to the period 1187–1232. Such can be seen in the lower courses of the so-called 'Agricola Tower', the finely decorated chapel of St Mary de Castro and parts of the inner bailey. The castle may at this stage have loosely resembled the inner ward of Ludlow Castle. The outer bailey was not rebuilt in stone until after 1245, but this was, during the twelfth and early thirteenth centuries, a baronial castle in the grand style, capable of housing one of the largest households in the country in impressive surroundings (Plate 10).

The death of Earl John in 1237 without male heirs provided an opportunity for Henry III to secure the county. He thereafter refurbished the castle as the administrative centre of his new lordship and as the springboard from which he and his son, Lord Edward, launched a series of campaigns against the Welsh. The *Annales Cestrienses* provides the local perspective:

> 1245: The king and queen of England came together to Chester on Sunday, August 13, and with them an abundant army, that is to say, Richard, earl of Cornwall, brother of the king; Simon, earl of Leicester; Roger, earl of Winchester; William, earl of Albemarle; [Hugh], earl of Oxford, and almost all the nobles of the whole of England; and they stayed there until the Sunday following. And on the morrow of S. Philibert the king set out with his army for Wales ...

Chester castle was retained in what perhaps approximated to good defensive order at least until the end of the fourteenth century, when it was still an occasional residence of King Richard II.

The Cheshire barons followed the lead given them by the earls and equipped themselves with castles, which became their normal residences in the twelfth century. The circular, flat-topped, earth motte which stands on the north-west side of Malpas Church is a substantial reminder of this phase of castle building and may have been raised on the orders of Robert fitzHigh, the

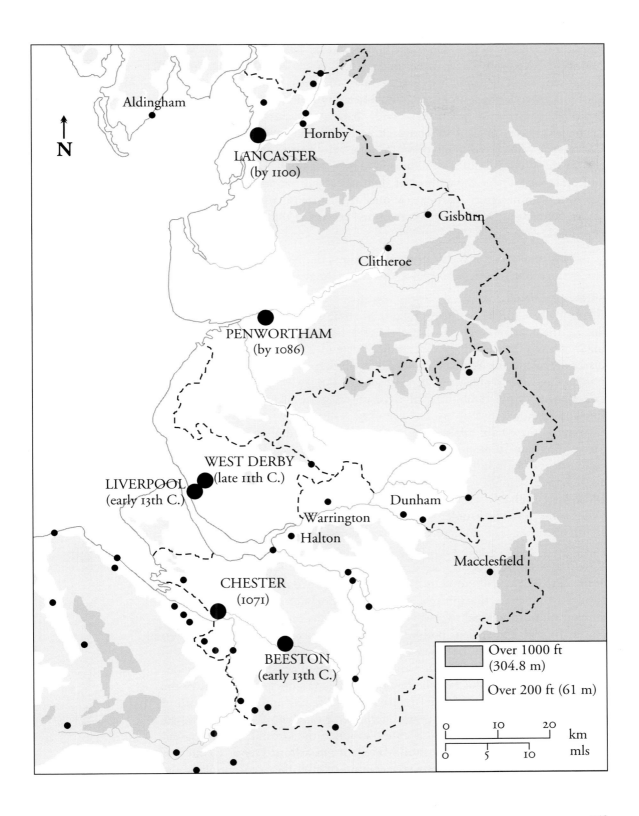

Aldingham

N

Hornby

LANCASTER
(by 1100)

Gisburn

Clitheroe

PENWORTHAM
(by 1086)

WEST DERBY
LIVERPOOL (late 11th C.)
(early 13th C.)

Dunham

Warrington

Halton

Macclesfield

CHESTER
(1071)

BEESTON
(early 13th C.)

Over 1000 ft
(304.8 m)

Over 200 ft (61 m)

0          10          20
km
0     5      10
mls

143

first baron (Plate 6). Elsewhere in Cheshire, many late eleventh and twelfth century castles were constructed in similarly obscure and undocumented circumstances. The earls had castles built on their principal manors, at Shotwick, Macclesfield, Frodsham, Shocklach and Aldford. All, in origin, were probably constructed as mottes with baileys attached, and substantial earthworks have survived at Shotwick and Aldford. Those on the west of Cheshire may have been intended to serve as a screen of strongholds held against the Welsh, along with Oldcastle (Thomson 1967), Dodleston, Pulford and other sites under the control of the earls in north and east Wales. Such defences were necessary, particularly once the Norman conquest of northern Wales faltered, as William of Malmesbury noted for the year 1093 (Mynors *et al.* 1998, 571):

> At this time too the Welsh broke out against the Normans, ravaged Cheshire and part of Shropshire, and seized Anglesey by force of arms.

Shotwick defended a crucial position on the estuary of the Dee and was later substantially refurbished, being rebuilt in stone with a ward and six towers during the border conflicts of the thirteenth century (Cullen and Horden 1986). There is a marked agglomeration of defended sites in areas of particular insecurity, as on the Welsh march, and in northern Lancashire (Higham, M. 1991), where the problems associated with the reign of King Stephen were exacerbated by the ambitions of Scottish kings to expand into northern England (Figure 45).

Many of these local castles were constructed at the administrative centres of pre-existing and substantial estates. Aldford (at Domesday referred to as the earl's estate of Farndon), Macclesfield and Frodsham are examples among the earls' estates, which were mirrored by Halton, Nantwich and Northwich, which were probably all constructed by his barons. At many of these sites, new towns were developed under baronial patronage during the twelfth and thir-teenth centuries. The close, physical juxtaposition of Norman castles and early, parochial churches is noticeable but not invariable on both sides of the Mersey. Where they do both occur, castle and church combine to give an impression of the twin bastions of Norman authority. For the incoming aristocracy, it was natural to integrate the spiritual with the trappings of secular power and to develop multi-functional foci within their estates as centres of patronage and power. Indeed, the ancient parishes seem to have been a major influence on the way that some at least of the early baronies were constructed, which should not surprise us given that parishes arguably originated as estates. Several exam-ples from Lancashire illustrate the point effectively (Figure 46). The core of the lordship of Hornby consisted of the parishes of Melling and Tunstall, both of which provided groups of townships offering very different resources, from the valley bottom to the fells. To this core was added the lordship of Tottington, making up the parishes of Bury and Middleton, in Salford Hundred, but it is very possible that these parishes were constructed after the event, bringing the ecclesiastical jurisdiction into line with the secular. Penwortham barony,

initially focused on the castle next to the chu[...] [...] Meols and
Penwortham (including the detached portion [...] Leyland, with the addition of a large part of Standish parish and a scatter of
individual townships in Amounderness, so had all of agricultural land, old

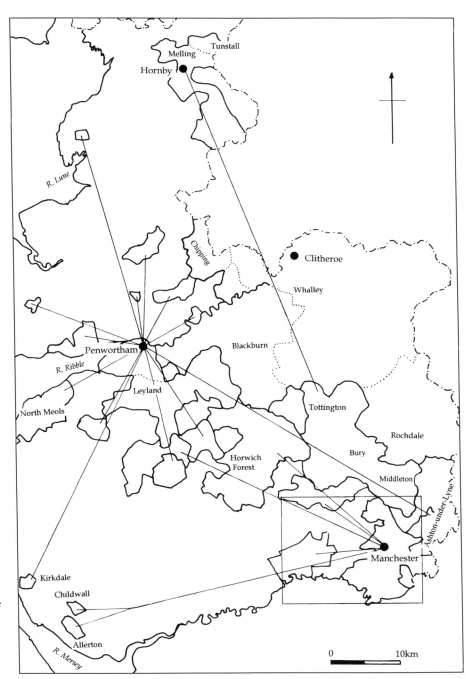

FIGURE 46.
The Lancashire
baronies of Hornby,
Penwortham, Clitheroe
and Manchester. The
inset rectangle
represents the inset
outline of Figure 50.

great Lacy honour of Clitheroe included the
ancient parishes of Whalley and Blackburn,
t of Ribchester parish and all Rochdale. The
racteristically long and thin, encompassing a
ile both Chipping and Whalley have bound-
phical terms. Makerfield barony was nearly
igan and Winwick, and included the whole
coterm...
of the post-Conqu..
Makerfield. In Cheshire, the Dunham
barony was clearly influenced ... omposition by both Bowdon parish and
the pre-existing holdings of Alfward, with which it was near coterminous, and
the Nantwich, Halton and Malpas baronies all continued, to an extent at least,
pre-existing parochial and secular territories.

The insecurity of the early to mid-twelfth century encouraged the construction, or retention, of small, fortified sites by other members of the local
aristocracy. Dunham Massey and Ullerswood were held by Hamo de Massey
against Henry II in 1173 (Renn 1968). There is some debate as to the precise
location of the castle of Dunham Massey but it should probably be equated
with the surviving earthworks near the artificial lake in the gardens of Dunham
Hall. There is, however, a motte and bailey on the banks of the Bollin, known
as Watch Hill, in the township of Bowdon, the bailey of which is, at *c.* 1.5 ha,
comparable in size and defences to Halton Castle (Lancashire): it should probably be seen as a castle of the Massey family. Stockport Castle also dates to
the twelfth century and was held in 1172–73 for Geoffrey, the second son of
Henry II, against his father. This was probably a timber castle. It may have
been refurbished in stone at about 1200, by the de Stockport family, and it is
probably this stone enceinte which survives in plan in the modern street
pattern (Dent 1977) as Castle Yard.

Of the surviving baronial castles of Cheshire, Halton was the most strongly
fortified. The castle was built by the hereditary constables of Chester Castle,
on an outcrop of sandstone overlooking the Mersey and the long abandoned
*burh* at Runcorn, where the parish church remained. It may have replaced a
Saxon thegn's fortified manor house on this or a closely adjacent site. The
earliest castle was a ring-work, within which stood a timber tower or keep,
inside an inner bailey, which exploited existing level differences on the apex
of the hill (Figure 47). Much of the surviving detail dates to the fourteenth
and fifteenth centuries (McNeil 1987). The site was maintained and periodic
rebuilding occurred into the sixteenth century, as the castle continued to act
as the local focus of estate administration for the Duchy of Lancaster.
Excavation of the site revealed that little stratigraphy had survived the successive refurbishments but pottery was recovered dating from the twelfth century
onwards. Halton Castle and borough, plus the minster churches at Runcorn
and Great Budworth, and Norton Priory, provided the key foci for a barony
which dominated northern central Cheshire.

A similar pattern emerges north of the Mersey. Penwortham ceased to be a
major centre during the late eleventh century, superseded by the construction

FIGURE 47.
Halton Castle
(Cheshire): a hilltop
already probably used
in the late Anglo-Saxon
period as a thegn's
residence, the Norman
castle was eventually
upgraded in the
fourteenth century and
provided with a stone
enceinte by the Duchy
of Lancaster.

of Lancaster Castle, the keep of which was raised on the outer defences of the Roman fort by 1102 (V.C.H. 1908). Whether or not Lancaster initially had an earth and timber phase is unclear but much of the development of the site as a masonry castle occurred during the reign of King John. It was virtually complete within the thirteenth century, eventually comprising a substantial, stone-built ward with a keep (the Lungess Tower). However, substantial rebuilding occurred when the castle became the administrative centre of the royal duchy in the late fourteenth and fifteenth centuries when the great gate was constructed (1403–13), and again when it was converted to a prison.

More typical of Norman construction are the 'primitive' castles of the Lune Valley, at Halton, Hornby, Whittingham, Sedbergh and Tebay (the last two in Cumbria). Those at Halton and Hornby are substantial, upstanding examples of motte and bailey construction, both of which were important sites, Halton being the administrative centre of the forests of the Lancaster lordship. Like Gisburn and Newton, both derived advantages from sites adjacent to natural waterways, the Halton site to particularly good effect, utilising a position of natural defence with parallels at Watch Hill and Castleton, Rochdale. The motte at Halton is unusually small but the bailey is comparable in size to those at similar sites. At Hornby, the early castle, 'Castlesteads' (Figure 48), was part

FIGURE 48. Castlestead, Hornby: a substantial motte and bailey in the Lune Valley was the early focus of the barony, near which both a priory and borough were later established.

PETER ILES, LANCASHIRE COUNTY COUNCIL

PLATE I.
Rainow, in the eastern, upland edge of Cheshire. A landscape of late medieval assarts and remnants of ancient woodland gives way in the hills to the rectilinearity of post-medieval enclosure.

PLATE 2. Lindow Moss, near Wilmslow, is the last mossland in the region to be commercially dug. Prehistoric trees which have been uncovered from low down in the peat litter the site.

PLATE 3. St Patrick's Chapel, Heysham: an eighth-century double church site on a coastal peninsula almost cut off from the mainland by marshes.

PLATE 4.
A pre-Conquest cross shaft at Halton (Lancashire), which arguably reflects the presence of a major church here in the late Anglo-Saxon period.

PLATE 5.
Ingleborough Hillfort, a major landscape feature and perhaps an important marker for a local people or tribal group in the early Middle Ages.

PLATE 6.
Malpas: a small
medieval urban
settlement which
developed around an
early church and
secular estate centre,
which attracted the
construction of a
Norman castle motte.

PLATE 7.
The valley of the Tarn
Wyre was colonised
during the thirteenth
century, with numerous
vaccaries established in
a ribbon along the
stream.

PLATE 8.
Marsh land beside the
river Douglas at
Longton offered the
medieval community
valuable seasonal
grazing.

PLATE 11.
Clitheroe, a town which was established at the foot of the crag on which a baronial castle was constructed. This is the core of the early town, with comparatively regular burgage plots laid out in two rows.

PLATE 12.
Lower Peover Church, Cheshire, which is a comparatively rare survivor of the common late medieval practice in this county of building minor churches as timber-framed structures erected on a stone plinth.

FIGURE 49.
Beeston Castle: a 'scientific' castle of the early thirteenth century constructed to defend Chester from the east and advertise the power of the earls.

of a group of seigneurial foundations, which eventually included a priory, half a mile away beside the Lune, and the comparatively regular urban settlement around the bridge, almost a mile away. However, the earthwork castle was eventually replaced by a new masonry one, closely adjacent to the new town but to the east, on high ground beside the river Wenning. This was still considered to be in good order in the late sixteenth century when it was the centre of a substantial establishment with farmyard buildings arranged in four yards outside the walls (Chippindall 1939).

It was probably castles of the simplest type that were constructed at the centre of the barony of Manchester, on the site of Chethams College, and at Warrington, on the now removed Mote Hill near St Elphin's Church (Grealey 1976). Both were replaced by more comfortable manor houses in the later medieval period. Clitheroe may have started as an earthwork around 1100, but was equipped in the twelfth century (perhaps in the 1170s) by the de Lacy family with a small stone keep and a stone enceinte.

Greater in scale were the royal, then comital castles at West Derby and Liverpool. At West Derby, King William and Roger of Poitou took over a preexisting hundredal and estate centre, the focus of what was, at the Conquest, the richest and most densely settled part of Lancashire. The site was equipped with a castle which twelfth- and thirteenth-century refurbishment developed into an impressive, stone-built and entowered enceinte. Liverpool was very different. It was a planted town or bastide but one that was not conceived until 1207, at the initiative of King John. The substantial, masonry, castle ward was constructed on the south side of the new borough (Figure 23) but no surface evidence of the defences now remains.

By far the most spectacular survivor of medieval castle construction in the region is Beeston Castle, constructed on a sandstone crag overlooking the Tarporley gap through the Central Cheshire Ridge (Figure 49). The site had been fortified in the prehistoric period but no Norman defences had been constructed. It belongs to a new generation of strategically sited castles of the Angevin era, of the new, 'scientific' type epitomised by Château Gaillard, which Richard I built to hold the Seine valley route into Normandy. Beeston was constructed at the orders of one of the richest, most powerful and most experienced politicians and military leaders of the day, earl Ranulph III of Chester. He had first hand knowledge of contemporary military developments in Angevin France and had held the castles of Vire, Semilly and Avranches until the loss of Normandy in the early years of the thirteenth century (Harris 1975). Construction began in 1225, using sandstone dug from quarries that were immediately adjacent and from the dry moat around the inner bailey, the work being funded by a local customs tax. The original design differed little from the structure as it survives, with an inner ward defended by a rock-cut moat and walls strengthened by half-round, flanking towers. Two of these protected the inner gate, with a large upper room running across between them. This inner ward was set at the apex of the rocky outcrop, with a walled outer bailey of *c.* 3.8 ha. occupying the entirety of the gentler, south-facing slopes. There is no upstanding evidence of medieval occupation within the outer bailey, which was probably intended to do no more than deny the obvious lines of approach to potential assailants. The whole outer defence probably depended heavily on those stationed at the gatehouse of the outer bailey wall (Hough 1978).

There can be little doubt that Beeston was constructed in response to a threat other than that posed by the Welsh. It guards Chester and the Dee valley from the east, perhaps serving a strategic function comparable to the *burh* at Eddisbury in the early tenth century. The castle was built for a great prince, anxious to protect his 'capital' from rivals within England. He was also presumably keen to impress those travelling to it by this unique manifestation of his power and wealth. It was not until after Ranulph's death that the site was taken into royal custody and thereafter used in the context of the Welsh wars, being refurbished successively by Henry III and Edward I (Colvin 1963), but the castle had little visible impact on the pattern of rural settlement in the area and failed to attract any urban development.

The surrender of the earldom to the crown and the subsequent absenteeism of most great lords in the later middle ages accelerated the process of neglect that overtook most of the region's castles. The infrequent visits of the Black Prince or John of Gaunt galvanised their local agents into refurbishing the residential facilities of the major sites but the Lancastrian usurpation of 1399 effectively ended further visits at this level. Changing expectations of comfort, social behaviour and architectural opportunities encouraged the shift from defensive works towards great or large houses, but many of the region's castles retained an administrative role well into the sixteenth century and were maintained sufficiently to allow them to perform these functions.

In many instances, the authority which these castles represented had a long term influence on the regional landscape by maintaining particular types of tenure and land use on different parts of the territory, and controlling the development of urban sites and various strategies for investment, such as the construction of mills, vaccaries or fisheries. If we take the comparatively well-documented barony of Manchester in the decades around 1300 as an example (Harland 1856–62, vol. 53), the lordship had at its core a castle (later manor house), an ancient church with an extensive parish and a borough with monopoly trading rights throughout the barony (Figure 50). Additionally, it maintained a small park around the castle site, a much larger one to the north at Blackley Park and a private chase, with eight vaccaries, at Horwich. Demesne lands and other assets were leased out in several townships, but mostly within the various hamlets in Manchester itself, with a second capital messuage at Kearsley providing a focus for the nearer, detached, portion of the barony to the north. Oxgangs were held in bondage in Gorton, Openshaw, Ardwick, and elsewhere inside Manchester. Other townships or large parts of townships were held of the barony as knights' fees, and these were typically at some distance. The total income in 1282 from secular assets was £131 7s. 8¼d. but this was dwarfed by the income from the three advowsons of Manchester,

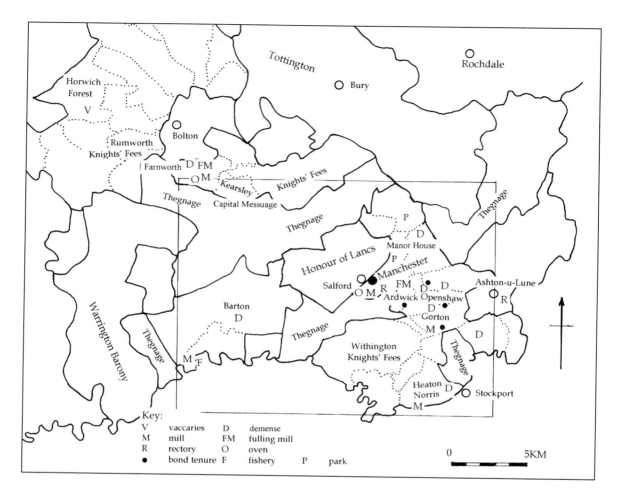

Key:
V	vaccaries	D	demense
M	mill	FM	fulling mill
R	rectory	O	oven
●	bond tenure	F	fishery	P	park

0		5KM

FIGURE 50.
The core of Manchester Barony, to illustrate the way the honour was focused on two sites, Manchester itself and the second but lesser capital messuage at Kearsley, around both of which investment in manorial monopolies was concentrated. Neighbouring lordships developed a ring of rival boroughs (open circles, named). The inset rectangle should be related to that on Figure 46.

Childwall and Ashton-under-Lyne, which the barony retained, which was more than double. However, the impact on the landscape was greatest at the core of the barony, in and around Manchester itself, and far less on the periphery. Like several other baronies both in Lancashire and Cheshire (such as Penwortham), the Grelley lordship also had small holdings close to the major castles to which they themselves owed knights' service, in this case in the close vicinity of West Derby.

Few local men could aspire to the wealth, status or privilege to own a true castle but most manorial lords expected to be housed in a dwelling that was distinguishable from those of inferior status and which offered a modicum of defensive potential in adversity. The interface between the castle and the manor house was never a simple one. The lord of the manor of Bury in the second half of the fourteenth century, constructed a stone house of *c.* 25 m by 20 m with walls nearly two metres thick, within an enclosure defined by a defensive moat, six metres wide and 1.5 m deep (Tyson 1986). The defences were refurbished by Sir Thomas Pilkington, who obtained a licence to crenellate in 1469, but demolition followed only two decades later. In 1403, a licence to crenellate was granted to James de Radcliffe for the reconstruction of Radcliffe Towers in stone, defended by towers (Tyson 1985), and a funnel-vaulted pele tower has survived from this phase. Similar pele towers were constructed in the late medieval period at Broughton, Wrayshole and Gawthorpe (Lancashire) and at Brimstage (1398) and Doddington (1365) in Cheshire, but they were far less numerous here than in Cumbria. Lathom House, since demolished, was perhaps the grandest example, but other fifteenth-century examples include Arden Hall (east of Stockport) and Turton Tower. Most such 'castles' and pele towers were in reality no more than manor houses, on which unusual resources has been expended by the more affluent and/or aspirational among the local aristocracy. Some were constructed during periods of weakened royal authority, when internal disturbances were commonly compounded by the threat or reality of border raids, from Scotland, or from the Welsh rebels of the early Lancastrian period. However, much of this rebuilding was primarily a fashion statement, designed to publicise the status and power of particular local figures, often at a point when they had achieved influence at court or in local government.

## The large house and the manor-house

In the eleventh century, timber building traditions dominated construction throughout the region, even in the manor-house, giving way to stone construction in the twelfth century only in a tiny minority of buildings of the very highest status, erected on the orders of great lords or wealthy ecclesiastical institutions. Thereafter, stone building replaced timber very slowly, adopted initially by wealthy townsfolk and a minority of manorial lords. Throughout the period, most buildings were probably built from the same materials and on the same basic principles as those of lesser status excavated at Tatton and Norton. At the social level of the manorial hall, however, they attained greater size and complexity and incorporated far more professional skills. Carpenters were not uncommon among lists of those owning suit to the great manorial courts and 'daubers' and 'lead-beaters' also occur quite widely. In contrast, masons are not often documented away from the major urban, castle and clerical sites.

Documentary references to rural buildings are rarely of sufficient descriptive value to determine whether a wooden or a stone building was in question. However, the incidence of surviving, timber-framed structures, mostly from the late fourteenth, fifteenth and sixteenth centuries, implies that a local tradition of building from timber was already dominant in the earlier period (Wood 1965), following the long-hallowed tradition of a hall with attendant structures in association. The basic design was constructed using cruck frames placed about four metres apart, tied together with horizontal tie beams pegged with oak dowels, with beam-supported wall plates on either side and purlins in between. The frames would arguably normally be prefabricated.

A surviving hall of traditional style is Chorley Hall, constructed on an oblong plan with both the solar and the service areas in the same building block as the hall, although they are covered by a separate, transverse roof. Baguley Hall is the most substantial survivor from the fourteenth century, substantially predating both Rufford Old Hall and Samlesbury. It has been claimed that the structure incorporates elements of pre-Conquest building traditions (Smith and Stell 1960), particularly as regards the bowing of the long sides, which suggests comparison with Viking Age buildings, but archaeological investigation has demonstrated that the stone stylobates on which the walls were supported were very nearly parallel, the bowing being a feature exclusively of the timber framing. The hall has two bays of near equal size and features planks rather than panelling as an exterior wall surface (Figure 51). Underlying post-holes of an earlier aisled hall, no later than the early thirteenth century, were identified archaeologically, which was at least 15 m long and 9.5 m wide (Dixon *et al.* 1989). The posts were earth-fast, set in massive post pits. Both here and at Old Abbey Farm, Risley (see below), we see evidence of aisled buildings of the early post-conquest period being replaced

FIGURE 51.
Baguley Hall: the north
wall of the great hall,
during restoration
work. The hall was
probably built by Sir
William Legh after he
inherited the estate in
1356, following the
death of John Baguley.
Note the cusped braces
to the panels, which
create the foil and
quatrefoil shapes. These
perhaps herald the
tradition of lightly
ornamented timber-
framing which is
common across the
North West down to
the late sixteenth
century.

W. JOHN SMITH

by aisle-less structures built with a developed, fully framed structure on dwarf stone walls.

Parallels between the later of these buildings and others in the region (Radcliffe Towers, Tabley Old Hall and Smithills Hall have been cited) suggest that a developing but persistently conservative tradition of timber construction existed locally into the late medieval period and beyond. Examples of this only now survive in a tithe of halls, constructed by men of 'gentry' status in the fourteenth to sixteenth centuries. Ordsall Hall provides the earliest example of a surviving solar wing, built to provide private accommodation by the Radcliffe family in 1360–62 (G.M.A.C. 1995). When complete, the wing measured 33 m by 5.5 m rising to six metres at the eaves, and was highly decorated inside with moulded ceiling beams and two ornate fireplaces.

The study of halls began early in the North West, with an excellently illustrated volume by Taylor published in 1884 finding a ready market among the owners of the great houses of the region. Even at that stage, many examples were in decline, as was Ordsall Hall, or Samlesbury, which in Taylor's opinion had suffered desecration when converted to a public house. Since his day there has been a substantial drop in the status of many of these great houses. Families without the resources to maintain them have tended to dispose of them or allow them to decay with the result that most of the best-kept survivors now depend upon public ownership in various guises, including the National Trust. Tabley Old Hall, for example, which was still preserved 'with great care' in 1884, is now a ruin.

The halls which remain offer a series of fundamental interpretive problems. It is unclear, for example, how representative surviving examples are, with high rates of loss in particular among buildings of lower status (Crossley 1976). Most surviving sites have had an extended history of occupation, during which wholesale demolition or alterations of early phases has been commonplace as building styles have changed to accommodate social needs and aesthetic tastes. Archaeology has proved to be a surprisingly problematic method of research in some instances where it has been attempted, because of the scale of work required and the thoroughness of late phases of rebuilding on most sites. As a result, the number of standing buildings with interpretable, medieval fabric is small.

The late medieval period, defined in architectural terms from *c.* 1350–1550, was the last period to witness a concentration of resources on the great hall. This was a traditional building of standardised design which derived ultimately from the halls of the pre-Conquest era, in which lord, family and retinue would habitually eat together, do business or merely congregate (Brunskill 1987). As such, it was the focus and core of the late-medieval great house. In Lancashire and Cheshire, most were open-roofed, timbered buildings built as a series of bays, supported by frames or base crucks. They generally had steeply pitched roofs, the beams of which were often ornamented by the type of surface decoration best seen at Smithills Hall, Adlington or Rufford Old Hall (Figure 52), which was visible from the ground. These timbers could be of

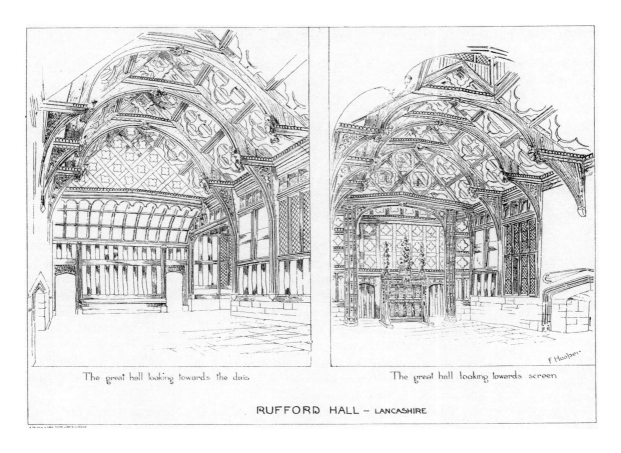

The great hall looking towards the dais                    The great hall looking towards screen

F Hooper

RUFFORD HALL – LANCASHIRE

considerable size. The demolition and reconstruction of Newton Hall, Hyde, allowed a detailed examination to occur. The crucks weighed about four tons (4064 kilos) apiece. Carbon dating established that the cruck blades were cut from oak trees in the late fourteenth century, which had been saplings in the Domesday period (Marsden 1971).

In plan timber-framed halls varied upwards from ten to 15 m long, by six to eight metres wide. Many were constructed on wall bases of sandstone, in some instances reaching a height of one or two metres, producing buildings of half-timbered style such as Adlington Hall. Some were, in contrast, constructed without a plinth of stone. The late fifteenth-/early sixteenth-century phase at Tatton Old Hall was based on isolated, untrimmed pieces of sandstone inserted under the timber uprights as padstones and there is no evidence of a proper stylobate until later reconstruction of the walls (Higham and Cane 1999; Higham, N.J. 2000). The height of halls like that at Adlington (c. 11.5 m to the ridge and c. 7.5 m to the eaves) made them structures of considerable grandeur, with much in common with the nave of a church. Rufford Old Hall was constructed or reconstructed in the mid Tudor period with fine speres and was richly panelled, the seven bays being separated by six hammer-beam principal rafters. Adlington was provided with windows, the

FIGURE 52.
Rufford Old Hall (Lancashire): two early views of the interior of one of the finest surviving late medieval buildings in the region, by F. Hooper (after Taylor (1884), plate XVII, facing p. 76).

ledges of which were two metres from the ground, guaranteeing privacy while admitting plenty of light. Little medieval glazing has survived. Leaded lights are present in the late examples of Bramhall Hall and Little Moreton Hall and medieval glass was retrieved from excavations at Tatton. Heraldic glass survives at Speke, Rufford and Ordsall.

The most durable element of the great hall has in many instances been the roof. Most were covered with 'grey slates' – heavy slabs of sedimentary rock, two to three centimetres thick, which came from numerous local quarries along the Pennines. A minority were probably thatched. The well-protected roof in many instances outlasted the wall timbers on which they rested as these became dilapidated, under attack from damp and decay. At Royle Hall, near Burnley, in the middle of the seventeenth century, the roof was propped up and the walls rebuilt in stone (Taylor 1884). Similar, drastic action was taken at Rainhill Hall Farm (Lewis 1986) and at Tatton Old Hall at the end of the century and there are signs that several other halls incorporate roof timbers which predate the buildings on which they rest.

Within the hall, the focus of artistry was the high table. In the better surviving examples, elaborate canopies were erected over the dais. That at Adlington (constructed *c.*1505) was decorated with various coats of arms of Cheshire families. The canopy at Rufford Old Hall (*c.*1540) is a magnificent example of late-medieval decoration, the coving ornamented with moulded ribs forming 36 panels, which rise to a battlemented and moulded beam (Wood 1965). Much of the roof decoration either ornamented the high table, or showed to best advantage from it, so that it would normally be visible to the owner and the more important of his guests.

The great hall was only one element within the gentry house, even if it was still the central focus into which most resources were directed. Late thirteenth-century buildings of comparable status, such as Stokesay Castle (near Ludlow), illustrate the elaboration of the manorial hall, to which retiring rooms (the solar) and kitchens were commonly appended. The late medieval gentry houses of the North West were also constructed with these facilities, although in fewer instances have these smaller rooms survived later refashioning. At Tatton Old Hall, excavation in 1979 outside the west end of the Old Hall established that the structure had originally been longer by several metres. A post-supported, plastered, interior division had separated off the far end. The continuous clay floor that this solar shared with the hall demonstrated that the whole had been constructed *in toto*, and the solar separated off only at a very later stage in the building process. At Tatton, no evidence was identified archaeologically of a kitchen area at the opposite end of the hall but the presence of a screens passage implies that such existed. However, structural evidence and cooking pottery of the period was uncovered outside the hall to the south, opposite the external door. It is probable that this was associated with the utility area of the house beyond the screens passage.

Elsewhere, a typical layout has been identified, with kitchens separated from the hall by a screens passage. Such was observed, for example, at Chorley Hall and at Peel Hall, Ince, when the latter was surveyed in 1983 (Walker and Tindall eds 1985). The earliest surviving example in Lancashire is Warton Old Rectory, constructed probably in the early fourteenth century, but the early element has been disguised by later structural changes.

By the mid-fifteenth century, growing pressure on the service wings and private quarters of halls was beginning to result in an 'H' shaped layout, in which the central hall was narrower than adjacent rooms. Perhaps the best, and arguably the most attractive, local example is Little Moreton Hall (Figure 53), where the hall and its wings have been retained within the substantial later additions to the house. The upper floors, which had later been inserted into the hall, have been removed. The architectural development visible on such sites was the necessary precursor of the shift away from the hall as a social focus that was to dominate new architectural styles in the Elizabethan period.

Large, rural houses of the region reached a level of complexity that is in itself impressive (see most recently Nevell and Walker 2002). Moorholm Manor House was described in the mid-fourteenth century as having a great

FIGURE 53.
Little Moreton Hall: a late medieval moated hall from the air. The grandiose gatehouse dates from the early seventeenth century, but the hall behind is substantially a fifteenth-century building.

chamber, a garderobe, pantry, buttery, kitchen, knights's chamber and a chapel. Outside were two granges, a kiln, a house for turves, a house for carpentry, a house for dogs, stable, smithy, two granges called the 'Westbernes', an oxhouse with a stable and a cottage near the "water of Ker", the whole valued at £100 (Farrer 1915). This description implies a substantial demesne operation centred upon a highly organised and functionally departmentalised group of buildings, at the centre of which was a hall of developed style.

Such houses were very numerous in the later Middle Ages, being constructed both over the foundations of existing buildings but also on 'green field' sites which had no previous history of high status settlement. At Tatton, successive halls seem to have been constructed on four different sites between *c.* 1200 and 1850, as different owners relocated and stamped their own particular needs and status on their *caput* manor. Similarly, Piers Warburton removed his principal residence from Warburton village to Arley in 1469, building a new moated hall within the core of his well-wooded and watered deer park. The setting itself offered considerable opportunities to an upwardly mobile gentleman, and the site was also well-placed at the centre of the family's various landed interests, which stretched into Great Budworth as well as Appleton, Sutton and Warburton. The main survivor from this building phase is the barn built with crucks, which presumably derived from the woodland of the estate, which was used in the nineteenth century as a riding school and is therefore known as 'The Ride'.

## Moats

It was among buildings of this status that the practice of construction within a moated enclosure proliferated. The chronology of moated sites is less than clear, particularly in the North West where the evidence derived from excavation has tended to be of late structural episodes (sixteenth century and later) where any has been identified (e.g. Peel Hall, Wythenshawe; Barrow Old Hall, Great Sankey). In the most general terms, the majority were arguably constructed within the period 1200–1500 but pottery which is thought to be of the twelfth century has come from two sites which have been excavated in Cheshire, at Northwoods Farm and Hale Barns. The possibility remains that earlier examples existed and there is occasional evidence of previous occupation, as at Timperley Old Hall, carbon-dated to the Anglo-Saxon period (Nevell 1997).

Moated sites are numerous, being identifiable in a significant proportion of townships in the region in association with manorial sites or significant sub-manors (Figures 25 and 26). The common but not invariable pattern of one moated site per manor/lordship has led in Cheshire to the suggestion that most examples were of manorial status (Wilson 1987) but this was by no means uniform and was even less the case in Lancashire. Even in Cheshire, in specific instances, it is clear that moated sites were of sub-manorial status. For example, the moated sites of Swineyard Hall and Northwood Hall at High

Legh were sub-manorial units carved out of one of the two primary manors of High Legh, neither of which is known to have been based on a moated site. These moated houses were, however, both holdings which were portrayed as of manorial status in the later Middle Ages, supporting the view that moats were connected with the social pretensions of their owners. They were also characteristic of an assarting landscape. Around Wigan and across much of western Lancashire, moated sites are far more numerous than manors and are more closely associated with the houses of the gentry than with the manorial aristocracy, particularly from the period after 1300 (now, in general, see Lewis 2000). The common occurrence of thegnage among landholders in this area means that families with modest pretensions to local power and influence were particularly numerous and it was that group who were primarily responsible for the proliferation of this class of monument.

Although widespread in the region, moated sites are scarce in the uplands and along the Pennine fringe. There were obvious, environmental constraints which conditioned their distribution, linked to the difficulty of digging them and the drainage properties of the soil. The few that occurred in east Lancashire, for example, are valley bottom sites, such as that at Holden Green, near Bolton by Bowland (Figure 54). In addition, moats are absent from the

FIGURE 54.
Holden Green Moat (Lancashire): a well-preserved moated platform with an inlet stream visible to the left and broad ridge and furrow immediately beyond the moat.

PETER ILES, LANCASHIRE COUNTY COUNCIL

FIGURE 55.
Toot Hill, Macclesfield
Forest (Cheshire): a dry
moated platform
overlooking the Forest
marks the centre of its
administration.
A chapel still stands
close by.

core of Cheshire's forests and were presumably not generally dug there, reflecting the early comital control over assarting within the forest area (Wilson 1987). That said, a site contained by a rock-cut moat, with associated chapel, on Toot Hill high up on the Pennine edge, served as the focus of the administration of Macclesfield Forest (Figure 55).

In most instances, the form is square or rectangular, with a moat between eight to 15 m across and a central platform of *c.* 1000 square metres, as is the case at Hough Hall (Figure 26). However, far larger and more elaborate examples occur, in association with fishponds (e.g. Bewsey Old Hall), or utilising expanses of open water, as at Tabley Old Hall. The larger moats may enclose an area of more than an acre (0.4 hectares), but never more than two.

The excavation of moats has rarely provided much information. Throughout their period of use, it was necessary to clean the moat regularly, a practice which has resulted in the dispersal of early occupation debris, which might otherwise have collected there. In addition, moated platforms are substantial and their wholesale excavation has tended to be beyond the resources of local groups, whether amateur or professional. Even so, extensive excavation of a minority, such as Bewsey Old Hall and Denton Hall, has both recovered the profile of the moat and revealed traces of late medieval, timber-framed buildings (Lewis 2000; Nevell and Walker 2002). Excavations at Northwoods Farm (Dodcott cum Wilkesley) and Hough Hall (Mere) have both revealed evidence of service buildings, ovens and other structures. Perhaps the most complete exploration of a moated site is that conducted at Old Abbey Farm, Risley by the then Lancaster University Archaeological Unit (Heawood 1999). The manor of Culcheth was divided into four at the death of Gilbert de Culcheth in 1246, leading to the establishment of several new manorial sites, including this one, which was clearly part of a dispersed settlement pattern in an assarting landscape. An aisled hall was initially built on padstones on a moated platform in the period 1246–1315, which was eventually replaced by a fully framed aisle-less structure built on sill beams. A timber bridge was constructed in the mid-fifteenth century across the moat, but this may merely have replaced an existing structure.

Moats performed more than a single function. In some instances they might be dug to protect hay yards or orchards. It has been suggested as a result of trial excavation that the moat at St Michael's House, Micklehead Green (Merseyside) was a landscape feature, constructed no earlier than the sixteenth century (Hollos 1987), and the example at Grafton (Cheshire) appears similarly to derive from landscaping, probably from the early seventeenth century. However, most surrounded, or partially surrounded, buildings of comparatively high status. On organic or clay soils, where drainage of the house platform might be a problem, they provided a well-drained base, sometimes with runoff enhanced by cut channels (Wilson 1983). They offered a built-in stew for fish farming and a fire break in case of accident. More significant, they provided a degree of protection from wild animals and from crime of the type that was so commonly recorded in contemporary court records involving breaking and entering, assault and robbery. To be able to equip a house with such a defence was a considerable status symbol and many were probably dug primarily for this purpose, particularly by families of rising fortune who believed themselves to be making enemies (e.g. Harrop 1983). It is worth noting that regions that enjoyed a particular notoriety for riots and local feuding were unusually well provided with moated sites. Such is the case, for example, in the Wigan area, where a particularly virulent series of feuds were fought out by rival groups of the local gentry in the early fourteenth century (see below and Tupling 1949). Elsewhere, fashion and consciousness of status were arguably of greater significance as motives.

Both the needs of security and the competition for high status encouraged the construction of gatehouses to protect the passage across the moat. These could be substantial structures in the late medieval period. Few medieval examples survive, being largely timber-built. A stone bridge still crosses the moat around the building platform at Peel Hall (Wythenshawe) and gatehouses exist at Wardley Hall and at the monastic grange of Saighton but the entrance arrangement at sites like Little Moreton Hall have been extensively altered or replaced since the fifteenth century. Bradley, in the late fifteenth century was described as (William Beaumont, quoted by Angus-Butterworth 1977):

> a new hall with three new chambers and a fair dining room, with a new kitchen, bakehouse and brewhouse, and also with a new tower built of stone with turrets, and a fair gateway, and above it a stone bastille well defended, with a fair chapel, ... all premises aforesaid, with the different houses, are surrounded by a moat with a drawbridge ...

By the mid-thirteenth century, some at least of the local aristocracy were abandoning their hereditary castles in favour of moated sites. Such would seem to be the origin of Bewsey Old Hall, from which excavation has retrieved pottery from *c.*1260 onwards, although the stratification is poor. Ightenhill and Frodsham moats belong to a similar context, both having been manor houses at the centre of major aristocratic or royal estates.

As habitual employers of masons, it is unsurprising that the monks of St Werburgh's Abbey built in stone even when constructing secular categories of building from the twelfth century onwards, both at Chester and on their principal manors. The guest house of the Abbey represents a twelfth century building of domestic style, incorporated into the monastic plan. It had a first floor hall (of the type becoming common in castles at this date) constructed over vaulted cellarage in four double bays, with a further three beneath the great chamber (Wood 1965). Outside Chester, their masonry is now only represented by the fifteenth-century gatehouse of Saighton manor and the more substantial remains of Ince manor (Figure 56), on a small sandstone outcrop on the Mersey marshes (Thompson 1983). Here there survives, in near ruinous condition, within a courtyard which was in part defined by a rock-cut, dry moat, a pair of buildings set at right angles, one of which is an open hall, *c.* 15.8 m by 6.4 m. A passage runs the length of the building within the inner wall, which used to provide access to a solar at the upper end. Stonework from several periods survives but the structural evidence is consistent with a primary building date in the late thirteenth or early fourteenth centuries. The second range of buildings was constructed in the fourteenth century as lodgings, with four separate chambers, in a style which can be compared to monastic lodgings at Dartington, or contemporary colleges at Oxford and Cambridge. These buildings were intended to house members of the Abbey when on business at the manor but they or their immediate predecessors were also deemed fit for the entertainment of the great – Edward I was accommodated at Ince in 1277.

FIGURE 56.
Ince (Cheshire): the stone buildings at the core of a grange of St Werburgh's Abbey in the thirteenth and fourteenth century. The site was originally moated.

Masons were little used by other patrons below the rank of the comital or baronial aristocracy. The residence of the foresters of Delamere was built on behalf of the prince in 1351. Archaeological evidence has been uncovered of successive rebuilding in stone thereafter by the Done family (Varley 1950) but most of their contemporaries lacked the resources or the motivation to make more than a minor use of masoned stone in their own residences. Timber building traditions were to remain the norm in the region up to the mid-Tudor period and the 'Great Rebuilding' reached the North West significantly later than the south and east of England.

# CHAPTER 6

# Boroughs, Markets and Fairs

Among the general run of medieval settlements, only a minority developed urban characteristics. There is, however, considerable ambiguity concerning recognition of a particular place as a rural settlement or a town. In some senses, all towns operated as villages, having field systems, for example, and livestock, and inhabitants who made their living from farming. Rather fewer villages, however, were in any sense towns. There have been two types of definition used to distinguish the town: in the early twentieth century, the institutional definition was prioritised, seeing the town as a place which had received a charter and was therefore a borough (e.g. Tait 1936; Beresford and Finberg 1973), but this has proved too legalistic to encompass the breadth of more recent debate. Scholars today generally prefer a broader definition which rests on socio-economic characteristics, giving consideration to the proportion of non-agricultural occupations, dependence on foodstuffs produced elsewhere and the sense in which communities thought of themselves, and were thought of by others, as different to the general run of rural settlements (Reynolds 1992, followed by Palliser 2000). This rather more elastic definition enables towns of many different types, in legal terms, to be considered together as a single category of settlement, which is easily justified when particular examples of chartered and non-chartered urban settlements are compared (e.g. Rigby 1984). There remains, however, a grey area at the bottom end where some settlements could be termed either a village with a market, for example, or some other urban characteristic, or a small market town. Medieval language does not help us here, since the terms vill and town were interchangeable, both being used for a settlement or township.

There were significant numbers of towns established in the region in the Middle Ages (Figure 57), but urbanisation came very late to the North West by comparison with other regions of England. This corner of the country can lay claim to no proto-urban communities in late prehistory, such as Hengistbury Head, for example, in Dorset, and maps of Roman towns leave the whole north-western region a blank (as Wacher 1995). Only Meols, at the northern end of the Wirral peninsula, developed as a beach head site in prehistory, which then functioned at least intermittently through the Middle Ages. Our understanding of this site has been adversely affected by changes in the topography of the beach itself since the Middle Ages and derives very largely from nineteenth-century collections of artefacts (Hume 1863), although new research on this important locality is now in process.

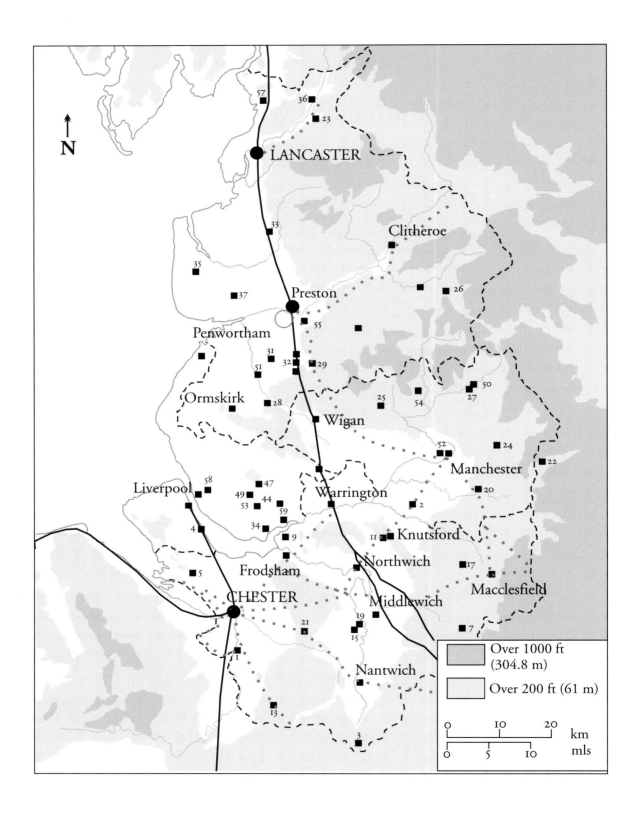

N

LANCASTER

57

36
23

Clitheroe

33

35

37

26

Preston
55

Penwortham

31
51 32
29

Ormskirk
28

25
54

27 50

Wigan

Liverpool 58
47
49 44
53

52

Manchester
24

22

Warrington

59
34

20

9

2

4

11
Knutsford

5

Northwich

17

Frodsham

CHESTER

Middlewich

Macclesfield

1

21

19
15

7

1

Nantwich

13

3

| | Over 1000 ft (304.8 m) |
| | Over 200 ft (61 m) |

0        10        20      km
0        5        10       mls

The first tentative rebirth of urban life in England occurred in the mid-Anglo-Saxon period, when particular locations developed as the foci of tribute collection and social and ritual gatherings connected with the exercise of royal and priestly power. While this was largely a rural phenomenon, the Rome-centric church of the Anglo-Saxons tended to reclaim old Roman sites, such as towns and forts, perhaps largely for symbolic reasons.

Thinking of this type may have brought about the initial reoccupation of Chester, where Roman remains must have been very visible in the seventh century. Chester was possibly already a Mercian monastic site before the Viking Age (Thacker 1982, 1985), but the British synod which occurred there or thereabouts *c.* 600 might alternatively indicate that pre-existing British cult was present at the same site, which could have had its roots in the Roman period. Very little 'Anglian' (pre-Viking Anglo-Saxon) archaeology has been uncovered there, and to date Chester has failed to produce evidence for pre-Viking defences such as have been found at Hereford. The ecclesiastical development of earlier Roman sites occurred at Lancaster, which, on the evidence of surviving sculpture, was probably a pre-Viking monastery (Shotter and White 1980), and Farndon, where an early church was established at the eastern end of a bridging point of the Dee which was well-used in the Roman period. Other pre-Viking churches or monasteries in the region, like Halton (Lancashire), Heysham and Sandbach, were, however, without Roman connections, and never developed urban characteristics within the Middle Ages.

## Chester

Chester's re-foundation in 907 by King Alfred's daughter, Æthelflæd, lady of the Mercians, signals the arrival of royal interest in defended sites in the region. At over 60 acres, the site was among the largest in the country (London excepted) and was clearly intended to act as a major regional centre. How urban it was, however, is open to question. Redevelopment during the tenth century occurred both inside and outside the walls, where leather working has been identified: the old fortress seems to have been occupied primarily by a new minster (St Werburgh's) plus the king's moneyers, although the mint is as yet unidentified. The new urban community probably consisted primarily of their dependants and the few artisans and traders necessary to supply an elite market (see Fleming 1993 for parallels). It is as a mint site that Chester seems to have been most successful. Some 1,550 coins survive from the period 973–1066, making it in this respect the sixth most productive mint in England, albeit London's output was ten times, and York's perhaps three times, greater (Hill 1981).

In some senses, Chester benefited from the Viking Age, which brought it important trading connections with Dublin (Wallace 1986) and York as part of the wider increase in mercantile activity which characterised northern and particularly eastern England. This did not, however, make much impact on the immediate locality. The lesser *burhs* founded by Æthelflæd and then her brother Edward the Elder, at Runcorn, Eddisbury, Thelwall and Manchester, were small forts which do not seem to have developed economically, although coin and other finds from the vicinity of Manchester's Roman fort may indicate some trading there. The proliferation of minor mints in southern England in the early eleventh century is generally interpreted as evidence for local markets. Such did not occur in the North West, or the North more generally, where minting remained the preserve of a very few major sites.

Chester does not, therefore, seem to have been at the apex of a regional pyramid of local markets, but a rather isolated oasis of urbanity and commercialism in a region which was otherwise even more rural in character than most. Its success depended in part on its role as a defended centre of government (a shire *burh*), in part on its role as a port. However, the latter role was probably in decline by the late tenth century. The arrival of a 'northern raiding ship army' in 980, as recorded by the *Anglo-Saxon Chronicle*, perhaps signalled the weakness of English authority in the northern reaches of the Irish Sea. Chester's extra-mural suburb was abandoned at about the same time, perhaps

FIGURE 58.
Chester and the Dee: the riverside city was the principal port of the region, despite the silting which affected the ability of ships to reach the walls in the later Middle Ages. Watergate Street is clearly visible on the right.

as a direct consequence, and the mint evidence suggests that south-western towns, such as Bristol and Exeter, were challenging the control of the Irish trade which Chester's ship-owners had earlier developed.

Chester seems to have shared in the general growth of urban communities which characterised the last three quarters of a century of Anglo-Saxon England, but it remained geographically on the very edge of that phenomenon. At Domesday, within the North West, Chester was by far the most significant town, termed a *civitas*. Otherwise, Penwortham had a mere six burgesses, which were even outnumbered by the manorial community attached to the lordship. No other centre was explicitly a town. Throughout the whole region, therefore, at the Conquest only at Chester was there a community that can be described as urban on socio-economic grounds, focused on its command of the lower estuary of the Dee and its port facilities (Figure 58).

Chester was a port of some consequence, providing by far the most important outlet to the Irish Sea for the English Midlands and the North West. As such, it acted as an entrepôt between the relatively sophisticated, English manufacturing economy and the suppliers of raw materials via sea traffic from the west. Regular trade links existed with Ireland and along other coasts of the Irish Sea. Among the products being traded in its markets in 1086 were marten skins. Although some may have derived from the region, this was probably indicative of an inflow to Chester from the so-called 'Celtic Fringe' of a wide range of animal-derived resources, including pelts, hides, horn and furs. As late as the mid-thirteenth century, an anonymous list of places and their associations, written probably by a merchant, was still to link Chester with the fur trade. However, Lucian, describing Chester in the late twelfth century, emphasised the maritime links with Aquitaine, Spain and Germany, as well as Ireland (Taylor ed. 1912). Such long distance trade required mercantile specialists who, in turn, employed servants, labourers, craftsmen and artisans, whose needs encouraged the growth of an urban market for more local, rural products such as grain and fish. Local industries certainly included the working of horn, antler and bone (McPeake *et al.* 1980).

The Domesday Survey of Chester recorded the presence in 1066 of 487 houses, including those in the bishop's borough, but this total had declined by 205 houses by 1086, presumably both as a direct and indirect result of King William's attentions in 1070. The city was of sufficient importance to have the permanent presence of reeves and officials of the earl and the crown, a mint, which, at Domesday, had seven moneyers, and a separate legal system, with 12 judges and doomsmen. The Conquest led to a strengthening of its governmental role, with the building of a castle (of which only 11 occur on urban sites in Domesday Book), at which the new Norman earldom was based. Additionally, William relocated the see of Lichfield to Chester, to St John's. There was, therefore, an exceptional concentration of elite households at Chester at this date, which will have encouraged others to both congregate and seek opportunities there.

The area occupied by the eleventh-century urban community was larger than that of the legionary fortress. On account of a shift in the course of the river, harbour facilities had been developed at the southern extremity of the site and it was here that traders and merchants were concentrated (Mason 1976). The distribution of housing in 1086 cannot be reconstructed but it is difficult to justify the decision to build St John's outside the walls if space was easily available within. It may be that the *burh* defences had already encompassed the port area (Dodgson 1968; Alldridge 1981). Whether or not, the walls constructed in the late twelfth or early thirteenth centuries were to do so. Observation and small-scale excavation has enabled parts of the now-demolished wall line on the south and west sides to be identified and its course verified (Ward 1985). Behind the wall, deposits of archaeological material lie up to six metres deep, including the Roman levels. The Roman fortress and its gates dictated the overall layout of the main streets, parts at least of which seem to have been laid out in the pre-Conquest period (Ward 2001). The remainder were established by the thirteenth century, forming the grid recognisable from the earliest map evidence. Watergate Street was at this stage the principal thoroughfare linking the core of the city with the wharf. Densely packed, timber-framed and thatched town houses, warehouses and other buildings in this area were particularly prone to the risk of fires, and major outbreaks devastated the commercial sector in 1140, 1180 and 1278 (Christie 1887). It is, however, worth noting that none of these incidents has yet been positively identified archaeologically.

In the late thirteenth and early fourteenth centuries major rebuilding occurred, elements of which have survived to adorn the modern city. It is unclear whether or not this was in response to the last of the great fires, since some rebuilding probably preceded it while other elements arguably post-dated it by half a century. The galleried system of two-tier retailing reflects a common style of split-level townhouse which was widespread nationally by 1200, continuing to be built up to the mid-fourteenth century (Brown 1999). The unique survival of the 'Rows' from this period is sufficient to earn for Chester the accolade for the best surviving group of medieval town houses in Britain (Ward 1984), even though medieval fabric is largely concealed by later work. Needless to say, these have not always been seen as an asset. After he had viewed them, Defoe (1725) suggested that 'they make the city look both old and ugly ... they make the shops themselves dark, and the way in them is dark, dirty and uneven'.

The shops to which he took exception are those two-level examples in the town centre, concentrated on Eastgate Street, Bridge Street and Watergate Street, which are constructed above vaulted basements or cellars, which, on stylistic and other grounds, can be dated to the half century around 1300 (Figure 59).

These were built in the common West European tradition of the raised hall and the Chester cellars represent the undercrofts of such buildings. They were constructed in stone as the lower floors of merchants' houses, serving variously

FIGURE 59.
Eastgate Street,
Chester, from the air.
Note the density of
roadside building,
much of which dates to
the Middle Ages, with
long burgage plots
behind.

as workrooms, shops or storage. Numerous examples have now been identified as a consequence of a major research project (Brown 1999), of which the more elaborate, like that beneath Number 11 Watergate Street, are divided into two aisles by, in this case, a row of octagonal columns.

An opportunity to examine one of these structures in detail presented itself in the case of Number 12 Watergate Street before and during demolition (Ward 1984). Sandstone walls at right angles to the street enclosed a simple undercroft of the late thirteenth century, or slightly before, on a road alignment onto which later rebuilding has encroached. It may have supported a first floor hall with chambers on two floors behind. In the rear yard, a substantial pit indicated occupation at least half a century before the fire of 1278.

Above basement level, many of these structures have been substantially remodelled or clad in stone and brick. However, numbers 48–50 Bridge Street were, several decades ago, recognised as surviving examples of medieval, stone town houses and a programme was established to examine in detail all standing remains. This has led to the recognition of several further examples, such as Numbers 38, 40 and 42 Watergate Street (Figure 60).

Here, behind the seventeenth-century façade, a medieval town house has been identified of double-range plan, built across three burgage plots on an 18 m long street frontage and parallel to the road (Brown *et al.* 1986). A 9.6 m × 7.2 m great hall occupies most of the space, which is at the front at row level but at the rear at ground level. The discrepancy between ground levels at front and rear may be due to the pre-existing accumulation of Roman building debris, which was never consistently removed by later occupants. The

FIGURE 60.
Numbers 38, 40 and 42 Watergate Street: a cutaway deconstruction of a late medieval town house.
RICK TURNER

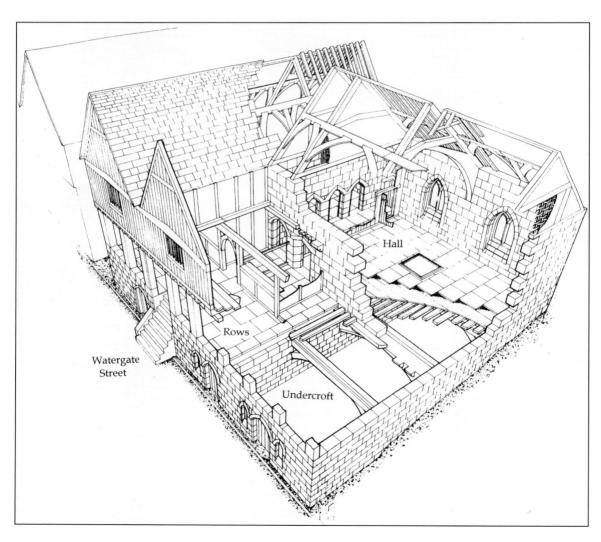

FIGURE 61.
Leche House, measured
three-dimensional
cutaway drawing of a
Chester townhouse.

RICK TURNER

substantial joists suggest that the original floor would have been stone flags, on which would have rested a central, open hearth. At the front of the hall was located a small shop opening onto the row. Dendochronological dating of structural timbers was consistent with a building date of *c.*1325.

The scale of this building, the stonewalling and the use of three adjacent plots imply that whoever commissioned its construction was a man of substance, be he a merchant, a manufacturer or a Cheshire manorial landlord. Henceforth he could expect an income from the rent of six shops and to this extent the building represents a business venture, but its residential purpose dominated its design and structure. Detailed survey work has continued to reveal fresh examples of medieval fabric, such as Leche House (17 Watergate St), where the original undercroft of good quality ashlar sandstone measures 14.6 m by 5.8 m internally and was erected in the late fourteenth century.

Moulded timber from the original street frontage survives with indications of close-studding and the original central doorway (Figure 61). The upper storeys consist of a late fifteenth-century timber-framed house.

Chester was represented on the Gough Map by a high and crenellated stone wall surrounding dense housing and the towering church steeple of St Werburgh's. The medieval walls were a powerful symbol of its primacy, providing security against attack but also serving to advertise the power and prestige of the community and so promote its markets. In 1322, a mason called John of Helpstone contracted with the city authorities to construct a spur to the circuit of the walls to give added protection to the old harbour area on the west of the city (Ward 1985; Thacker 2000). At the western end he built the Water Tower, which is externally cylindrical but internally octagonal, with parallels at Conway and Rhuddlan, which may have been the prototypes. This added defence was the response of a successful and wealthy commercial community, made anxious by the hostile activity of Scottish fleets in the northern reaches of the Irish Sea during the decade following the disaster of Bannockburn. Wealthy the leaders of this community certainly were. The high-medieval, urban elite included such families as the Doncasters, engaged in the wine trade with Gascony, the wool trade with Flanders via Ipswich, corn shipments from Ireland, minerals from North Wales, customs farming throughout the North West and land ownership in Rhuddlan and elsewhere. The Doncasters resided in Watergate Street and had shops in Bridge Street. In the fourteenth century, the family had more servants than most members of the local aristocracy (Hopkins 1950).

Trading interests linked members of this community via coastal and river craft with Runcorn, Frodsham and Middlewich, via sea-going ships to Dublin and the new walled towns of North Wales and by horse and/or wagon into the west, east and south Midlands. The urban community drew for its necessities not only on the Cheshire hinterland, but also on corn and cloth from Ireland, corn from England and fish (herrings, salmon, ray, oysters, whelks and eels) from the neighbouring rivers, coasts and estuaries. By the fourteenth century, slates from quarries in Wales were in use in roofing the city, replacing the more hazardous thatch and shingles, which had hitherto abetted the risk of fire (Jope and Dunning 1954). As surnames developed in the thirteenth and fourteenth centuries, some Chester families or individuals were distinguishable by their place of origin. Recorded examples included Ireland, Dublin, the Midlands and many nearer places. After *c.* 1300, surnames derived from Welsh place-names became increasingly common.

Within the city there developed a complex community, operating within a highly differentiated economy, lubricated by the ready use of money in most transactions. Occupations typical of seafaring employment augmented those of a trading and artisan community to produce a bewildering variety that took in the full gamut from the medical professions to entertainers and retailers (for parallels, see Dyer 2002). As was normal in such communities, particular trades concentrated in sectors, resulting in frequent references in the rolls of the City Courts to Ironmongers' Row, Baxster Row and Cooks Row. More widespread was the production of ale, which was a female-dominated industry catering for local consumption and the regular influxes of incomers attending the bi-weekly markets and bi-annual fairs (Laughton 1995).

Chester had a unique position among English provincial towns, which provided an extra stimulus to the urban economy. The authority of the earls was exercised on a wider and more exclusive scale than that of any other twelfth- or early thirteenth-century magnate and Chester was their regional capital, as well as being a major port and shire town. The principal castle of the earl lay on the edge of the town, dominating the crucial port area and access up-river. Although the earls were themselves only occasionally resident, they brought with them a vast retinue of servants, adherents and guests whose needs can only have stimulated the urban economy. Even in their absence, the town was the focus of the earldom for judicial and social purposes, and his functions exercised through lieutenants. Those seeking justice from outside the immediate environs must perforce have sought lodgings in the town. Those acting as officers of the administration or who were drawn for social reasons to this the principal centre of local society brought to the town the profits of their rural holdings and spent them there on buildings, lodgings and consumption of many kinds. A substantial impetus to the commercial success of Chester derived from growing royal interest in the facilities it could offer. This process was initiated by Henry II, who campaigned against the northern Welsh from Chester, then accelerated as a result of the interest of Prince John (subsequently King John) in Ireland. In 1195, 200 'great men' were said to have assembled in the city to take ship to Ireland, and the prince himself arrived intending to take ship later in the same year (Christie 1887). Although we should not take too much notice of the figures offered by the author of the *Annales Cestriensis*, it is clear that direct royal control of Cheshire, after the death of Earl John in 1237, brought King Henry III to the city on several occasions. His son and other lieutenants, with their retainers, came frequently with armies for the wars in Wales (in 1245, 1256, 1257, 1277). The subsequent consolidation of the Welsh conquest between 1282 and *c*. 1310 led to a massive building programme in the newly founded boroughs and castles beyond the Dee, the labour and materials for which were concentrated at, and managed from, Chester.

With this level of governmental activity, it is not surprising that the late thirteenth and early fourteenth centuries should have been one of the most successful periods for the mercantile community, providing them with access to the capital and artisans to rebuild major parts of the city. It is unlikely to be coincidence that the abbey of St Werburgh's was able to conduct a major re-building programme, from which are extant the choir (Jansen 2000) and the Lady Chapel of the present day cathedral (Maddison 2000), along with the refectory with its surviving stone pulpit of *c*.1280. A new chancel was added to the church over the next 2 decades and, by 1340, the extension of the long, south transept was underway (Crossley 1976).

Despite these stimuli, however, the town of Chester may have expanded relatively little by the early fourteenth century above the population levels already achieved in 1066. Russell (1948) estimated that the urban population in 1348 might be not much in excess of 2,000, in which case there had been no appreciable population growth, and it had declined in relative terms from fourth largest town in England in 1086 to forty-second. However, Russell's figures may err on the side of caution. There are reasons for thinking that the town had exceeded this estimate in the period around 1300. Because it was exempt from national taxation, so was excluded from the poll taxes of the last quarter of the fourteenth century, it is a notoriously difficult town to assess in this respect. However, recent estimates suggest that it might have had something like 1,200 tax payers in 1377, had it been assessed, placing it at around thirty-third in the ranks of English towns, alongside Stamford, Newark and Ludlow (Dyer, A. 2000). There is general agreement that the population stood at around 3,500 throughout the later Middle Ages, so was probably significantly higher in 1300, when the city was arguably of about the same size and general shape as that mapped by John Speed in 1610 (Figure 62).

Although Chester did not experience the growth of some towns in southern England, so probably slipped down national league tables, it still retained its

FIGURE 62.
John Speed's map of Chester in 1610.

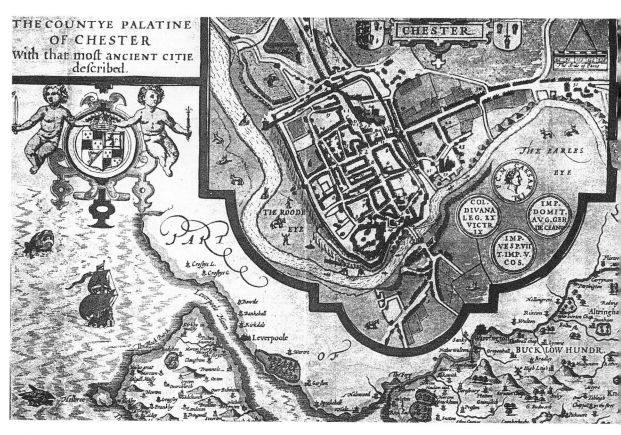

early pre-eminence in the urban hierarchy of the North West. No Lancashire town was assessed at a high enough level at any point during the period 1150–1334 to feature among the hundred most populous urban communities (Dyer, A. 2000). Nor could any other town in the region boast the range of features which Chester enjoyed and which singled it out as a uniquely urban space within the North West. To take churches as an example, by comparison other towns were characteristically late, and had only a single parish church (as Manchester), one which was at a distance but within the township (as Frodsham) or none at all (like Nantwich, or Macclesfield until 1278). By 1300, Chester, in contrast, had nine parish churches. Of these, two had large parishes, those of St John's and St Oswald's, the latter being extended to encompass the local estates of St Werburgh's. St Chad's was certainly already there at Domesday and several of the remainder may already then have been founded, albeit that, of the lesser churches, only St Mary's was well-endowed. The proliferation of churches indicates a local community of exceptional wealth and size, even before 1100, even though the number of foundations was small by southern standards: Winchester, for example, had around 50 churches by 1100. Of course, church institutions were not limited to parochial foundations. A house of Benedictine nuns was founded *c.* 1150, a hospital (the leper asylum of St Giles) in the last decade of the century and houses for each of the four mendicant orders in the course of the thirteenth century. No other town in the region could boast so many. All in all, Chester had a uniquely urban landscape. Comparatively numerous stone churches and several other religious foundations, including a major Benedictine house, were interspersed with large numbers of substantial town houses ranged around densely-occupied streets. Massive stone defences cordoned off the heart of the urban community – and this was the only walled town in the region – but on several sides medieval development spilled out and spread along the roads outside the gates.

### Smaller towns

From the twelfth century onwards, a new impetus to focus central place functions at particular sites encouraged the development of numerous small towns or *bastides* in the region. The key stimuli were often castles, which functioned both as elite residences and as the foci of baronies, so encouraged the congregation of the better-off, in particular, for a variety of social and political purposes. As groups of artisans and traders took root to profit from this concentration of buying power, markets naturally developed. However, these were not the only new towns. Trading settlements developed at route nodes such as major cross-roads and river crossings, at the borders of major lordships and at meeting places between different types of landscape, where one type of surplus could be exchanged for another. This proliferation of towns was part of a very general phenomenon, witnessed elsewhere in England, and also in Wales, with the period from *c.* 1180 to *c.* 1250 experiencing the most rapid urban growth. This expansion brought markets within reach of most peasant farmers within the region (Figure 57), often for the first time, and led to a dramatic expansion of the market economy and commercialisation of society.

To a large extent, the North West reflected the national picture in this broad process of urbanisation but there were some particular local features. For one thing, the baseline for urban development was exceptionally low in the region at the opening of the twelfth century, when Lancashire still had hardly any settlements which warrant the term 'town'. So, too, the economy was markedly devoid of coin use at this date. Although the Domesday Survey was couched in terms of particular values and estimates of income, in practice most transactions in the late eleventh century outside Chester probably involved the giving and receipt of commodities or services without cash changing hands. Another local phenomenon was the presence of salt extraction and particular, proto-urban settlements which had developed or were developing to cater for that industry. These settlements, the *wiches*, are paralleled elsewhere in England, as at Droitwich, but they are unusual and warrant close attention.

## The *wiches*

Despite Oxley's (1982) interpretation of these sites as towns, it is unclear to what extent the salt extraction centres of Nantwich, Northwich and Middlewich should be thought of as urban centres in the eleventh century. Each was a centre of industry, certainly, and complex levies on the removal of salt recorded in Domesday Book hints at substantial traffic in this primary product. Even so, it must be doubted whether or not there was a proliferation of trades, such as mark out an urban community, as opposed to a single industry, at any of these sites. At Nantwich in 1066 an enclosed space contained the eight demesne salthouses of the king and the earl, one attached to Earl Morcar's manor of Acton and an unspecified number owned by men of the district, grouped around a salt-pit (Morgan 1978). The other Domesday sites were probably similar. Salt extraction had presumably occurred in the past at Leftwich, near Northwich, *Chapmonswiche*, near Knutsford, and Wychough and Fulwich near Malpas, but by 1066 had apparently ceased.

The dispersal of the salt from all three sites was subject to tolls overseen by officials who were presumably resident at or close to the site (discussed by Oxley 1982). Current evidence supports no more than the assertion that these sites occupied a proto-urban role, providing local and distant communities, and itinerant traders, with a single commodity. At Middlewich, this role was supplemented by the site acting as the hundredal centre but it was already in decline as a 'central place' by the eleventh century and lost hundredal status in the following centuries to Northwich, where a castle was also built. The latter was treated separately in the Domesday Survey, as regards the dues paid by the proprietors of the salthouses. In addition, it was the very antithesis of a central place in 1086, lying within the *parochia* of Great Budworth, which extended into four Domesday hundreds. Like some other new urban settlements of the Middle Ages (e.g. Stockport, Preston), it lay in a frontier zone between different lordships.

Like Middlewich, Nantwich had associated with it the pleas of the hundred but it was not a parish centre, lying within the *parochia* of Acton, the centre of a substantial, comital estate in 1066. The presence of a manorial hall of considerable size at Acton in 1086 reflected its status as an elite residence in the late Anglo-Saxon period, when it was held by Earl Morcar. The fuel for the boiling of brine in the eleventh century probably came from the substantial woodland resources of his Acton estate (which were six leagues by one league). The economies of *wich* and estate were, therefore, meshed together at this stage. It was only after the Conquest that Nantwich developed as a baronial centre and castle site, in this respect displacing Acton, which remained, however, the parish church to which the *wich* community paid tithes. There was a chapel in the *wich* by 1130, which was progressively rebuilt and enlarged, but the abbey of Combermere's appropriation of Acton church and its dependencies ensured that the borough remained within the parish of Acton throughout the period.

The dislocation that accompanied the Conquest effectively destroyed the pre-existing salt industry. Only a single salthouse was said to have been operative at Nantwich when William Malbank took control. The process of reconstruction had not by 1086 re-established the profitability of the *wiches* to pre-Conquest levels. At this date Nantwich centred upon the district known as Snow Hill (*Snore Hyll*), whence issued the brine spring, adjacent to the market. Its urban characteristics seem to have developed rapidly under the patronage of successive Malbank barons and, after the foundation of Combermere early in the twelfth century, also under the abbot of that house.

Redevelopment within the town has provided opportunities for a programme of archaeological investigation on several sites. The most informative revealed two salt-houses, constructed with stake and wattle walls with limited support of external walls by untrimmed posts set in individual post-pits. One of the houses was short-lived and was demolished but the second example was successively re-equipped until the sixteenth century (McNeil 1983). The latter measured 11.7 m by 7.9 m and was supported by five load-bearing posts down each side in a trapezoidal plan, part of which may have been roofed. Timbers dated by dendrochronology gave estimated felling dates of 1177–1191, substantiating the dating evidence derived from the very large quantities of pottery found on site. The process of salt production was systematic and uniform across several sites and space allocated for specific processes. Brine was brought by wooden pipes across the river into troughs of puddled clay or hollowed-out tree trunks, then boiled in lead pans over open hearths, of which there were six per house. Salt was then dried and stored in separate areas before dispatch. Nantwich prospered and was arguably Cheshire's second urban community around 1500.

Middlewich emerged as an urban community during the thirteenth century, although it remained under the proprietorship of the earls, being leased at farm. In the mid-century, as many as 75 salt-pans were operating, suggesting a total of 12 or 13 salt-houses. A market was established in 1260 and a charter had probably been granted before 1288, the same year from which a borough can be traced at Northwich (Beresford and Finberg 1973). References to burgesses occur from the 1280s onwards but they were unable to secure control of the *wich* against the interests of numerous religious houses and the local aristocracy (Thompson 1981a). The core of the medieval town lay around the church and to the east of it, with the salt industry concentrated at two salt pits, one on each side of the River Weaver. Like those at Nantwich, the buildings were built of wood; a fire caused considerable damage in 1281. A series of small-scale excavations have revealed evidence of timber-framed buildings (e.g. Bestwick 1974).

The medieval history of Northwich closely paralleled that of Middlewich and it was similarly retained as comital demesne throughout the period. The *wich* lay in the chapelry of Witton – literally the 'ton of *wich*'. Proprietorial rights over the manufacturing of salt at this site were in the hands of numerous members of the local aristocracy, most of whom, like the Massey family of Tatton, probably derived their interests by descent or purchase from rights enshrined in Domesday. In 1066, thegns of unspecified number had held salthouses in the *wich*.

It is a feature of all these relatively early Cheshire urban centres so far described that they were constructed on Roman sites, and the Roman road system was clearly influential in their re-development in the central Middle Ages. However, only a minority of the later boroughs of the region were Roman in origin (Lancaster is the obvious example), with others either re-sited close by (as Warrington, Preston and Manchester) or quite distinct from the pattern of Roman settlements. It is to these later sites which we now turn our attention.

## Royal and seigneurial boroughs, markets and fairs

Between *c.* 1180 and the Black Death, numerous commercial privileges were conferred on communities in the North West to encourage the development of trading activity, to the ultimate profit of the manorial lord and the site of his choice. Some at least of these grants were speculative ventures, offered by members of the local elite as incentives to encourage development, on occasion in a defensive move designed to challenge towns founded on neighbouring estates. Others were reactive, conferred on communities which clearly already had urban characteristics. It is this period which witnessed the greatest expansion of market provision in the region. This proliferation of specialist trading communities had its beginnings in the late eleventh century but the evidence flatters only to deceive. Excepting Chester, within the region only Penwortham had burgesses in Domesday Book (see above) and the *wiches* otherwise provide the only plausible candidates as even proto urban centres. Place-names which derive from trade may be significant, such as the several Davenports (of which only one occurs in Domesday as a rural manor near Congleton), Stockport (first recorded in the twelfth century) or *Chapmonswiche* but none is known to have been a town. There is no evidence that the Mersey *burh* sites or the Scandinavian 'moot' sites of Wirral or West Lancashire evolved as commercial centres at this date. Of the latter, only Thingwall in Wirral was listed as a manorial site in Domesday Book. Nor is there much evidence that commerce had managed any significant penetration of the hinterland of the North West. The beach market of Meols seems to have seen some activity during the Viking Age. Otherwise, if local markets occurred within this context, they should probably be identified with those centres which emerged as significant estate, parish and governmental centres in Domesday – the hundredal centres of Lancashire and the great estate foci south of the Mersey. The urban population of Lancashire seems, therefore, to have been a mere 30 or so individuals, with Cheshire, excluding Chester, not much higher.

It was upon this unpromising base that the Norman aristocracy began to promote urban development, spurred on by the need to maximise revenues from estates that were initially of little more than potential value. The powerful demographic expansion which coincided with their efforts provided circumstances in which many such centres could survive and even develop, and the new towns in turn provided the market facilities which facilitated the commercialisation of the economy, here as elsewhere in England, which further encouraged population increase by encouraging economic specialisation and so raising productivity. The spread of new towns and the associated growth in the size of the urban population probably shadowed the wider demographic expansion which was occurring, with all three reaching a peak around 1300. Nationally, the urban share of the overall population increased between 1086 and 1300, rising from approximately ten per cent to something like 15–20 per cent (Palliser 2000). Given the small size of the total population of the region, an increase in the proportion seems unlikely, given that Chester's population (*c.* 2,400) may have been around 20 per cent of the total in 1086. There was, however, a substantial rise in the total urban population of the region by 1300. If it conformed to the national norm, as seems quite possible, it will then have been something around 20,000–30,000. This statistic has no specific validity but it does reflect the probable rate of increase and provides an illustration of the greater complexity of the economy and its enhanced dependence on exchange mechanisms and occupational specialisation by 1300.

New foundations were often dictated by landed proprietors with specific aims in mind and able, in many instances, to offer local commercial privileges such as freedom from tolls on their own estates (cf. the situation in Derbyshire; Coates 1965). The ultimate success of the site depended on more fundamental factors. There was a clear link between commercial viability and the site chosen. Major river crossings, road intersections and ports provided the best chance of success, with even pairs of towns succeeding, such as Manchester and Salford, one on each side of a major bridging point, where two major lordships met. Where the route was less well-used, such competing foundations struggled and one often failed, as Knutsford Booths, by Knutsford, both of which received charters in the same year from competing landowners. So too did early foundation matter, since established markets had advantages over those attempting to establish themselves, which generally needed real advantages in other respects to make much headway. While Preston successfully supplanted Penwortham, Walton le Dale, established on the opposite side of the Ribble from Preston over a century later never flourished. The local practice of using tidal routeways across estuarine sands probably stimulated the growth of such sites as Bolton-le-Sands and Grange-over-Sands, on Morecambe Bay, but neither these nor such hamlets as Hillam, from where another route crossed the Cocker estuary, ever attained urban status. Other relevant factors were the capacity of the local agrarian community to respond to market stimulus and generate a surplus and the extent to which the chosen site had other central place characteristics – as a centre for estate administration, baronial or hundredal government or parochial organisation. The changing status of the *wiches* has already been noted in this respect. Other sites were less exclusively tied to a specific resource and were prone to suffer from the competition of neighbouring communities with similar privileges as these proliferated in the thirteenth century.

A minority of sites were established in estuarine locations and were intended *a priori* to offer port facilities. This was the case at Lancaster, where the town developed below the Norman castle and church. By the late twelfth century its local pre-eminence as a port can have been in no doubt. Even so, the grant of borough status made by John as Count of Mortain in 1193 does look very speculative and was presumably intended to further stimulate urban development. It conferred on the community the customs enjoyed by Bristol – the premier port of the west coast and by this date a major English town. The royal charter that followed upon John's subsequent ascent to the throne substituted the customs of Northampton. Around 1300, Lancaster probably differed little in size and layout to the settlement mapped by John Speed in 1610 (Figure 63).

The earliest borough in the North West was probably the six burgesses at Penwortham, noted in Domesday Book, on the south bank of the Ribble, downstream from Preston. The site enjoyed a high pre-Conquest status as a royal manor but it is unclear whether or not it should be considered a *burh* in the late Anglo-Saxon period. As the status of the castle and lordship declined in the twelfth century, however, the physical disadvantages of a site without good natural port facilities and set away from the Roman road system from the Mersey crossings up towards Lancaster (the modern A6) told against its success. Preston emerged, initially as a rival and ultimately as successor, with a royal charter based on that of Newcastle-under-Lyme granted in 1179.

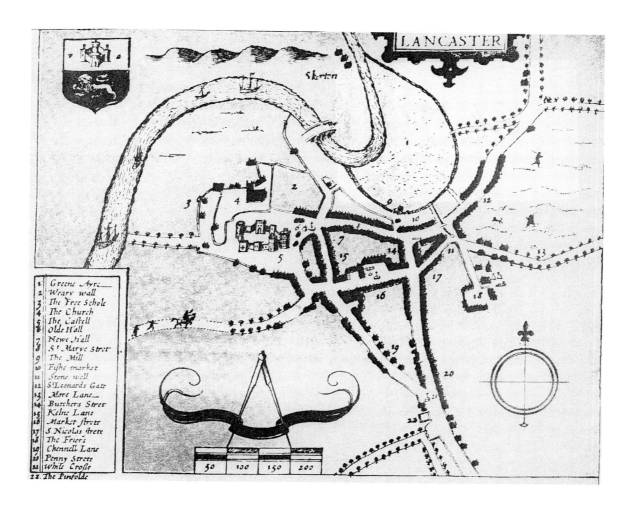

Key on map:

1. Greene Ayre
2. Weary wall
3. The Free Schole
4. The Church
5. The Castell
6. Olde Hall
7. Newe Hall
8. St Marye Stret
9. The Mill
10. Fish market
11. Stone well
12. St Leonards Gate
13. More Lane
14. Butchers Stret
15. Kelne Lane
16. Market Strete
17. S Nicolas Strete
18. The Friers
19. Chennell Lane
20. Penny Strete
21. White Crosse
22. The Pinfolde

FIGURE 63.
John Speed's map of
Lancaster in 1610.

Access to the Roman road system and to coastal trade created circumstances in which the borough of Frodsham flourished in the late thirteenth century. A two-row town on the site of the modern high street received several grants of commercial and judicial privileges in the early thirteenth century from Ranulph de Blundeville but the haven for ships lay about a half mile distant on the lower Weaver. The combination of seigneurial control, the presence of the Chester to Warrington road and the poorly drained nature of the banks of the Weaver in this vicinity seem to have been sufficient to discourage settlement drift to the area of the haven. The borough was complimented by a comital castle or fortified manor house but the parish church remained outside on higher ground, at Overton, which was probably the earlier centre of both parish and estate.

By far the most important of these new ports was Liverpool. Created on a green field site with no existing, central place functions, Liverpool was a new town planned in 1207 by King John, beside his new castle there (Figure 23). It was intended to serve as a port to give the king access to his interests in

183

Ireland. The castle was completed by 1235 and the borough probably recruited a new urban population particularly freely at an early stage – the attitude of Henry III's regime to the community was markedly less paternalistic when he conferred a second charter in 1229. The initial layout centred on three roads forming an 'H' plan, which probably changed little until the seventeenth century. A ferry connected the new port with the Wirral peninsula at Birkenhead but control of this had to be shared with Birkenhead Priory. All indications point to Liverpool remaining subordinate to Chester as a port throughout the Middle Ages (Jarvis 1950). In Liverpool, as in all the lesser urban centres of the region, a substantial proportion of the urban population retained interests in local agriculture. Even so, numerous trades were evidenced in the surnames of both Liverpool and its less successful precursor at West Derby, from which many may have migrated to the new site in the early thirteenth century.

While towns which were certainly planted, such as Liverpool, are in a small minority, others display a degree of regularity of plan and a close reliance on lordship that suggests something similar. So, for example, at Clitheroe, the medieval layout centred on Castle Street, running east from the castle, plus Castle Gate and Wellgate at opposite ends (Plate 11), and seems to have been laid out on a previously unoccupied site. However, most communities developed at existing settlements, in part by a process of 'organic' growth, in part under the active encouragement of self-interested landlords. 'Organic' towns developed where routes intersected, at river crossings and at other sites where local people met travellers from a distance. At many, the grant of borough privileges post-dated the acquisition of some, at least, of the functions of an urban centre, as arguably occurred at the *wiches*, at Macclesfield and Preston, and possibly at Frodsham. Similar circumstances encouraged the growth of a series of communities along the old Roman roads south of Preston, as at Wigan (charter dated 1246), where roads from the south and from Liverpool converged to cross the River Douglas, and at Warrington (earliest charter by 1176; Carter 1953) where the Roman road crossed the Mersey. In the far north, the great parochial centre at Warton developed urban characteristics during the later Middle Ages but it was described by Leland (IV, 1964, 11) in the 1530s as 'a preati streat for a village'.

South of the Mersey, Stockport, with a name derivative of trade, emerged as a small urban site located between a minor baronial castle and church, on the valley edge, and a major ford (later, an important bridge) across the Mersey, on the main road from Manchester to the Midlands and London (charter 1260). Similarly, sites such as Malpas – the mid-point between Whitchurch and Holt – had burgages by 1280 (Beresford and Finberg 1973), grouped around the castle and church sites, and the regularity of the layout may imply a planned town. Macclesfield grew up outside the earl's castle at a major route meeting point, based on Jordangate, Chestergate and Wallgate (Tonkinson 1999, 11), which betray a degree of regularity and a hint of planning. Altrincham, mid-way along the Roman road between Northwich and

Manchester, was provided with a borough charter in 1290 by the baron of Dunham, and again looks to have been laid out.

Such small boroughs certainly owed more to the income derived from the provision of services to travellers and local farmers coming in to the markets than to manufacturing. The salt trade may have been of particular importance in this respect, generating a flow of packmen and hauliers across Cheshire. However, even the establishment of the basic route network is far from simple (e.g. Hindle 1982). The bare bones of the road network are shown on the Gough Map (Figure 57), which clearly prioritises the Roman road now represented by (from north to south) the A6/A559/A530. However, many more routes existed beyond the Roman system by the thirteenth century, if not before.

Some sites lay at a distance from the major routes and depended heavily on the interest and influence of particular patrons. Halton (Cheshire), for example, lay neither on the Mersey nor on the Chester – Warrington road. Any of Runcorn, Preston-on-the-Hill or Daresbury offered greater commercial attractions but the site was presumably predetermined by the concentration on the hill at Halton of the business of justice and estate management at the centre of the barony. With the disadvantages of this location, it is not surprising that the borough never attained more than very local significance and ultimately failed.

Outside of Chester, and to an extent Nantwich, Middlewich, Lancaster and Preston, the medieval towns of the region have received comparatively little archaeological attention. Massive urban redevelopment in the post-war period has left very little upstanding from the late medieval period, with structures like Staircase House, Stockport, representing tiny numbers of fifteenth- to seventeenth-century houses in a sea of later buildings. In Manchester, wholesale removal and re-erection of the earliest surviving buildings, known as the Shambles, has left them out of context, both archaeologically and topographically.

The use of early map evidence has therefore assumed considerable significance in attempts to illustrate the types of urban settlement present. Early post-medieval evidence exists only for Lancashire and Cheshire (as above). For other, lesser towns, the evidence is generally later, so the degree of alteration potentially much greater, but Kuerden's map of Preston in 1684 and a map of Manchester and Salford made 'about 1650' but not drawn up until 1822 (Figure 64) provide indications of the scale of these centres in the later Middle Ages (Morris 1983). Other examples are generally later, but even so it is often possible to detect the basic topography of the medieval foundation in later cartographic evidence. With the exceptions already made, most were single street settlements dependent either on an elite settlement, a river crossing or a major route intersection, consisting primarily of a few rows of burgage plots, laid out with very varying degrees of regularity and divided in most instances by hedges. Many, like Preston, must have seemed isolated nucleations in a landscape otherwise characterised by dispersed moated sites, farms and

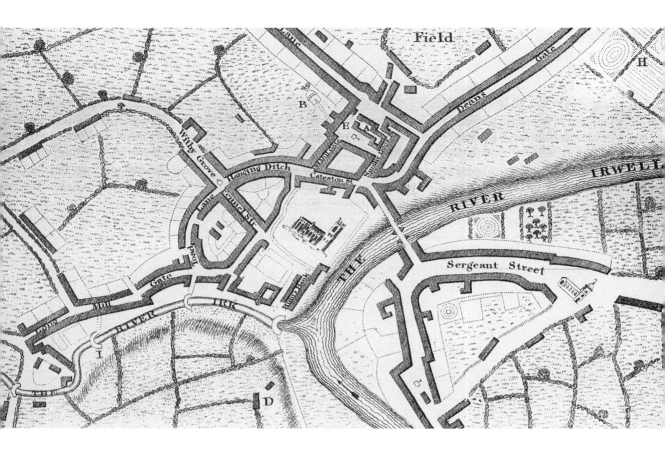

FIGURE 64.
A plan of Manchester
and Salford, supposedly
originally made about
1650 and drawn from
an original in the
possession of William
Yates Esq. by John
Palmer, Architect, in
1822.

hamlets, such as proliferated throughout Fulwood, Ribbleton, Brockholes and Fishwick, with open mosses still interspersed with woods and agricultural land.

By the 1340s, the North West was arguably as well-provided with markets as any other region of England and this despite the slow start in the late pre-Conquest period. It was also despite the comparative poverty of the region as revealed by the low levels of tax assessment in those parts where estimates can be made (Glasscock 1975; illus. Morris 1983). By the Black Death, at least thirty five communities with some of the characteristics of a town had been established in medieval Lancashire south of the Sands, and twenty two in Cheshire. The distribution of those north of the Mersey was heavily influenced by the lines of the A6 and A49, and perhaps also by the presence of an agrarian surplus in parts of the western lowlands. There was also the opportunity to profit from exchange between predominantly agricultural produce in western Lancashire and pastoral in the east. In areas distant from either agricultural surplus or through-routes, boroughs were scarce and the needs of the local community were served by markets established within less urbanised communities. Such predominated on the Fylde and in the uplands of Blackburnshire (Tupling 1933), where the level of exchange was apparently inadequate to support very many specialist communities.

# Table 4. Urban settlements in the North West.

The Gough Map may also have represented and named Bentham, Cockersand Abbey, Burscough Priory, Winwick and (?) Knowsley, none of which displays urban characteristics, but see Higham, M. 1993, for the problems of assignation.

| Name | Urban character from: | Charter date | 11th-century church? | Castle? | Port? | River crossing/major road? | On Gough map? | Survival to 17th century? |
|---|---|---|---|---|---|---|---|---|
| **Pre-1974 Cheshire** | | | | | | | | |
| 1. Aldford | ?12th C. | 1254 | – | y | – | y | – | – |
| 2. Altrincham | 13th C. | c. 1290 | – | – | – | y | – | y |
| 3. Audlem | 13th C. | 1295 | – | – | – | y | – | – |
| 4. Bromborough | ?13th C. | 1278 | y | – | ? | – | – | Replaced by Ellesmere Port |
| 5. Burton | ?13th C. | 1299 | y | – | ? | – | – | – |
| 6. Chester | ?10th C. | Civitas 1086 | several | y | y | y | y | y |
| 7. Congleton | ?13th C. | 1282 | – | – | – | y | – | y |
| 8. Frodsham | ?12th C. | 1208x15 | y | y | y | y | – | y |
| 9. Halton | ?12/13th C. | – | – | y | – | – | – | – |
| 10. Knutsford | 13th C. | 1292 | – | – | – | y | – | y |
| 11. Knutsford Booths | 13th C. | 1292 | – | – | – | – | – | – |
| 12. Macclesfield | ?12th C. | 1237–38 | – | y | – | y | y | y |
| 13. Malpas | ?13th C. | 1281 | y | y | – | y | – | y |
| 14. Middlewich | ?11th C. | – | y | y | – | y | – | y |
| 15. Murifield | 14th C. | By 1319–20 | – | – | – | – | – | Replaced by Winsford |
| 16. Nantwich | ?11th C. | By 1319–20 | – | – | y | y | y | |
| 17. Nether Alderley | 13th C. | 1254 | – | – | – | y | – | – |
| 18. Northwich | ?11th C. | 1288 | – | y | – | y | y | y |
| 19. Over | ?13th C. | 1294x1306 | – | – | – | y | – | Replaced by Winsford |
| 20. Stockport | ?12th C. | c. 1260 | – | y | – | y | – | y |
| 21. Tarporley | ?13th C. | 1282 | – | – | – | y | – | – |
| 22. Tintwistle | 14th C. | 1358–9 | – | – | – | y | – | – |
| **Pre-1974 Lancashire South of the Sands** | | | | | | | | |
| 23. Arkholme | 13th C. | 1279 | – | – | – | – | – | – |
| 24. Ashton u Lyne | 14th C? | ?1413 | ? | – | – | y | – | y |
| 25. Bolton | 13th C. | 1253 | – | – | – | y | – | y |
| 26. Burnley | 13th C. | 1294 | – | – | – | y | – | y |
| 27. Castleton | ?14th C. | 1311 | – | y | – | y | – | Replaced by Rochdale |
| 28. Charnock Richard | 13th C. | 1284 | – | – | – | y | – | – |
| 29. Chorley | 13th C. | By 1257 | – | – | – | y | – | y |
| 30. Clitheroe | ?12th C. | By 1258 | – | y | – | – | y | y |
| 31. Croston | 13th C. | 1283 | – | – | – | – | – | – |
| 32. Euxton | c. 1300 | 1301 | – | – | – | y | – | – |
| 33. Garstang | 14th C. | 1310 | – | – | – | y | – | y |

*Table 4 continued*

| Name | Urban character from: | Charter date | 11th-century church? | Castle? | Port? | River crossing/major road | On Gough map? | Survival to 17th century? |
|------|------|------|------|------|------|------|------|------|
| 34. Hale | 13/14th C. | 1304 | – | – | – | – | – | – |
| 35. Hardhorn | 14th C. | 1348 | – | – | – | – | – | – |
| 36. Hornby | 13th C. | 1285 | – | y | – | y | – | y |
| 37. Kirkham | 13th C. | By 1296 | ? | – | – | – | – | y |
| 38. Lancaster | 12th C. | 1193 | y | y | y | y | y | y |
| 39. Lathom | 14th C. | 1304 | – | – | – | – | – | – |
| 40. Layton | 13th C. | By 1257 | – | – | – | – | – | – |
| 41. Liverpool | 1207 | 1207 | – | y | y | – | y | y |
| 42. Manchester | ?13th C. | 1301 | y | y | – | y | y | y |
| 43. Netherton | 14th C. | 1338 | – | – | – | – | – | – |
| 44. Newton le Willows | 13th C. | 1257 | – | – | – | y | – | y |
| 45. Ormskirk | 13th C. | 1286 | ? | – | – | y | – | y |
| 46. Penwortham | 10/11th C. | Burgesses in 1086 | – | y | ? | – | – | – |
| 47. Prescott | 13/14th C. | 1333 | ? | – | – | ? | y | y |
| 48. Preston | 12th C. | 1179 | y | – | y | y | y | y |
| 49. Roby | 14th C. | 1372 | – | – | – | ? | – | – |
| 50. Rochdale | 13th C. | 1251 | – | nearby | – | y | – | y |
| 51. Rufford | 14th C. | 1339 | – | – | – | y | – | – |
| 52. Salford | 12/13th C. | 1231 | – | – | – | y | – | y |
| 53. Tarbock | 13th C. | 1257 | – | – | – | – | – | – |
| 54. Tottington | 13th C. | – | – | – | – | y | – | – |
| 55. Walton le Dale | 13th C. | 1301 | – | – | ? | y | – | – |
| 56. Warrington | 13th C. | – | y | y | ? | y | y | y |
| 57. Warton | 13th C. | 1246x1271 | – | – | – | – | – | – |
| 58. West Derby | 11/12th C. | – | – | y | – | y | – | Replaced by Liverpool, 1207 |
| 59. Widnes | 14th C. | 1355–6 | – | – | – | y | – | y |
| 60. Wigan | 13th C. | 1246 | – | – | – | y | y | y |

South of the Mersey, no royal boroughs existed because of the exclusive authority of the earls. They appear to have been niggardly in granting to their barons the right to confer borough status on communities which might have competed with their own foundations or with Chester. However, the majority which can be identified were the foundations of members of the Cheshire baronage or senior clerics. Outside the Weaver valley, the incidence of foundations was lower than in the richer parts of Lancashire.

Accurate figures are not available to assess the total urban population at any stage, although, as occurred nationally, it will certainly have risen as a proportion of the whole in most hundreds between 1086 and 1350. The number of tenements can in some instances be calculated from burgage rents. There were, for example, 168 burgages in the borough of Liverpool in 1346, suggesting a population of 650–850. At Manchester in 1282 the burgage rents suggest a total of about 143 burgages, or 550–700 individuals on the assumption that the number of burgages was approximately equivalent to the number of families. In practice, the number of families may have far outnumbered the number of burgages, accommodated by sub-letting and fragmentation, and one recent estimate has suggested that Manchester and other larger chartered towns had populations of 1–3,000 in the mid-thirteenth century. Other borough communities were far smaller. Knutsford had 38 burgages in 1294, for example, and it is unlikely that, excluding Chester, the average can have exceeded between 40 and 80, in which case the burghal population of the region in the 1340s should fall within a very conservative estimate of 12,400–24,800, to which should be added at least 2,000–4,000 to account for Chester. In practice, the total could have been considerably greater than these figures would suggest.

Such figures do not have any absolute credibility. They do, however, illustrate both the increasing commercialisation of the region and the level of population increase which should be anticipated in the period between 1066 and the Black Death. In the decades around 1300 the region was supporting a widespread network of modest seigneurial boroughs, a handful of royal foundations and a single town of national significance. These represent a level of economic activity which, although perhaps still poor by national standards, was significantly upwards in both qualitative as well as quantitative terms, and this had both direct and indirect impacts on the landscape in many ways. The contrast with 1066 or 1086 hardly need be stated.

## Trade

The identification and interpretation of medieval trade patterns requires an unlikely combination – the survival of adequate quantities and types of documentary evidence alongside the investigation and recording of well-stratified archaeological deposits. In practice, the situation in the North West falls far short of the ideal. Before 1350 the documentary evidence for trade is at best anecdotal. The archaeological evidence is dominated by a corpus of sites which are far from being typical either as habitations or as places of consumption. These comprise Chester itself, the *wiches* and a handful of castles and religious houses. In these the likely patterns of trade both within the region and with neighbouring or distant trading partners are only occasionally discernable.

Cheshire salt provided a valuable and exportable product. Salt-ways emanated from the Weaver valley in all directions, taking this local product by pack-horse over the Pennines via Macclesfield and Longdendale, and by the same means, wagons and shoulder-pack across the plain. Salt was probably being shipped out from the ports of north Cheshire throughout the period.

It may have been the local availability of salt which encouraged the export of meat from Cheshire's forests and farms. Perhaps as important to the local economy was the production of leather which again may have been exported to other regions in some quantities even before documentary evidence becomes available from Chester in the fifteenth century. References to shoe-makers are not uncommon even among Lancashire's rural communities. The area is unlikely to have exported significant quantities of grain, despite the high rents derived from the flour mills at Chester and elsewhere. Rather, it seems often to have been a net importer.

The region was arguably, in general terms, an exporter of bulk, low value raw materials to southern England and beyond, and an importer of much smaller quantities of high value, manufactured goods. In this respect at least, the terms of trade are unlikely to have favoured the local community. However, in the Irish Sea trade, this relationship was to an extent reversed, with bulk raw materials entering England via Chester and Liverpool.

Leather goods are only found on excavations in anaerobic conditions. Even then it is impossible to establish a source for the raw materials. To trace trade links, the archaeologist falls back on types of artefact which are both less resistant to ageing processes and easier to trace to a source. By far the most accessible in this context are discarded sherds of pottery. There are, however, major problems inherent in this type of material as a basis for wider interpre-tation of trading partnerships. In a group of sites where castles and monasteries are numerically significant, it is possible that pottery distribution may reflect the behaviour of the secular and religious aristocracy and the origins of their garrisons, rather than trade as such. It may well be that the peregrinations of such as the earl of Chester and his household, for example, around his far-flung estates in Britain and France may have been directly responsible for the arrival of individual vessels in the region.

At the Conquest, the southern half of the region was within a pottery producing and using province, possibly centred in Staffordshire, stretching down the West Midlands and Marches. The product is termed 'Chester Ware' after the hoard pot found on the Castle Esplanade in 1950 (Webster *et al.* 1953) but this should not imply that manufacture was necessarily present in the county. Pottery of this type has been found on several sites within Chester. However, it is rare elsewhere in the region, and so far absent north of Mercia, beyond the Mersey.

The tradition represented by 'Chester Ware' signalled a departure from what had hitherto apparently long been an aceramic society. The diagnostic products were cooking vessels, wheel-thrown in a hard, brown or orange fabric. It has been suggested that this tradition of manufacture continued to produce cooking vessels into the Norman period, with finds for example coming from the Cistercian Grange at Ellesmere Port in a twelfth-century context. The same tradition may be traceable into the thirteenth or even four-teenth centuries (Laing 1977). However, cooking pottery of East Midland origin or style was reaching Chester by the late twelfth century and other

Midland traditions were having an impact by the thirteenth century. Straight-sided pots in sandy grey fabric were deposited by early occupants of the timber phase of the priory at Norton in the mid-twelfth century and these can be paralleled at Chester. By *c.*1250 significant similarities were developing between cooking wares at Chester and those of Ulster.

There is little evidence that twelfth- and even early thirteenth-century pottery reached a significantly wider group of users. Glazed tablewares first made an appearance in the early thirteenth century at the Cistercian Abbey of Valle Crucis (Clwyd: Butler 1976) and the short-lived castles of the period at Dyserth, Deganwy and Rhuddlan have yielded small groups of decorated and glazed jugs and a few cooking vessels (Davey and Rutter 1977). Royal interest in these sites makes them inappropriate examples from which to interpret the dispersal of pottery within the regional community. To emphasise the distinction, it is on these same sites that there have been found the region's earliest examples of wares from Normandy and south-west France, the latter of which mirror the well-known development of Gascon wine imports to England after the loss of Normandy and Anjou. Such may easily have been brought to the castles by individuals from a considerable distance without any local trading taking place.

It was not until the late thirteenth century that there was a marked increase in the quality and range of pottery in use in the region. Much of the evidence for this has come from excavations on the castles of North Wales. Again, these represent an unprecedented intrusion into the region of royal interest and resources. Polychrome and fine, green-glazed vessels from Saintonge in south-west France provided the most successful product at the luxury end of this range of fabrics (Davey and Rutter 1977). Cheaper goods included red wares, much of which probably derived from industries local to Chester. Finds of Saintonge wares in Chester are of a quantity to suggest that that port became one of the principal points of entry into Britain for this luxury product.

Local manufacture in the Chester region appears to have responded to the much improved market opportunities, which developed in the late thirteenth century. With Chester in use as a royal arsenal and entrepôt, local manufacturers took the opportunity to capture a share of the trade into the new, English colonies in Wales. A stone-built, triple flued kiln at Ashton, excavated in 1933 (Newstead 1934), was producing a range of vessels including squat jugs decorated with rouletting, spatula impressions and comb hands in the years around 1300 (Davey 1977). A kiln at Deanery Field, Chester, was in production only slightly later and another kiln has been identified by a pit-group, which included kiln furniture, found at Frodsham Street. A pair of kilns located at Brereton Park, Foulk Stapleford, were arguably in production in the thirteenth century. The Ewloe industry began during the fourteenth century, producing a variety of vessels and ridge tiles, still within the tradition common to the whole West Midlands. Production there was not destined to finish until 1940. Chester deposits bear witness to a veritable explosion in the quantities of pottery being broken and thrown away. Even so, quantities are less than can be identified on comparable sites in the east of England and the number of sources represented is significantly fewer.

Pottery provides some indication of trade links across the Irish Sea. Pottery from the ceramic traditions exemplified at Chester had reached Rathmullen Castle, Co. Down, by the first quarter of the thirteenth century (Hurst 1985). By midway through the century squat jugs made in the Chester area were reaching Dublin. These were characterised by a high degree of decoration, some sporting zoomorphic design. However, local wares were not the only ones reaching Ireland. Ham Green wares made near Bristol have been found in some quantities at Dublin, reflecting the strong links established between these two ports in the late twelfth century. Ham Green wares are no more than marginally represented at Chester. Bristol merchants were the natural competitors of the Chester men and probably generally had the upper hand.

The Irish Sea trading system was not exclusively dependent on English products. Scottish pottery was reaching the Isle of Man in the fourteenth century, probably particularly during the period of Scottish dominance early in the century. It is also worth noting that vessels from south-west France reached Dublin in considerable quantities. They did not, however, penetrate as far as many of the inland sites of the North West. Only trace quantities of imported wares have been identified at Beeston Castle and Nantwich and no imports at all were represented at Bury (Davey 1983).

It was not only the role of Chester in the Welsh wars which provided the stimulus to expand production. Elsewhere in the region, there was an approximately contemporary upturn in the quantity and range of pottery being used. For example, a vigorous local industry developed in the later thirteenth century in the Nantwich region, with kilns at Audlem and probably elsewhere (Roberts 1977) producing part-glazed wares typically with gritty fabrics. Structural fragments of a kiln and wasters have been identified at Eaton-by-Tarporley, in central Cheshire, which would appear to belong to the same period. At Norton Priory the same type of technology was being used to manufacture tiles of a style with parallels in the products from one of the Deanery Field kilns at Chester and from Warrington and Lancaster friaries (Greene and Johnson 1978; Penney 1982). An as yet unidentified kiln was supplying Speke Hall by the late fourteenth century (Higgins 1982). The Butler household at Bewsey Old Hall were buying local wares as well as imports from France from the late thirteenth century (Lewis and Smart 1988); similar wares were being deposited in Wigan by c. 1300.

Such industries were probably typical of a developing local demand, with growth in commerce and industry reflected in, and stimulated by, the growth in population and also of the borough network at precisely this time. All the signs are that the local community was passing across a series of economic thresholds in the late thirteenth century, which encouraged a significant increase in individual specialisation within an increasingly complex and exchange-based economy.

The region lay on the periphery of two traditions of pottery manufacture. In east Cheshire, the West Midlands tradition of manufacture met a rival tradition which was rooted in the West Riding of Yorkshire and which has been dubbed the Pennine gritty wares. Pottery of both types was reaching Tatton in the early fourteenth century, if not before, presumably by way of the new market facilities at Knutsford and Altrincham.

North of the Mersey, the quantity of pottery recovered is small and no tradition of manufacture has been identified which predates the Conquest. The same east–west divide as occurs in Cheshire can be identified in southern Lancashire. Vessels from the ditch silt of West Derby Castle belong to the tradition represented by kilns such as that at Ashton, in the West Midlands tradition (Davey and Rutter 1977). Further east, close to the Pennines at Bury, this tradition was absent and the presumed fourteenth century assemblage was dominated by Pennine gritty wares with no obvious parallels elsewhere (Tyson 1986) and therefore probably of local manufacture.

Beyond the Ribble, kilns have been identified, either archaeologically or from documentary reference at Silverdale, Docker Moor, Caton, Ribbleton, Ellel and Warton. Where pottery has been recovered the affinities are more obviously with the West Riding or the North East of England than with Cheshire (White 1977), while significant quantities have now been recovered from both Preston and Lancaster but not from any other town north of Manchester (McCarthy and Brooks 1988).

These patterns of pottery distribution are coincident with the bi-focal organisation of the region as enshrined in Domesday Book but it is probable that this zonation has as much to do with the cross-Pennine holdings of magnates such as the de Lacy's as with older provincial loyalties.

Pottery was only one minor object of trade within the region, however easily identifiable to the archaeologist. The goods passing over the bridges at Warrington in the early fourteenth century give a more realistic impression of the range of trade that was occurring (Beaumont 1872). Numerous types of sea fish and shellfish contrasted with bacon and a wide range of vegetables and consumables – cheese, butter, lard, wine, cider, honey, grain, barley, onions, etc., and with the pelts of domesticated and wild animals, metal wares, coal, and a variety of cloth. Much suggests local production, including the linen and canvas and the pelts of deer, hares, rabbits, cats and foxes. Other items such as silks, wine and East Anglian worsted were part of a wider network of trading links which connected the region, however indirectly, with the east coast, France and the Mediterranean. It is noticeable that goods of intrinsically high value were almost entirely imported to the region, if not to the country.

### Towns, trade and textiles: 1350–1540

Across the Later Middle Ages, the regional community remained a scattered and predominantly rural one, as might also be said of the population nationally. Despite the rapid growth of the late twelfth and thirteenth centuries, towns of whatever sort had never been more than a small proportion of the total number and range of settlements. The number of urban dwellers had, of course, increased dramatically, but the majority still lived in rural settlements. In most towns, there were fewer than 2,500 inhabitants. The success of particular sites was very variable during the population decline of the later Middle Ages: some successfully replenished their populations by immigration while some declined in size, or reverted to villages or hamlets. In Cheshire, of the 22 urban settlements identified up to the late fourteenth century, half no longer had urban characteristics by the seventeenth century (table 4), although this does include several replaced by neighbouring urban developments. In historic Lancashire, the corresponding figure is 17 out of 38.

Chester was always by far the largest town in the region, but its population and its prosperity seem to have peaked during the reign of Edward I. By the mid-fourteenth century, Chester was exhibiting signs of decline as a port, independent of any share in plague losses. The port was excluded from the legal export of wool to Europe during the century. It was in any case ill placed for such a trade, although wine ships from Gascony might have valued wool as a return cargo. Lancashire wool in 1343 was apportioned to the middle price band, but exports were neither substantial nor carried on local vessels. The Lancashire monasteries (Furness aside) were not among those making substantial contributions to wool exports, although St Werburgh's at Chester did feature consistently.

By the 1320s, many cargoes destined for Chester were being unloaded in the Dee estuary on account of the accumulation of silt higher up the river. Henceforth, vessels could only reach the town with difficulty when tidal conditions were favourable. This impediment probably derived both from re-deposition by coastal currents and from river-borne silt, the two forces coalescing in the estuary to deposit large banks of silt and sand.

The extent to which this process inconvenienced the Chester community is difficult to assess. Small craft were regularly used to carry merchandise from the port to the estuary and the City certainly survived as an entrepôt and continued as the principal maritime outlet for the region. However, by the mid-fifteenth century, ships of sea-going size were unable to approach within 12 miles of the city and the fee farm was progressively reduced from the £100 of Edward I to £20 (Hewitt 1929). North-western trade was increasingly diverted to Yorkshire ports during the latter part of the period.

The assumption of the town's poverty, which lay behind these reductions, may not have been all the citizens claimed. The successful petitions by which the citizens extracted these concessions from the crown each occurred at a time when the king of the day was peculiarly vulnerable (1445, 1484, 1486), and consequently prepared to trade a reduction in tax for support. The successful revival of the wine trade into an out-port of Chester in the period after 1510 seems not to have been seriously inconvenienced by the problems of silting. In consequence, there has been an attempt to explain away the apparent difficulties of the port as opportunistic bargaining with central authority by the urban elite.

It has been suggested that other factors lay behind the apparent decline of Chester in the fifteenth century and that the decline has been exaggerated. It was patently in the interests of the citizens to exaggerate any decline so as to obtain fiscal concessions (Wilson 1965) but it is unlikely that such could be obtained even from an embattled central government except where the case was credible.

That said, the city continued to attract applicants for entry as free-men in undiminished numbers and maintained the municipal buildings without apparent difficulty. However, the rate of ecclesiastical building or rebuilding does not appear to have matched other parts of the region, particularly if the still energetic community of St Werburgh's be omitted. For example, 43 miserichords survive from the late fourteenth century in the Cathedral, the style of which implies significant connections with work done at Lincoln (Grössinger 2000). Henry Bradshaw, a monk of St Werburgh's *c.* 1500, described the city in glowing terms (1887 edition): 'Proued by the buyldynge of olde antiquite. In cellers and lowe volutes, and halles of realte. Lyke a comly castell, mighty, stronge and sure. Eche house like a toure, ...'

To an extent, the decline of Chester was predictable. The reign of Edward I saw an unprecedented flow of goods and services through the city for specific, political reasons. It could not be expected that this stimulus to the local economy would be maintained. The Edwardian conquests in Wales left members of the local community in a privileged position in trade and in the exploitation of minerals in North Wales. However, the revolt of Owain Glyn Dŵr in the early fifteenth century reduced this trade markedly over several decades, to the detriment of Chester merchants. There are signs that Chester men found it particularly difficult to re-establish their previous trading network in North Wales once the rebellion had subsided.

Much of the shipping which linked the port to Gascony, to Ireland and to other English ports was owned throughout the fourteenth century by aliens — non-freemen of the city. It may be that local ship-ownership and construction were discouraged by the problems of the Dee and the inability of seamen to bring their ships into the city's harbour. With little direct revenue from carrying, the community may have obtained less income from seafaring than hitherto and the role of the port and its outposts within the economy of the city may well have declined. In a sample survey of occupations in the city in the reign of Henry V, Bennett (1983) found that merchants and shipmen comprised a mere four per cent of the total. 13 per cent of all tradesmen were engaged in leather working, against 39 per cent in clothing and the textile trades and 25.2 per cent in victualling. Textiles were by these criteria the most important local product but the leather working trades that were to distinguish this community in the Elizabethan period were already significant (Woodward 1967). Chester was probably at this date an important entrepôt for the import of pelts and hides from the Irish Sea basin.

Despite the decline in home-based carrying, goods continued to flow through Chester. Cloth was exported to Ireland in return for wool, flax and hides, much of the flax destined for the nascent linen industry which was taking root in the townships on the south side of Manchester during the fifteenth century, where it supplemented home grown supplies. A trading and familial network linked the Chester community and some of the lesser boroughs such as Nantwich and Manchester to London via Coventry where local men were prominent as clothiers and skinners.

The Gough map (probably a product of the early fourteenth century) identifies the major roads linking the region to others. Chester was linked via Shrewsbury to Bristol, along the north coast to Caernarvon and via the Birkenhead ferry to Liverpool. Lancaster was connected via Warrington with Coventry and London, connecting in the Weaver valley with the major Cheshire boroughs (Figure 57). A network of lesser roads and tracks can be adduced from a variety of evidence. Plotting the itineraries of kings and other notables results in map evidence which appears extremely complex and even self-contradictory, probably because insufficient points on each route are identifiable by this means (Hindle 1982).

The region was not, by national standards, a significant exporter of cloth in the late Plantagenet period (Carus-Wilson and Coleman 1963; Lloyd 1983), despite the gradual spread of water-powered fulling mills into the regional countryside. However, by the second half of the fifteenth century, a network of local men was trading north-western textiles to the east coast ports and to London. Such activities sucked into commercial centres some of the lesser gentry of eastern Cheshire and Lancashire and stimulated the growth of markets there. The goods of two Rochdale merchants, James Brerelegh and William Merlande, were distrained for debt in the middle of the century (Shaw 1960). The total value was £152 10s., which included bows and arrows, tools, grain, money, muniments and bonds but the bulk comprised cloth of linen and wool. The merchants were engaged in the export of bed blankets, carpets, coverlets and cloths including cottons – coarse woollen cloth. Their stock suggests that Rochdale had already emerged at this stage as an important trading market, at the western end of a network covering much of what was to become the heartland of the West Riding and east Lancashire woollen manufacturing area.

The merchandising of textiles lay firmly in the hands of indigenous traders by this period. Robert Shaw, *mercator* of Quick (Saddleworth) in 1379, held a sub-manor at 'the Shagh' and he and his peers were engaged in carrying cloth, blankets and coverlets to Kingston-upon-Hull, where some local families established branches (Shaw 1958). Robert's sons retained an interest in the cloth trade. A younger son, Robert, was described as 'mercer' at Dukinfield and was probably engaged in export via Hull. When he died (1444) his executors were left to collect his commercial debts from those with whom he had dealt, including such a prominent local gentleman as Sir Nicholas of Longford of Withington. The activities of John 'the mercer' demonstrates the economic links which were developing between the townships on the south and east of Manchester and along the Pennine edge, from which goods were increasingly exported eastwards via pack-horse tracks across the Pennines and along Longdendale.

The most successful of Robert's descendants was to be that Sir Edmund Shaw who established himself as a goldsmith in London and served as mayor in the auspicious year when Richard III usurped the throne. From his grateful king, Shaw obtained substantial rewards and established himself and his family in Rainford (Essex). However, the less spectacular branches of the family whom he had left behind in the North West stayed in the cloth business in the Stockport area, in the vicinity of the parish church where his father, John Shaw, mercer, was buried.

At the centre of the expanding textile trade lay the market of Manchester. There is some evidence to suggest that the number of burgages had undergone a modest increase since the late thirteenth century, totalling by 1473 something in the order of 155 plots (Harland 1856–62). Whether the population had increased is a moot point, since the level of sub-tenancies at either period is unknown, but it does seem clear that Manchester on the eve of the Tudor period was a community which was, demographically at least, buoyant and possibly already expanding. In 1473 large numbers were holding fractions of a tenement, perhaps implying expansion, and about half were single properties. 11 have been identified with local country gentlemen and the ownership of town property was probably commonplace among the local squirarchy (Lloyd 1983). The increasing size and wealth of the community was reflected in the decision by the last de la Warre baron and rector to re-found the parish church in 1422 as a collegiate institution. At the same time, he converted the manor house to accommodation for the new community of priests – resulting in the structure of the older parts of what is now Chetham's School. The Chetham family after whom that school was named were already recognised as cloth merchants of Manchester in 1540.

By the reign of Henry VIII, Manchester Parish had emerged as the highest taxed part of Lancashire. There are difficulties in making comparisons between the lay subsidy returns of the fourteenth century and taxation figures for the sixteenth, but the relative advance of Manchester in comparison with West Derby Hundred is probably significant (Sheail 1968; followed by Morris 1983). Satellite markets had become established for which there is no pre-plague evidence at important centres local to Manchester, such as Ashton-under-Lyne and Bury (Tupling 1933). This was occurring in the same period which elsewhere in the region was witnessing the decay of smaller and late-established markets, such as Croston on Lancashire's western plain, and Hornby in Lonsdale. The economic divide which could be identified in pottery distribution, for example, between the west and east of southern Lancashire in the decades around 1300 was still present but now beginning to operate to the advantage of the east, despite all the physical problems of exporting via the Pennine trails.

A local involvement in textiles was not new. A fulling mill existed at Manchester at least as early as the late thirteenth century and several others can be identified during the same period among the vills of the Pennine fringe and Bucklow Hundred. Recent research in Bowland and Lonsdale has established the location of place-name evidence for textile working, often associated with field evidence of tenter banks, the dams and sluices of walkmills and potash kilns (Higham, M. 1988). In addition, retting ponds and other evidence of flax treatment have been identified. At Greystonegill, documentary evidence suggests that features associated with flax retting and woollen cloth manufacture should be dated back at least as early as the fourteenth century. The provision and exploitation of such facilities probably provided many medieval landowners with some income but they were of no more than local significance. What was new in the later Middle Ages was the organisation of local cloth manufacturing to take advantage of growing trade opportunities. Merchants organised the collection of finished goods from the numerous, scattered, rural weavers, marketed them and delivered bulk orders to more or less distant markets or ports. The trade enabled a plethora of local families to supplement inadequate revenues from poor farms by home-working but only a very small minority to grow rich through trade.

Despite its promise for the future (Willan 1980), the rise of Manchester was of very modest proportions by 1540 (Figure 64) and Chester retained for the moment its prominence in the region's trade and remained the largest single concentration of manufacturing. Even so, the economic development of the upland parts of Lancashire, and particularly the Manchester region, had already begun to suck in wool and flax to support local textile working, and the buoyancy of rural manufacturing had an impact on local demography. Communities such as Ashton-under-Lyne were well populated during the fifteenth century, with a knock-on impact on the local demand for land and pressure to enclose.

No other urban community was more than perhaps a quarter the size of Chester. Preston was the largest town in central Lancashire in the late medieval period, its role dependent on its central position on the communication network. In 1397 more than 300 individuals were members of the guild merchant there (Abram 1884), suggesting a total population well in excess of 1,500 and perhaps considerably larger. This suggests substantial expansion since the extent made in the reign of Henry III, in which the seigneurial proceeds from farming and fishing combined at Preston were reckoned to be worth £14 13s. 4d., but the strictly urban profits of markets, tolls and stallage a mere £5. The rich fishing grounds and cockle beds of the Lancashire estuaries were clearly significant but the figures are low by any standard.

Elsewhere, Nantwich was probably the largest of the Cheshire *wiches* and the third borough of the region. However, most towns may have had difficulty retaining their pre-plague levels of population and several were lost in the changing economic climate of the post-plague era (Table 4). With 86 taxpayers in 1379, Liverpool was probably typical of the modestly successful boroughs,

*Table 5. The profits of Preston, based on the Extent of Preston, 28 Henry III (Farrer 1901).*

|  |  |  | Sub–total |
|---|---|---|---|
| **Profits from farming and fishing** |  |  |  |
| 4 ploughlands | £6 |  |  |
| Fisheries | £6 |  |  |
| Mills | £2 |  |  |
| Meadows |  | 5s. 4d. |  |
| Pasture |  | 8s. – | £14 13s. 4d. |
| **Profits from trade** |  |  |  |
| Markets | £3 |  |  |
| Toll | £1 10s. |  |  |
| Stallage |  | 10s. | £5 |
| **Other manorial profits** |  |  |  |
| Perquisites of the pleas |  | 13s. 4d. |  |
| Escheats |  | 6s. 8d. | £1 |

where economic opportunities remained to be realised, but there is little sign of major expansion here before the later sixteenth century. Many rural market centres like Knutsford were assessed for purposes of taxation at a rate below that of surrounding agricultural communities, despite the undoubted presence of several families engaged in trade.

The degree of specialisation within the towns continued to vary from site to site. The port of Liverpool had 49 out of its total assessment of 86 taxpayers in 1379 described as tradesmen, against 26 peasant cultivators (Bennett 1983). More local records demonstrate that considerable specialisation continued to be present in the countryside with building trades and textiles well documented, particularly in the more affluent lowland areas. Occupational surnames remained common and it must be significant that about a quarter of the tradesmen identified in Bennett's sample came not from boroughs at all but from large villages like Sandbach. In northern Lancashire, large numbers listed in the Poll Tax returns of 1379 were fishermen, reminding us the extent to which food collecting still featured within the north-western economy in the later Middle Ages. Evidence of the diverse types of fish being consumed comes, for example, from early sixteenth-century accounts from Millom, North of the Sands, which refer to herrings, a turbot, 'cokfish' (?salmon), eels and salted porpoise (Winchester 1983).

# CHAPTER 7

# The Church and the Landscape

It is easy to view the North West as a region which changed only very slowly during the 1,000 years of the Middle Ages. The structure of the church, however, exhibits both considerable continuity and also major alteration. Assuming that the scatter of 'Eccles' place-names do indicate an early strata of churches from the Dee northwards (Figure 11), it is noticeable that none of these names is that of a major church in late Anglo-Saxon England. Only Eccleston, near Chester, Eccleston, near Standish, and Eccles near Manchester either survived or revived as church sites in the post-Conquest period, but none were dominant parishes within their hundreds, either in terms of area or in terms of the valuation of 1291 (Table 6). In some instances it is possible to speculate regarding the timing of this shift: so, for example, Manchester's church is likely to have been a by-product of the construction of a royal fortification (a *burh*) at Manchester's Roman fort site in the early tenth century, when it may, perhaps, have displaced Eccles. Other changes were probably associated with the upheavals of, first, the inclusion of the region within Anglo-Saxon kingdoms during the seventh and eighth centuries, then the re-ordering which accompanied the Scandinavian impact and incorporation into an enlarged English kingdom. Re-naming of existing church sites may have been widespread, as Kirk Lancaster, Ormskirk, Kirkham (Lancashire) and Lymm and Rostherne (Cheshire), all of which have Old Norse elements within their names, and new churches were being founded, by kings and queens (as at Chester, Runcorn and perhaps Manchester and Warrington), by bishops (at Burton, perhaps, and Wybunbury) and by the estate-holding laity. These processes had begun to produce a pattern of manorial churches with comparatively small parishes in the Wirral and Dee valley by the eleventh century, but elsewhere many *parochiae* remained very large, with dependent chapels coming into existence. This was particularly true north of the Mersey, where each hundred seems to have had only one, two or at most three major churches (as Warrington, Manchester, Winwick, Wigan, Whalley, Preston and Blackburn). If we take the 45 Lancashire churches named in the *Taxatio* of 1291, 26, or some 58 per cent, provide evidence, in terms of stone sculpture, place-name or Domesday entry, that they were already in existence in 1086. Given the poor status of the documentary record, this is an impressive proportion, particularly given that pre-Conquest sculpture also survives at several other church sites which were not included, such as Bolton-le-Sands and Gressingham.

## Table 6. North West churches listed in the Papal Taxatio of 1291 (based on data provided by Professor Jeffrey Denton).

| No. | Church | Value: £ s. d. | No. | Church | Value: £ s. d. |
|---|---|---|---|---|---|
| **13th-century Cheshire** | | **Cheshire total: 841–2–4** | | | |
| 1 | Chester, Holy Trinity | 6–13–4 | 31 | Rostherne | 13–6–8 |
| 2 | Chester, St Mary on the Hill | 13–10–8 | 32 | Bowdon | 11–6–8 |
| 3 | Chester, St Oswald | 16–0–0 | 33 | Lymm | 4–13–4 |
| 4 | Hawarden | 13–6–8 | 34 | Grappenhall | 5–0–0 |
| 5 | Dodleston | 6–4–8 | 35 | Astbury | 33–18–8 |
| 6 | Eccleston | 5–6–8 | 36 | Sandbach | 22–13–4 |
| 7 | Waverton | 6–17–4 | 37 | Over | 9–6–8 |
| 8 | Plemstall | 12–0–0 | 38 | Warmingham | 6–13–4 |
| 9 | Thornton le Moors | 10–13–4 | 39 | Middlewich | 53–6–8 |
| 10 | Ince | 5–0–0 | 40 | Davenham | 20–0–0 |
| 11 | Christleton | 13–3–0 | 41 | Prestbury | 26–13–4 |
| 12 | Barrow | 6–13–4 | 42 | Stockport | 18–13–4 |
| 13 | Tarporley | 5–0–0 | 43 | Mottram in Longdendale | 10–0–0 |
| 14 | Chester St John | 26–13–4 | 44 | Cheadle | 8–0–0 |
| 15 | Shotwick | 8–0–0 | 45 | Northenden | 7–10–8 |
| 16 | Neston | 13–6–8 | 46 | Wilmslow | 8–0–0 |
| 17 | Heswall | 5–0–0 | 47 | Barthomley | 10–0–0 |
| 18 | West Kirby | 13–6–8 | 48 | Audlem | 10–0–0 |
| 19 | Burton | 10–0–0 | 49 | Acton | 53–0–0 |
| 20 | Woodchurch | 9–6–8 | 50 | Bunbury | 20–0–0 |
| 21 | Bebington | 8–13–4 | 51 | Marbury | 5–0–0 |
| 22 | Bidston | 5–6–8 | 52 | Wybunbury | 31–13–4 |
| 23 | Wallasey | 12–2–0 | 53 | Malpas | 26–13–4 |
| 24 | Bromborough | 16–0–0 | 54 | Tilston | 6–13–4 |
| 25 | Stoke | 6–13–4 | 55 | Coddington | 6–16–4 |
| 26 | Backford | 5–6–8 | 56 | Tattenhall | 6–16–4 |
| 27 | Frodsham | 24–0–0 | 57 | Aldford | 10–0–0 |
| 28 | Runcorn | 20–0–0 | 58 | Hanmer | 10–0–0 |
| 29 | Great Budworth | 24–13–4 | 59 | Bangor-is-y-coed | 10–0–0 |
| 30 | Weaverham | 13–6–8 | 60 | Tarvin prebendary | 33–6–8 |
| **13th-century Lancashire** | | **Lancashire total: 1307–0–0** | | | |
| 61 | Bolton | 13–6–8 | 84 | Huyton | 10–0–0 |
| 62 | Standish | 13–6–8 | 85 | Winwick | 26–13–4 |
| 63 | Eccleston | 12–0–0 | 86 | Leigh | 8–0–0 |
| 64 | Croston | 33–6–8 | 87 | Wigan | 33–6–8 |
| 65 | Penwortham | 20–0–0 | 88 | Lancaster | 80–0–0 |
| 66 | Leyland | 10–0–0 | 89 | St Michael's-on-Wyre | 66–13–4 |
| 67 | Manchester | 53–6–8 | 90 | Preston | 66–13–4 |
| 68 | Eccles | 22–13–4 | 91 | Ribchester | 22–0–0 |
| 69 | Prestwich | 18–13–4 | 92 | Chipping | 10–13–4 |
| 70 | Bury | 13–6–8 | 93 | Kirkham | 183–6–8 |
| 71 | Middleton | 13–6–8 | 94 | Poulton-le-Fylde | 66–13–4 |

Table 6 *continued*

| No. | Church | Value: £ s. d. | No. | Church | Value: £ s. d. |
|---|---|---|---|---|---|
| 72 | Rochdale | 23–6–8 | 95 | Garstang | 40–0–0 |
| 73 | Ashton-under-Lyne | 10–0–0 | 96 | Cockerham | 22–6–8 |
| 74 | Flixton | 4–13–4 | 97 | Lytham | 4–0–0 |
| 75 | Blackburn | 33–6–8 | 98 | Halton | 12–0–0 |
| 76 | Whalley | 66–13–4 | 99 | Claughton | 6–13–4 |
| 77 | Warrington | 13–6–8 | 100 | Tatham | 6–13–4 |
| 78 | Prescott | 40–0–0 | 101 | Melling | 40–0–0 |
| 79 | Childwall | 40–0–0 | 102 | Tunstall | 34–13–4 |
| 80 | Walton-on-the-Hill | 44–0–0 | 103 | Heysham | 10–0–0 |
| 81 | Sefton | 26–13–4 | 104 | Whittington | 16–0–0 |
| 82 | Halsall | 10–0–0 | 105 | Warton | 66–13–4 |
| 83 | Ormskirk | 13–6–8 | | | |

The Normans took over a church which was impoverished, poorly equipped with buildings, conservative in structure and thinly staffed. No buildings of the earlier period survive excepting only the twin churches at Heysham (Plate 3). Parochial framework can only be reproduced in outline but all the indications from later evidence suggest that most parishes were focused on modest structures but were multi-settlement and multi-estate in composition. Many in the centre and east of the region were among the largest such units in England, with Great Budworth, Prestbury, Mottram in Longdendale, Wybunbury, Manchester and Whalley, for example, each presiding over a parish which included at least half of a Domesday hundred (Figure 65). The bishop of Lichfield and the archbishop of York shared responsibility for the area, with a boundary (which probably dates to *c.* 920–4) on the Ribble. For both the late Saxon dioceses, the North West constituted a peripheral zone which provided them with little revenue, to which bishops probably rarely travelled, and which were normally administered by archdeaconries at Chester and Richmond and a comparatively early network of rural deaneries.

King William's transfer in 1075 of the Lichfield diocese to relative safety, beneath the walls of Chester, proved short-lived. It seems unlikely that the move was ever popular with the bishop and his staff, whose estates and revenues were centred in the West Midlands. Chester was abandoned in 1102 by the second post-Conquest bishop in favour of Coventry where he had obtained the wealthy Abbey of St Mary's. Although the bishops of Coventry henceforth retained Chester in their title, in practice the region reverted to its previous, peripheral status. Without the income which might have accrued from the seat of a bishopric, the canons of St John's were henceforth to be reliant on their local resources. These included only relatively small estates. Their income from the influx of pilgrims to their chief relic, the crucifix of Chester, was a source of revenue which belongs to the High Middle Ages,

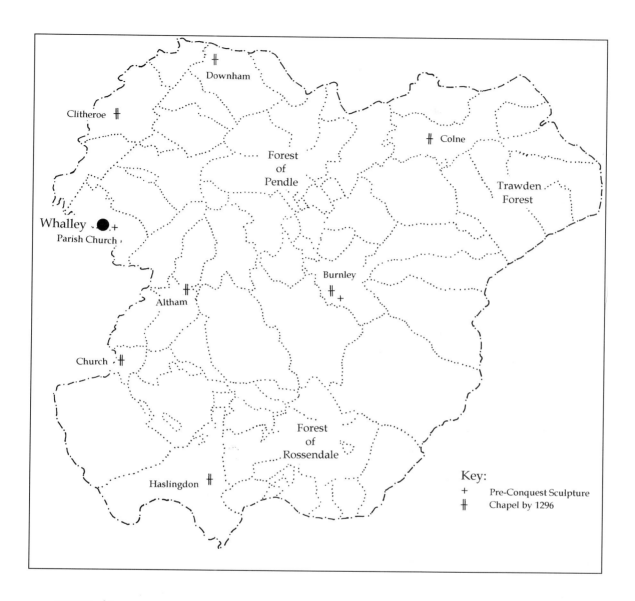

FIGURE 65.
The parish of Whalley,
comprising the larger,
eastern part of
Blackburn Hundred,
with its dependent
chapels.

rather than the Norman period. The result was the temporary abandonment of their cathedral part-built, until sufficient funds were available for work to be completed after 1150. The second phase was undertaken in an early gothic style, with pointed arches and narrow shafts on top of the undecorated, Norman drum pillars erected in the late eleventh century.

## The monasteries

During the Norman period, what wealth there was in the region was concentrated in the hands of a small aristocracy. Most were initially immigrants, and brought with them notions about church patronage and organisation which they derived from their recent experience in north-west France. This was an increasingly monastic church, but only two significant clerical communities existed in the North West, both at Chester. There was a strong tendency, therefore, to look to immigrant institutions and personnel to satisfy their needs. The weak economic condition of much of the region may explain the dilatory interest shown by the early Normans in the church, although it must be said that change nationally was not immediate on the Conquest. It was not until *c.* 1093 that Earl Hugh re-founded St Werburgh's as a monastery 22 years after he had, himself, been enfeoffed with his Cheshire estates. The re-foundation was undertaken with the advice of St Anselm of Bec, and the newly enriched community was staffed by monks drawn from his Abbey. The endowment of the pre-Conquest canons was transferred to the new, Benedictine house. Grants by the earl and countess Ermintrude included miscellaneous trading privileges, substantial demesne lands in Cheshire, North Wales, Derbyshire and Lincolnshire and the tithes of numerous of their manors (Tait 1920). Their military tenants in Cheshire were encouraged to grant lands not exceeding 100s. and their free tenants to bequeath their bodies and a third of their goods to the house. Numerous of the Earl's tenants did as he requested. For example, William Malbanc gave *Witeberiam*, a third of Wepre, the church and tithe of Tattenhall, a salthouse in Nantwich, two bovates of land and the tithes of Slachale, *Caitona* and *Yraduc*.

The foundation charter of the Abbey is a late fabrication but probably represents an approximately genuine tradition of that event and the measures taken to underpin the economy of the house. The charter refers to more than a dozen individuals or groups to whom the foundation was dedicated, and for whom the monks should pray (Cownie 1998, 157). A salient point is the extent to which the house was expected to serve as a sepulchre for the whole Cheshire aristocracy, whose exclusive, close-knit and hierarchical society was thereby to be preserved beyond death.

A second important factor was the wholesale granting of parochial tithes to the house (Figure 66). The transfer of tithes offered the secular aristocracy an inexpensive and therefore attractive method of endowment, which gave the religious community responsibility for providing a competent incumbent to parishes in a region where there was a dearth of trained, religious personnel. This practice offered the local aristocracy considerable advantages and it was followed wholesale, as more religious foundations were created, with the eventual result that parochial revenues formed an unusually large proportion of the income of the houses of the North West as late as the Dissolution.

Robert of Rhuddlan was among the many who enriched Norman houses with English property, in his case granting churches, which included Kirkby (Wirral), Hilbre and St Peter's (Chester) to the Abbey of Utica. Despite this display of individual patronage, when he was killed by the Welsh he was buried in his cousin's foundation of St Werburgh's. It was not until the second, third or even fourth generations from the Conquest that the Cheshire barons and their families broke with this tradition, preferring in most instances

FIGURE 66.
The foundations of St Werburgh's and Lancaster Priory: St Werburgh's already had substantial estates (cross-hachered), to which Earl Hugh (circle cross-hachered) and his tenants (circle dotted) added, but churches (solid small circle), agricultural tithes (open small circle) and tithes on fisheries (star) made up a major part of the resources of both from an early date.

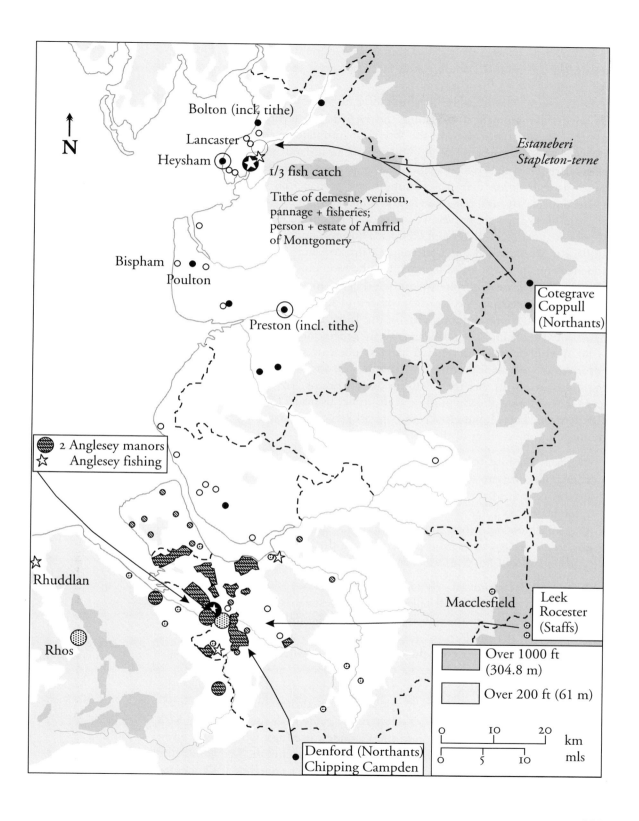

**N**

Bolton (incl. tithe)

Lancaster

Heysham

1/3 fish catch

Tithe of demesne, venison,
pannage + fisheries;
person + estate of Amfrid
of Montgomery

*Estaneberi
Stapleton-terne*

Bispham

Poulton

Preston (incl. tithe)

Cotegrave
Coppull
(Northants)

⊘ 2 Anglesey manors
☆ Anglesey fishing

Rhuddlan

Rhos

Macclesfield

Leek
Rocester
(Staffs)

Denford (Northants)
Chipping Campden

Over 1000 ft
(304.8 m)

Over 200 ft (61 m)

0    10    20    km
0    5    10    mls

to be interred in their own foundations as these came into existence. The earls continued to be buried among their ancestors until their line was ended by the death of John le Scot in 1237.

St Werburgh's was at the forefront of land improvement, enclosure and economic development throughout the twelfth, thirteenth and early fourteenth centuries, particularly in the Wirral, the immediate environs of Chester and the Dee–Mersey mosslands. Unenclosed heathland and commons were particularly at issue. Their neighbours were concerned at the abbots' bringing land into cultivation from the common at Upton in the second half of the thirteenth century, and both sought and obtained right of pasture on his newly enclosed land after the harvest (Tait 1920, 359). The heath lying between the abbot's manors of Eastham and Childer Thornton and a neighbour's estate at Willaston was divided up and mered (marked out) in 1305, with shares attached equally to the three manors. For the moment it remained as common pasture, but the owners were to confine digging for peat to their own shares and full-scale assarting was clearly envisaged (Tait 1920, 97). The area consists of low-lying land now dominated by the Birkenhead railway line, but such names as 'Heath Lodge' and 'Heath Farm' reflect the earlier condition.

St Werburgh's also developed interests in east Cheshire, particularly in connection with their rectory of Prestbury. A document of the 1270s (Tait 1920, 570) confirms that the township boundaries of Peover Superior, Snelson and Chelford were already in place at this time. In places the arable of adjacent vills actually abutted, but elsewhere local pockets of mossland were undergoing drainage by the cutting of ditches. The boundary

> begins at the ford below the water supply for the mill of Chelford then climbs up a certain valley called *Merecloh* to the double hedge which lies between the fields of the said vills [Snelson and Chelford], and from the same hedge via a certain syke outside the enclosure of Snelson even into the deep moss, and then following that syke through the said deep moss towards *Faudon* even to the *Leylache* where the bounds of Chelford, of *Faudon* and of Old Warford meet together.

Astle Hall lies approximately on the site of Chelford Mill and the township boundary still runs up a small valley or clough westwards onto reclaimed heath and common between Snelson and Chelford. The line of the double hedge may represent the modern township boundary. Moss Farm on the edge of Peover Heath is suggestive of old mossland and Bowden Bank Farm perhaps reflects the lost place-name *Faudon* (Dodgson 1970, ii, 86–7).

Roger of Poitou chose a comparable method by which to introduce the reformed church to his lordship. Roger had inherited from his late Saxon predecessors a pre-Conquest minster church, as evidenced by its name, Kirk Lancaster, in Domesday Book, and pre-Conquest carvings, which may, given its location on Roman ruins, have been an early stone church. The Lancashire estates beyond the Ribble may have had as few as eight churches at Domesday (three were recorded as dependent on Preston), all of which were probably as impoverished as the remainder of the community. These were a poor basis for the exercise of new ecclesiastical patronage. In 1094, Roger granted the church of Lancaster to the monks of Sées in Normandy. In return, they undertook to staff a priory to be founded beside his new castle, and this too was presumably built of the dressed stone which the Roman fort provided.

The new foundation was to be supported by an income which included the rectories of nine of his churches and a moiety of another, in Lancashire and Nottinghamshire, and the tithes on livestock from a further 19 townships (V.C.H. 1908; Figure 66). His example was followed by some of his principal tenants, including Sheriff Geoffrey and Ralph Gernet. In the early twelfth century, further grants of churches were received from the families of de Montebegon, de Walton, Gernet, de la Ware, de Balista and de Stalmine (Lacy) and numerous gifts of land from others, although the latter were generally small and limited to the various dispersed parts of Lancaster parish. As a result of these ecclesiastical grants, St Mary's Priory at Lancaster obtained an interest in, or ownership of, a substantial scatter of the parish churches of the lordship, particularly in the area which was eventually to emerge as the county of Lancashire (but see Cownie 1998). The resulting network of ecclesiastical patronage reflected closely the secular pattern of lordship, which it was to long out-live.

These two foundations apparently satisfied the religious ambitions of, or perhaps soaked up the resources available to, the first generation of the Normans. After their deaths, the monks could be relied upon to bury them in sepulchres which were safe, socially prestigious, accessible to their relicts and spiritually advantageous. In both instances, they were also within a short distance of their castles. During their lives, their abbots or priors would take over much of the daunting responsibility for staffing the local church, rebuilding its structures and supplying its needs.

The gradual economic recovery of the region in the twelfth century coincided with the arrival in Britain of new orders of religious, whose economic expectations were rather different to those of the now traditional, Benedictine houses. Successive monarchs and their court aristocracies patronised several of these orders. The Savignacs and Cistercians competed for advancement in the reigns of Henry I, after which the former were incorporated into the latter. Later in the century, the Augustinian and Premonstratensian Canons attracted considerable patronage.

These orders preferred to follow variants of the religious life which were more or less compatible with isolation, if not desolation, and could, therefore, be established on waste and unproductive land, on the edge of cultivated terrain, on isolated islands in lowland marshes, or in upland valleys. Such needs lent themselves to the conditions of the North and to Wales. The twelfth century saw a significant flow of patronage to the reformed religious in the north-western counties, where secular lords who were themselves not necessarily particularly wealthy saw positive advantages available to themselves in return for a relatively small investment. The initial endowment usually comprised ecclesiastical revenues, combined with land which was under-utilised and therefore under-productive of seigneurial income. The new foundations performed a central role in the economic development of many parts of the region, in collaboration with local lords and their tenants, and this was arguably part and parcel of their role.

The new wave of foundations was initially sponsored by the vassals of the earl of Chester (Figure 67). It was begun by the baron of Halton, who, in 1115, founded an Augustinian priory at Runcorn. This was a small, late-Anglo-Saxon minster church, which was probably served by two priests in 1086 and had a parish extending across the northern half of *Tunendune* Hundred, but the priory soon moved to Norton. Thereafter new religious communities proliferated. In 1123, Count Stephen of Blois, nephew and favourite of Henry I, founded a community of Savignacs at Tulketh, west of Preston and on the edge of the marshes which flank the northern side of the Ribble estuary. Of its own volition, the community transferred to the furthest reaches of his lordship, at Furness in 1127, where they became one of the most expansive and eventually one of the wealthiest of the Cistercian houses of the North. Another of the barons of Cheshire, Hugh Malbanc (second Baron of Nantwich) founded a Savignac house at Combermere before 1130 on the extreme southern borders of his barony, in an area of widespread woodland (Ormerod 1882, iii). The foundation grant included the manor of Wilkesley and the rich and important church of Acton (with its chapels at Nantwich, Wrenbury and Minshull), to which Earl Ranulph added various, valuable, legal and financial privileges. The effect was to make the monks responsible, as institutional rectors, for spiritual administration in the core of the barony and for the provision of a family chantry and sepulchre for the Malbanc dynasty.

This and similar examples led to a wave of foundations in the region, by which the majority of the local aristocracy became associated as principal patrons with one or more religious establishments. The Cistercian house of Poulton (Chesh.) was founded from Combermere *c.* 1146–53 under the patronage of the butler of the Earl of Chester (Barraclough 1957; Emery *et al.* 1996). There followed a Benedictine nunnery at Chester (founded by the Earl, c. 1150) and a Benedictine priory founded at Birkenhead by Hamo de Mascy about the same date. Perhaps the least attractive site was that chosen for the Cistercian house at Stanlaw, founded by the Constable of Chester, in the 1170s, on a rocky promontory in the marshes of the lower Mersey which he renamed *locus Benedictus*. Here, if anywhere, a community of enthusiasts could practice a well-regulated regime of asceticism in the spirit of the order's founders (for a survey, Williams and Mackinder 1986). The community benefited from grants of disafforestation, an annuity, quittance from tolls and other benefits from the earldom (Barraclough 1988, pp. 210–16, nos. 208–15), presumably via the good offices of their founder.

The late twelfth century witnessed a comparable group of foundations in Lancashire. Most recent patronage had been directed towards houses that lay

FIGURE 67.
Monastic foundations, friaries and hospitals in the North West, showing their re-foundations on different sites as appropriate.

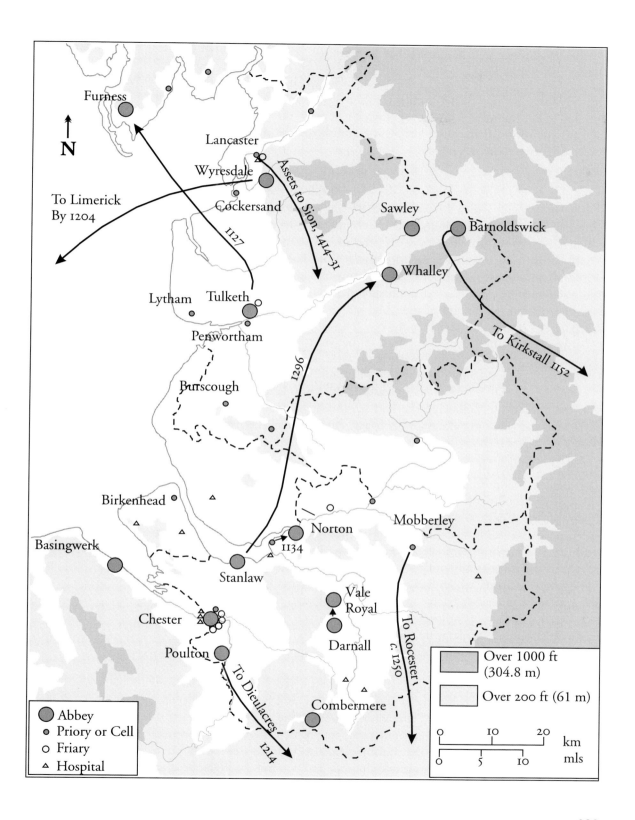

Furness

N

To Limerick
By 1204

Lancaster
Wyresdale
Cockersand
1127

Assets to Sion, 1414–31

Sawley
Barnoldswick
Whalley

To Kirkstall 1152

Lytham
Tulketh
Penwortham

Burscough

1296

Birkenhead

Basingwerk

Norton
1134

Mobberley

Stanlaw

Vale
Royal

Chester

Darnall

To Rocester

Poulton

To Dieulacres

1214

Combermere

c. 1250

Over 1000 ft
(304.8 m)

Over 200 ft (61 m)

0          10          20    km

0        5        10    mls

Abbey
Priory or Cell
Friary
Hospital

outside the region, such as the grant of Cockerham manor and church to the Augustinians at Leicester in the 1150s (France 1954). Such continued, resulting, for example, in a cell or priory of the Abbey of Evesham at Penwortham under the patronage of the Bussel family (Hulton 1853), and one of Durham at Lytham. The foundation grant of Lytham reveals the type of marginal, lowland environment in which this was established. The monks of Durham received (Farrer 1902, p. 348):

> all my land of Lythum, with the church of that town ... within these bounds to wit from the ditch on the western side of the burial yard of Kilgrimol, above which I have erected a cross, westwards unto the sea; and again from that ditch and cross, over towards the east along by the Cursidmere, over the great moss and the stream unto Balholm, which said stream runs towards Suinebrigg; again from Balholm in a straight line over the moss, which lord John, Count of Moreton, divided between himself and me, unto the northern side of Estholm-ker, following eastward unto the margin of the water which comes from Bircholm, and separates Estholm-ker and Brining-ker, following that division of water between us southward unto the ford [?] between Estholme and Couburgh, thence returning towards the west, and fetching a compass southward over the moss into the Pull beyond Snarte'salte where it falls upon the sea shore, and so going towards the south across unto the Ribill at the mid-stream, following the mid-stream of that water westward unto the sea, and so to the aforesaid ditch and cross; and all the marsh between the said bounds with the eyes [or holmes] which are therein.

A picture emerges of farms and hamlets scattered on islands of dryer land (holmes), in a landscape dominated by mosslands, some mered but some still undivided, carrs (boggy land), open water and marshland.

Conishead, Cockersand, Wyresdale and Burscough were all founded as independent houses by local families in the last decade of the century, all in landscapes where little agrarian development had so far occurred. Cockersand started in the 1180s as a hermitage, from which there developed a hospital for lepers and the infirm, which had been founded on a small and isolated pocket of sands and gravels between extensive mosses and the sea. The hospital received a handful of properties, including a fishery on the Lune, from Henry II's steward, William de Lancaster, Lord of Garstang, then a series of grants from the lords of Thurnham. Clement III responded by granting a Bull of Protection in 1190, which gave official status to the community as a house of Premonstratensian Canons. By 1200, it had attracted a significant flow of local lands (albeit in small parcels) and other assets, and had come under the active patronage of Theobald Walter who granted Pilling to the canons in 1194 (Brooke 1898). One of the several industries into which the canons ventured was salt production, along the coastal marshes, which developed as a significant coastal industry in Amounderness and around Morecambe Bay during the Middle Ages.

Like many houses of its order, the Augustinian house of Burscough (near Ormskirk) was sited in an area of late economic development, where assarting was still widespread in the late thirteenth century and land improvement by drainage was a necessary prerequisite of cultivation. The boundaries of numerous grants refer to sykes and ditches, revealing low-lying terrain in danger of water-logging, as the following example suggests (Webb 1970, 55, no. 43, dated *c.*1229–*c.*1260):

> a certain part of my land of Hawkshead which is contained within these boundaries, namely starting from Hawksheadsyke to a certain ditch towards the south, following that ditch towards the north up to the corner of another ditch next to *le Quytegore* and then following that ditch up to *le Quytegore* towards the east up to *Muscarsiche* and then following *Muscarsiche* climbing up to Hawksheadsyke and then following Hawksheadsyke climbing up to the aforenamed ditch in the south part …

The original grant was small but the patrimony grew for about a century, competing successfully with the houses at Cockersand and Warburton, in which the Lathom family also had interests (Webb 1970). Their estates were heavily concentrated within the immediate locality but numerous references to wind- and watermills in documents of the early thirteenth century suggest that this was slowly becoming a profitable, grain-growing area. The three churches of Ormskirk, Huyton and Flixton all formed part of the original grant and served throughout the history of the house to underpin the income of the canons. Most of the later grants to the community were donated by men below the rank of manorial lords and comprised small parcels in the agricultural lands of neighbouring communities.

Such houses were never to be of more than local significance but they typify the monastic establishment of the North West. From the beginning, much of their revenue from land was arguably from rents paid by tenants holding small and dispersed parcels of land. At the dissolution, Whalley, for example, was found to have lands leased in small parcels as very large numbers of farms, each of which contained arable and pasture in approximately equal amounts, with lesser quantities of meadow and woodland.

Where significant grants did not coincide with the exclusivity of occupation, which was a condition of the Cistercian rule, existing communities might be displaced. The process could destroy holdings, or even whole vills, as occurred in 22 cases around Fountains Abbey in the West Riding. The aim was to create granges where the monks or their lay brethren could pursue a strategy of direct exploitation, as was established from Poulton at Churton (where the settlement pattern has been affected: see Figure 38) and perhaps Dodleston. A religious community was founded by Henry de Lacy in 1147 at Barnoldswick, which he renamed 'The Mount of St Mary' (Clarke 1895). The foundation grant included Barnoldswick Church, the four parochial vills of East Marton, West Marton, Bracewell and Stock and two further small vills. The locals who had been evicted do not appear to have moved far away, for it was their custom to meet at the church on feast days with their priest and clerks. The Abbot responded to this recurrent disturbance by pulling down the church; the ensuing court case was awarded to the monks by the papal curia.

The monks claimed to be plagued by persistently wet weather and by robbers and so in 1152 removed to Kirkstall (West Yorkshire), retaining Barnoldswick as a grange. In the early 1190s they attempted to similarly reduce their lands at Accrington to a grange but met there with resistance, which was less constitutionally minded. The monks recorded that:

> certain malignants who lived in the neighbourhood whose ancestors had held Accrington before, at the instigation of the Devil, utterly burnt up the same grange with all its furniture and cruelly slew three lay brethren who were managing the grange, namely Norman, Humphrey and Robert (Clark 1895).

The issue was once again resolved in favour of the monks, on this occasion at the intercession of their patron, Robert de Lacy.

Given the widespread availability of under-used land in the region, such conflicts were probably the exception rather than the rule. The grange system did provide secure work for one group within society. Lay brethren were a normal part of the work force of houses of the Cistercian order and probably outnumbered the monks by a factor of two or three times during the high water mark of direct exploitation in the late twelfth century. Recruitment to their numbers provided a valuable safety valve in a period of rapid population rise and took a significant number of young men out of the reproductive cycle. However, since the Cistercians were exempt from episcopal visitation, information concerning the composition of their houses is not generally available.

The grange system allowed the Cistercians to establish themselves as the most effective direct exponents of new management techniques among the monastic communities. While not matching the wool production of the Yorkshire houses or Furness, Basingwerk (now in Clwyd) and Stanlaw were among the houses exporting wool via the Florentines in the late thirteenth century (Donkin 1958). Wool from St Werburgh's was reaching the Boston wool fair by the same period, and this older house also had granges. Monastic sheep flocks were presumably grazing lands along the estuaries of both the Dee and Mersey.

Another papal privilege to the Cistercians created a further fertile area for dispute, this time with the local parochial clergy. In 1132, lands held by the Cistercians were exempted from tithes. In 1215 this was relaxed but only as regards new grants. The flow of grants to the monasteries dried up during the thirteenth century with the earliest founded, in general, the first to lose the patronage of the secular community. The last, and most spectacular Cistercian house was that founded initially at Darnhall by Lord Edward, son and heir of Henry III, in August 1270, as he set out on crusade, and removed to Vale Royal in 1277 (Denton 1992). As befitted a foundation by the heir to the throne, it was destined to have the longest, Cistercian church in the country but its construction was to be a major drain upon the county revenues for a generation to come (Thompson 1962). The landed endowment was inadequate for the size of community originally envisaged.

Several other religious communities found themselves accommodated in such adverse conditions that they successfully petitioned to be allowed to move. The migration from Tulketh to Furness established a local precedent, which was in 1134 followed by the canons at Runcorn who moved within the barony to Norton. The Poulton community was re-established at Dieulacres (Rudyard, Staffordshire) in 1214. The daughter-house of Furness at Wyresdale removed to the Irish lands of its patron, Theobald Walter, within a few years of its foundation. A short-lived and impoverished monastic foundation at Mobberley was annexed to Rocester in Staffordshire in the thirteenth century.

Such moves to less remote or more advantageous sites with prospects of better patronage coincided with a gradual abandonment of the extreme asceticism, which characterised early generations of inmates in the twelfth-century orders. It is a reflection of contemporary attitudes to the region, and perhaps also to the concept of asceticism in a 'desert' space, that no houses moved in to balance the loss of the several which departed to new sites outside. However, in many case the original lands continued to be exploited and developed, with Norton Priory, for example, further developing low-lying lands along the south bank of the Mersey by a series of drainage works.

Perhaps the most celebrated removal was that of the Stanlaw Cistercians to Whalley in the late thirteenth century, carried out with the active co-operation and encouragement of their patron, Roger de Lacy, the Earl of Lincoln. The house at Stanlaw shared in the benefits that derived from the improving fortunes of their patrons, when the barony of Halton was amalgamated by inheritance with the substantial estates of the de Lacy family. This placed within their sights the rectories of the vast parishes of the east of southern Lancashire, centred at Whalley, Eccles, Blackburn and Rochdale, all of which they eventually obtained.

Their remove from Stanlaw was stimulated by a series of putative disasters: floods, the collapse of the tower (1287) and a ruinous fire (1289). In 1296 they obtained possession of the old deanery and advowson at Whalley, moved in and began to build, but the new church was not begun until 1330 and the dormitory was not completed until 1425, because of shortage of funds. In the meantime, the community gave serious thought to the possibility of moving to an even less remote site, in the developed agricultural belt of Lancashire at Toxteth, near Liverpool, where the earls had a valuable park.

By the time the Stanlaw community was on the move to Whalley and Vale Royal was coming into existence, the Cistercians had begun to abandon the grange system which had been such a distinctive feature of their organisation a century before. By 1336 large amounts of the comparatively recent Vale Royal granges were at rent and the numbers of lay brethren declining. The early fourteenth-century conflicts between the Abbot and his tenants centred not on any threatened extension of the grange economy but on the nature of their tenurial obligations to him as their manorial lord (see above).

Whalley in 1336 held a compliment of 29 monks and only a single lay brother. The estates were very largely at farm and an unusually high percentage of their income was to come throughout the late medieval period from parochial revenues (Hulton 1847). Where granges continued, monks were being placed in them and therefore were acting as estate managers or farmers. The monasteries themselves were the foci of very extensive engineering, with banks and boundaries, and conduits feeding water for various purposes including milling, cooking and sewage. Sawley Abbey, then in Yorkshire, provides an example where the earthworks of these several activities survive virtually intact (Figure 68).

The religious houses played a full part in the economic exploitation of the region and on occasion fell foul of the law. The abbots of Chester, Basingwerk and Whalley were among the principal defaulters listed for non-payment of fines for trespass against the Forest of Wirral in 1351 (Irvine 1949). The fourteenth-century monasteries were increasingly becoming corporate land-owners whose aims and operations were difficult to distinguish from those of other local land-holders, from whose families most inmates derived. These same local families were the principal beneficiaries of changing patterns of monastic estate management, taking up tenancies and employment as stewards. Even so, there is good reason to believe that the reputation of monasteries in the region survived rather better into the late medieval period than was the case across much of the south of England (Haigh 1969).

By the late thirteenth century, much of the remaining trickle of benefactions reaching the monasteries were for chantries. John Arneway, for example, Mayor of Chester, died in 1278, leaving bequests to provide for masses for his soul at St Werburgh's but most such offering went to the Chester nuns, local parish churches and the friars, rather than the monasteries.

To an extent friaries replaced monasteries as foci of secular patronage from the thirteenth century onwards but the friars remained a phenomenon of the more urban communities. All four orders were established in Chester and houses were founded in addition at Warrington, Preston and Lancaster. The Carmelites at Chester were established in 1289–90, originally with a grant of seven messuages in a suburb of the City. A cemetery was established within a quarter century thereafter (Bennett 1935). Some friaries attracted the patronage of the local gentry. At Lancaster, for example, the friars were established in typically modest premises under the patronage of Sir Hugh Harrington. Excavations on the long demolished site have recovered ceramic tiles comparable to those from Warrington Friary, Norton Priory and elsewhere. Such imply that some modest adornment was normal within the churches of local friaries but the mendicants retained their reputation for preaching and asceticism up to the Reformation. During the later Middle Ages and into the sixteenth century, the local friars were generally successful in attracting small bequests and mortuary payments and many wills required that they should officiate at the funeral of the deceased.

## Parish and church

At the Conquest, the region was characterised by extensive parishes, some of which were served by minster churches with very small groups of clergy taking responsibility for the cure of souls and operating over a wide area from a single focus (for minsters, see Blair 1988). The size of these parishes was exceptional. In Whalley, Great Budworth and Prestbury, the North West had the three largest parishes in England below the Tyne (Sylvester 1969). These represented the survival of mid- to late Anglo-Saxon parishes, such as had been divided up via the establishment of manorial or estate churches in most regions of

FIGURE 68.
Sawley Abbey, a small Cistercian house in the upper Ribble valley, showing the extensive earthworks associated with a monastic community in the Middle Ages.
ADRIAN OLIVIER

England. Their presence should be seen as a reflection of the low levels of population and prosperity that characterised the North West in the eleventh century.

Some inroads had already been made in adjusting this parochial structure, inroads which were at their most marked in the rather more prosperous west of Cheshire, where St Werburgh's arguably provided a second force for parochial reorganisation. Where they had not obtained the relevant church, the canons or their successors used their access to the patronage of the powerful to remove their estates from the parochial jurisdiction of the local clergy. However, where they were granted the rectories of the great parochial churches – as in the case of St Werburgh's at Prestbury, or Norton Priory at Great Budworth – then the religious houses became committed and self-interested opponents of parish fragmentation. By 1200, not much less than half the parish churches of Lancashire had passed into the hands of the monasteries and more were to follow in the next century and a half. The situation in Cheshire was not markedly different: the *Valor Ecclesiasticus* included mention of twenty six held by monasteries, of which St Werburgh's held eighteen, dwarfing any other houses in this as in other respects. Particularly in the case of Lancashire, many were held by houses which lay outside the region although some recipients used such grants to establish local priories or cells.

Monasteries either took a pension from the parish revenues and presented to the living, or they appropriated the whole and made provision for the cure of souls by the employment of a chaplain or vicar. Where a church was converted to be the conventual church of a new foundation, - appropriation was the norm, as at Lancaster or Penwortham, but there was a gradual increase in the practice during the latter half of the twelfth century (V.C.H. 1908), motivated in all probability by the financial benefits it conferred.

Other churches remained under the control of secular patrons (e.g. Venables at Rostherne and Grelley at Manchester), but the rights of lay patrons were ill-defined. In Lancashire hereditary rectories were in existence, under religious patronage at Walton and Kirkham and under the protection of lay patrons at Whalley and Blackburn. The huge size of Whalley parish set the rector apart from his peers and successive incumbents in the thirteenth century, if not before, adopted the title of dean. The clerical abuses that such priests represented may have encouraged lay patrons to grant rectories to the religious, and it was just such a transfer that brought an end to the independent deans of Whalley. The Cistercians were enabled to appropriate its revenues only by appeal to the Pope over the head of the Bishop of Coventry. Henceforth it was to be served by a monk and a vicarage was established of exceptional value to include a competent manse, 30 acres of land, rights in the abbey's wood and the altarage of the church, although this generous endowment was adjusted downwards in favour of the monks during the fourteenth century.

As estates proliferated and population increased in the twelfth and thirteenth centuries, so pressure grew to extend the parochial system so as to make churches and the basic services they provided more accessible to the widely scattered gentry classes. New parishes already seemed to have been carved out of existing ones in the late pre-Conquest period (as seems to have occurred at Thornton-le-Moors, Cheshire, for example) and the process continued thereafter, with the foundation of new parochial churches at sites such as Aldford, in association with a castle and nucleated settlement, which was founded in the first half of the thirteenth century. A proliferation of new, smaller parishes was particular prevalent in Cheshire west of the Central Ridge, where the putative ancient multi-township parishes of such churches as Farndon, with its near circular churchyard (Figure 69), virtually disintegrated. Even within the existing parish structure, much could be achieved by the establishment of parochial chapels, subordinate to and dependent on the mother church. Some chapels may have been already in existence at Domesday but there is no way of assessing what proportion. Others came into existence as a result of negotiations between local lords and the parochial rectors, who were often able to legislate so as to retain their rights to parochial income and superiority over the new benefice.

217

So, for example, by a series of agreements in the thirteenth century with the deans and then the monks at Whalley, the de Stapleton lords of Quick (now Saddleworth) at the extremity of Rochdale parish established a chapel and chaplain to celebrate divine office on the estate. The Stapletons had to provide a manse, land and livestock for their priest and build the chapel. In the following century the local community took on much of the responsibility for maintaining the chapel the Stapletons had built, leaving the monks to find books and vestments and repair the chancel.

Some chapels gradually became independent parish churches. The Blackburn chapel of La Law had become a parish church in all but name by *c.*1200, with full burial rights and rights of baptism. Its elevated status owed much to the influence of the important local family of Banestre. Bowdon parish extended across 13 manors. By around 1300, a chapel at ease had been established in Ashton-upon-Mersey, which acquired parochial status under the patronage of two local manorial families just 50 years later. Warburton church, the timber framing of which may be sixteenth century (Nevell 1997, 29), began life as a chapel of ease of Lymm, from which it was detached, becoming a priory in 1187–90 and then a parochial church in 1270–71. Elsewhere in Cheshire, Lawton and Swettenham originated as parochial chapels of Astbury but had emerged as independent parish churches before the Black Death, Lawton like Astbury under the patronage of St Werburgh's. Baddiley was a one township parish entirely surrounded by the multi-township parish of Acton, from which it fairly obviously derived. The status of other foundations seems to have been obscure or controversial. For example, Barrow was on occasion listed as a church, but appears to have been a chapelry of Tarvin until the reign of Elizabeth. It was probably a manorial foundation of the fitzNigel lords, which exercised full parochial rights and responsibilities but did not have full parochial status (Davnall 1985). Across Lancashire, there was a strong connection between townships held in thegnage or drengage and the creation of single township parishes, as, for example, at Tatham, Claughton and Ireby, in Lonsdale. Some of these may predate the Conquest. By the end of the Middle Ages, many local gentry had their own private chapels served by chaplains and attached to their principal houses, but this practice developed the provision of ecclesiastical services very much in the private sphere, alongside the parochial framework.

The precise position of such foundations was a compromise between the influence and support that local needs could muster and the ability of existing rectors to defend the *status quo* and the growing revenues that brought them. Few secular lords were as powerful as the de Lacy family, whose chapel at Clitheroe Castle was entirely free of parochial jurisdiction. In general, religious rectors were more able to wrest privileges for their chapels from the parochial authorities. Chapels remained far more numerous in Lancashire than Cheshire, where even the large parishes based at Prestbury and Gt Budworth had only four and one chapels respectively by 1300.

FIGURE 70.
The distribution of churches taxed in 1291 (after Phillips and Phillips 2002, 39, and additional data for Lancashire provided by Professor Jeffrey Denton). The churches are named in Table 6 on pages 201–2.

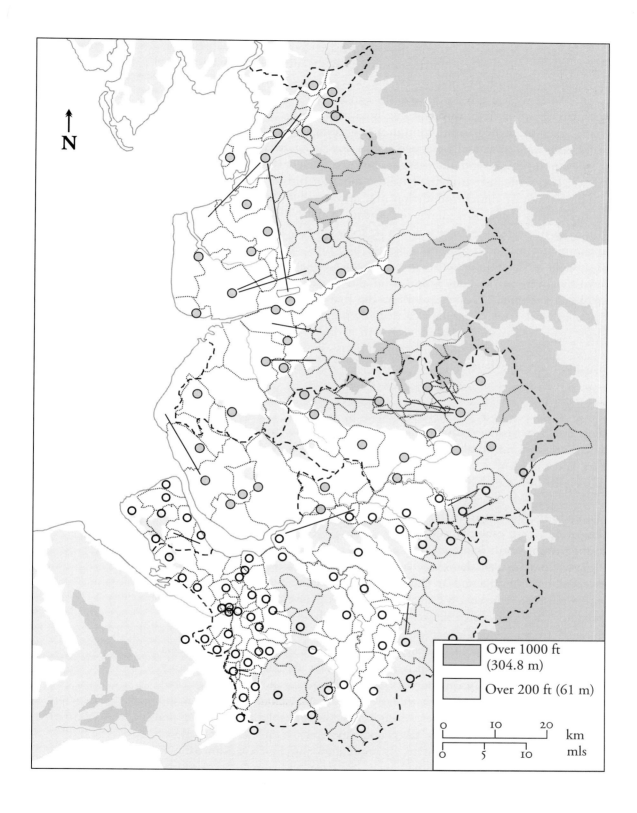

Although such privileges might prove expensive, local access to a place of worship and burial was substantially improved by the infilling that occurred in the twelfth and thirteenth centuries. The rural population in the poorer parts of the North West was never to have the benefit of a church on every manor, but many families lived within a one hour walk of a church or chapel by *c.*1300. Even so, many parishes continued to encompass numbers of vills which could be as high as 22 and were regularly in double figures (Figure 70). From the view-point of a bishop, the result cannot have been entirely satisfactory but the scattered settlement structure left little room for further change.

This pattern of church foundation did, however, have a profound impact on the general shape of medieval settlement. In the North West, there were numerous nucleated settlements which lacked a church, a situation which was uncommon throughout southern England, and these even included comparatively large urban foundations. An even higher proportion of non-nucleated townships were in the same position. In this respect, stereotypes concerning medieval settlements, which prioritise the juxtaposition of church, manor house or castle and village, are particularly inappropriate to this landscape. Once again, the particularity of the region is driven home, as is the need to interpret this society without preconceptions derived from very different circumstances elsewhere.

## Church fabric

Only at Chester is there any significant survival of early Norman architecture. The short-lived cathedral at Chester is still to be seen in the lower part of the nave and the main arch over the crossing at St John's. The triforium above belongs to the second half of the twelfth century and above that is masonry of the thirteenth century. At St Werburgh's elements of the Norman abbey church in the Romanesque style were integrated into subsequent rebuilding in the period *c.*1250 onwards, surviving as an arch and triforium in the east wall of the present north transept (Gem 2000).

Away from Chester, there is little work that dates before *c.* 1150 – Heysham excepted, but from the mid- to late twelfth century there is a scatter of survivors, which must be representative of a substantial local investment in ecclesiastical building. The groin vaulted chapter-house at Birkenhead and the west door of the so-called chapel, behind the parish church at Prestbury (Figure 71), provide evidence of late-Norman architecture and the churches at Shocklach and Bruera retain wide-jointed masonry which may date from the later twelfth century (Crossley 1938). Late Norman doorways survive at Bispham and Gressingham, and the twelfth-century chancel north wall at Ormskirk. At Acton, 12 loose stones are richly carved with religious scenes, which include the Almighty, a bishop with his staff and winged saints. Fonts of the period survive at the same site, and also at Grappenhall, Eastham and Mottram. By implication, the church at Barnoldswick was of stone when it was demolished in the late 1140s, and many other parochial foundations were presumably constructed in stone during this period.

FIGURE 71.
The late twelfth-
century oratory at
Prestbury, largely
reconstructed in the
Victorian period, which
stands behind the later
medieval parish church
on the banks of the
river Bollin.

The first call upon the building resources of the new monasteries were their own conventual churches. Of these, only St Werburgh's and Lancaster survive as medieval structures and associated buildings have been retained only at the former. St Werburgh's reflects the ambitions and skills of many generations of abbots, their masons and their wood carvers. Much of the church, including the Lady Chapel and Choir, was conceived and executed in the second half of the thirteenth century. The south transept was remodelled to make space available for altars in the fourteenth century and the nave was rebuilt in the mid-fourteenth century (Figure 72). Lancaster Priory Church dates to the fifteenth century, after the suppression of the alien priories and the removal of the community to Syon in Middlesex. The monastic buildings lay on the north side of the church but did not survive the removal of the religious community by the Lancastrian kings.

Of the region's monastic sites, only the Priory at Norton has been the subject of extensive, modern excavations, carried out under the auspices of

FIGURE 72.
St Werburgh's, Chester,
from the air. The
Abbey church, now the
Cathedral, dominated
the medieval skyline, as
depicted also on the
Gough map,
emphasising the wealth
and importance of the
Benedictine house in
the region's premier
urban settlement.

Runcorn New Town Development Corporation during the 1970s (Greene 1989). Of the medieval fabric, only the south wall of the nave of the church and the west range of the undercroft are upstanding, having been incorporated into later houses occupying the site. Otherwise the structure of the priory was completely demolished after the sale of the whole to the Brookes family in 1545. The surviving doorway is in un-weathered condition, with sharp chevron decoration of the late twelfth century (Figure 73), comparable in age to the doorway of Shotwick church, which it otherwise excels.

Around the stone-built complex, archaeology uncovered the remnants of an early, timber phase of occupation (Figure 74a). Those remains substantial enough to be interpreted were thought to represent a gate-house or gate-keeper's house and two phases of accommodation, comprising an initial structure at least 12 m by 7 m, which was replaced by a larger building, 11 m wide by at least 14 m long, with two rows of aisle posts, a thick clay floor and a stone hearth. These buildings were constructed of relatively mature oaks with panels of wattle and daub, suggesting the local availability of plentiful supplies of standing timber and managed woodland. A possible temporary church was also identified but not fully excavated.

FIGURE 73.
An elaborate Romanesque doorway of the late twelfth century at Norton Priory, leading to the nave from the western cloister walk, which is in pristine condition having been protected by the cloister walk roof, then, post-dissolution, a succession of stately homes.

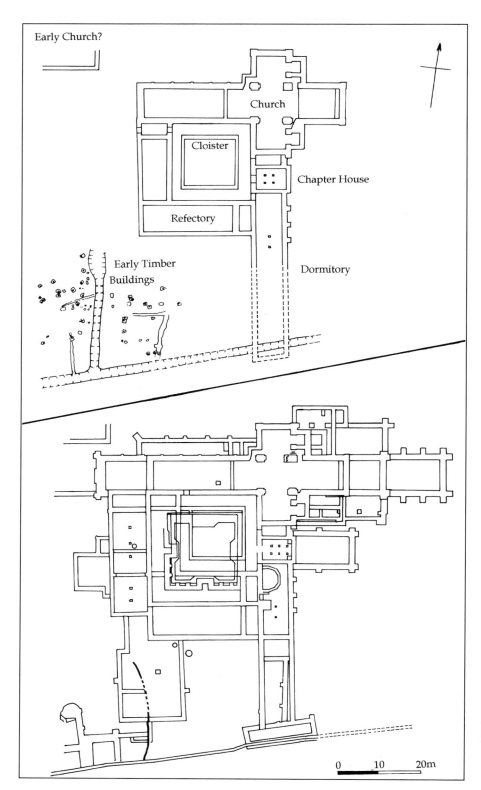

Early Church?

Church

Cloister

Chapter House

Refectory

Dormitory

Early Timber
Buildings

0    10    20m

FIGURE 74.
Plans of Norton Priory.
*Above:* its early phases
with timber buildings
being replaced by a
small, twelfth-century
stone layout;
*below:* the Abbey on
the verge of dissolution
in the sixteenth century
(after Greene 1989, xi,
80).

The timber phases were abandoned and demolished by *c.* 1190, by which time the masonry church was constructed. As was customary, this was the first part of the permanent fabric to be erected, using local red sandstone throughout, with ashlar facing containing a core of rubble and mortar. The church was far enough advanced to be consecrated in 1157 although it had to be substantially rebuilt after a fire in 1236. Beneath the floors of the church, the east cloister walk and the chapter house, numerous, often highly decorated sandstone coffins and grave slabs were discovered, containing or covering the remains of the privileged members of the community and their principal patrons. In burial grounds to the north and east were large numbers of further graves. There could not be a more comprehensive reminder of the sepulchral role of such foundations for patrons and inmates alike (Figure 75). By 1175, the community had completed a small range of buildings set around a cloister, which included the chapter house, refectory cellarer's range, with the dormitory running south from the south-east corner. Over the following 350 years, the basic plan was retained but substantial rebuilding occurred, involving large-scale extensions to the church and a large thirteenth-century kitchen range, as well as changes in the cloister area which effectively moved the southern range further away from the church. Building was still underway in the decades which preceded the reformation (Figure 74b).

At Norton, the foundations, and parts of the physical fabric which supported the buildings of a modest monastic community, bear witness to the periodic maintenance and improvements on which the canons spent a part of their revenues. As such, it is probably representative of the monastic communities of the North West.

The canons offered a substantial stimulus to numerous crafts and trades. For their church they required floor tiles, which were made on site (Greene and Johnson 1978), for various buildings they employed the skills of the mason, the carpenter and artificers in glass and lead and a variety of roofing trades, as well as unskilled labour. Work on this site and others employed the services of wagoners and quarrymen, nail manufacturers and blacksmiths (e.g. Thompson 1962). At least during periods of substantial building activity, monastic communities provided one of the most substantial and wide-ranging series of market opportunities for local suppliers. Even so, much of their raw materials, be it stone, timber or clay, came from their own estates or those of their patrons. By the end of the period it is clear that building timber was becoming increasingly hard to come by, available only by the grace and favour of those lords with major woodland and/or forest rights. In this respect and in their appetite for laths, wattles and other woodland products, the local religious houses were part of the general and growing pressure on woodland in the region.

There is little evidence of a comparable level of commitment to construction among the parish churches of the region before the late fourteenth century. Elements of earlier fabric do occasionally survive, but most major

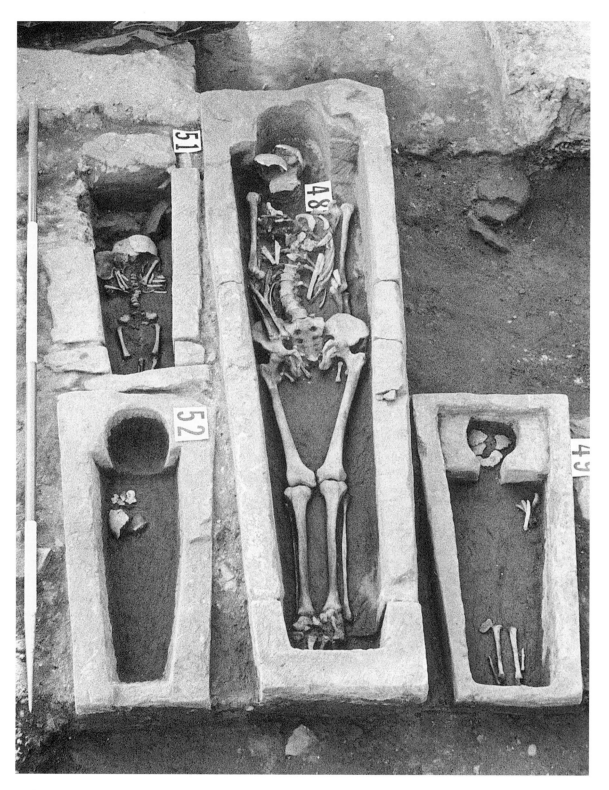

building episodes should probably be associated with the wealth of a particular patron. For example, the building of a substantial chapel at Nantwich in the late thirteenth century should be linked with the accident of patronage by Robert Burnell, Bishop of Bath and Wells, Chancellor of England and a keen patron of church building. The parish churches of the North West were probably in general small, relatively undecorated and ill-maintained, symptomatic of the comparative poverty of local patrons. It was not until significant numbers of local men were able to exploit the unusual range of opportunities offered by the patronage of the Black Prince, Richard II and (more specifically in Lancashire) the Lancastrian Kings that widespread signs appeared of an upturn in church construction, producing a plethora of late decorated and perpendicular styles, as at Bunbury, Malpas (Plate 6), Nantwich, Great Budworth, Frodsham, Manchester, Middleton, Wigan and Lancaster. To that point, many local churches probably remained timber-framed, and particularly those which originated as chapels and attained parochial status only in the fourteenth or fifteenth centuries, with meagre revenues. Something close to a score of timber-framed or partially timber-framed churches were still standing in Cheshire in 1800, but few survived the major rebuilding phase of the next century. Warburton and Siddington retain individual walls, Chadkirk and Holmes Chapel are part timber-framed but Lower Peover (Plate 12) and Marton have survived as black and white buildings, the latter with the remnants of painted plaster on the interior west wall. In the Middle Ages, timber-framed churches will have been far more numerous throughout the shire, as they were in Shropshire and Herefordshire, and may equally have occurred in lowland Lancashire.

## The Church in the later Middle Ages

Several of the ecclesiastical institutions experienced severe financial difficulties in the later medieval period. St Werburgh's and the nuns of St Mary's at Chester were hard hit by the Welsh rebellion and the black monks were adversely affected by the changing economic conditions for farming. St Werburgh's sought to compensate for the financial shortfall by wholesale appropriation of benefices and the suppression of vicarages at such valuable livings as Prestbury and Astbury. The *Valor* recorded that nearly a third of the revenues of the house were from parochial tithes. By 1540 only the manors of Huntington and Sutton were held in demesne. Elsewhere their wide estates were leased and much had been converted to pasture with the reduction of income that such conversion implied. In addition, the value of their estates had been adversely affected by coastal erosion in the Wirral peninsula. The poverty of St Werburgh's was relative, and probably compounded by a period of poor management. That of St John's and, more particularly, the nuns was absolute. By the middle of the fifteenth century the nunnery was in a poor condition, the buildings in need of urgent repair and the income inadequate even for the daily needs of the inmates.

FIGURE 75.
Norton Priory stone coffins found in the original chapter house but only deposited there, apparently all at the same time, after it had become the vestibule to the new one. The skeletons are of an adult male and three children, who may have been his, and they were presumably from an important local family of patrons, given this location and the impressive coffins.

PATRICK GREENE AND
JOHN ASTIN, NORTON
PRIORY MUSEUM TRUST

As far as can be judged, a similar picture emerges elsewhere in the region, with the religious heavily reliant on leases and parochial revenues. Penwortham, for example, was leasing for life land at Farington in the mid-fourteenth century and by the beginning of the reign of Henry VIII the house was leasing its tithes of corn and hay for the exceptional period of 60 years to two generations of local farmers (Hulton 1853). Those houses with substantial resources (as Combermere and Whalley) were able to weather the difficult economic conditions of the late four-teenth century comparatively well, while small and poorly-endowed houses were less buoyant. A major problem for the institutional religious lay in the changing pattern of endowment among the secular community. In general, monasteries received little or no fresh lands or other assets from this source after *c.* 1320 and as profits from land and tithes declined so their total revenues were affected.

During the later medieval period, the laity chose several alternative methods of facilitating their passage to the afterlife. Religious fraternities flourished in the major towns. Two existed in Chester in the fourteenth century, dedicated to St Anne (based on St John's) and St George (at St Peter's), with the purpose of augmenting church services, providing mutual support to members and intercessional prayer. Neither long survived the middle years of the fifteenth century, by which time chantries had become increasingly popular amongst those who could afford them.

Only the rich, or well-off, and childless could afford perpetual chantries. Few could afford to establish them on the scale envisaged at Upholland, where Sir Robert de Holland founded a college in 1310 but it is noteworthy that this had suffered severe financial difficulties within a decade and was replaced by a Benedictine priory in 1319. His eventual successor as the leader of the gentry of south-west Lancashire, the first earl of Derby, founded an almshouse at Lathom in 1500. Chantries – generally on a less ambitious scale – were very numerous in the region by the Reformation, both in the parochial churches and in monasteries (Baines 1868).

A by-product of the late-medieval popularity of chantries among gentry and burgesses was the endowment of a rash of grammar schools. This process had its beginnings before the Black Death and made a little headway in the Lancastrian period (e.g. Middleton Grammar School) but became increasingly popular after 1500, with a steady stream of testamentary foundations throughout the region by 1525. The result was a much improved provision of basic education for the boys of the poor not only in the rising commercial centres, such as Manchester, Warrington and Liverpool, but also in outlying townships, such as Farnworth near Bolton.

Parochial churches and friaries emerged as by far the commonest recipients of testamentary generosity and friars were frequently preferred to bury the deceased. Many like Randle 'Whytlof' (died 1361) left small bequests to several religious institutions, in his case to the friars at Warrington and Chester, St Mary's at Prestbury, St Mary's at Macclesfield and St Peter's at Prestbury. All of these were in addition to the chaplain who was to celebrate mass for half a year on his behalf (Ferguson 1896).

FIGURE 76.
The tomb of Sir Hugh de Calverley, in Bunbury Parish Church, which he refounded and to an extent rebuilt (after Ormerod (1882), II, plate facing p. 264).

Despite the bequests that they attracted, the friaries did not flourish financially. The Franciscans and Dominicans in Chester were in debt when dissolved to the value of two or three times their annual income and the Franciscan church had been in use in the early sixteenth century as a store for maritime equipment in return for upkeep of the fabric (Jones 1957). The Chester house of Carmelites was in better financial shape at the dissolution, despite a period of decline throughout the fifteenth century (V.C.H. 1980). Even so, all three orders maintained themselves in the esteem of the secular community up to the dissolution and beyond. The friary at Warrington, which has now been extensively excavated, enjoyed a scholastic reputation and Bishop Bird complained, after the suppression, of the high regard in which the local friars were still held by the civic community.

The late fourteenth century witnessed substantial reconstruction, renovation and embellishment of Cheshire's parochial churches. Local figures who had made good in France and/or in royal service were largely responsible. Sir Hugh de Calverley provides an apt example, obtaining royal consent in 1386 to re-found Bunbury church as a college or chantry staffed by a master and six chaplains. He repaired and enlarged the fabric (the crown supplied 20 tree trunks from Cheshire's forests for scaffolding poles), and his tomb still dominates the building (Figure 76). In the fifteenth century this movement became a flood throughout the region. Several of the surviving parish churches were extensively refashioned, whether always on original sites or nearby is not clear. Gt Budworth, Frodsham and Malpas provide examples of new fabric constructed on elevated sites visible for miles around, in the perpendicular style. Malpas was remodelled in the last years of the fifteenth century with alterations to the upper portions (Crossley 1936a).

As secular patrons emerged to new-found wealth under the patronage of princes and kings, so they chose both to advertise their success and attend to the needs of their souls. Many elected to patronise their own, local parochial churches. The church of Mottram-in-Longdendale, for example, was constructed in the reign of Henry VII. The part of the fabric which offered the most eye-catching possibilities was the tower. The late fifteenth century through to the dissolution has been aptly described as the 'age of tower building' with numerous examples still extant, including several, such as Tarvin, Macclesfield and Wybunbury, which appear to have been constructed by the same 'school' of masons (Crossley 1936b; 1940). The rebuilding of Hornby church tower was still underway under his patronage when Lord Mounteagle died in 1523.

The towns were equally the scene of investment in church fabric. The Abbey of St Werburgh's was not so greatly inconvenienced by the shortcomings of their revenues that they had to cease construction. Much of the cathedral at Chester dates to the period after the Black Death. The south transept was underway in the 1340s but the crossing tower was constructed and the nave completed in the fifteenth century.

In Lancashire little has survived from the late thirteenth or fourteenth centuries and little new was attempted until the fifteenth century. The outstanding example of a late-medieval church in the pre-1974 shire is the collegiate church at Manchester, undertaken in the years after 1422 when re-foundation occurred under the patronage of Thomas de la Warre. The unusually wide church was then extensively enlarged and embellished by successive, wealthy, wardens from the Langley and Stanley families and by the chantries of several local patrons later in the century. Slightly later (1431), the rebuilding of the priory and parish church at Lancaster was undertaken.

It is in their craftsmanship in wood that the region's church builders excelled. A local tradition of ornamentation can be discerned in the great halls of the late Middle Ages (see above) but it is in the embellishment of church interiors that these artists most fully demonstrated their accomplishments. There survives from this outpouring a wealth of carving, albeit only a fraction of what must have been present in the years before the Civil War. The Chester stalls with their misericords were undertaken about 1380. There followed stalls at Nantwich (*c.*1390), Middleton, Manchester (*c.*1506) and Lancaster. The rood screens at Mobberley and Astbury belong to the same period. The miserichords from Whalley Abbey were salvaged and can now be seen in the parish church. In all cases, the workmanship is characterised by a great variety of design and execution (Crossley 1976). It became customary to replicate in stone the decorative motives carved in wood. For example, the rudimentary quadrefoils at Smithills Hall find an echo in the approximately contemporary stone decorative panels on the exterior of Middleton Church and on carved wooden details within.

## The community and the Dissolution

The regional community in the early Tudor period was reactionary in its attitudes and conservative in its tastes. The same patrons who funded the building of late examples of the medieval hall listened to locally composed ballads, such as *Bosworth Fielde* and *The Ladye Bessie*, which would have been anachronistic in southern England. That the custom of founding chantries was still alive in the 1530s is consistent with an ongoing commitment to traditional catholicism. No evidence of Protestantism has been discerned in the region before the mid-century at earliest and the continuing strength of papism in the reign of Elizabeth in Lancashire is, and was then, widely recognised.

The community was poorly served by a parochial clergy who were, by national standards, ill-educated and under-funded. That is not to deny that graduates were reaching the region by the reign of Henry VIII but they were competing for the patronage of local patrons with others whose family connections compensated for their poorer scholastic attainments. The late medieval rectors of Winwick and the archdeacons of Chester, to offer two examples, were frequently members of the Stanley family whose paths to rich preferment were smoothed by the accident of their birth.

Literacy began to percolate from the church, the land-owning classes and urban elites into lower social strata during the later Middle Ages, arguably as a by-product of the raised standard of living. Concern to provide basic education was common among the gentry and civic aristocracies and encouraged their commitment to the proliferation of the new grammar schools (see above). By 1540, some members of the laity were better educated than the local clergy. However, the resulting tension did not lead locally to nonconformity, although there were disputes of a traditional kind between clerics and their parishioners, which generally centred on mortuary payments and tithes.

When they reached this region, both the Dissolution and the Reformation were imposed from outside on a society which was at best apathetic and at worst highly antagonistic towards government sponsored changes, which were viewed within the region with marked suspicion.

Within local society, the larger monasteries retained a status and a value which their counterparts in southern Britain had largely forfeited. The moral reputation of several houses was high: Cockersand was attracting new recruits and expanding in the years before the Dissolution (Haigh 1969) and the condition of Whalley Abbey appears to have been satisfactory, despite the sumptuous fare which commonly reached their table (Ashmore 1962). St Werburgh's, by contrast, was weakened by faction and by a lengthy contest for the abbacy, the protagonists within the cloister reflecting the struggle for political patronage and influence which was occurring more widely in the shire.

The Dissolution was a national phenomenon, organised centrally by a government which was enabled by national legislation to interfere in the affairs of the church, irrespective of local opinion. A hostile fact-finding visitation occurred in February 1535. The rulers of the monastic community were in no doubt of their incapacity to deflect the coming storm and some made what short-term gains they could. The Prior of St John the Baptist, Laund, Leicestershire, gave John Leghe of Norbury Booths (near Knutsford) a 60 year lease of 'all and singles there tithe corne and hey, pygges, gesse, hemp and flax growying, coming or being w(ith)in the cyrcutt of the lordshippe and demeanes of Norbury Boothes ...' (Taylor 1950). Soon after, there began the suppression of those houses with an income of less than £200 per annum. In Cheshire, this process involved the dissolution of all the religious houses excepting only St Werburgh's, Combermere and Vale Royal, on grounds of affluence, and Chester Nunnery owing to a lack of suitable places elsewhere for the inmates. In Lancashire south of the sands, of the independent houses, only Whalley and Cockersand remained, the latter because there was nowhere else within the order to send the canons.

Within weeks of the suppression of Sawley, Holland and Burscough, the commons of Lancashire beyond the Ribble rebelled against royal policy. The rising, known popularly as the Pilgrimage of Grace, began east of the Pennines, spreading into the north and east of Lancashire in the early months of 1536. The Earl of Derby lost control of his tenants in these areas and his son, Lord Mounteagle, and Sir Marmaduke Tunstall abandoned the north to the insurrection, which had considerable gentry backing.

Causal links between the Dissolution and the rising were close (Haigh 1969). The Pilgrims reinstated the monks of Sawley and expected support from the other religious, many of whom found their benefactors a severe embarrassment. Local communities objected to the destruction of religious houses which routinely accommodated members of their own families or employed or succoured their own relatives as servants, stewards, or tenants, or with fees or alms. Houses such as Whalley and Sawley were particularly important as providers of alms and of hospitality in areas in which travel was a necessary but comparatively difficult activity, with few alternative places to overnight that were secure (Figure 77). The buildings of the greater houses were the most splendid, the best served and the best provided of a region in which most churches, their furnishings and their incumbents left much to be desired.

The attitude of the earl of Derby was probably critical in halting the spread of insurrection. An unenthusiastic but cautiously loyal nobleman, constrained by debt to the crown as much as he was attracted by a substantial royal commission, Derby gathered his affinity in southern Lancashire on behalf of the government. It seems reasonable to assume that his sympathies and those of many of his supporters lay with the insurgents. The Stanleys had close links with most local monasteries and the earl was already in a better position to exploit their resources with them in being than he was to be after the Dissolution.

By the end of the winter of 1536, the rebellion had collapsed, outfaced by a determined government and in fear of government reprisals of the kind meted out at Carlisle. Derby was joined by an enthusiastic supporter of the

FIGURE 77
Whalley Gate House: the massive walls and two gate houses reflect both the status of the Abbey and also the insecurity of this north-western corner of England in the later Middle Ages, when the building of defensive residences, such as pele towers, spread widely through Cumbria to central and even southern Lancashire.

government, the earl of Sussex, and a series of strategic, judicial executions confirmed the victory of the crown, with Abbot Paslew at Whalley conspicuous among the victims.

Only isolated outbreaks of violence had occurred south of the Ribble, such as that which accompanied the abbot of Norton's meeting with the dissolution commissioners in October 1536. Despite having a gross income of more than £200, Norton was dissolved at this point. A force reckoned at several hundreds gathered from the locality to the abbey's support and the insurgents were able to reoccupy much of the house before the sheriff arrived and rescued the commissioners.

The greater houses and those that survived the suppression of 1536 gave way rapidly thereafter, in an atmosphere of fear and trepidation. Whalley was deemed to have fallen to the crown by reason of the treason of its abbot. Cockersand was the last Lancashire house, surrendering to the crown in January 1539, by which time both Combermere (July 1538) and Vale Royal (September 1538) had done the same south of the Mersey. Bar only the nunnery at Chester and a handful of hospitals, St Werburgh's was the last north-western house to surrender, last as it had been first, as befitted the richest and most influential house, falling to the crown on the 20 January, 1540.

Monastic property passed either to the Duchy or, more often, to the new Court of Augmentations. The role of the land-hungry Duchy as a recipient of many erstwhile monastic estates in Lancashire kept an unusual quantity of local property in royal hands. This was not the case south of the Mersey, where access to royal patronage gave Ralph Worley, a member of the royal household, the opportunity to buy the site and much of the lands of Birkenhead Priory. Similar circumstances enabled George Cotton to convert Combermere to a country house and Thomas Holcroft, the royal commissioner, to build at Vale Royal, where he dismantled the church and incorporated the ruins in his new mansion. At Norton, Sir Richard Brooke purchased the site in a fairly ruinous condition nine years after it was dissolved, and set about redeveloping the buildings of the outer courtyard into a grand house, around which the medieval moats and water courses were retained (Beaumont 1873; Green 1989). To the North of the Mersey, Sir William Paget and several merchants obtained grants or purchases but most sales of land went to established Lancashire men with an existing record of government service. Thomas Holcroft was again among the purchasers, with new lands from the estates of Lytham Priory and Whalley. His colleague, John Braddyll, was another beneficiary.

Despite their entry to the monastic land market, recent examination has been unable to identify aggressive new estate management practices among the markedly protestant incomers, such as characterised many men in a similar position elsewhere in England. The 'new monastics' were arguably as conservative in this sense as most other elements in this regional society (Haigh 1969).

Unlike most monastic sites, St Werburgh's was retained for spiritual purposes. In August 1541, the formalities were completed by which the church was converted to a cathedral and Chester diocese was created out of the archdeaconries of Chester and Richmond. The last abbot became the first dean, with nine of his monks among the new cathedral staff, at the centre of a critically under-financed see now almost devoid of landed estates.

CHAPTER 8

# Postscript

In 1066 the North West was a peripheral part of an England which was only loosely unified under the leadership of the West Saxon dynasty, and its landscapes reflected that fact. Outside of Chester, comparatively small settlements predominated, often of just one or two farms, sometimes with five or six, with a patchwork of arable strips laid out around them. Outside these relatively restricted pockets of intensive land-use, much of the terrain was only lightly used for pasture or food-gathering activities of various kinds. Substantial amounts of the land surface were virtually unused, consisting of lowland mossland or marshes, or upland hill country, and woodland was very widespread. Some areas were already set aside for hunting and there were numerous beasts of the chase and probably also wolves, which were their natural predators. Within a national context, this was a marginal land in pretty well every meaning of the term, be it geographic, demographic, economic or environmental. This was a true frontier landscape.

The period from 1086 to 1349 witnessed perhaps the most important and far-reaching changes in this landscape to have occurred between the last Ice Age and the industrialisation of the region in the late eighteenth and early nineteenth centuries. This was a period of unprecedented, if ill-understood, population increase and colonisation, which witnessed the expansion of pretty well all the settlements within the region, and the foundation or transformation of very many more, including a whole raft of new, small urban foundations and villages as well as numerous hamlets and dispersed farms and cottages.

Although the bare bones of the manorial structure existed in 1066 in the estates and tenurial organisation of the late Saxon aristocracy, it was in this period that those bones had flesh put on them, both in terms of population and of territorial expansion of land in agrarian use. Numerous new manors or sub-manors were formed from lands which were previously waste or just seasonal pastureland, often based on moated sites, while peasants cut out a plethora of small holdings in the woods and wastes, both with and without manorial support. New religious houses were founded, often in comparatively under-used terrain, bringing yet more pressure for assarting and land reclamation. New settlements – vaccaries – based largely on cattle rearing were established in the uplands. Woodland progressively declined in extent during this epoch under the pressure of assarting, the pasturing of livestock and felling for timber. Much of what remained was managed intensively and harvested regularly, via pollarding or coppicing. Vast numbers of new enclosures were created from the commons and new town fields laid out and ploughed up as ridge and furrow. While it would still be fair to describe this as a woodland landscape, few really extensive woods existed by 1500 and numerous small stands, copses and river or stream bank woodland made up a high proportion of the total.

This is not to imply that the region had lost much of its marginality. The uplands offered a harsh environment suited only to extensive land-use, while the lowland landscape remained throughout one dominated over significant areas by extensive mosslands too deep and broad to be reclaimed in their totality by the technologies available. These had little value beyond their use as a source of fuel. Nor was the region particularly successful in economic or demographic terms when measured against parts of southern England, either in terms of wealth per unit area or density of population. The Middle Ages did, however, witness a major episode of catch up, which saw regional levels of population and of economic activity rise faster than many other parts of England, albeit to quite modest levels. The comparatively rapid process of colonisation and land-use intensification which occurred was of crucial importance in terms of the regional community and the landscape which it shaped.

This period saw the development of numerous nucleated settlements. Some had urban characteristics, as well as agrarian ones, and it fair to say that the basic framework of market towns (but not industrial towns) was laid down during the Middle Ages, and has altered comparatively little since, despite some losses. Many more nucleated settlements had few or none of the characteristics of towns, and were always agrarian communities. Most of these, too, have survived to the modern period, albeit a few villages and some hamlets were deserted as a consequence of the establishment of monastic granges, or between *c.* 1350 and 1800. At the same time, many areas retained or developed a dispersed pattern of settlement, which was particularly dominant in old woodland parts, such as central southern Lancashire.

There were arguably several important factors determining the pattern of settlement, none of which answers all cases. One seems to have been the attitudes of land-owners (although these are not often directly ascertainable), who were responsible for numerous new towns and the recognition and encouragement of urban developments at numerous sites where organic development was already occurring due to geographical or economic factors. Many agricultural villages look as though they were planned, and this is unlikely to have occurred without manorial support, at least, and may have derived from lordly initiative. Many of the small manorial hamlets which were characteristic of the eleventh century developed into open field villages by the fourteenth, and landlords were presumably accepting of this process, at the very least, and keen to expand their rent rolls where appropriate. The availability of suitable soils in sufficient acreages to facilitate large expanses of arable was also important, since open fields and the nucleation of settlement seem to have been strongly linked. Larger parcels of better-drained lowland soils were, therefore, generally occupied by one or more nucleated settlements. Manorial interest in the actual organisation of the landscape seems often to have been weak, however, perhaps because the early scarcity of labour then the comparative absence of week work discouraged lords from engaging in demesne farming. There is comparatively little evidence of manorial demesne intermingled in the open field with the strips of the peasantry. Furthermore, two factors weakened the impulse to organise open field into just two or three great fields each used exclusively in any one year: one was the widespread availability of summer pasture on the marshes, moss skirtlands and uplands, which reduced the pressure on collectively organised fallow to provide pasture for the livestock of lord and peasantry alike; the other was the variability and marginality of so much of the terrain, that encouraged the organisation of open field in small parcels rather than great swathes, with enclosed land, woodland, or stretches of mossland, etc. in between. The result was a system of open field unlike that of the Midlands both in scale and organisational rigidity, characterised by either one large single field or numerous, scattered units, or, where only very limited areas of agricultural land were accessible, a small scale, infield/outfield pattern of utilisation.

Where the landscape was ill-suited to the development of open field, alternative strategies were available to manorial lords. Some chose to found religious houses on outlying islands of dry terrain within the lowland mosses, and leave the task of colonisation and improvement largely to them. Others founded vaccaries in the valleys of the uplands, sometimes in quite large numbers. Small scale assarting by peasant families, of wet bottom land, woodland or moss edge sites, often resulted in numerous new tenancies, which brought new rents and services to the manor. Such resulted in dispersed patterns of settlement, with crofts and messuages interspersed with new enclosures and pockets of moss, heath or woodland, but not incorporated into open field.

However, where manorial lords chose to sub-infeudate or let substantial parcels of land capable of colonisation and improvement, then entire new economic units with their own settlements took root on the margins of existing townships. In these circumstances, the renting of land to members of the community with the resources to invest in improvement encouraged the development of a large and influential class of substantial farmers, 'yeomen' and lesser gentry. Such families often had a portfolio of lands and other assets, but at their core was generally a comparatively compact estate of a few hundred acres, with land of various different categories (including both enclosed and common land), within which they generally lived. Like the monastic foundations, these aspiring gentry families invested in land improvement, drainage and enclosure, built new mills and developed commercial herds capable of yielding a surplus for sale. They also created scatters of new peasant holdings, not generally in large villages but in hamlets and dispersed farms set in among pastures, woods and arable fields, and alongside the surviving moss-, wood-, hill- or heathland from which such estates had generally been carved out.

re-organised over the next two centuries, to produce the comparatively regular, rectangular fields which, over significant areas, betray signs of having been planned with the cheese industry in mind, and losing in the process many pre-existing field-names. The attack on the great lowland mosses was still only beginning, and numerous lowland, as well as upland communities retained shared rights of common, albeit access was comparatively limited. There were numerous smaller commons as well, which had so far resisted complete enclosure where the ground was very wet or deep peat survived, and which were often on the boundaries of several townships. As, for example, the First Edition Ordnance Survey Six Inch map of Preston and its environs records in 1849 of the 108 acre Ribbleton Moor, it was 'Land common to the townships of Ribbleton and hamlet of Brockholes. The township boundary between A and B is undecided.' The stone plinths of crosses marked the approximate line of the Clitheroe road from Preston as it crossed the common, and habitations ringed it, but its elongated 'L' shape had to this date survived the pressure to enclose. To the south lie the irregular fields of Brockholes, which were probably piecemeal assarts from Brockholes Wood (the name, which has a British stem, recalls a badger sett). To the west are regular fields derived from the enclosure of part of Preston's open field, and behind them more moorland, which had been emparked by this date for municipal use. To the north are variously the late and highly regular fieldscapes of central Fulwood, which had been medieval forest, and the far less regular fields around Ribbleton Hall. This sort of diversity is characteristic in an area where communities, in the lowlands at least, rarely used parliamentary procedures to achieve township-wide re-planning, but instead undertook numerous smaller scale re-organisations affecting just one estate within a township, a particular common or park, or a small number of farms. The consequent pattern of farms and fields obscures the medieval landscape more thoroughly than in the champion areas, where change was better documented and on a more monumental scale. In addition, the growth of industry and the rapid rise in the regional population later encouraged the ploughing up of land, with the result that medieval ridges survive less well here than in parts of the Midlands or the North East.

It would be trade, then manufacturing, that would further change this landscape, but in 1540, that was only just beginning. The antiquarian Leland remarked variously that Manchester men were buying Irish yarn at the port of Liverpool, that canal coal was being mined near Wigan and sea coal around Bolton, and that several towns were prospering, among which he singled out Warrington for the excellence of its market. In other respects, however, it was still predominantly an agricultural landscape of great variation, a landscape of extraordinarily flat lowlands with extensive mosslands and marshes, but mossland from which the rising land of the old woodland areas were always visible, with the uplands and fell country behind.

# Bibliography

## Abbreviations in use in the Bibliography

| | |
|---|---|
| *Ag.H.R.* | *Agricultural History Review* |
| A.M.S. | Ancient Monuments Society |
| *Ant. J.* | *Antiquaries Journal* |
| *Arch. Camb.* | *Archaeologia Cambrensis* |
| *B.J.R.L.* | *Bulletin of the John Rylands Library* |
| *C.A.B.* | *Cheshire Archaeological Bulletin* |
| *C.B.A.* | *Council for British Archaeology* |
| *Chesh.H.* | *Cheshire History* |
| C.R.O. | Cheshire Record Office |
| *C.S. 1, 2, 3* | *Chetham Society, First Series, etc.* |
| *Ec.H.R.* | *Economic History Review* |
| *E.H.R.* | *English Historical Review* |
| G.M.A.C. | Greater Manchester Archaeological Contracts, University of Manchester |
| *G.M.A.J.* | *Greater Manchester Archaeological Journal* |
| *J.C.&N.W.A.S.* | *Journal of the Chester and North Wales Archaeological Society* |
| *J.C.A.S.* | *Journal of the Chester Archaeological Society* |
| *J.Ecol.* | *Journal of Ecology* |
| *J.E.P.N.S.* | *Journal of the English Place Name Society* |
| *J.Med.H.* | *Journal of Medieval History* |
| *Med.Arch.* | *Medieval Archaeology* |
| *M.H.* | *Midland History* |
| *N.H.* | *Northern History* |
| *N.Phytol.* | *New Phytologist* |
| n.s. | new series |
| o.s. | old series |
| *P.M.Lit.&Phil.Soc.* | *Proceedings of the Manchester Literary and Philosophical Society* |
| *P.P.S.* | *Proceedings of the Prehistoric Society* |
| *R.C.H.M.* | *Royal Commission on Historical Monuments* |
| *R.S.L.C.* | *Record Society of Lancashire and Cheshire* |
| *T.C.W.A.A.S.* | *Transactions of the Cumberland and Westmorland Antiquarian and Archaeological Society* |
| *T.H.S.L.C.* | *Transactions of the Historical Society of Lancashire and Cheshire* |
| *T.L.C.A.S.* | *Transactions of the Lancashire and Cheshire Antiquarian Society* |
| *V.C.H.* | *Victoria County History* |

Abram, W. A. (1884) *Preston Guild Merchant 1882*, Memorials of the Preston Guilds, Preston.
Alldridge, N. J. (1981) 'Aspects of the Topography of Early Medieval Chester' *J.C.A.S.* 64: 5–31.
Anderson, O. S. (1934) *The English Hundred-Names*, Lund, Lunds Universitets årsskrift.

*Bibliography*

Angus-Butterworth, L. M. (1977) 'Early Lancashire Brasses' *A.M.S.* n.s. 22: 90–103.

Angus-Butterworth, L. M. (1982) 'Some Old Lancashire Halls' *A.M.S.* n.s. 26: 194–209.

Appleby, J. C. and Dalton, P. eds (1997) *Government, Religion and Society in Northern England, 1000–1700,* Stroud, Sutton.

Arrowsmith, P. (1997) *Stockport: A History,* Stockport, Stockport Metropolitan Borough Council.

Ashmore, O. (1962) 'The Whalley Abbey Bursars' Account for 1520' *T.H.S.L.C* 114: 49–72.

Ashmore, O. (1982) *The Industrial Archaeology of North West England,* Manchester, Manchester University Press.

Astill, G. (1988) 'Rural Settlement: the Toft and the Croft' in G. Astill and A. Grant eds, 36–61.

Astill, G. and Grant, A. eds (1988) *The Countryside of Medieval England,* Oxford Basil Blackwell.

Astill, G. and Langdon, J. eds (1997) *Medieval Farming and Technology: The Impact of Agricultural Change in Northwest Europe,* Brill.

Aston, M., Austin, D. and Dyer, C. eds (1989) *The Rural Settlements of Medieval England: Studies Dedicated to Maurice Beresford and John Hurst,* Oxford, Basil Blackwell.

Atkin, M. A. (1985) 'Some Settlement Patterns in Lancashire' in D. Hooke ed., 171–185.

Axon, W. E. A. (1884) *Cheshire Gleanings,* Manchester and London.

Aybes, C. and Yalden, D. W. (1995) 'Place-name Evidence for the Former Distribution and Status of Wolves and Beavers in Britain' *Mammal Review* 25.4, 201–27.

Bailey, M. (1989) *A Marginal Economy? East Anglian Breckland in the Later Middle Ages,* Cambridge, Cambridge University Press.

Bailey, R. N. (2003) '"What Mean These Stones?" Some Aspects of Pre-Norman Sculpture in Cheshire and Lancashire,' in D. Scragg, ed. *Textual and Material Culture in Anglo-Saxon England: Thomas Northcote Toller and the Toller Memorial Lectures, Woodbridge,* Boydell and Brewer, *213–39.*

Baines, E. (1868) *The History of the County Palatine and Duchy of Lancashire,* vol. 1 (a new, revised and improved edition, ed. J. Harland), London and Manchester.

Baker, A. R. H. and Butlin, R. A. eds (1973) *Studies in Field Systems in the British Isles,* Cambridge, Cambridge University Press.

Ballard, A. and Tait, J. (1923) *British Borough Charters 1216–1307,* Cambridge, Cambridge University Press.

Bankes, G. H. A. and Haworth, J. P. (1965) 'School House Farm, Up Holland' in 'Three Church Buildings in Lancashire and Cheshire', by R. F. Taylor, *T.H.S.L.C.* 117: 47–52.

Barker, E. E. ed. (1953) *Talbot Deeds, 1200–1682,* R.S.L.C. 103.

Barker, P. A. and Higham, R. A. (1982) *Hen Domen, Montgomery,* vol. 1, London Royal Archaeological Institute.

Barraclough, G. (1951) 'The Earldom and County Palatine of Chester' *T.H.S.L.C.* 103: 23–57.

Barraclough, G. ed. (1957) *Early Cheshire Charters* R.S.L.C. 76.

Barraclough, G. ed. (1988) *The Charters of the Anglo-Norman Earls of Chester, c. 1071–1237,* R.S.L.C. 126.

Barrow, G. W. S. (1969) 'Northern English Society in the Early Middle Ages' *N. H.* 4: 1–28.

Barrow, G. W. S. (1973) *The Kingdom of the Scots,* London, Edward Arnold.

Barrow, G. W. S. (1975) 'The Pattern of Lordship and Feudal Settlement in Cumbria' *J. Med. H.* 1, 2: 117–138.

Bartley, D. D. (1975) 'Pollen Analytical Evidence for Forest Clearance in the Upland Area West of Rishworth, West Yorkshire' *N. Phytol.* 74: 373–381.

Bartley, D. D., Jones, I. P. and Smith, R. T. (1990) 'Studies in the Flandrian Vegetational History of the Craven District of Yorkshire: the Lowlands' *J. Ecol.* 78: 611–632.

Bassett, S. (1992) 'Church and Diocese in the West Midlands: the Transition from British to

Anglo-Saxon Control' in J. Blair and R. Sharpe eds *Pastoral Care before the Parish*, Leicester Leicester University Press, 13–40, 423–37.

Bates, D. (1982) *Normandy before 1066*, Harlow Longman.

Bean, J. M. W. (1962–3) 'Plague, Population and Economic Decline in the Later Middle Ages' *Ec. H. R.* 15

Beaumont, W. (1872) *Annals of the Lords of Warrington*, vol 1, C.S. 186.

Beaumont, W. (1873) *A History of the Castle of Halton, and the Priory or Abbey of Norton*, Warrington.

Beck, J. (1969) *Tudor Cheshire*, Chester, Cheshire Community Council.

Bede, *Ecclesiastical History of the English People*, ed B. Colgrave and R. A. B. Mynors (1969), Oxford, Oxford University Press.

Bellamy, J. G. (1964–5) 'The Northern Rebellions in the Later Years of Richard II' *B.J.R.L.* 47: 254–274.

Bennett, J. H. E. ed. (1906) *The Rolls of the Freemen of the City of Chester*, R.S.L.C. 51.

Bennett, J. H. E. (1935) 'The White Friars of Chester' *J.C.A.S.* 31: 5–54.

Bennett, M. J. (1979) 'Sources and Problems in the Study of Social Mobility: Cheshire in the Later Middle Ages' *T.H.S.L.C.* 128: 59–75.

Bennett, M. J. (1979) 'Sir Gawain and the Green Knight and the Literary Achievement of the North-west Midlands: The Historic Background' *J. Med. H.* 5: 63–88.

Bennett, M. J. (1983) *Community, Class and Careerism: Cheshire and Lancashire Society in the Age of Sir Gawain and the Green Knight*, Cambridge, Cambridge University Press.

Beresford, M. W. and Finberg, H. P. R. (1973) *English Medieval Boroughs: A Handlist*, Newton Abbot, David and Charles.

Beresford, M. and Hurst, J. (1971) *Deserted Medieval Villages*, Woking, Lutterworth Press.

Bestwick, J. D. (1984) 'Excavations at Middlewich 1972–3 Site J, Kings Street' *C.A.B.* 2: 29–30.

Bettey, J. (2000) 'Downlands' in J. Thirsk ed. 27–49.

Birks, H. J. B. (1963–4) 'Chat Moss, Lancashire' *P. M. Lit & Phl. Soc.* 106: 22–45.

Birks, H. J. B. (1965a) 'Late-glacial Deposits at Bagmere, Cheshire and Chat Moss, Lancashire' *N. Phytol.* 64: 270–285.

Birks, H. J. B. (1965b) 'Pollen Analytical Investigations at Holcroft Moss, Lancashire, and Lindow Moss, Cheshire' *J. Ecol.* 53, 299–314.

Blair, J. (1985) 'Secular Minsters in Domesday Book' in P. H. Sawyer ed. *Domesday Book: A Reassessment*, London, 104–142.

Blair, J. (1987) 'The Local Church in Domesday Book and Before' in J. C. Holt ed. *Domesday Studies*, Woodbridge, 265–278.

Blair, J. ed. (1988) *Minsters and Parish Churches: The Local Church in Transition 950–1200*, Oxford, Oxford University Committee for Archaeology.

Blair, J. and Sharpe, R. eds (1992) *Pastoral Care Before the Parish*, Leicester, Leicester University Press.

Blair, P. H. (2nd edn, 1977) *Anglo-Saxon England*, Cambridge, Cambridge University Press.

Booth, P. H. W. (1976) 'Taxation and Public Order: Cheshire in 1353' *N. H.* 12: 16–31.

Booth, P. H. W. (1979) 'Farming for Profit in the 14th Century: The Cheshire Estates of the Earldom of Cheshire' *J.C.A.S.* 62: 73–90.

Booth, P. H. W. (1981) *The Financial Administration of the Lordship and County of Cheshire 1272–1377* C.S. 3, 28.

Booth, P. H. W. (1984) 'Calendar of the Cheshire Trailbaston Proceedings, 1353' *Chesh. H.* 13: 22–28.

Booth, P. H. W. ed. (1984) *Burton in Wirral, a History*, Burton and S. Wirral Local Hist. Soc.

Booth, P. H. W. (1993) 'From Medieval Park to Puritan Republic', in A. G. Crosby ed., 63–83.

*Bibliography*

Booth, P. H. W. and Carr, A. D. (1991) *Account of John de Burnham the Younger, Chamberlain of Chester, of the Revenues of the Counties of Chester and Flint, Michaelmas 1361 to Michaelmas 1362*, R.S.L.C. 125.

Booth, P. H. W. and Dodd, J. P. (1979) 'The Manor and Fields of Frodsham' *T.H.S.L.C.* 128: 27–57.

Booth, P. H. W. and Jones, R. N. (1979) 'Burton in Wirral: From Domesday to Dormitory, Part Two' *Chesh. H.* 4: 28–42.

Bott, O. (1984) 'Cornmill Sites in Cheshire 1066–1850: 3, Medieval Mills and Agriculture' *Chesh. H.* 13: 33–38.

Bowman, W. M. (1960) *England in Ashton-under-Lyne*, Altrincham, Sherratt for the Aston-under-Lyne Corporation.

Bradshaw, H. (1887) *The Life of Saint Werburge of Chester*, ed. C. Horstmann for the Early English Text Soc. O.S., 88, London.

Britnell, R. H. (1993) *The Commercialisation of English Society 1000–1500*, Cambridge, Cambridge University Press.

Brook, D. (1992) 'The Early Christian Church East and West of Offa's Dyke' in N. Edwards and A. Lane eds *The Early Church in Wales and the West*, Oxford Oxbow Monograph 16, 77–89.

Brooke, T. ed. (1898) *The Chartulary of Cockersand Abbey* C.S. 2, 38.

Brotherston-Ratcliffe, E. H. (1975) 'Excavation at Grange Cow Worth, Ellesmere Port, 1966 and 1967' *J.C.A.S.* 58: 69–80.

Brown, A. N. (1984) 'The Rows Debate: Where Next?' *J.C.A.S.* 67: 77–84.

Brown, A. N. (1999) *The Rows of Chester: The Chester Rows Research Project*, London, English Heritage.

Brown, A. N., Howes, B. and Turner, R. C. (1986) ' A Medieval Stone Town House in Chester', *J.C.A.S.* 68: 143–153.

Brownbill, J. (1901) 'Cheshire in Domesday Book' T.H.S.L.C. 155: 1–25.

Brownbill, J. (1913) *A Calendar of the Collection of Deeds and Papers of the Moore Family*, R.S.L.C. 67.

Brownbill, J. ed. (1914) *The Ledger-book of Vale Royal Abbey*, R.S.L.C. 68.

Brunskill, R. W. (1962) 'The Clay Houses of Cumberland' *A.M.S.* 57–80.

Brunskill, R. W. (3rd edition, 1987) *Illustrated Handbook of Vernacular Architecture*, London Faber and Faber.

Bryson, B. (2000) 'Introduction' in P. Forty (project manager) *The English Landscape*, London, Profile Books, 1–13.

Bu'Lock, J. D. (1958) 'Pre-Norman Crosses of west Cheshire and the Norse Settlements Around the Irish Sea' *T.A.S.L.C.* 68: 1–11.

Bu'Lock, J. D. (1960) 'Celtic, Saxon and Scandinavian Settlement at Meols in Wirral' *T.H.S.L.C.* 112: 1–28.

Bu'Lock, J. D. (1970) *Pre Conquest Cheshire*, Chester, Cheshire Community Council.

Burne, R. V. H. (1948) 'The Dissolution of St Werburgh's Abbey', *J.C.A.S.* 37: 5–38.

Burne, R. V. H. (1957) 'Cheshire under the Black Prince', *J.C.&N.W.A.S.* 44: 1–18.

Burne, R. V. H. (1961) 'Richard II and Cheshire', *J.C.&N.W.A.S.* 48: 27–34.

Bushell, W. F. (1956) 'The Ancient Graveyard of Birkenhead Priory', *T.H.S.L.C.* 108: 141–146.

Butler, L. A. S. (1976) 'Valle Crucis: An Excavation 1970', *Arch. Camb.* 125: 80–126.

Cameron, K. (1968) 'Eccles in English Placenames', in M. W. Bailey and R. P. C. Hanson eds *Christianity in Roman Britain*, Leicester, 87–92.

Campbell, B. M. S. (2000) *English Seigneurial Agriculture 1250–1450*, Cambridge, Cambridge University Press.

Cantle, A. (1937) *The Pleas of Quo Warranto for the County of Lancaster*, C.S. 2, 98.

Cantor, L. (1983) *The Medieval Parks of England: A Gazetteer*, Loughborough, Department of Education, University of Loughborough.

Carrington, P. ed. (1994) *From Flints to Flower Pots: Current Research in the Dee-Mersey Region*, Papers from a seminar held at Chester, February 1994, Chester City Council Archaeological Services Occasional Paper no. 2.

Carter, G. A. (1953) 'The Free Borough of Warrington in the Thirteenth Century', *T.H.S.L.C.* 105: 25–44.

Cathcart King, D. J. (1988) *The Castle in England and Wales*, London, Croom Helm.

Chambers, F. M. and Wilshaw, I. W. (1997) 'A Reconstruction of the Post-glacial Environmental History of Tatton Park, Cheshire, from Valley Mire Sediments', University of Keele Dept. of Geography Occasional Papers, 13.

Chapman, V. (1953) 'Open Fields in West Cheshire', *T.H.S.L.C.* 104: 35–60.

Chibnall, M. ed. (1969) *The Ecclesiastical History of Orderic Vitalis*, Oxford, Oxford University Press.

Chippindall, W. H. (1939) *A 16th Century Survey and Year's Account of the Estates of Hornby Castle, Lancashire*, C.S. 2, 102.

Christie, R. C. ed. (1887) *Annales Cestrienses or Chronicle of the Abbey of S. Werburg, at Chester* R.S.L.C. 14.

Clarke, E. K. (1895) 'The Foundation of Kirkstall Abbey', *Thoresby Society Transactions*. 4: 169–208.

Clayton, D. J. (1980) 'The 'Cheshire Parliament' in the 15th Century', *Chesh. H.* 6: 13–27.

Clayton, D. J. (1990) *The Administration of the County Palatine of Chester, 1442–85*, C.S. 3, 35.

Clayton, K. M. (1979) 'The Midlands and Southern Pennines', in A. Straw and K. Clayton eds *Eastern and Central England*, London, Methuen 143–231.

Coates, B. (1965) 'The Origin and Distribution of Markets and Fairs in Medieval Derbyshire', *Derbyshire Archaeological Journal* 85: 92–111.

Coates, R. and Breeze A. (2000) *Celtic Voices English Places*, Stamford, Shaun Tyas.

Collens, J. (1999) 'Flying on the Edge: Aerial Photography and Settlement Patterns in Cheshire and Merseyside' in M. Nevell ed., 36–40.

Colvin, H. M., Brown, R. A. and Taylor, A. J. (1963) *The History of the King's Works: the Middle Ages,* vols I and II, London, H.M.S.O.

Cooke, A. M. ed. (1901) *Act Book of the Ecclesiastical Court of Whalley 1510–38*, C.S. 1,44.

Cordingley R. A. and Wood-Jones, R. B. (1959) 'Chorley Hall, Cheshire', *A. M. S.* n. s. 7: 61–86.

Coward, B. (1983) *The Stanleys, Lords Stanley and Earls of Derby 1385–1672* C.S. 3, 30.

Cowell, R. (1990) 'Current Prehistoric Work on Merseyside: Greasley and other Prehistoric Sites', *C.B.A. Grp 5 Newsletter* 60: 3–4.

Cowell, R. W. and Innes, J. B. (1994) *The Wetlands of Merseyside*, North West Wetlands Survey 1 Lancaster, Lancaster University Archaeological Unit.

Cowell, R. W. and Philpott, R. A. (2000) *Prehistoric, Romano-British and Medieval Settlement in Lowland North West England*, Liverpool, National Museum and Galleries on Merseyside.

Cownie, E. (1998) *Religious Patronage in Anglo-Norman England 1066–1135*, Woodbridge, Royal Historical Society, Boydell Press.

Croom, J. (1988) 'The Fragmentation of the Minster *Parochiae* of South-East Shropshire', in J. Blair ed. 67–82.

Crosby, A. G. ed. (1993), *Lancashire Local Studies*, Preston, Carnegie Publishing.

Crosby, A. G. (1996) *A History of Cheshire*, Chichester and London, Phillimore.

Crosby, A. G. (1998) *A History of Lancashire*, Chichester and London, Phillimore.

Crossley, F. H. (1936) 'Cheshire Church Towers', *J.C.A.S.* 2, 31: 89–112.

*Bibliography*

Crossley, F. H. (1937) 'On the Importance of 14th Century Planning in the Construction of the Churches of Cheshire', *J.C.A.S.* 2, 32,1: 5–52.

Crossley, F. H. (1938) 'Cheshire Churches in the 12th Century', *J.C.A.S.* 32,2: 73–97.

Crossley, F. H. (1940) 'The Renaissance of Cheshire Church Buildings in the late 15th and early 16th Centuries', *J.C.A.S.* 2, 34,2: 53–160.

Crossley, P. (1976) *Medieval Architecture and Sculpture in the North West*, Manchester, Whitworth Art Gallery.

Crowe, P. R. (1962) 'Climate' in *Manchester and its Region: A Survey Prepared for the Meeting in Manchester August 29th to September 5 1962*, Manchester, Manchester University Press for the British Association, 17–46.

Cullen, P. W. and Horden, R. (1986) *The Castles of Cheshire*, Liverpool, C and H. Publishers.

Curry, A. E. (1979) 'Cheshire and the Royal Demesne 1399–1422' *T.H.S.L.C.* 128: 113–138.

Danbury, E. (2000) 'The Intellectual Life of the Abbey of St Werburgh, Chester, in the Middle Ages' in A. Thacker ed., 107–120.

Darby, H. C. and Maxwell, I. S. eds (1962) *The Domesday Geography of Northern England*, Cambridge, Cambridge University Press.

Darby, H. C. and Terrett, I. B. (1954) *The Domesday Geography of Midland England*, Cambridge, Cambridge University Press.

Darlington, R. R. (1933) 'Aethelwig, Abbot of Evesham', *E.H.R.* 48: 1–22, 177–85.

Davey, P. J. ed. (1977) *Medieval Pottery from Excavations in the North West*, Liverpool, Institute of Extension Studies, University of Liverpool.

Davey, P. J. (1983) 'Later Medieval Imported Pottery in the Irish Sea province', in P. Davey and R. Hodges eds *Ceramics and Trade*, Sheffield, University of Sheffield, 209–230.

Davey, P. J. and Rutter, J. A. (1977) 'A Note on Continental Imports in the North West 800–1700 AD', *Medieval Ceramics* 1: 17–30.

Davies, C. S. (1960) *The Agricultural History of Cheshire* C. S., 3, 10.

Davies, C. S. (1976) *A History of Macclesfield*, Manchester J. Morten.

Davies, R. R. (1987) *Conquest, Coexistence and Change: Wales 1063–1415*, Oxford, Oxford University Press.

Davnall, S. A. (1985) *The Development of the Parochial System in Mid Cheshire, 1086–1292*, unpublished M. A. Thesis, University of Manchester.

de Figueiredo, P. and Treuherz, J. (1988) *Cheshire Country Houses*, Chichester.

Defoe, D. (1725) *A Tour through England and Wales*, Repr. in Everyman's Library, 820, 821, London.

Dent, J. S. (1977) 'Recent Excavations on the site of Stockport Castle', *T.A.S.L.C.* 79: 1–13.

Demarest, E. B. (1923) 'Inter Ripam et Mersham', *E.H.R.* 38; 161–70.

Denton, J. (1992) 'From the Foundation of Vale Royal Abbey to the Statute of Carlisle: Edward I and Ecclesiastical Patronage', *Thirteenth Century England* 4: 123–37.

Dickinson, S. (1985) 'Bryant's Gill, Kentmere: Another 'Viking-Period' Ribblehead?' in J. R. Baldwin and I. D. Whyte eds *The Scandinavians in Cumbria*, Edinburgh, 83–8.

Dixon, P., Hayfield C. and Startin, W. (1989) 'Baguley Hall, Manchester: the Structural Development of a Cheshire Manor house', *Archaeological Journal* 146: 384–422.

Dodd, J. P. (1982) 'The Population of Frodsham Manor 1349–50' *T.H.S.L.C.* 131: 21–33.

Dodd, J. P. (1986) 'Domesday Cheshire: Some Agricultural Connotations' *J.C.A.S.* 68: 85–95.

Dodgson, J. McN. (1957) 'The background of Brunanburh' *Saga-Book of the Viking Soc.* 14: 303–316.

Dodgson, J. McN. (1966–81) *The Place-Names of Cheshire*, in five parts, Cambridge, English Place-Name Society at Cambridge University Press.

Dodgson, J. McN. (1967) 'The English Arrival in Cheshire' *T.H.S.L.C.* 119: 1–37.

Dodgson, J. McN. (1968) 'Place-Names and Street Names at Chester' *J.C.A.S.* 55: 29–62.

Dolley, R. H. M. (1955) 'The Mint of Chester, I' *J.C.&N.W.A.A.&H.Soc.* 42: 4–5.

Donkin, R. A. (1958) 'Cistercian Sheep farming and Wool Sales' *Agr.H.R.* 6: 2–8.

Donkin, R. A. (1963) 'The Cistercian Order in Medieval England: Some Conclusions', *Trans. Institute of British Geographers* 22: 181–98.

Donnelly, J. S. (1954) 'Change in the Grange Economy of English and Welsh Cistercian Abbeys, 1300–1540', *Traditio* 10: 399–458.

Driver, J. T. (1970–1) 'The Mainwairings of Over Peover: a Cheshire Family in the 15th and early 16th Century' *J.C.A.S.* 57: 27–40.

Driver, J. T. (1971) *Cheshire in the Later Middle Ages, 1399–1540*, Chester, Cheshire Community Council.

Dyer, A. (2000) 'Appendix: Ranking Lists of English Towns in Medieval England', in D. Palliser ed. *The Cambridge Urban History of Britain*, vol I, Cambridge, 747–768.

Dyer, C. C. (1989) *Standards of Living in the Later Middle Ages*, Cambridge, Cambridge University Press.

Dyer, C. C. (1991) *Hanbury: Settlement and Society in a Woodland Landscape,* Leicester, Leicester University Press.

Dyer, C. C. (2000) 'Woodlands and Wood-Pasture in Western England', in J. Thirsk ed. 97–121.

Dyer, C. C. (2002) *Making a Living in the Middle Ages: The People of Britain 850–1520*, New Haven and London, Yale University Press.

Earwaker, J. P. (1877) *East Cheshire Past and Present*, London, the author.

Earwaker, J. P. (1890) *The History of the Ancient Parish of Sandbach, Co. Chester*, London.

Edwards, B. J. N. (1998) *Vikings in North West England: The Artefacts*, Lancaster, Centre for North-West Regional Studies, University of Lancaster.

Edwards, N. and Lane, A. eds (1988) *Early Medieval Settlement in Wales*, Oxford, Oxbow.

Ekwall, E. (1918) *Scandinavians and Celts in the North-West of England*, Lund, Lunds Universitets årsskrift.

Ekwall, E. (1922) *The Place Names of Lancashire*, C.S. 2, 81.

Elliott, G. (1973) 'Field Systems of North-West England', in A. R. H. Baker and R. A. Butlin eds, 41–92.

Emery, M. M., Gibbins, D. J. L. and Matthews, K. J. (1996) *The Archaeology of an Ecclesiastical Landscape*, Chester Archaeology Excavation and Survey Report. 9

Fairburn, N. (2002) 'Birch Heath, Tarporley: Excavation of a Rural Romano-British settlement', *J.C.A.S.* 77: 58–114.

Fairclough, G. J. (2002) 'Understanding and Managing the Landscape: The English Heritage Historic Landscape Characterisation Programme', *Society for Landscape Studies Newsletter* Spring/Summer 2002.

Fairclough, G. J. ed. (1999) *Historic Landscape Characterisation*, London, English Heritage.

Farrer, W. (transl. and transc.) (1897) *The Court Rolls of the Honour of Clitheroe in the County of Lancaster*, 1, Manchester and Burnley, Emmott and Co.

Farrer, W. ed. (1899) *Final Concords of the County of Lancaster*, vol. 1, R.S.L.C. 39.

Farrer, W. ed. (1901) *Some Court Rolls of the Lordships, Wapentakes and Demesne Manors of Thomas, Earl of Lancaster in the County of Lancaster*, R.S.L.C. 41.

Farrer, W. ed. (1902) *The Lancashire Pipe Rolls*, Liverpool, Young.

Farrer, W. (1903) *Lancashire Inquests, Extents and Feudal Aids*, vol. 1, R.S.L.C. 48.

Farrer, W. ed. (1907) *Abstracts of Lancashire Inquests Post Mortem and Ad Quod Damnum, Feudal Aids, Rentals and Extents*, vol. 2, R.S.L.C. 54.

Farrer, W. ed. (1915) *Lancashire Inquests, Extents and Feudal Aids*, vol. 3, R.S.L.C. 70.

*Bibliography*

Feilitzen, O. von (1937) *The Pre-Conquest Personal Names of Domesday Book*, Uppsala, Almqvist and Wiksells Boktryckeri-a-b.

Fellows-Jensen, G. (1983) 'Scandinavian Settlement in the Isle of Man and North-West England: The Place-name Evidence', in C. Fell *et al.* eds *The Viking Age in the Isle of Man*, London 37–52.

Fellows-Jensen, J. (1985) *Scandinavian Settlement Names in the North West*, Copenhagen, Komission hos akademisk forlag Navnestudier udgiver af Institut for Navneforskning.

Fellows-Jensen, G. (1992) 'Scandinavian Places-Names of the Irish Sea Province', in J. Graham-Campbell ed. 31–42.

Fenwick, C. (1998) *The Poll Taxes of 1377, 1379 and 1381*, Part 1, Records of Social and Economic History n. s. 27 for British Academy, Oxford, Oxford University Press.

Ferguson Irvine, W. M. ed. (1896) *A Collection of Lancashire and Cheshire Wills 1301–1752* R.S.L.C. 30.

Fishwick, H. (1871) *History of the Parochial Chapelry of Goosnargh*, Manchester, C. Simms.

Fishwick, H. ed. (1896) *Pleadings and Depositions: Duchy Count of Lancaster*, vol. 1, R.S.L.C. 32.

Fleming, R. (1993) 'Rural Elites and Urban Communities in Late Saxon England', *Past and Present* 141: 3–26.

Flenley, R. ed. (1911) *Six Town Chronicles*, Oxford, Clarendon Press.

Floyer, J. K. (1905) 'Warton Old Rectory, Lancashire', *T.L.C.H.S.* n.s. 21: 28–47.

Fowler, P. J. (2002) *Farming in the First Millennium AD*, Cambridge, Cambridge U.P.

Fox, Sir C. (1932) *The Personality of Britain: its Influence on Inhabitants and Invaders in Prehistory*, Cardiff, National Museum of Wales and the Press Board of the University of Wales.

Fox, Sir C. (1955) *Offa's Dyke: A Field Survey of the Western Frontier Works of Mercia in the Seventh and Eighth centuries*, London, Oxford University Press for the British Academy.

Fox, H. S. A. (1981) 'Approaches to the adoption of the midland system', in R. T. Rowley ed. *The Origins of Open Field Agriculture*, London, Croom Helm, 64–111.

Fox, H. S. A. (1992) 'The Agrarian Context' in *The Origins of the Midland Village*, Papers prepared for a Discussion Session at the Economic History Society Annual Conference, Leicester, April 1992, unpublished and privately circulated.

France, R. S. (1938) 'A History of Plague in Lancashire', *T.H.S.L.C.* 90: 1–76.

France, R. S. (1950) *Lancashire Acts of Parliament 1415–1800*, Lancashire County Council Record Publication no. 3, Preston.

France, R. S. (1954) 'Two Custumals of the Manor of Cockerham, 1326 and 1483', *T.A.S.L.C.* 64: 38–54.

Freke, D. J. and Thacker A. T. (1987) 'Excavations at the Inhumation Cemetery at Southworth Hall Farm, Winwick, Cheshire, in 1980', *J.C.A.S* 70: 31–8.

Garrett, J. V. (1982) *Reconstruction of the Field Pattern of the Swinehead Estate, High Legh, Cheshire, from a 17th Century Terrier*, Unpublished Project, Certificate of Landscape History, University of Manchester Department of Extra-Mural Studies.

Gastrell, F. (1845) Notitia Cestriensis, *or Historical Notices of the Diocese of Chester*, ed. F. R. Raines, Manchester.

Gelling, M. (1990) *The Place Names of Shropshire*, vol. 1, Cambridge, English Place-Name Society at Cambridge U.P.

Gelling, M. (1991–2) 'Paganism and Christianity in Wirral' *J.E.P.N.S.* 25: 11.

Gelling, M. (1992) *The West Midlands in the Early Middle Age*, Leicester, Leicester U.P.

Gelling, M. (1995) 'Scandinavian Settlement in Cheshire: the evidence of place-names' in B. E. Crawford ed. *Scandinavian Settlement in Northern Britain*, Leicester, Leicester U.P. 187–194.

249

Gem, R. (2000) 'Romanesque Architecture in Cheshire *c.* 1075 to 1117' in A. Thacker ed., 31–44.

Giles, P. M. (1950–1) 'The Enclosure of Common Lands in Stockport', *T.H.S.L.C.* 62: 73–110.

Gillepsie J. C. (1974) 'Richard II's Cheshire Archers' *T.H.S.L.C.* 125: 1–39.

Glass, A. ed. (1982) *Historic Buildings Register*, vol 1, London, H.M.S.O.

Glasscock, R. E. ed. (1975) *The Lay Subsidy of 1334*, Oxford, Oxford University Press for the British Academy.

G.M.A.C. (1995) *The East Wing, Ordsall Hall, Salford*, unpublished and privately circulated.

Graham-Campbell, J. ed. (1992) *Viking Treasure from the North-West: The Cuerdale Hoard in its Context*, Liverpool, National Museums and Galleries on Merseyside, Occasional Papers no. 5.

Graham-Campbell, J. (2001) 'The Northern Hoards from Cuerdale to Bossall/Flaxton', in N. J. Higham and D. H. Hill eds, 212–229.

Grant, R. (1991) *The Royal Forests of England*, Stroud, Alan Sutton.

Gray, H. L. (1915) *English Field Systems*, Cambridge, Mass.

Grealey, S. ed. (1976) *The Archaeology of Warrington's Past*, Warrington, Warrington Development Corporation.

Greene, J. P. (1989) *Norton Priory: The Archaeology of a Medieval Religious House*, Cambridge, Cambridge University Press.

Greene, J. P. and Hough, P. R. (1977) 'Excavation in the Medieval Village of Norton, 1974–6' *J.C.A.S.* 60: 61–93.

Greene, J. P. and Johnson, B. (1978) 'An Experimental Tile kiln at Norton Priory, Cheshire', *Medieval Ceramics* 2: 30–42.

Griffiths, D. (2001) 'The North-West Frontier', in N. J. Higham and D. H. Hill eds, 167–187.

Griffiths, D. (2004) 'Settlement and Acculturation in the Irish Sea Region', in J. Hines *et al.* ed.: 125–38.

Grössinger, C. (2000) 'Chester Cathedral Miserichords: Iconography and Sources' in A. Thacker ed., 98–106.

Hadley, D. M. and Richards, J. D. eds (2000) *Cultures in Contact: Scandinavian Settlement in England in the Ninth and Tenth Centuries*, Brepols, Turnhout.

Haigh, C. (1969) *The Last Days of the Lancashire Monasteries and the Pilgrimage of Grace*, C.S. 3, 17.

Hall, D. (1995) *The Wetlands of Greater Manchester*, Lancaster, Lancaster University Archaeological Unit, Lancaster Imprints.

Hall, J. ed. (1896) *The Book of the Abbot Of Combermere 1289–1529*, R.S.L.C. 31.

Hall, J. (2nd edition 1972) *A History of the Town and Parish of Nantwich*, Manchester, Morton.

Hall, R. (2001) 'A Kingdom too far: York in the Early Tenth Century' in N. J. Higham D. H. Hill eds, 188–99.

Hallam, H. E. (1958) 'Some Thirteenth Century Censuses' *Ec.H.R.* 2, 10: 340–361.

Hallam, H. E. (1961) 'Population Density in the Medieval Fenlands' *Ec.H.R.* 2, 14.

Hallam, H. E. ed. (1988) *The Agrarian History of England and Wales*, vol. 2, Cambridge, Cambridge U.P.

Hamilton, N. E. S. A. ed. (1870) *Wilhelmi Malmesbiriensis Monachi de Gestis Pontificem Anglorum*, London.

Harding, S. (2002) *Viking Mersey : Scandinavian Wirral, West Lancashire and Chester*, Birkenhead, Countyvise Ltd.

Harland, J. (1856–62) *Mamecestre*, 3 vols. C.S., 53, 56, 58

Harland, J. ed. (1868) *Three Lancashire Documents of the 14th and 15th Centuries* C.S., 74.

Harvey, B. F. (1991) 'Introduction: the 'Crisis' of the Early Fourteenth Century' in B. M. S. Campbell ed. *Before the Black Death: Studies in the Early Fourteenth Century* Manchester, Manchester U.P. 1–24.

Harris, A. (1967) 'A Note on Common Fields in North Lancashire' *T.H.S.L.C.* 119: 225–228.

Harris, B. E. (1975) 'Ranulph III, Earl of Chester' *J.C.A.S.* 58: 99–114.

Harrison, B. E. and Clayton, D. J. (1979) 'Criminal Procedure in Cheshire in the Mid 15th Century' *T.H.S.L.C.* 128: 161–172.

Harrop, S. A. (1983) 'Moated Sites in North East Cheshire and their Links with the Legh Family in the Fourteenth Century' *Chesh.H.* 2: 8–15.

Harvey, S. P. J. (1976) 'Evidence for Settlement Study: Domesday Book' in P. H. Sawyer ed. *Medieval Settlement*, London, Edward Arnold, 195–199.

Haselgrove, C. (1996) 'The Iron Age', in R. Newman ed., 61–74.

Hawkes, J. (2003) *The Sandbach Crosses: Sign and Significance in Anglo-Saxon Sculpture*, Dublin, Four Courts Press.

Hawkes, J. and Hawkes, C. (1947) *Prehistoric Britain*, London, Chatto and Windus.

Heawood, R. for Lancaster University Archaeological Unit (1999) *Old Abbey Farm, Risley, Warrington Borough. Building Survey and Excavation at a Medieval Moated Site*, Pre-publication report deposited at Cheshire Sites and Monuments Record.

Hewitt, W. (1923) 'Marl and Marling in Cheshire', *Proceedings of the Liverpool Geological Society* 13, 1: 24–28.

Hewitt, H. J. (1929) *Medieval Cheshire: An Economic and Social History of Cheshire in the Reigns of the Three Edwards*, C.S. 2, 88.

Hey, D. (1986) *Yorkshire from A.D. 1000*, Harlow, Longman.

Hibbert, F. E., Switzur, V. R. and West, R. G. (1971) 'Radiocarbon Dating of Flandrian pollen zones at Red Moss, Lancashire', *Proceedings of the Royal Society, London*, B, 177: 161–176.

Higden, R. *Polychronicon*, ed. C. Babington and J. R. Lumby, 9 Vols, London, Rolls Series, 1865–86.

Higgins, D. A. (1982) 'Excavations at Speke Hall, Merseyside 1981/2' Unpublished Report by the Rescue Archaeology Unit, University of Liverpool.

Higham, M. C. (1988) 'Early Textile Processing: The Archaeological Evidence' *C.B.A. Reg. Group 5, Newsletter* 56:10.

Higham, M. C. (1991a) 'The Mottes of North Lancashire, Lonsdale and South Cumbria' *T.C.W.A.A.S.* 91: 79–90.

Higham, M. C. (1991b) 'The Archaeology of Flax Retting' *University of Lancaster Centre for North West Regional Studies Regional Bulletin* n.s. 5: 20–25.

Higham, M.C. (1993) '*Through a Glass Darkly – the Gough map and Lancashire*', in A. Crosby ed.: 29–41.

Higham, M. C. (1995) 'Scandinavian Settlement in North-West England, with a Special Study of *Ireby* names', in B. E. Crawford ed. *Scandinavian Settlement in Northern Britain*, Leicester, Leicester U.P., 195–205.

Higham, M. C. (1999) 'Names on the Edge: Hills and Boundaries', *Nomina* 22: 61–71.

Higham, M. C. (2003), 'Place-names and Local History', *T.L.C.A.S.* 99, 205–13.

Higham, N. J. (1978/9) 'Tatton Old Hall: A Preliminary Report on Excavations Conducted at Easter 1979' *C.A.B.* 6: 72–74.

Higham, N. J. (1979a) 'An Aerial Survey of the Upper Lune Valley' in N. J. Higham ed., 31–38.

Higham, N. J. (1979b) 'Continuity in North West England in the First Millennium A.D.' in N. J. Higham ed., 43–52.

Higham, N. J. ed. (1979) *The Changing Past*, Manchester, Manchester University Department of Extra-Mural Studies.

Higham, N. J. (1980) *Excavations at Ordsall Hall Demesne Farm 1978–1979,* Greater Manchester Archaeological Group Publication No. 2.

Higham, N. J. (1982a) 'Bucklow Hundred: The Domesday Survey and the Rural Community', *C.A.B.* 8: 15–21.

Higham, N.J. (1982b) 'Medieval Tatton: The Reconstruction of a Landscape', *Chesh. H.* 9: 31–44.

Higham, N. J. (1984/5) 'Tatton Park: Interim Report on the 7th Season of Excavations of the Deserted Village' *C.A.B.* 10: 75–82.

Higham, N. J. (1986a) *The Northern Counties to A.D. 1000,* Harlow, Longman.

Higham, N. J. (1986b) 'Tatton: Settlement and Land-Use in One Cheshire Township c. A.D. 1000–1400' *The Manchester Geographer* n.s. 7: 2–17.

Higham, N. J. (1987) 'Landscape and Land-Use in Northern England: a Survey of Agricultural Potential, *c.* 500 B.C.–A.D. 1000' *Landscape History* 9: 35–44.

Higham, N. J. (1987–88) 'Hough Hall: the Trial Excavation of a moated platform in Mere Township, Cheshire' *J.C.A.S.* 70: 87–97.

Higham, N. J. (1988a) 'The Cheshire Landholdings of Earl Morcar in 1066' *T.H.S.L.C.* 137: 139–147.

Higham, N. J. (1988b) 'Dispersed Settlement in Medieval Cheshire: Some Causal Factors', *Medieval Settlement Research Group, Annual Report* 2: 9–10.

Higham, N. J. (1988c) 'The Cheshire Burhs and the Mercian Frontier to 924', *T.A.S.L.C.* 85: 193–221.

Higham, N. J. (1992) 'Northumbria, Mercia and the Irish Sea Norse 893–926', in J. Graham-Campbell ed., 21–30.

Higham, N. J. (1993) *The Origins of Cheshire,* Manchester, Manchester University Press.

Higham, N. J. (1995) 'Territorial Organisation in pre-Conquest Cheshire', in T. Scott and P. Starkey eds *The Middle Ages in the North West,* Liverpool, Leopard's Head Press, 1–14.

Higham, N. J. (1997a) 'The Context of *Brunanburh*', in A. R. Rumble and A. D. Mills eds *Names, Places and People: an Onomastic Miscelllany for John McNeal Dogson,* Stamford, Paul Watkins, 144–156.

Higham N. J. (1997b) 'Patterns of Patronage and Power: The Governance of Late Anglo-Saxon Cheshire', in J. C. Appleby and P. Dalton eds, 1–13.

Higham, N. J. (2000) 'The Tatton Park Project, Part 2: The Medieval Estates, Settlements and Halls', *J.C.A.S.* 75: 61–133.

Higham, N. J. (2001a) '*Bancornaburg*: Revisiting Bangor-is-y-coed', in N. J. Higham ed. *Archaeology of the Roman Empire: A Tribute to the Life and Works of Professor Barri Jones,* Oxford, British Archaeological Reports, International Series 940, 311–318.

Higham, N. J. (2001b) 'Britons in Northern England in the Early Middle Ages: Through a Thick Glass Darkly', *N. H.* 38, 1: 5–25.

Higham, N. J. (2004) 'Viking-age Settlements in the North-Western Countryside: Lifting the Veil?', in J. Hines *et al.* ed. 297–312.

Higham, N. J and Cane, T. (1999) 'The Tatton Park Project, Part 1: Prehistoric to Sub-Roman Settlement and Land Use', *J.C.A.S.* 74: 1–61.

Higham, N. J. and Hill, D. H. eds *Edward the Elder: 899–924,* London, Routledge.

Higham, N. J. and Jones, G. D. B. (1974–5) 'Frontiers, Forts and Farmers: Cumbrian Aerial Survey', *Archaeological Journal* 132: 16–53.

Higham, N. J. and Jones, G. D. B. (1983) 'The Excavations of two Romano-British Farm Sites in North Cumbria', *Britannia* 14: 45–72.

Higham, N. J and Jones, G. D. B. (1985) *The Carvetii,* Gloucester, Alan Sutton.

Highet, T. P. (1960) *The Early History of the Davenports of Davenport,* C.S. 3, 9.

Hill, D. H. (1981) *An Atlas of Anglo-Saxon England,* Oxford, Basil Blackwell.

*Bibliography*

Hindle, B. P. (1982) 'Roads and Tracks', in L. Cantor ed. *The English Medieval Landscape* London, Croom Helm, 193–217.

Hines, J., Lane, A. and Redknap, M. ed. (2004) *Land, Sea and Home* Leeds, Maney Publishing for The Society for Medieval Archeology.

Hodgkinson, D., Huckerby, E., Middleton, R. and Wells, C. E. (2000) *The Lowland Wetlands of Cumbria*, Lancaster, Lancaster University Archaeological Unit, Lancaster Imprints.

Hodson, H. (1974) *The Old Community: A Portrait of Wilmslow*, Wilmslow, Hampsfell Press.

Hollos, D. (1987) 'Excavations by the North West Archaeological Trust, 1986–7' *Liverpool University Archaeology Newsletter* 3: 3–8.

Hooke, D. ed. (1985) *Medieval Villages,* Oxford University Committee for Archaeology Monograph no. 5.

Hopkins, A. (1950) *Selected Rolls of the Chester City Courts*, C.S. 3, 2.

Hornyold-Strickland, H. (1935) *Biographical Sketches of the Members of Parliament for Lancashire, 1290–1550*, C.S. 1, 93.

Hoskins, W. G. (1955) *The Making of the English Landscape*, London, Hodder & Stoughton.

Hough, P. R. (1978) 'Excavations at Beeston Castle, 1975–77', *J.C.A.S.* 61: 1–24.

Hoyle, R. W. (1987) 'An Ancient and Laudable Custom: the Definition and Development of Tenant Rights in North-Western England in the 16th Century', *Past and Present*, 116: 24–55.

Hulton, W. A. (1847) *Coucher Book of Whalley Abbey*, vol. 1, C.S. 1, 10.

Hulton, W. A. ed. (1853) *Documents Relating to the Priory of Penwortham and Other Possessions in Lancashire of the Abbey of Evesham*, C.S. 1, 30.

Hume, A. (1863) *Ancient Meols: or Some Account of the Antiquities Found Near Dove Point, on the Sea-Shore of Cheshire*, London, J. R. Smith.

Hurst, J. G. (1985) 'The Dating of Late 12th- and Early 13th-Century Pottery in Ireland', *The Ulster Journal of Archaeology* 48: 135–141.

Husain, B. M. C. (1973) *Cheshire under the Norman Earls*, Chester, Cheshire Community Council.

Iles, P. and Newman, R. (1996) 'Priorities and Challenges', in R. Newman ed., 177–86.

Irvine, W. F. (1949) 'Trespasses in the Forest of Wirral in 1351', *T.H.S.L.C.* 101: 39–45.

Irvine, W. F. (1953) 'The Early Stanleys', *T.H.S.L.C.* 105: 45–68.

Ives, E. W. (1969–70) 'Patronage at the Court of Henry VIII: the Case of Sir Ralph Egerton of Ridley', *B.J.R.L.* 52: 346.

Ives, E. W. (1971) 'Court and County Palatine in the Reign of Henry VIII: The Career of William Brereton of Malpas', *T. H. S. L. C.* 123; 1–38.

Ives, E. W. (1981) 'Crime, Sanctuary and the Royal Authority under Henry VIII: the Exemplary Sufferings of the Savage Family', in M. S. Arnold and S. D. White eds *On the Laws and Customs of England*, North Carolina Press: 296–320.

Jansen, V. (2000) 'Attested but Opaque: The Early Gothic East End at St Werburgh', in A. Thacker ed., 57–65.

Jarvis, R. C. (1950) 'The Head Port of Chester, Liverpool, its Creek and Member' *T.H.S.L.C.* 102: 69–84.

Jolliffe, J. E. A. (1926) 'Northumbrian Institutions', *E.H.R.* 161: 1–42.

Jones, A. (1979) 'Land Measurement in England', *Ag.H.R.* 27: 10–18.

Jones, D. (1957) *The Church in Chester, 1300–1540*, C.S., 3, 7.

Jones, G. R. J. (1976) 'Multiple Estates and Early Settlement' in P. H. Sawyer ed. *Medieval Settlement*, London, Edward Arnold, 15–40.

Jones, M. (1986) *England Before Domesday*, London, Batsford.

Jope, E. M. and Dunning, G. C. (1954) 'The Use of Blue Slate for Roofing in Medieval England', *Ant.J.* 34: 209–217.

Kapelle, W. E. (1979) *The Norman Conquest of the North: the Regions and its Transformation, 1000–1135*, London, Croom Helm.

Keats-Rohan, K. S. B. (1999) *Domesday People: a Prosopography of Persons Occurring in English Documents, 1066–1166*, Woodbridge, Boydell.

Keen, L. (1976) 'Baguley Hall, Manchester' *J.C.A.S.* 59: 60–66.

Kennett, A. M. (1984) 'The Rows in the City Records' *J.C.A.S.* 67: 47–54.

Kenyon, D. (1974) *Rural Settlement Patterns in Medieval Cheshire*, Unpubl. M.A. Thesis, University of Manchester.

Kenyon, D. (1979) 'Aerial Photography and the Open Fields: Open Field Agriculture in Medieval Cheshire', in N. J. Higham ed., 59–66.

Kenyon, D. (1986a) 'Notes on Lancashire Place-Names I: the Early Names', *J.E.P.N.S.* 18: 13–37.

Kenyon, D. (1986b) 'The antiquity of -*ham* Place-Names in Lancashire and Cheshire', *Nomina* 10: 5–10.

Kenyon, D. (1991) *The Origins of Lancashire*, Manchester, Manchester University Press.

Kermode, J. (1997) 'New Brooms in Early Tudor Chester?' in J. C. Appleby and P. Dalton eds, 144–158.

Kershaw, I. (1973a) *Bolton Priory: the Economy of a Northern Monastery, 1286–1325*, Oxford, Oxford U.P.

Kershaw, I. (1973b) 'The Great famine and Agrarian Crisis in England, 1315–22', *Past and Present* 59: 13–50.

Kettle, A. J. (1980) 'Religious houses', in B. E. Harris ed. *A History of the County of Chester*, vol. 3, London, Victoria County History, 124–187.

King, A. (1978) 'Gauber High Pasture, Ribblehead – an Interim Report', in Hall R. ed. *Viking Age York and the North*, London, C.B.A. Research Report 27: 21–5.

Laing, L.R. (1976) 'Some Pagan Anglian Finds from Deeside', *J.C.A.S.* 59: 50–1.

Laing, L. R. (1977) 'The Origins and Affinities of Chester Medieval Cooking Pots', in P. J. Davey ed. *Medieval Pottery from Excavations in the North West*, Liverpool, Institute of Extension Studies Liverpool Univeristy, 115–117.

Lamb, H. H. (1972–7) *Climate, Past, Present and Future*, London, Methuen.

Laughton, J. (1995) 'The Alewives of Later Medieval Chester', in R. E. Arthur ed. *Crown, Government and People in the Fifteenth Century*, Stroud, Alan Sutton, 191–208.

Leadam, I. S. (1897) *The Domesday of Inclosures, 1517–18*, vol. 2, London, Longmans.

Leah, M. D., Wells, C. E., Appleby, C. and Huckerby, E. (1997) *The Wetlands of Cheshire*, North West Wetlands Survey 4, Lancaster, Lancaster University Archaeological Unit.

Leland, T. (1535–43) *Leland's Itinerary in England and Wales*, ed. L. Toulmin-Smith, 5 vols. London, Centaur Press Ltd. 1964.

Le Patourel, J. (1978) 'Documentary Evidence', in A. Abeg ed. *Medieval Moated Sites*, York, C.B.A. Res. Rep. 17, 21–28.

Lewis, C., Mitchell-Fox, P. and Dyer, C. (1997) *Village, Hamlet and Field: Changing Medieval Settlement in Central England*, Manchester, Manchester University Press. Republished (2001) in Macclesfield by Windgather Press.

Lewis, C. P. (1982) 'Herbert the Jerkin-Maker: A Domesday Tenant Identified', *T.H.S.L.C.* 131: 159–160.

Lewis, C. P. (1985) *English and Norman Government and Lordship in the Welsh Borders, 1039–1087* Unpubl. D.Phil. Oxford.

Lewis, C. P. (1991a) 'An Introduction to the Cheshire Domesday', in A. Williams and G. H. Martin eds *The Cheshire Domesday*, London, Alecto Historical Editions, 1–25.

Lewis, C. P. (1991b) 'An Introduction to the Lancashire Domesday' in A. Williams and G. H. Martin eds *The Lancashire Domesday*, London, Alecto Historical Editions, 1–41.

*Bibliography*

Lewis, C. P. (1991c) 'The Formation of the Honor of Chester, 1066–1100', in A. T. Thacker ed. *The Earldom of Chester and its Charters*, Chester, 37–68.

Lewis, J. (1986) 'Medieval Merseyside: a Summary of the Evidence for the post-Conquest Period' Seminar Paper for Merseyside Archaeological Society, privately circulated.

Lewis, J. (2000) *The Medieval Earthworks of the Hundred of West Derby: Tenurial Evidence and Physical Structure*, Oxford, British Archaeological Reports, British Series 310.

Liddiard, R. (2003) 'The Deer Parks of Domesday Book', *Landscapes* 4.1: 4–23.

Lloyd, J. (1983) 'The Medieval Economy', in M. Morris ed., 35–44.

Lodge, E. C. and Sumerville, R. eds *John of Gaunt's Register, 1379–83*, Camden Soc., 3, 56, 57.

Lowe, N. (1972) *The Lancashire Textile Industry in the 16th Century*, C.S. 3, 20.

Lowndes, R. A. C. (1963) '"Celtic" Fields, Farms and Burial Mounds in the Lune Valley' *T.C.W.A.A.S.* n.s. 63: 77–95.

Lowndes, R. A. C. (1964) 'Excavations of a Romano-British farmstead at Eller Beck' *T.C.W.A.A.S.* n.s. 64: 6–13.

Loyn, H. R. (1991) *Anglo-Saxon England and the Norman Conquest*, Second Edition, Harlow, Longman.

Lumby, J. H. ed. (1939) *A Calendar of the Norris Deeds*, R.S.L.C. 93.

Lyons, Rev. P. A. (1884) *Two Compoti of the Lancashire and Cheshire Manors of Henry de Lacy, Earl of Lincoln*, C.S. 1, 112.

MacKay, A.W. and Tallis, J.H. (1994) 'The Recent Vegetational History of the Forest of Bowland, Lancashire, U.K.', *N. Phytol*, 128: 571–84.

Maddison, J. (2000) 'Problems in the Choir of Chester Cathedral', in A. Thacker ed., 66–80.

Maitland, F. W. (1907) *Domesday Book and Beyond*, Cambridge U.P.

Marsden, T. L. (1971) 'Newton Hall, Hyde, Cheshire' *A. M. S.* 18: 65–76.

Mason, D. J. P. (1975) 'Chester: Lower Bridge Street' *C.A.B.* 3: 40–41.

Mason, D. J. P. (1976) 'Chester: the Evolution of its Landscape' *J.C.A.S.* 59: 14–23.

Mason, D. J. P. (1985) *Excavations at Chester, 26–42 Lower Bridge Street, the Dark Age and Saxon Periods*, Chester, Grovesnor Museum Archaeological Excavation and Survey Reports 3.

Mason, D. J. P. (1988) '*Prata Legionis* in Britain', *Britannia* 19: 163–89.

Mate, M. (1985) 'Medieval Agrarian Practises: the Determining Factors' *Ag. H. R.* 33: 22–31.

Matthews, K. (1997) 'St Plegmund: Cheshire's Archbishop of Canterbury', *Chesh. H.* 36: 1–8.

Matthews, S. (2003) 'William the Conqueror's campaign in Cheshire in 1069–70: ravaging and resistance in the North-West', *N. H.* 40: 1: 53–70.

Maxwell, I. S. (1962) 'The West Riding', in H. C. Darby and I. S. Maxwell eds *The Domesday Geography of Northern England*, Cambridge, Cambridge U.P.

McDonnell, J. (1986) 'Medieval Assarting Hamlets in Bilsdale, North East Yorkshire' *N.H.* 22: 269–279.

McKenna, L. (1980/81) 'From Post Hole to Timber-framed Building', *C.A.B.* 7: 22–27.

McKenna, L. (1994) *Timber Framed Buildings in Cheshire*, Chester, Cheshire County Council.

McNeil-Sale, R. (1980/81) 'Nantwich, 3 years of excavations and observations' *C.A.B.* 7: 30–33.

McNeil, R. (1983) 'Two 12th century wich houses in Nantwich, Cheshire', *Med. Arch* 27: 40-88.

McNeil, R. (1987) *Halton Castle: 'A Visual Treasure'*, Liverpool, North West Archaeological Trust, Report no. 1.

McNiven, P. (1969–70) 'The Cheshire Rising of 1400' *B.J.R.L.* 52: 375–396.

McNiven, P. (1980) 'The Men of Cheshire and the rebellion of 1403' *T.H.S.L.C.* 129: 1–30.

McNulty, J. ed. (1939) *Thomas Sotheton v Cockersand Abbey: A Suit as to the advowson of Mitton Church, 1369–70*, C.S. 1, 100.

McPeake, J. C., Bulmer, M. and Rutter, J. A. (1980) 'Excavations in the Garden of No. 1 Abbey Green, Chester, 1975–77: Interim Report', *J.C.A.S.* 63: 15–38.

Middleton, R., Wells, C. E. and Huckerby, E. (1995) *The Wetlands of North Lancashire*, North West Wetlands Survey 3, Lancaster, Lancaster University Archaeological Unit.

Miller, E. (1964) 'The English Economy in the 13th century: Implications of Recent Research', *Past and Present* 28: 21–40.

Miller, E. (1975) 'Farming in Northern England during the 12th and 13th centuries' *N.H.* 10: 1–16.

Mills, M. H. and Stewart Brown, R. (1938) *Cheshire in the Pipe Rolls, 1158–1301, R.S.L.C.* 92.

Millward, R. (1955) *The Making of the English Landscape, Lancashire*, London, Hodder and Stoughton.

Morgan, P. J. ed. (1978) *Domesday Book, vol. 26: Cheshire*, from a draft translation prepared by A. Rumble, Chichester.

Morgan, P. J. (1979) 'Cheshire and the Defence of the Principality of Aquitaine', *T.H.S.L.C.* 128: 139–60.

Morris, C. ed. (1947) *The Journeys of Celia Fiennes*, London, Cresset Press.

Morris, M. ed. (1983) *Medieval Manchester*, Manchester, Greater Manchester Archaeological Unit.

Muir, R. (2000) *The New Reading the Landscape: Fieldwork in Landscape History*, Exeter, University of Exeter Press.

Musty, J. (1974) 'Medieval Pottery Kilns' in V. I. Evison, H. Hodges and J. G, Hurst eds *Medieval Pottery from Excavations*, London, John Baker, 2–65.

Mynors, R. A. B., Thomson, R. M. and Winterbottom, M. eds (1998) *William of Malmesbury: Gesta Regum Anglorum*, vol. 1, Oxford, Clarendon Press.

Nevell, M. (1991) *Tameside 1066–1700*, Tameside, Tameside Metropolitan Borough Council.

Nevell, M. (1992) *Tameside before 1066*, Tameside, Tameside Metropolitan Borough Council.

Nevell, M. (1997) *The Archaeology of Trafford*, Trafford, Trafford Metropolitan Borough Council.

Nevell, M. (1999) 'Great Woolden Hall: A Model for the Material Culture of Iron Age and Romano-British Rural Settlement in North West England?', in M. Nevell ed. 48–63.

Nevell, M. ed. (1999) *Living on the Edge of Empire: Models, Methodology and Marginality*, Manchester and Chester, Council for British Archaeology North West, the Field Archaeology Centre, University of Manchester and Chester Archaeology.

Nevell, M. (2000) 'A Bibliography of North West Archaeology, 1991–2000' *Archaeology North West* 5: 33–41.

Nevell, M. and Walker, J. (2002) *Denton and Dukinfield Halls and the archaeology of the Gentry and Yeoman House in North West England 1500–1700*, Tameside, Tameside Metropolitan Borough Council.

Newman, R. (1996) 'The Dark Ages' in R. Newman ed., 93–108.

Newman, R. (1996) 'Medieval Rural Settlement' in R. Newman ed., 109–124.

Newman, R. ed. (1996) *The Archaeology of Lancashire, Present State and Future Priorities*, Lancaster, Lancaster University Archaeological Unit.

Newstead, R. (1934) 'Medieval Pottery and Kiln at Ashton, near Chester', *A.A.A.* Liverpool, 21: 5–26.

Oldfield, F. (1963) 'Pollen Analysis and Man's role in the Ecological History of the South-east Lake District', *Geografiska Annaler* 45,1: 23–40.

Oldfield, F. (1969) 'Pollen Analysis and the History of Land use', *Advancement of Science* March 1969: 298–311.

Oldfield, F. and Stratham, D. C. (1965) 'Stratigraphy and Pollen Analysis on Cockerham and Pilling Mosses, North Lancashire', *P. M. Lit. Phil. S.* 107: 70–85.

*Bibliography*

Omerod, G. (2nd edition, 1882) *The History of the County Palatine and City of Chester*, T. Helsby ed. 3 vols., London. George Routledge.

Orwin, C. S. and Orwin, C. S. (1938) *The Open Fields*, Oxford, Oxford University Press.

Oschinksky, D. (1948) 'Notes on the Lancashire Estates in the 13th and 14th Centuries', *T.H.S.L.C.* 100: 9–32.

Owen, H. W. (1997) 'Old English Place-Name Elements in Domesday Flintshire', in A. R. Rumble and A. D. Mills eds *Names, Places and People: An Onomastic Miscellany for John McNeal Dodgson*, Stamford, Paul Watkins, 269–278.

Oxley, J. (1982) 'Nantwich: an 11th-century salt town and its origins', *T.H.S.L.C.* 131: 1–20.

Palliser, D. (2000) *The Cambridge Urban History of Britain*, vol. 1, Cambridge, Cambridge University Press.

Parker, J. (1904) *A Calendar of Lancashire Assize Rolls*, R.S.L.C. 47.

Pelham, B. A. (1969) 'The Fourteenth Century', in H. C. Darby ed. *A Historical Geography of England before A.D. 1800*, Cambridge, Cambridge U.P. 230–265.

Penney, S. H. (1982) 'Excavations at Lancaster Friary, 1980–81', *Contrebis* 10: 1–13.

Phillips, A. D. M. and Phillips, C. B. (2002) *A New Historical Atlas of Cheshire*, Chester, Cheshire County Council and Cheshire Community Council Publications Trust.

Phillips, C. B. and Smith, J. H. (1994) *Lancashire and Cheshire from AD 1540*, Harlow, Longman.

Philpott, R. A. (1999) 'Recent Anglo-Saxon Finds from Merseyside and Cheshire and their Archaeological Significance', *Med. Arch.* 43: 194–202.

Porter, J. (1978) 'Waste Land Reclamation in the Sixteenth and Seventeenth Centuries: the Case of South-eastern Bowland, 1550–1630', *T.H.S.L.C.* 127: 1–23.

Postan, M. M. (1973) *Essays on Medieval Agriculture and General Problems of the Medieval Economy*, Cambridge, Cambridge University Press.

Potter, T. W. and Andrews, R. D. (1994) 'Excavation and Survey at St Patrick's Chapel and St Peter's Church, Heysham, Lancashire, 1977–8', *Ant. J.* 74: 55–134.

Rackham, O. (1986) *The History of the Countryside*, London, Dent.

Rahtz, P. H. (1977) 'The Archaeology of West Mercian Towns', in A. Dornier ed. *Mercian Studies* 109ff.

Razi, J. (1980) *Life, Marriage and Death in a Medieval Parish*, Cambridge, Cambridge U.P.

R. C. H. M. (1975–82) *County of Northampton, Archaeology Sites* vols 1–3, London.

Renaud, F. (1876) *The Ancient Parish of Prestbury in Cheshire*, C.S. 1, 97 Manchester.

Renn, D. F. (1968) *Norman Castles in Britain*, London, John Baker Publishers.

Reynolds, S. (1992) 'The Writing of Medieval Urban History in England', originally published in *Historiography and Theory*, 19, republished in S. Reynolds, *Ideas and Solidarities of the Medieval Laity in England and Western Europe,* Aldershot, 1995, 43–57.

Richards, J. (2000) 'Identifying Anglo-Scandinavian Settlements', in D. M. Hadley and J. Richards eds, 295–310.

Richards, R. (1947) *Old Cheshire Churches*, London.

Rigby, S. H. (1984) 'Boston and Grimsby in the Middle Ages: an Administrative Contrast', *J. of Med. H.* 10: 51–66.

Rigby, S. H. (1995) *English Society in the later Middle Ages: Class, Status and Gender*, Basingstoke, Macmillan.

Roberts, B. C. (1968) ' A study of Medieval Colonisation of the Forest of Arden, Warwickshire', *Ag.H.R.* 16: 101–113.

Roberts, B. K. (1985) 'Village Patterns and Forms: Some Models for Discussion', in D. Hooke ed., 7–26.

Roberts, B. K. (1987) *The Making of the English Village*, Harlow, Longman.

Roberts, B. and Wrathmell, S. (2000) *An Atlas of Rural Settlements in England*, London, English Heritage.

Roberts, P. A. (1977) 'Nantwich 1974–6', in P. J. Davey ed. 106–107.

Robinson, H. (1968) 'Cheshire River Navigations with Special Reference to the River Dee', *J.C.A.S.* 55: 63–87.

Robinson, J. M. (1990) *A Guide to the Country Houses of the North-West*, London.

Roffe, D. (2000) *Domesday: The Inquest and the Book*, Oxford, Oxford U.P.

Roskell, J.S. (1937) *Knights of the Shire for the County Palatine of Lancashire, 1377–1460*, C.S. 3, 96.

Rowley, T. (1978) *Villages in the Landscape*, London, Dent.

Russell, J. C. (1948) *British Medieval Population*, Alberquerque, The University of New Mexico Press.

Russell, P. B. (1992) 'Place-Name evidence for the survival of British Settlements in the West Derby Hundred (Lancashire), after the Anglian invasions', *N.H.* 28: 25–41.

Rutter, J. A. (1984) 'Lifestyle in the Rows with particular reference to a collection of Pottery From 11 Watergate Street, found in 1894', *J.C.A.S.* 67: 55–75.

Saunders, V.A. (1954) 'Shropshire', in H. C. Darby and I. B. Terrett eds *The Domesday Geography of Midland England*, Cambridge.

Sawyer, P. H. ed. (1979) *Charters of Burton Abbey*, Cambridge, Cambridge University Press for the British Academy.

Shaw, R. C. (1949) *Kirkham in Amounderness*, Preston, Seed.

Shaw, R. C. (1956) *The Royal Forest of Lancashire*, Preston, privately printed.

Shaw, R. C. (1958) 'Two 15th Century Kinsmen', *T.H.S.L.C.* 110: 15–30.

Shaw, R. C. (1960) 'The Goods of Two Rochdale Merchants in the Mid-15th Century', *T.H.S.L.C.* 112: 155–158.

Sheail, J. (1968) *The Regional Distribution of Wealth in England as indicated in the lay subsidy returns 1524–5*, unpublished PhD thesis, University of London.

Shimwell, D.W. (1985) 'The Distribution and Origins of the Lowland Mosslands', in R.H. Johnson ed. *The Geomorphology of North-West England*, Manchester, Manchester U.P., 299–312.

Shotter, D. and White, A. (1980) *The Roman Fort and Town of Lancaster*, Lancaster, Centre for North-West Regional Studies, University of Lancaster.

Sidebottom, P. (2000) 'Viking Age Stone Monuments and Social Identity in Derbyshire', in D.M. Hadley and J. Richards eds. 212–35.

Singleton, F. J. (1963) 'The Influence of Geographical Factors on the Development of the Common Fields of Lancashire', *T.H.S.L.C.* 115: 31–40.

Singleton, W. A. (1952) 'Traditional House-Types in Lancashire and Cheshire' *T.H.S.L.C.* 104: 75–92.

Singleton, W. A. (1955) 'Traditional Domestic Architecture in Lancashire and Cheshire', *T.L.C.A.S.* 65: 33–47.

Smith, E. H. (1958) 'Lancashire Long Measure', *T.H.S.L.C.* 110: 1–14.

Smith, J. T. and Stell, C. F. (1960) 'Baguley Hall: the Survival of Pre-conquest Building Traditions in the 14th century' *Ant.J.* 40: 131–151.

Smith, L. P. (1976) *The Agricultural Climate of England and Wales, Areal Averages 1941–70*, London, H.M.S.O.

Smith, R. (2002) 'Plagues and Peoples: The Long Demographic Cycle, 1250–1670', in P. Slack and R. Ward eds *The Peopling of Britain: The Shaping of a Human Landscape, the Linacre Lectures*, Oxford, Oxford U.P., 177–210.

Smith, W. and Webb, W. (1656) *The Vale-Royall, of England* published by D. King and sometimes attributed to him, London.

*Bibliography*

Somerville, R. (1953) *History of the Duchy of Lancaster, I (1265–1603)*, London, Chancellor and Council of the Duchy.

Stead, I. M., Bourke, J. B. and Brothwell, D. (1986) *Lindow Man: The Body in the Bog*, London, British Museum.

Steane, J. M. (1960) 'Excavations at a Moated Site near Scarisbrick', *T.H.S.L.C.* 112: 147–154.

Stenton, F. M. (1943) *Anglo-Saxon England*, Oxford, Oxford U.P.

Stephens, G. R. (1985) 'The Roman Aqueduct at Chester', *J.C.A.S.* 68: 59–69.

Stewart-Brown, R. (1916) 'The Townfield of Liverpool, 1207–1807', *T.H.S.L.C.* 67: 1–51.

Stewart-Brown, R. (1922) 'The Domesday Roll of Chester', *E.H.R.* 37: 481–500.

Stewart-Brown, R. ed. (1925) *Calendar of the County Court, City Court and Eyre Rolls of Chester, 1259–1297 with an Inquest of Military Service, 1288*, C.S. 2, 84.

Stewart-Brown, R. ed. (1938) *Cheshire in the Pipe Rolls, 1158–1301*, R.S.L.C. 92.

Stone, D. (1997) 'The Productivity of Hired and Customary Labour: Evidence from Wisbech Barton in the Fourteenth Century', *Ec.H.R.* 50: 640–656.

Strickland, T. and Rutter, J. (1980/1) 'The Castle: Colonnade and Archway', *C.A.B.* 7: 39–40.

Studd, J. R. (1979) 'The Lord Edward's Lordship of Chester, 1254–72', *T.H.S.L.C.* 128: 1–26.

Swarbrick, J. (1923) 'The Abbey of St Mary-of-the-Marsh at Cockersand', *T.L.C.A.S.* 40: 163–193.

Sylvester, D. (1956) 'The Open Fields of Cheshire', *T.H.S.L.C.* 108: 1–34.

Sylvester, D. (1958) 'A Note on Medieval Three-Course Arable Systems in Cheshire', *T.H.S.L.C.* 110: 183–186.

Sylvester, D. (1960) 'The Manor and the Cheshire Landscape', *T.L.C.A.S.* 70: 1–15.

Sylvester, D. (1967) 'Parish and Township in Cheshire and North East Wales' *J.C.A.S.* 54: 23–36.

Sylvester, D. (1969) *The Rural Landscape of the Welsh Borderland: A Study in Historical Geography*, London, Macmillan.

Sylvester, D. and Nulty, G. (1958) *The Historical Atlas of Cheshire*, Chester, Cheshire Community Council.

Tait, J. (1908) 'Political History to the End of the Reign of Henry VIII', in W. Page ed. *A History of the County of Lancashire*, vol. 2, London, Victoria County History, 175–217.

Tait, J. (1916) *The Domesday Survey of Cheshire* C.S. 2, 75.

Tait, J. ed. (1920) *The Chartulary or Register of The Abbey of St Werburgh Chester*, vol. 1, C.S. 2, 79.

Tait, J. (1924) *Taxation in Salford Hundred 1524–1802*, C.S. 2, 83.

Tait, J. (1936) *The Medieval English Borough,* Manchester, Manchester University Press.

Tait, J. ed. (1939) *The Foundation Charter of Runcorn (Later Norton) Priory*, C.S. 2, 100.

Tallis, J. H. and McGuire, J. (1972) 'Central Rossendale: The Evolution of an Upland Vegetation', *J.Ecol.* 60: 721–737.

Tallis, J. H. and Switsur, V. R. (1973) 'Studies on Southern Pennine Peats', *J.Ecol.* 61: 743–751.

Taylor, C. (1983) *Village and Farmstead*, London, George Philip.

Taylor, F. (1950) 'Hand-lists of the Legh of Booths Charters in the John Rylands Library', *B.J.R.L.* 32,2: 229–300.

Taylor, H. (1884) *Old Halls in Lancashire and Cheshire*, Manchester, Cornish.

Taylor, H. M. and Taylor, J. (1965) *Anglo-Saxon Architecture*, 2 vols Cambridge, Cambridge University Press.

Taylor, J. (1966) *The Universal Chronicle of Ranulf Higden*, Oxford, Oxford University Press

Taylor, M. V. ed. (1912) *Liber Luciani de Laude Cestrie*, R.S.L.C. 64.

Terrett, I. B. (1948) 'The Domesday Woodland of Cheshire', *T.H.S.L.C.* 100: 1–8.

Terrett, I. B. (1962a) 'Cheshire', in H. C. Darby and I. S. Maxwell eds 330–391.

Terrett, I. B. (1962a) 'Lancashire', in H. C. Darby and I. S. Maxwell eds 392–418.

Thacker, A. (1982) 'Chester and Gloucester: Early Ecclesiastical Organisation in two Mercian Burghs', *N.H.* 18: 199–211.

Thacker, A. (1985) 'Kings, Saints and Monasteries in Pre-Viking Mercia', *M.H.* 10: 1–25.

Thacker, A. T. (1987) 'Anglo-Saxon Cheshire' in B. E. Harris ed., *Victoria County History of Cheshire*, vol. 1, London, 237–292.

Thacker, A. T. ed. (1991) *The Earldom of Chester and its Charters: a tribute to Geoffrey Barraclough*, *J.C.A.S.* 71.

Thacker, A. T. ed. (2000) *Medieval Archaeology, Art and Architecture at Chester*, Leeds, The British Archaeological Association, Conference Transactions 22.

Thirsk, J. (1964) 'The Common Fields', *Past & Present* 29: 3–25.

Thirsk, J. (1966) 'The Origin of Common Fields', *Past & Present* 33: 142–147.

Thirsk, J. (1987) 'The Farming Regions of England', in J. Thirsk ed. *The Agrarian History of England and Wales*, 4, Cambridge, Cambridge U.P.: 1–112. London.

Thirsk, J. (1967–2000) *The Agrarian History of England and Wales*, 8 vols. Cambridge, Cambridge U.P.

Thirsk, J. ed. (2000) *The English Rural Landscape*, Oxford, Oxford U.P.

Thompson, A. (1999) 'The Archaeology of Manchester Airport's Second Runway' *Archaeology North West* 4: 6–7.

Thompson, Sir E. M. ed. (1904) *Chronicon Adae de Usk, AD 1377–1421*, Oxford, Oxford U.P.

Thomson, F. H. (1962) 'Excavations at the Cistercian Abbey of Vale Royal, Cheshire, 1958', *Ant. J.* 42: 183–207.

Thomson, F. H. (1967) 'Excavations at Castle Hill, Oldcastle near Malpas, 1957', *J.C.A.S.* 54: 5–8.

Thomson, F. H. (1969) 'Excavations at Linenhall Street, Chester, 1961–62' *J.C.A.S.* 56: 1–22.

Thompson, P. (1980) *Frodsham: The Archaeological Potential of a Town*, Chester, Cheshire Monographs 1.

Thompson, P. (1981) *Middlewich, The Archaeological Potential of a Town*, Chester, Cheshire Monographs 2.

Thompson, P. (1981) *Congleton: The Archaeological Potential of a Town*, Chester, Cheshire Monographs 3.

Thompson, P. (1983) *Ince Manor: Medieval Monastic Buildings on the Mersey Marshes*, Chester, Cheshire Monographs 5.

Thompson, P., McKenna, L. and Mackillop, J. (1982) *Ploughlands and Pastures*, Chester, Cheshire County Council.

Thorn, F. R. (1991a), 'Hundreds and Wapentakes', in A. Williams and G.H. Martin ed. *The Cheshire Domesday*, London, Alecto Historical Editions, 26–44.

Thorn, F. R. (1991b), 'Hundreds and Wapentakes', in A. Williams and G.H. Martin ed. *The Lancashire Domesday*, London, Alecto Historical Editions, 42–54.

Titow, J. Z. (1965) 'Medieval England an the Open Field System', *Past and Present* 32: 86–102d.

Titow, J. Z. (1969) *English Rural Society 1250–1350*, London, George Allen & Unwin.

Tolkien. J. R. R. and Gordon, E. V. eds (2nd edition, 1967) *Sir Gawain and the Green Knight*, Revised by N. Davis, Oxford, Oxford University Press.

Tonkinson, A. M. (1999) *Macclesfield in the Later Fourteenth Century: Communities of Town and Forest, C.S.* 3, 42.

Toulmin Smith, L. ed. (1906–10) *The Itinerary of John Leland*, 5 vols. London, Centaur Press.

Towneley, C. and Dodsworth, R. eds (1875) *Abstracts of Inquisition Post Mortem, Edward II – Henry V, C.S.* 1, 95.

Tupling, G. H. (1927) *The Economic History of Rossendale*, Manchester, Manchester University Press.

*Bibliography*

Tupling, G. H. (1933) 'Markets and Fairs in Medieval Lancashire', in J. G. Edwards, V. H. Galbraith and E. F. Jacob eds *Historical Essays in Honour of James Tait*, Manchester, by subscription, 345–356.

Tupling, G. H. (1949) *South Lancashire in the Reign of Edward II*, C.S. 3, 1.

Tyson, N. (1985) 'Excavations at Radcliffe Tower, 1979–80', *G.M.A.J.* 1: 39–54.

Tyson, N. (1986) 'Excavations at the site of Bury Castle, Greater Manchester 1973–1977' *G.M.A.J.* 2: 89–130.

Varley, J. ed. (1941) *A Middlewich Chartulary*, vol. 1, C.S. 2, 105.

Varley, W. J. (1950) 'Excavations at the Castle Ditch, Eddisbury, 1935–38' *T.H.S.L.C.* 102: 1–68.

V.C.H. (1908) *Lancashire*, vol. 2, ed. W. Farmer and D. Brownbill. London.

V.C.H. (1979) *A History of the County of Chester*, vol. 2, ed. B. E. Harris, for University of London Institute of Historical Research by Oxford U.P.

V.C.H. (1980) *A History of the County of Chester*, vol. 3, ed. B. E. Harris, for University of London Institute of Historical Research by Oxford U.P.

V.C.H. (1987) *A History of the County of Chester*, vol. 1, ed. B. E. Harris, for University of London Institute of Historical Research by Oxford U.P.

Vibond, P. (1992–3), 'Harrow Fields in Heswall-cum-Oldfield', *J.E.P.N.S. 25, 9–10*.

Vincent, J. A. C. ed. (1893) *Lancashire Lay Subsidies, I, Henry III – Edward I*, R.S.L.C. 27.

Wacher, J. S. (2nd edition, 1995) *The Towns of Roman Britain*, London, Batsford.

Wadsworth, A. P. (1919–22) 'Enclosure of the Commons in the Rochdale District', *Rochdale Lit. & Sci. Soc. Trans.* 14: 98–110.

Wainwright, F. T. (1945–6) 'Field-Names of Amounderness Hundred', *T.H.S.L.C.* 97 repr. In H. P. R. Finberg ed. (1975) *Scandinavian England*, Chichester, 229–279.

Walker, F. (1939) *Historical Geography of South-West Lancashire*, C.S. 2, 103.

Walker, J. S. F. with Bryant, S. and Morris, M. (1986) *Roman Manchester, a Frontier Settlement* Manchester, Greater Manchester Archaeological Unit.

Walker, J. S. F. and Tindall, A. S. eds (1985) *Country Houses of Greater Manchester*, The Archaeology of Greater Manchester 2, Manchester, Greater Manchester Archaeological Unit.

Wallace, P. F. (1986) 'The English Presence in Viking Dublin', in M. Blackburn ed. *Anglo-Saxon Monetary History*, Leicester, Leicester U.P. 201–221.

Walsh, A. C., Allan, A. R. and Harris, B. E. (1983) *The History of the County Palatine of Chester: A Short Bibliography and Guide to Sources*, Chester, Cheshire Community Council.

Ward, S. (1979–80) 'Chester: Princess Street Area', *C.A.B.* 7: 43–44.

Ward, S. (1984) 'The Rows: the Evidence from Archaeology', *J.C.A.S.* 67: 37–46.

Ward, S. (1985) 'Recent Work on the Medieval City Wall', *J.C.A.S.* 68: 79–84.

Ward, S. (1994) *Excavations at Chester, Saxon Occupation within the Roman fortress,* Chester, Archaeological Service Excavation and Survey Reports 7.

Ward, S. (2001) 'Edward the Elder and the Re-establishment of Chester' in N. J. Higham and D. H. Hill eds, 160–166.

Webb, A. N. ed. (1970) *An Edition of the Cartulary of Burscough Priory*, C.S. 3, 18.

Webster, G. Dolley, R. H. M. and Dunning, G. C. (1953) ' A Saxon Treasure Hoard found at Chester, 1950' *Ant. J.* 33: 22–32.

Wells, C., Huckerby, E. and Hall, V. (1997) 'Mid- and late-Holocene vegetation history and Tephra studies at Fenton Cottage, Lancashire, UK' *Vegetation History and Archaeolbotany* 6,3: 153–166.

White, A. J. (1977) 'Kiln Sites and Documentary Evidence in North Lancashire', in P. J. Davey ed. 121.

White, G. (1981) 'Aldersey, Chowley and Coddington: A Study of the medieval landscape' *Chesh. H.* 7: 32–49.

261

White, G. (1983) 'On the Dating of Ridge-and-Furrow in Cheshire' *Chesh. H.* 12: 20–23.

White, G. (1995) 'Open fields and Rural settlements in Medieval West Cheshire' in T. Scott and P. Starkey eds *The Middle Ages in the North West*, Liverpool, Leopard's Head Press, 15–36.

Whitelock, D. ed. (1955) *English Historical Documents I c. 500–1042*, London, Eyre and Spottswoode.

Willan, T. S. (1980) *Elizabethan Manchester*, C.S. 3, 28.

Williams, C. and Mackinder, R. (1986) 'Stanlow Abbey', *Liverpool University Archaeology Newsletter* 2: 17–18.

Williams, J. M. (1979) *The Stanley family of Lathom and Knowsley, c. 1450–1504: A Political Study*, unpubl. M. A. Thesis, University of Manchester.

Willams, M. (1970) *The Draining of the Somerset Levels*, Cambridge, Cambridge University Press.

Williams, R. S. (1979) 'Aerial Photography in Cheshire' in N. J. Higham ed., 53–58.

Williams, R. S. (1984) 'Aerial Photography and the Evidence for Medieval Farming in West Cheshire' *T.H.S.L.C.* 133: 1–24.

Williamson, T. (1984) 'The Roman Countryside: Settlement and Agriculture in N. W. Essex', *Britannia* 15: 225–230.

Williamson, T. (1987) 'Early Co-axial field systems on the East Anglian boulder clays', *P.P.S.* 53: 419–432.

Williamson, T. (2003) *Shaping Medieval Landscapes*, Macclesfield, Windgather Press.

Williamson, T. and Bellamy, L. (1987) *Property and Landscape*, London, George Philip.

Wilson, D. (1983) 'Excavation of a Medieval Moated Site at Buttery House Lane, Davenport Green, Greater Manchester', *T.A.S.L.C.* 82: 121–146.

Wilson, D. (1985) 'A Note on Old English *hearg* and *weoh* as Place-name Elements Representing Different Types of Pagan Saxon worship sites', *Anglo-Saxon Studies in Archaeology and History*, 4: 179–83.

Wilson, D. (1987) 'The Medieval Moated Sites of Cheshire', *T.A.S.L.C.* 84: 143–154.

Wilson, D. M. and Hurst, J. G. (1968) 'Medieval Britain in 1968: Aldingham Castle, Lancashire, report on excavation by B. K. Davison', *Med. Arch.* 15: 258.

Wilson, K. P. (1965) 'The Port of Chester in the 15th Century', *T.H.S.L.C.* 117: 1–16.

Wilson, K. P. ed. (1969) *Chester Customs Accounts 1301–1566*, R.S.L.C. 101.

Winchester A. J. L. (1978) 'The Medieval Vill in the Western Lake District: Some problems of definition', *T.C.W.A.A.S.* ns. 78 55–70.

Winchester A. J. L. (1983) 'The Castle Household and Demesne Farm at Millom in 1513–14', *T.C.W.A.A.S.* ns 83, 85–100

Winchester, A. J. L. (1987) Landscape and Society in Medieval Cumbria, Edinburgh, John Donald.

Winchester, A. (1993) 'Field, Wood and Forest: Landscapes of medieval Lancashire', in A. Crosby ed., 7–27.

Wood, M. (1965) *The English Mediaeval House*, London, Phoenix House.

Woodward, D. M. (1967) 'The Chester Leather Industry, 1558–1625', *T.H.S.L.C.* 119: 65–111.

Wrigley, E. A. and Schofield, R. S. (1981) *The Population History of England, 1541–1871*, London Edward Arnold.

Yalden, D. (1999) *The History of British Mammals*, London. Academic Press.

Youd, G. (1961) 'The Common Fields of Lancashire' *T.H.S.L.C.* 113: 1–42.

# Index

Where identical names occur, additional information is provided to aid location, either by reference to a nearby place, a district or the pre-1974 shire.